Latino Communities

Emerging Voices: Political, Social, Cultural, and Legal Issues

Edited by

Antoinette Sedillo Lopez
University of New Mexico

A Routledge Series

Latino Communities

Emerging Voices: Political, Social, Cultural, and Legal Issues

Antoinette Sedillo Lopez, *General Editor*

Latinos and Local Representation
Changing Realities, Emerging Theories
Florence Adams

Puerto Rican Newspaper Coverage of the Puerto Rican Independence Party
A Content Analysis of Three Elections
Maria Cristina Santana

Colegio Cesar Chavez, 1973–1983
A Chicano Struggle for Educational Self-Determination
Carlos S. Maldonado

Latinos in Ethnic Enclaves
Immigrant Workers and the Competition for Jobs
Stephanie Bohon

Telling Our Stories
The Lives of Midwestern Latinas
Theresa Barron McKeagney

Dominicans in New York City
Power From the Margins
Milagros Ricourt

Latino National Politial Coalitions
Struggles and Challenges
David Rodriguez

Creating Tropical Yankees
Social Science Textbooks and U.S. Ideological Control in Puerto Rico, 1898–1908
Josẽ-Manuel Navarro

Brown Eyes on the Web
Unique Perspectives of an Alternative U.S. Latino Online Newspaper
Maggie Rivas-Rodriguez

Pregones Theatre
A Theatre for Social Change in the South Bronx
Eva C. Vásquez

The Quest for Tejano Identity in San Antonio, Texas, 1913–2000
Richard A. Buitron, Jr.

Caribbean Spanish in the Metropolis
Spanish Language among Cubans, Dominicans, and Puerto Ricans in the New York City Area
Edwin M. Lamboy

Skin Color and Identity Formation
Perceptions of Opportunity and Academic Orientation among Mexican and Puerto Rican Youth
Edward Fergus

Inviting Latino Voters
Party Messages and Latino Party Identification
Stacey L. Connaughton

Leaving Latinos Out of History
Teaching U.S. History in Texas
Julio Noboa

Gay Hegemony/
Latino Homosexualities
Manolo Guzmán

Latino-Anglo Bargaining
Culture, Structure, and Choice in Court Mediation
Christine Rack

Latino-Anglo Bargaining

Culture, Structure, and Choice in Court Mediation

Routledge
Taylor & Francis Group
LONDON AND NEW YORK

Published in 2006 by
Routledge
Taylor & Francis Group
711 Third Avenue
New York, NY 10017

Published in Great Britain by
Routledge
Taylor & Francis Group
2 Park Square
Milton Park, Abingdon
Oxon OX14 4RN

First issued in paperback 2012

International Standard Book Number-13: 978-0-415-64962-9 (Papercover)

International Standard Book Number-13: 978-0-415-97458-5 (Hardcover)
Library of Congress Card Number 2005024511

Library of Congress Cataloging-in-Publication Data

Rack, Christine.
Latino-Anglo bargaining : culture, structure, and choice in court mediation / by Christine Rack.-- 1st ed.
p. cm. -- (Latino communities)
Includes bibliographical references and index.
ISBN 0-415-97458-5
1. Dispute resolution (Law)--United States--Social aspects. 2. Negotiation--United States--Social aspects. 3. Hispanic Americans. 4. WASPs (Persons) I. Title. II. Series.

KF9084.R33 2005
347.73'9--dc22 2005024511

informa
Taylor & Francis Group
is the Academic Division of Informa plc.

Visit the Taylor & Francis Web site at
http://www.taylorandfrancis.com

and the Routledge Web site at
http://www.routledge-ny.com

For peacemakers seeking justice

Contents

Foreword

In *Latino-Anglo Bargaining: Culture, Structure, and Choice in Court Mediation,* Christine Rack makes some deeply complex and multi-faceted contributions to the studies of Latinos, Latinas, gender, race, ethnicity, and class relations. But more than these interests appear in its pages. A layered narrative effectively interweaves orders of abstraction and condition that are customarily given independent treatment in disparate disciplines.

The analysis of race/gender/class "intersection" speaks for itself. I would humbly venture the prediction that it will considerably help to soften the canonical assumption in intersection studies that quantitative research is inimical to clarifying the interplay amongst these fundamental "vectors" of inequity. Reflecting on this dimension of the book, I am reminded of the injunction of the ecological psychologist Roger Barker, endorsed by the sociologist Erving Goffman—keep a watch on the public sites through whose portals random people enter to engage among themselves under certain formally established rules; behold the wondrous patterns of interface behavior that will there crystallize. From this perspective, to measure, as author Rack does, the relative and shifting power associations, based on varying dyadic combinations, is to present on stage the ballet of race, gender, and class effects through the lens of statistical insight.

As for the Latino experience, nuance rules. Considerable research has described the overtly political and cultural forms and creative artistry, the identity variations and contestations, associated with Mexican American, Chicano, and *Nuevomexicano* action. But do Latinos act according to their own collective sensibility in primal, face to face negotiation with Anglo men and women? Does a Latina exude a style distinctive to her ethgender within an encounter of implied contention over everyday resources? The analysis contained in this work succeeds in identifying such subtle patterns of response and initiation which means that it necessarily uncovers the how

Anglos act, by gender, sitting across the table from someone who is different by race and/or sex.

With original findings such as these, *Latino-Anglo Bargaining* is sure to make its mark and we can all look forward to the enhancements it will bring to several discourses.

Phillip B. Gonzales
Professor and Chair, Department of Sociology
University of New Mexico

Acknowledgments

Many people and institutions contributed to the MetroCourt Project and my formal and informal education. Gary LaFree was an investigator on the Project fifteen years ago, becoming my advisor in the Sociology doctoral program, the Chair of my dissertation committee. He was a consistent mentor and colleague, through data collection, analysis, and presentation, from the very inception of my work in the MetroCourt Project. I am grateful to take with me his constant question, "What are you trying to *say?*" and his emphasis on truthfulness as the final criterion for speech. At the University of New Mexico Sociology Department, Professors Phillip (Felipé) Gonzales and Susan Tiano provided crucial intellectual, professional, and personal support and challenge over more than a dozen years. Felipé Gonzales, Sociology Chair and New Mexico scholar by reputation and birth, served on my committee and generously remained involved in shaping these ideas, including reading drafts of this book and providing valuable insight and criticism. I was fortunate to know the late Everett Rogers, Communications scholar extraordinaire and member of my dissertation committee, who provided timely and open-hearted encouragement. I am also grateful to the many scholars, classmates, and faculty members who dared to speak their truths so that I could think with them. All of these mentors provided guidance and ideas that influenced the analyses and interpretations in this book. The errors, however, are mine alone.

The MetroCourt Project and I are indebted to the Albuquerque Mediation Center and the Bernalillo County Metropolitan Court (BCMC) for agreeing to be the site for this research. I am inspired to know Susan Barnes Anderson, her steady presence and profound commitment to mediation: she supported the research project at its inception, interviewed disputants, responded to the results with constructive change, and directs the BCMC Mediation Center to this day. A band of sociology and law students with a few mediators conducted more than 1,000 detailed initial telephone interviewers, *then* they tracked down 850 people *again* for follow-up. Financial support from the UNM Department of Sociology and the Center for Regional Studies enabled me to carry out the detailed analyses shown in this book. I am grateful to all of them.

Colleagues, friends, family and neighbors gave me support, encouragement, assistance and camping companionship throughout my graduate academic career, my years in Indiana as an assistant professor at Marian College, and my return to New Mexico where I became involved in the UNM Peace Studies Program. I did *nothing* to deserve the blessing of my siblings who have sustained me in every way.

The 1,009 disputants and 129 mediators who provided the data that I analyzed over seven years will probably never know how often, as I read their words, I speculated about their attitudes and feelings, and wondered about their hopes and fears, during a dispute process that has probably long since ceased to be meaningful in their lives. Nevertheless, it is an irrefutable fact that, without them, this work would never have been done. So I am grateful to the real people who took the risk and the time to contribute their thoughts and self-presentations to these data.

Neither words nor treasure can express my gratitude to my brilliant, exacting, gracious and wholly undeserved editor, Mary Beath.

Introduction

We humans are in a pickle. The many books examining our current predicament (war, climate change, environmental degradation, growing inequality, and resource depletion, to name just a few) try to end hopefully with a "what we can do" section. Invariably, the authors suggest cooperation, diplomacy, and united efforts instead of the deadly competition that currently holds sway. When we resolve to end the short-sighted violence, we immediately encounter three interrelated problems: the competitors are usually claiming "justice," for their "rightful" share of the pie in the face of a badly-intentioned opponent; the power to prevail by force lies beneath the surface give-and-take we associate with negotiated settlement; and thus we are left with a world where justice is sacrificed to power. In the final analysis, the only consensual alternative to coercion is for power to *choose* to relinquish force, to willingly subordinate itself to the common good, to forego the amoral *right* of *might*.

The MetroCourt study is a microcosm of that dilemma: how to have peace *with* justice, how to share power, to work with adversaries as colleagues, so we can move together to solve the problems that underlie the fight, while maintaining the kind of justice that gives all sides their due. The microcosm shares the crucial elements of the larger dilemmas: what *is* their due? Who and what determines it? What perversions of perception intercede to make our view of the conflict so vulnerable to distortion? How do members of the "other" side become the dastardly enemy, even as they go home to similar human lives, with the painfully common aspirations and disappointments that fill our inevitably *human* existence? Can anyone *help* the fighters to transcend the quintessentially human tendency to see only our own point of view? Unfortunately, this book provides no easy answers. However, it does offer a rather detailed look at the possibilities, mirages, and stumbling blocks, as well as moments of grace and kindness, encountered in cross-cultural and cross-gender dispute resolution.

This tension between harmony and the relations of force emerges in the language of this book: the voice alternates between description and criticism, between telling a story and revealing injustice, between objectivity and outrage. A similar tension has been distinctly personal. I continue to ask myself whether my membership in a group complicit in the economic injustice of the study may undermine my capacities to find an integrative point of view. Here too I found no easy answers.

In the eight years since I completed this research, I have come to see "cultural individualism" as a euphemism for the cultural patterns enabled by and enabling modern, first-world privilege. That privilege allows fulfillment of what Weber called our "peculiar philosophy of avarice" while shielding our mass consumption lifestyles from discomfort in the midst of absolute, not just relative, deprivation. Meanwhile, many of us bemoan our loss of community and grow weary of our frantic pace, even as we accelerate. But considering the alternative complicates the picture more than some analyses suggest. "Cultural collectivism" is not singular, but plural. Many human groups live within a variety of cultural systems capable of providing the loyalty, sensitivity, and generosity necessary for human survival in the *absence* of affluence.

Lately, I see the radical independence made possible by industrial capitalism as anomalous and probably short-lived: we've had a run of two hundred years to consume our planetary inheritance of fossil fuels. A recent book and its title reflect my current viewpoint: *the party's over* (Heinberg 2003). Heinberg reports on a number of geologists who explain that, though we might have softened the blow had we been listening, peak oil is *now.* We cannot sustain our *current* energy addiction, much less the hyper growth global capitalism demands. Global warming adds an exclamation point to the geologists. This impending endpoint makes it all the more necessary to become allies rather than enemies, cooperate rather than compete, relinquish privilege and practice restraint, and invent new cultural forms.

When I began working as the coordinator in the mediation study that came to be the MetroCourt Project, I was still aglow with the optimism generated by mediation training—almost invariably a hopeful, empowering experience. Mediation training conveys the idea that conflicts *can* be approached and even resolved by disputing parties themselves, and that mediation can assist in this process by using a few simple strategies to move the process forward. I was co-mediating regularly, fulfilling my training obligation to the Albuquerque Mediation Center

(AMC) when the mediator newsletter carried a notice of the research coordinator position. Recently graduated and looking for work, I applied and was hired in August 1990.

From the beginning, there were perplexing paradigm problems. The research question posed by the University of New Mexico Law School sought to test the proposition that *discrimination* would be greater in the informality of mediation compared to the formality of court. But who is discriminating? Unlike a judge, the mediators are only guardians of the process; mediators don't make decisions, disputants do. I believed this cornerstone idea presented at the training: if mediators just worked the process, there could be no opportunity to negatively affect outcomes. Confident that the study would reveal no mediator bias, I began my task of data collection and the AMC scheduled unwitting mediators to 280 study cases according to a protocol providing for relatively equal ethnic and gender balances in the mediator pairs.

Eighteen months later, the first statistical analyses showed that, indeed, minority claimants, largely Latino, left mediation with significantly reduced monetary outcomes compared to both similar adjudication cases and Anglo claimants in mediation.[1] Furthermore, mediator ethnicity and gender appeared to influence these outcomes so that there was no significant difference between Latino and Anglo claimant outcomes when the mediators were both Latino. Then we realized a very important fact: *all* the mediation cases had lower claimant outcomes than court cases *except* Anglo claimants with Anglo mediators. We were looking not at discrimination against Latinos but at *privilege* in favor of Anglos, with substantive effects facilitated by well-meaning, justice-seeking Anglos.

How did this happen? Who was to blame? Mediators? Claimants? Respondents? Should anyone *be* blamed for consensual outcomes? Thus began my seven years of analysis, probing reams of data to try to clarify what had happened. By this time I was in the UNM Sociology doctoral program and had the benefit of faculty mentors and courses to direct my queries.

Interviewing disputants and looking at early results, many of my cherished notions about mediation eroded under the weight of the evidence. Mediation disputants did not think relationships are more important than money, they did not always enjoy transformative experiences through their participation in the dispute dyad, but they did generally prefer the mediation process over adjudication. This was true even for Latino claimants who seemed to have been poorly served in the process. Despite the mediation rhetoric of win-win outcomes, monetary outcomes in small claims court *were* zero-sum: any reduction in claimant outcomes was *in fact* a benefit to the respondent. An almost endless stream of questions dogged me. Did the apparent "losers" realize that they "lost?" Did the "losers" *choose* altruistically to give benefit to the other party? How did the mediators affect outcomes? Were the Latino claimants and mediators just more even-handed? Maybe Latino claimants were more generous with Latino respondents? What about class differences? Maybe those privileged Anglos were lawyers? How did it happen that consensual outcomes came to reflect and even to accentuate the inequalities in the larger society?

While this book is a case study of one mediation program, the interest-based mediation model used here is common to most court-annexed programs. I completed these analyses for my 1997 dissertation in Sociology. The story I am telling in this book is on its simplest level a snapshot of Latino and Anglo bargaining in a southwestern small claims court mediation program in the early 1990s. The outcome data supporting this story are quantitative and based on court documents; the process variables are derived from semi-structured interviews and questionnaires providing disputant and mediator points of view[2]. In this way, the analyses are both quantitative and qualitative, the approach inductive as well as deductive.

The MetroCourt study offered a very complete dataset with very high response rates, multiple sources for validation and analysis of apparent contradictions, and little missing information. In my seven years of active involvement in the project and analysis, I learned a number of ways to view these data and the truths they represent. I continually asked questions and often learned that my assumptions/hypotheses were naive, misguided, or quite simply wrong. In this sense, the data have provided an empirical resource to my own theory-building about conflict resolution and mediation in the best objectivist tradition.

However, I personally interviewed more than 200 of the disputants in the initial or follow-up interviews and I encouraged an attitude of field research among the 15 law and sociology students and five mediators who conducted the other 1,500 interviews. I can see my footprints and theirs in the interview data. Even including the follow-up interviews, the data represent a portrait of a localized sample of small claims disputes, frozen in the years from 1990 to 1992. In this sense, the study also represents a fiction, a snapshot vulnerable to a host of situational influences and human error.

I became intimate with these data. I read patterns in frequencies, chi-square tests, linear regressions, and factor analyses as well as stories. It is as if each group, mostly defined into dualisms by what they were not, took shape as ghostly conversation partners. In one group especially, I saw myself. As you will see, most of the research team, interviewers, mediators, and disputants were Anglo women. The mediation training, the process, and the academic critiques emerged from Anglo women. I am an Anglo woman and I was a mediator as well an observer. Thus, the data and analysis are profoundly constructed from an Anglo female "point of view," is especially complicated because Anglo women play a decisive role in the story.

I feel these stories were entrusted to me in more than 2000 voices; I believe they want to be heard. I take responsibility for attempting to shape fragments of sentences, muffled suggestions, and blurry mathematical reflections into group portraits—generalizations inevitably falling into cognitive schema, always threatened by stereotype takeover in my psyche and yours.

OVERVIEW

Over the past twenty-five years, mediation has been increasingly used as an alternative to adjudication within the U.S. justice system. Civil cases filed in small claims courts with the expectation of judicial rulings are often diverted to the mediation forum where mediators facilitate a process that encourages parties to negotiate resolutions to their disputes. This forum suggests many questions we might ask about justice institutions. Specifically, rather than determining whether all persons are treated equally before the law, as written or practiced, the question in mediation is whether all parties are comparably situated and equally capable in the negotiation process.

Small claims mediation involves three interrelated elements that make it well suited to explore and analyze this issue. First, these cases are economic disputes, pursued at the public and structural level. Second, they involve personal interaction, enabling insight into whether the relationship was perceived as an interpersonal or inter-group encounter. Third, the outcome depended on mutual agreement, thus one explicitly based on choice.

This book teases out the influence of race-ethnicity, gender, and class that shaped negotiation behavior in mediated small claims disputes in the Metro Court, Bernalillo County, New Mexico between September 1990 and October 1991[3]. Using bargaining positions, reported goals and rationales, I asked questions about the sources of unequal effects in mediation: to what degree, if at all, were choices influenced by socialized patterns in approaching conflict, structured behavior based on role expectations, exploitation by the other party, and/or mediator influence or coercion? In trying to answer *these* questions, I ended up engaging questions about patterned ways different genders, ethnicities, classes, and occupations *handled* a situation in which the decision to cooperate or compete, to give or take, was, at least nominally, voluntary—a matter of choice.

Weber & Messick (2004) propose thinking about how culture affects choices as answers to the explicit or implicit question: What does a person like me do in a situation like this? The answer depends on a person's definition of the situation, his/her cognitive frame: What kind of situation is this? Social identities (race-ethnic, gender, class and occupation) play a major role in both answers. Cognitive scientists studying negotiation (see Gelfand & Brett 2004) have demonstrated that cultural differences in self-concept and cognitive framing associated with the cultural construct of individualism-collectivism have a significant effect on negotiating choices.

Supported by extensive and sometimes contradictory research, gender and cultural theories suggest that individuals socialized into collectivist and female social patterns are more like to show enhanced concern for the other party and would concede more readily. Many scholars, using value and conflict style inventories as well as game-based experimental designs, have clarified how individualist and collectivist cultural patterns, or "cultural syndromes" correspond to individual traits (Tiandis et al. 1995) and self definitions or "self-construals"—independent and interdependent (Ting-Toomey, Oetzel & Yee-jung 2001). Independent self-construal is predominant among people from individualistic cultures, while interdependent self-construal is predominant among people from collectivistic cultures. Although the construct is not unitary—that is, individualistic and collectivistic patterns are not polar opposites—the two dimensions tend to be negatively correlated. Individual assessment is clarified when "primed" by a scenario situation evoking ethnic/cultural identity, or by various situations that suggest individual or collective responses are more appropriate.

At the core of my own curiosity was whether minority people and women actually made the less individualistic and less self-interested negotiating decisions predicted by culture and gender theories. As a corollary, I was curious to know how closely Anglo men fit the cultural image that outsider groups have of them. In Vila's (1996) study, Mexicans and Mexican Americans defined Anglos and their own group's acculturation to Anglo culture not in terms of individualism, but in terms of materialism and striving. I wondered whether this construction was a valid generalization about Anglo and male culture in mixed-motive bargaining sessions like those examined here.

I placed the negotiation process in the foreground to examine the influence of ethnicity and gender on the negotiation process: how cultural vs. structural patterns influenced individual expressive and instrumental choices, and the relationship of these choices to exploitation. I examined the three major contributing elements to negotiation behavior—goals, alternatives, and motives.

The midground shows how class and professional roles interacted with race-ethnicity and gender in the negotiation process. In the near background, I placed the influence of the Southwest region, small claims court and the mediation situation, with court outcomes presented as the logical alternative to a negotiated agreement. I generalized the mediation environment as an ideology to which differing disputant responses might be likely, without attempting to specify unique mediator influences[4].

The larger social world is the far background for this portrait and, like all backgrounds, defines the influences shaping the detail observed in disputants, even as disputant behavior helps to illuminate the shape of the background.

Mediation: Negotiating Justice

A variety of social influences could have a heightened effect in mediation: context sensitivity, message vulnerability, role autonomy, and prejudice/exploitation. Latinos and women are likely to be more susceptible to any environment, and may be particularly vulnerable to the mediation message of cooperation and concession-making rather than competition. Latinos and women are usually situated differently from Anglo men in the negotiation process due to their lack of role autonomy and their vulnerability to the other party's discriminatory assumptions and practices.

Context sensitivity is a heightened response to the messages of the social environment. Called in earlier studies the cognitive style of "field dependence" (Witkin et al. 1962), context sensitivity varies both individually and by group-level socialization. Specifically, women and persons from cultures that Hall (1976) described as "high context"—in which more attention was given to the surrounding information—are theoretically likely to be more easily influenced by the environment surrounding them (Hui 1988; Gilligan 1982; Jordan et al. 1991). This contrasts with "low context" cultures like that of the United States where people are relatively immune to contextual influences.

In comparison to the adversarial court process that disputants anticipated when filing and answering a claim, the mediation environment introduces a drastic change of frame. Rather than a process focused on blame, liability, and argument, mediation reshapes the interaction. Mediators are trained and ideologically motivated to encourage disputants to reframe their disputes into resolvable problems, to consider context and relational aspects of their disputes, and to entertain solutions using nonmonetary elements despite original monetary definition. Susceptibility to problem-solving approaches—explicitly related to variation in cooperative versus competitive interaction—is unlikely to be evenly distributed in the population of small claims disputants. In a voluntary negotiation process like mediation, one or both parties must give, or concede, for an agreement to be reached. But motivation to reach agreement or to conciliate is also variable. Based on relational and collectivistic orientations in conflict and negotiating styles in other environments, women and Latino disputants are likely to give more readily than men and Anglos (e.g., Hui 1988; Bryan 1992).

A sense of personal agency is the foundation of negotiations based on bargaining choices. However, individual agency is questioned for women because they are more likely to internalize a dependent role and, in fact, more often function in less empowered positions even in professional roles (Kolb 1994). A similar argument based on lower professional status can be made for Latino disputants. Thus, although the concept that an actor is willing to and capable of making decisions in his/her own best interest is assumed to be a common human characteristic, it is inherently opposed to relational psychology ascribed to women and collectivistic patterns related to Latino cultural norms.

Based on wide-scale patterns of ethnic and gender stereotyping, women and Latino disputants face particular risks arising from discriminatory bargaining by the other party. Scholars (see Berreman 1972 and Bryan 1992 for relevant reviews) have documented such unequal outcomes in institutional settings as well as prejudice in interpersonal social processes. Delgado et al. (1985) review psychodynamic, sociohistorical and cognitive theory and research on prejudice to conclude that, although prejudices rarely change after the teen-age years, the *expression* of prejudice is situationally specific. They argue that, compared to adjudication, the mediation environment is less likely to suppress bias because it "allow[s] wider scope for the participants' emotional and behavioral idiosyncrasies; in these settings majority group members are most likely to exhibit prejudicial behavior" (Delgado et al. 1985:1391).

The notion of exploitation assumes an illegitimate use of power. Court outcomes are the likely alternative to a negotiated agreement and thus are rational negotiating realities, despite the obvious fact that institutionalized power may, in itself, be exploitative. I use the notion of exploitation to mean that a negotiator consciously manipulates the other party into a disadvantaged position based not on realistic negotiation alternatives but on the other party's personal qualities apparent during negotiations. Specifically, I examine evidence for an instrumental and materially self-interested party taking unfair advantage of the other party during the mediation process where the exploitation is enabled by relational or collectivistic values. In particular, I evaluate exploitation as "imbalanced reciprocity" (Gouldner 1960).

I attempt to distinguish consciously imposed exploitation from that which is allowed through an unwarranted deference that can be called "internalized oppression." In Chapter Nine I review evidence that suggests whether unwarranted deference arises from ignorance of alternatives or reduced expectations versus cultural and gender socialized choices that may be based on alternative values.

These broadly defined issues—context sensitivity, negotiation process with the assumption of concession-making and choice, and bias/exploitation—are complicated in various ways. First, ascriptive differences intersect with structural roles: Anglos and men—as members of dominant groups—are also likely to be in higher socioeconomic categories and professional roles than members of subordinate groups. Second, ascriptive status itself intersects in individual persons—"ethgender[5]" categories that are, arguably, unique and non-reducible to what Crenshaw (1990) refers to as the "single axis analyses" of either race-ethnicity or gender. Third, ascriptive effects are differentially active based on the similarity (insider status) or dissimilarity (outsider status) of the other party in a dispute[6]. Although organized within interestingly different theoretical models of causation, scholars largely agree that group boundaries are critical to negotiation and exchange dynamics and that people give more readily to insiders than outsiders.

Analytic Strategy

I address justice questions concerning the differential impact of court-annexed mediation on people socialized in nondominant cultural and gender identities. Are women, Latinos, lower class actors, and/or nonprofessional actors disadvantaged by the substitution of a negotiation for an adjudicatory process? I critically explore fundamental theoretical assumptions about gender and ethnic cultures when embedded in status-based differences.

My immediate interest is to examine the negotiation process and the critical act of giving or conceding, and their opposites—taking or resisting—found in these data. My larger concern is the influence of individual, group, and role socialization on facilitated negotiating behavior in the mediation forum, specifically as it is patterned by culture and social status.

My interactive analytic strategy highlights the status boundary effects between the two disputants. I examine gender and ethnic effects within two overlapping conceptual frames of culture and hierarchical rank which I summarize under the term "status." Disputants were placed in dichotomous categories as "higher" (HI) or "lower" (LO) in five status dimensions. Two of the categorical dimensions are *ascriptive* that is, those that are assigned at birth and are more or less permanent: ethnicity (Anglo or Latino) and gender (male or female). Three dimensions are achieved: class (higher or lower socioeconomic status), corporate (business or individual) and legal (represented or *pro se*[7]). Each case is identified by the claimant-respondent relationship in one of four possible interactive status conditions (HILO, HIHI, LOLO, or LOHI) in each of the five dimensions. The outcomes for these status relationships and the bargaining processes by which they were achieved are examined with reference to the order Black (1989) argues will predict discrimination patterns in criminal justice situations (see Chapter Six). Thus, this analysis examines the effects of each status dimension, as well as its impact on the status differentials between the disputing parties.

The analyses are based on data collected from 603 small claims cases (Hermann & West 1990) that were either adjudicated (N = 323) or mediated (N=280), in the Bernalillo County Metropolitan Court in Albuquerque, New Mexico between September 1990 and October 1991. First, I position this study in the matrix of negotiated justice (Chapter One) and explore the often unexamined intersection of culture and hierarchy (Chapter Two). The third chapter sets out the cultural context: the historical and law-related pattern of Latino-Anglo relationships, the environment of the Bernalillo County small claims court, and the mediation program. Chapter Four describes the research process and data used in this analysis. In Chapter Five I discuss culture and materialism and compare stated disputant goals after adjudication and mediation for evidence of a differential susceptibility to the mediation environment. Divergences between adjudicated and mediated outcomes are clarified in Chapter Six so that the reader can appreciate the alternatives to a negotiated agreement for disputants in mediation; and the consistent effects of mediator gender and ethnicity are summarized. Using negotiation and conflict styles research as interpretive frameworks, Chapter Seven displays the bargaining process in mediation and examines the changes in bargaining pattern based on the mediation environment and the ethnicity/gender of the other disputant. Chapter Eight shows analyses of reported motivations for disputant bargaining decisions, the distribution of disputant reports that the process was unfair, and the relationship of reported strategy and coercion on monetary outcomes. Chapter Nine clarifies the bargaining process for specific ethgenders and the evidence for bias and privilege. Chapter Ten tells stories showing how the mathematical patterns were expressed in a number of cases. A summary of the data and conclusions and implications follow in Chapters Eleven and Twelve.

This study of voluntary mediation offers data that both supports and refutes various theoretical propositions and laboratory tests in less naturalistic settings. First, are women vulnerable to exploitation because they are more relationally motivated than men? Second, are Latinos culturally socialized toward collectivistic disputing and allocation norms, and do these norms shift according to the group membership of the other party? Third, do structural relationships determine intra-individual interaction more than culturally socialized choices? This larger concern is the inverse of the meta-theoretical sociological problem of causation: how radically individual is choice? How much are choices determined or constrained by social structure in contrast to culture and gender socialization?

In a nutshell, I found that women's relationality may be the source of biased behavior but, in mediation, was *not* materially exploited; Latino collectivism was *not* biased but *was* exploited. Latinos seem to be living in a world with more dignity and less avarice than Anglos. Anglos, not Latinos, have insider dynamics that discriminate against outsiders. People often clothe their structural roles in ethgender styles, with varying commitment to the overt task of the role. Disputants sometimes were unprepared for the choices they *did* have, and socialization affected their response.

If cognitive science has taught us anything, it is that we must frame experience in order to receive it. The Enlightenment and Modernism offered the protection of the scientific method, insurance against the arrogance of speaking for more than oneself, and I use these tools, a scientific frame, in this book. But I am aware the shield is naught but a figleaf, easily shredded by the radical postmodern question of authorship to *anyone's* story. I present *evidence* for my point of view, but I am also constructing it. The whole enterprise is riskier than outright ethnography, where the person *is* the research instrument, because it is apparently self-validating by the very cultural tools I critique: rationality, calculation, distance.

I have come to see these data as a very particular text I have read and re-read, shaped by my questions and person, answered by my analytic strategies, and interpreted in light of my own shifting knowledge and experience. Compared to the weight of this awareness for me, I rarely mention the degree to which my personal perspective may have influenced the analyses presented. It should be understood, however, that the story presented here is ultimately my own version, and is probably more accurately critiqued as a researcher's viewpoint than many, because I am insider and outsider, participant and observer. My hope is that I have been able to approach the reflexivity that Rodriquez (1992) suggests for the problem of objectivity in native ethnography, and the synergy Morris et al. (1999) claims is possible with an interplay of insider-outsider viewpoints.

Chapter One

Small Claims Court & Mediation: Public Justice & Private Choices

SMALL CLAIMS COURTS

The first U.S. small claims courts, defined by relatively small amounts of money claimed and relaxation of the rules requiring legal representation, were established in Kansas in 1912 and Cleveland in 1913. The move toward informality, originally akin to what Weber described as Khadi justice (Rheinstein 1969), spread across the country. Small claims courts, like other legally informal institutions (Harrington 1982), were expected to supply a more substantive rationality to courts grown rigid, and to give small businesses and private citizens in civil disputes (i.e., non-criminal, monetarily defined conflicts) access to the power of the state.

The first attempts to assess whether this goal was actually accomplished did not begin until the 1950s. Then, as now, the evidence shows that the courts are more likely to be used by larger corporations against private, individual debtors in relatively inexpensive collection actions. The party filing the claim (the claimant) is more likely than the respondent to prevail (Yngvesson & Hennessey 1975).

Many of the cases filed in small claims court, like many criminal and civil cases of larger jurisdiction, are never formally adjudicated (Galanter 1983). The majority are routine collection actions that settle under threat of judgment, or remain unanswered and receive automatic "default" judgments that assume the non-answering respondent is fully liable. With the majority of cases out of the way, the cases that go to a formal court hearing more often reflect the party composition originally intended for small claims courts: private citizens with noncommercial disputes like car sales, loans, vandalism, auto accidents, consumers against small businesses, landlords and tenants filing against one another, and tradespeople filing for unpaid bills. In the Bernalillo County Metropolitan Court, less than one quarter of the cases formally adjudicated were composed of corporate creditors and individual debtors (i.e., collections), or involved lawyers for the claimant but not the respondent. It is important to remember, however, that these kinds of cases represent a sizeable majority of initial filings, and the majority of judgments awarded by the court (Vidmar 1984; Hermann et al 1992).

The cases that remain to be formally adjudicated in small claims courts, like the kinds of conflicts handled by other "specialized" courts created in the same era of reform (e.g., domestic relations, juvenile, and landlord-tenant courts), are notoriously complicated, often involve lower status issues and parties—even the lawyers using small claims courts are in the lowest ranks of their profession—and are rarely amenable to the kind of logic to which legal decision-makers aspire. They are more reflective of social problems than legal ones, and the informality of the courts is intended to provide a social rather than a legal cure (Harrington 1982; Yngvesson & Hennessey 1975).

COURT-ANNEXED MEDIATION

Mediation is a harmony- or conciliation-based process. It is one of several procedures that have entered the courts over the past twenty-five years described under the general category of Alternative Dispute Resolution (ADR). Court-annexed mediation is a more recent attempt to "de-calcify" (Merry 1987) the judicial system to increase flexibility and efficiency. The emphasis, especially in mediation, is the resolution of cases without reliance on the adversarial process. Goldberg, Sander and Rogers (1992) described mediation as the most "soft" of the ADR procedures. In contrast to arbitration that results in a third party decision, mediation is at least nominally a voluntary and consensual decision-making process because, like counselors, mediators have no overt decision-making power.

Court-annexed mediation grew from instrumental, expressive, and bureaucratic rationales. It combines negotiation, essentially an instrumental process, with peace advocacy, essentially an expressive motivation, and personal interaction, a less alienating social process. These three elements of mediation are precisely those that are at issue in mediation analyses.

As negotiation, mediation developed from diplomacy and deterrence policies formed in response to the imperatives of nuclear warfare. International diplomacy is a game of strategy (Schelling 1963). In cold war strategy, the goal is to *avoid* any implementation of negative consequences for the simple reason that nuclear war has no winners. Strategies, organized by the paradigm of behavioral psychology, are thus instrumentally aimed at manipulating the "enemy" by controlling the enemy's consequences (via threats/punishments and promises/rewards). Thus, the *other party's* outcome alternatives are manipulated in order to control the adversary's presumably rational choices. The strategy of implementing an escalating sequence of consequences, demonstrated perfectly by the preliminaries to the first Gulf War in 1991, is designed to show that the threats are credible and ideally inevitable consequences of the other party's undesired behavior. An atmosphere of a chess game with varying amounts of psychological sophistication pervades theoretical writing on the topic. Strategic use of the relationship between choice and alternatives is a focus in game and exchange theory, and, notably, trial and business practices.

Peace advocacy is rooted in an expressive and moral motivation[1]. Conflict resolution in contemporary times is based on the same nuclear age logic, intertwined with justice concerns raised during the Vietnam War. Avoidance of all-out nuclear war is rational. That military personnel should not be asked to die without justification is a moral argument. Analogous issues are common in the history of small claims disputes. Debtors' prison was eliminated because it was irrational (i.e., imprisoned debtors could not pay and actually cost more) but assessing blame and liability is an essentially moral act. Mediation combines rational bargaining with moral expression in the notion of "principled negotiation" popularized by Fisher & Ury (1981) as a strategy resulting in "win-win" or Pareto optimum agreements.

The growth of impersonal and relatively faceless bureaucratic social processes has been the target of wide public criticism over the past century. The more personal and narrative-tolerant mediation process is justified as an antidote to the chilling effect of modern social organization, specifically the cool rituals of Anglo jurisprudence (Resnick 1986). From international conflicts to zoning disputes to small claims cases, personal interaction and an opportunity to be heard (Lind, Tyler & Huo 1997) are the magic ingredient to successful peacemaking. Folger & Baruch Bush (1994; see also Putnam & Folger 1988), for example, place a primary focus on participant interaction by stressing verbal techniques of empowerment and recognition to achieve what they call "transformative mediation." In addition to legal studies and social psychology, relevant literature on mediation as an interpersonal process is found in anthropology and communications.

Contemporary use of mediation as an alternative to formal litigation emerged in response to these larger trends. These three elements of mediation—instrumental, expressive and interpersonal—answered social frustrations by posing an alternative to lose-lose violence, a potential for moral negotiation, and a counterfoil to impersonal justice. Mediation is a negotiation process with strategy and assumptions of rational self interest at its analytic core, infused with a softness associated with popular justice (Merry 1992). Although mediation is an ancient practice of third party conciliation, its present expression, generically called "interest-based mediation," is framed within the cultural language of modern capitalism.

Process in Mediation: Interest-based Negotiation

The most common model of mediation, and the one used at this research site, is patterned on principled negotiation, also known as interest-based mediation. In this language, dispute goals are reframed into economic language of interests, strategy is unstated, and conflict is muted, arguably silenced (Nader 1993) by the courtesies of negotiation dialogue. Avruch (1991) notes that interest-based mediation makes the assumption that interests are deeper than positions, a value judgment consistent with the amorality of western capitalism.

The idea of principled negotiation is that when negotiators release "positions" and redirect their attention to their real "interests" in a dispute, they will be able to release competitive attachment to win-lose outcomes. Without emotional attachment to positions, negotiators will be able to perceive new exchange possibilities, thus "expanding the pie." In this way, the negotiators will be able to find a mutually agreeable resolution within the expanded field of possible outcomes, or settlement points. In more recent formulations, this motivational higher ground is called "problem-solving" (Pruitt & Carnevale 1993) negotiation leading to integrative or optimum agreements.

The moral need answered by "principled negotiation" is not a moral *outcome* but a moral *process* focusing on interests, rather than winning or overcoming the other party. The model assumes a rational actor making self-interested choices among the possible alternatives. Fisher & Ury (1981) coined the acronym BATNA to refer to the need for the negotiators to keep their "Best Alternative To a Negotiated Agreement" firmly in mind so that they can negotiate without "giving in." The assumed goal of principled negotiation is integrative solutions answering both parties' interests. The alternatives to informal settlement are the defining limit of self-maximizing strategy. In court-annexed programs, the BATNA is usually the most likely court ruling.

Like choices, the interest-based *process* of mediation includes instrumental and expressive dimensions. Instrumentally, mediation includes rational elements of law (court alternatives, see McEwen 1991) and bargaining. Expressively, mediation is situated between justice and psychotherapy

(Harrington & Merry 1988; Grillo 1991:1588–94). Mediators act as facilitators in verbal negotiations between people who are in conflict. Mediators are trained in (usually) forty hours to reframe positional arguments into statements of interests, to divert blame, accusations and defense ("recognition," "venting," and "restating"), and generally to encourage the parties to find a solution themselves (Garcia 1991; Olsen 1989). However, because mediators are not psychologists and their intervention is brief, the healing is mostly limited to relieving immediate distress. Because mediators are most often not legal professionals, and are often proscribed from giving legal opinions, they are limited to generalized statements about the risks of win-lose court rulings in which the disputants have no control over the outcome. In mediation, rules of evidence are usually ignored.

On the level of social organization, court-annexed and interest-based mediation is part of a larger trend to reduce the complex issues of justice to disagreements over interests that might be "resolved" in polite conversation. Nader (1991, 1993) is eloquent on the effects of "harmony ideology" in legal settings, but hers is not the only voice suggesting that justice may not be served by this reduction. Criticism stems from concerns for economic justice (e.g., Abel 1982; Kairys 1990 [1982]; Hofrichter 1982; Lazerson 1982), psychological justice (e.g., Grillo 1991; Bryan 1992), cultural justice (e.g., Delgado et al 1985; Avruch 1991) and basic effectiveness (e.g., Burton 1990; Scimecca 1991; Baruch-Bush & Folger 1994). The thrust of all these concerns is that justice can not and should not be reduced to a negotiation process. Implicitly or explicitly, the argument is that negotiated justice is unfair to nondominant parties.

THE BARGAINING PROCESS

Figure 1.1 shows the negotiation process as bargaining positions reported by disputants in the MetroCourt data in a format that will be used in later chapters (Chapters Seven and Nine) for the bargaining analysis. Figure 1.1 graphically displays the differences between adjudicatory and mediated processes The *y* axis is the mean percentage of the original claim plotted at five points (positions) on the *x* axis for claimants and respondents: the initial claim and admitted liability (position 1), the reported amounts "really" owed (position 2), reported changes in position during intervention (position 3), and final adjustments (position 4). Note that the final outcomes taken from court rulings and mediated agreements (position 5), calculated as the mean percentage on the initial claim, are identical in the two fora. However, the outcomes for categorical

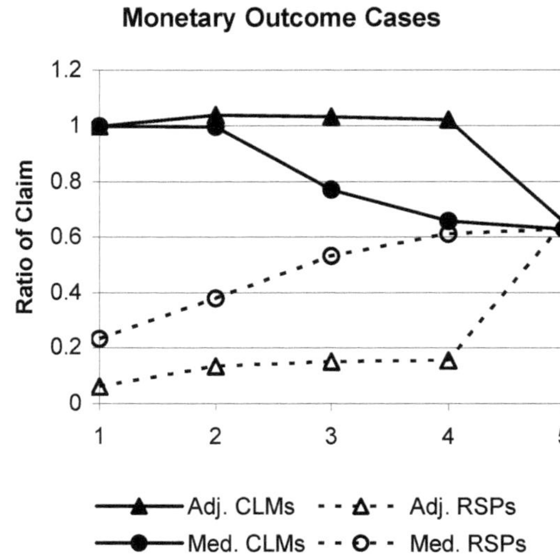

Bargaining Positions: 1 initial claim and admitted liability from court record; 2 reported amounts "really" owed; 3 reported changes during intervention; 4 reported final adjustments; 5 final outcomes taken from court rulings and mediated agreements

Figure 1.1 Positional Changes During Court and Mediation Processes

groups, as will be discussed throughout this work, are statistically divergent, both from other groups in the same forum and from the same groups in adjudication. The thrust of this work is to clarify how the mediation environment, and the interest-based negotiation process, operated for ethnic, gender, class, and professional categories of claimants (upper lines) and respondents (lower lines). This clarification rests heavily on theory and research in negotiations, discussed below and again in Chapter Seven.

Negotiation Assumptions

On the day-to-day level of practice, small claims mediation is a form of facilitated negotiation that assumes all parties are equal to the bargaining task, that the mediators themselves have no investments and do not influence outcomes, and that finding a negotiated solution to the conflict at hand (problem solving) is preferable to placing decision-making power in the hands of a judge, who, in turn, is theoretically ruling in the light of evidence, law and precedent. Negotiation, in turn, assumes self-interested negotiators are making rational choices.

Narrowly-defined rational choice assumptions are "productive assumptions" (Schelling 1963), especially in mathematical modeling of decision-making, because they assume quantifiable goals ("utilities") and an instrumental rationality that makes the design of laboratory tests more convincing. An example of this is the way that experimental subjects are manipulated into instrumental motivation by cash rewards for "winning." Citing the common financial plight of students to affirm that self-maximizing motivation was likely, careful exchange researchers like Molm (1991) specify the amounts of money that student-subjects can win from their negotiation performance. However, this narrow theoretical frame clearly misses important individual and group-level differences in goals, strategies, and identities. More broadly-defined rational choice theory assumes that non-material, expressive goals and psychological outcomes are pursued (weighed, compared and strategized) in the same instrumental fashion. For example, in a strategy not unlike Durkheim's *Homo duplex,* theorists posit that expressive (Collins 1981; Etzioni 1988), equity (Blalock & Wilken 1979), or group (Margolis 1982) interests are simply additional utilities, and use these concepts to account for measurable divergences from individually self-maximizing social behavior.

Exchange theorist Freidman (1987) pointed out that this theoretical practice is ultimately tautological, that is, the achieved outcome explains any bargaining behavior because the negotiator is presumed to have been seeking it. The MetroCourt data allows us to examine the relationship of stated goals to bargaining behavior to assess how closely the self-maximizing model approximated the empirical reality.

Dual Concern Model

As researchers in the mediation process, and in explicit recognition of the limitations in the rigid rational choice model, Pruitt & Carnevale (1993) proposed a "dual concern model" of negotiations. The dual concern model generates a matrix for understanding individual conflict styles: Low concern for one's own and other's outcomes leads to avoiding; high self-concern with low other-concern results in competition/contending; low self-concern with high other-concern leads to conceding/obliging; moderate concern for self and other leads to compromise; and high self-concern with high other-concern, according to this research, leads to the ideal problem-solving style able to create integrative, win-win outcomes.

Within the dominant, self-interested negotiation paradigm, Pruitt & Carnevale describe how negotiators operate between two poles: on the one hand, a negotiator seeks to maximize outcomes in light of alternatives to get the "best" outcome, and on the other, a negotiator specifically does not want to have been a "sucker." Between these limits (the best and the exploited), negotiating behavior is conceptualized on a continuum of *soft* to *firm* depending on the negotiators' willingness to concede during negotiations.

FIRM AND SOFT BARGAINING

Firm negotiators, also called "tough" bargainers, are likely to make large initial demands and resist reciprocal concession making. Logically and empirically, if agreement is reached at all, firmer negotiators achieve better outcomes. As a strategy, bargaining resistance risks lack of agreement but can also cause a negotiator eager for resolution to overmatch slight or no concessions. Positional commitment, a specific strategy in tough bargaining, is theoretically described by Schelling (1963): negotiators are paradoxically strengthened if they can claim a *lack* of agency because if they are bound to specific positions and consequences, they gain credibility and their "final position" carries more weight.

Since bargaining resistance is a successful self-maximizing strategy, it is associated with higher self-concern and implied instrumental motivation. However, positional commitment and rigidity are also likely for negotiators with positive alternatives and therefore willing to end negotiations without an agreement, and for those unwilling to compromise strong beliefs and justice principles.

Soft bargainers are likely to overmatch and concede early, without exploring the full range of options. Early conciliation diminishes final outcomes for the conciliator due to "tracking." In tracking, parties tend to match concessions, contentiousness, and take bargaining positions within a consistent distance from the other party. Soft negotiators who cooperate regardless of the other party's moves, are most effective if the other party is also soft. They would lose more if the other party is exploitative.

Because over-matching and early concession-making is a less successful self-maximizing strategy, especially if the other party is exploitative, a logical interpretation is higher other-concern and implied expressive motivation. However, soft bargaining could also indicate the perception or reality of poor alternatives. Other psychological motivations that might be considered expressive, such as discomfort with disputing, have no immediate relational connection to the other party.

Pruitt & Carnevale argue that problem solving is more likely when the bargaining strategy is balanced between soft and firm for both bargainers, and both negotiators hold a balanced and lively concern for their own outcomes as well as those of the other party. The dual concern model spells out the processes leading to imbalanced outcomes and the probability of reaching an agreement. In general, greater taking is likely when self-interest is higher than concern for the other party and/or the bargainer is firmer with a softer negotiation partner. Greater giving is likely when concern for the other is higher than self-concern and/or the bargainer is softer with a firmer negotiating partner. Two firm negotiators often fail to reach agreement; two soft negotiators are usually able to agree, but their outcomes may be less than the optimal point of highest joint benefit.

In zero-sum bargaining such as one based on a strictly monetary dispute like those examined here, exchanging concessions with the other party—reciprocal concession-making—is the essential ingredient in problem-solving negotiation processes. However, although reciprocity norms are powerful motivators in negotiations (Axelrod 1984; Blalock & Wilken 1979; Molm, Quist & Wisely 1993), bargainers often match frequency without matching magnitude. Typically, more powerful negotiators undermatch the concessions made by weaker parties. End stage "close the gap" concessions are particularly decisive when the other party is resistant or tough, indicating an investment in reaching an agreement. Gouldner (1960) defines exploitation as a failure to reciprocate.

Pruitt & Carnevale identify three variables affecting bargaining behavior: *fairness* refers to culturally sensitive norms concerning the proper way of disputing (process) and deciding outcomes (distribution); *power* refers to the dyadic relation, especially determined by the negotiators' alternatives; and the *relationship* between the parties. All of these variables are open to ethnic and gender patterning.

FAIRNESS NORMS

Fairness is at the heart of justice claims and shared fairness norms facilitate resolutions. Pruitt & Carnevale argue that common fairness rules provide the basis for tacit bargaining leading to a rapid resolution (see also Schelling's 1963 discussion of "focal points" for decision-making within a field of possibilities). However, when disputants do not share a fairness rule, research and theoretical speculation suggest divergent probabilities. If the fairness rules point in opposite directions, agreements reached by lengthy and complex bargaining might be truly balanced and integrative. However, divergent fairness rules could also narrow negotiations through positional rigidity.

Fiske (1991, 1992) argued that fairness rules, the normative expectations that structure exchange behavior and justice perceptions, are culturally learned and situationally evoked. He synthesized theory from Weber, Piaget & Ricoeur with anthropological research to demonstrate four identifiable and inherent patterns of relational exchange he calls "structures." These could also be called distributional norms.

The first, "communal sharing" is a need-based distributional norm. Examples of this are the exchange relationship found in the family, "primordial" collectivism (Van den Berghe 1981), traditional and gift-based economies (Mauss 1990 [1950]), and what Durkheim conceived of as "mechanical solidarity." As an ethic, it underlies the ideals of communism, communitarianism (e.g., Etzioni 1988; Bellah et al. 1985) and the mystical unity found in most theologies and metaphysical traditions. As a memory, communal sharing evokes images of colonial America, preconquest pueblos, and *Nuevomexicano* village interdependence.

Fiske's second exchange structure, "authority-ranking," is a distribution norm in which an unequal exchange that favors the superior is usually accepted as legitimate inequality by the subordinate. Status trumps all. As an ethic, it underlies the ideals of kingship, patriarchy, jurisprudence, pedagogy and the devotional practices of virtually all religions. Social relations based on authority deference are the exchange relation expected from ideologies supporting the Great Chain of Being (Takaki 1979), the meaningfulness of sacrifice and restraint (Gans 1985), the power-dependent relationship, and vertical cultural patterns (Triandis & Gelfand 1998). It characterizes the psychological dynamics of authoritarian regimes, and may be indistinguishable from Marxian "false consciousness" where disadvantaged people accept status differences as a reflection of merit and competence (Delgado et al. 1985; Ridgeway 1993).

Fiske's third exchange pattern, "equality matching," is a strictly in-kind reciprocity, in which the distribution norm is tit-for-tat, eye-for-eye. As an egalitarian ethic, it can be as competitive as it is even-handed. Leung & Iwakwaki (1988) explain that the "generous allocation norms" said to be an insider dynamic in collectivist cultures result from an equality distributional norm applied by parties who have actually contributed more, and an equity distribution when they have contributed less. The authors cite research using a Chinese sample suggesting that collectivist cultures stress the equality distribution norm with insiders.

Fiske describes the fourth model, "market pricing," as the equity exchange in modern capitalist society. Rewards are distributed according to input, and input is valued in accordance with a market metric. The ethic is

Smithian and the motivational base is individually self-maximizing and opportunity driven (Davis & Moore 1945). Fiske argues that the tendency of western thinkers to see exchange *only* through this equity structure is an ethnocentric and historically peculiar conception of human nature, one that banishes all other motives to social or moral arenas. This misses the point that economic self interest is culturally formulated.

In addition to cultural learning, Fiske specifies that the situation will determine which exchange norm or fairness rule will be applied. In this book, I will describe the environment and mediation context, and specifically address the negotiation situation in light of the similarity by category (insider-outsider) of the other party during the mediation session.

Based on Hofstede's ranking of national cultures (see Smith & Bond 1993: 40), compared to acculturation in the United States, Latin American cultures are more collectivistic, more likely to socialize individuals toward greater concern for the other. Furthermore, Latin American cultures are ranked as accepting greater distance between higher and lower status individuals (i.e., greater acceptance of social hierarchy), socializing members toward a greater willingness to legitimate unequal power relations. U.S. acculturation on the same scales is likely to encourage higher self-concern (individualistic) and a willingness to challenge superiors. Triandis & Gelfand (1998) suggest that the acceptance or rejection of hierarchy in a culture is actually an attribute, or subtype termed vertical and horizontal respectively. Latino culture as described by Hofstede is thus "vertical collectivism" and U.S. culture by this description is "horizontal individualism" (see Triandis 1995). Transposed to fairness norms, these cultural patterns suggest that Latino bargaining would be guided by authority ranking in imbalanced conditions and by equality-based exchange with equals (Leung & Iwakwaki 1988). This combination of rules is essentially the definition of generous allocation (see Chapter Seven). Anglo bargaining, by contrast, would be guided by equity fairness rules, regardless of the status relationship.

POWER DIFFERENCES

Structural exchange research (Molm 1987, 1988; see generally, Cook 1987) has more clearly addressed questions of power difference using game research techniques. Negotiating decisions were examined in dyads in which the power differentials between the negotiators (i.e., the negotiators' dependence on one another) were specifically manipulated by structuring the quality and number of alternatives for each negotiator (Molm 1991). Results suggest that power relations influenced the negotiations, but these influences were modified by reciprocity norms, equity values, and a relative aversion to using loss-inflicting ("punishment") strategies by more advantaged actors. Weaker parties were less likely to retaliate when stronger parties used loss-inflicting strategies. However, contrary to the hypotheses that more advantaged actors would gladly use their power, Molm (1991) found that their reported satisfaction was directly proportional to *increases* in the disadvantaged parties' outcomes, and decreased with the losses to disadvantaged negotiation partners.

Interestingly, in other research, parties who were ignorant of the structural power dynamics strove harder to "win." But when players were privy to the way that power was structured, consistently advantaging one and disadvantaging the other, stronger parties were found to take less, and weaker parties lost motivation to strive for more (Cook & Hegtvedt 1986). These research results are consistent with theoretical clarifications associated with the power dependent relationship and the internalized oppression thesis described in Chapter Two and Chapter Nine.

Based in Emerson's (1962) work on power dependent relations, Janeway (1980) pointed out that hierarchical relationships are in fact mutually dependent. These relationships are organized less on fear, than on mutual construction of hierarchical dependencies. More powerful parties rely on weaker parties to affirm the legitimacy of their dominance. In a thesis similar to the historical argument that slave-owners moderated their behavior out of fear of slave revolt, theorists have explained a self-interested reason for stronger party concessions based on fear of retaliation (see Blalock & Wilken 1979; Molm 1991; Molm Quist & Wisely 1994; Schelling 1963; Knight & Kagan 1977). Stronger claimants with weaker respondents might have more subtle motivations for other-concern, because they depend on weaker respondents for compliance (McEwen & Maiman 1984, 1989). In summary, power dependent relationships may have normative proscriptions on power use, materially-based fear of reprisal, and/or expressive psychological needs for legitimacy that can stimulate the stronger party to show concern for the weaker.

Acceptance or rejection of hierarchy would likely affect disputants' responses to power differences. Pruitt & Carnevale note that negotiations are often most difficult in the face of small power differences, a condition likely to engage a "power struggle." By contrast, negotiations proceeded with less contention when the negotiators hold relatively equal power or when the power discrepancy is extreme. The authors interpret the latter situation as due to the recognition by weaker parties that struggle is hopeless.

Positive & Negative Relationships

Like the positive and negative relationships with which they are associated, trust and distrust tend to be matched and to persist over time. Pruitt & Carnevale speculate that trusters tend to worry less about looking like suckers and would be more likely to make concessions to fill the gap produced by the other party's failure to concede at a deadline. Distrust is central to negative negotiating relationships, where bargainers tend to match contentious strategies (i.e., bargaining resistance and threats). In the absence of data, Pruitt and Carnevale theorized that past competition would result in less negativity if the competition was kept within normative boundaries that exclude taking unfair advantage.

The interpersonal relationship between the negotiators has a strong influence on the bargaining process. Pruitt & Carnevale describe positive and negative relationships, noting that the two negotiators tend to perceive and enact the same kind of relationship with one another. That is, if one party perceives a positive relationship with the other, the other is likely to describe the relationship similarly. The authors cite research documenting that, once established, the positivity or negativity of relationships tends to persist over time.

Positive relationships increase problem solving and concession making and negotiations are less likely to include contentious tactics (i.e., resistance and threats). Positive relationships imply that negotiators trust one another: they expect that the other party will cooperate in the future and will not consistently exploit concessions in the present. As an individual trait, trust appeared to be the difference between negotiators who matched the other party's contentious tactics and those who did not reciprocate or match contention.

Bonds of perceived similarity, kinship, common group membership, and a history of prior cooperation encourage positive relationships. Positive relationships that do not result in over-conceding (a problem in, for example, new romantic relationships) are called "working relationships" and may be expressively or instrumentally motivated. For example, positive concern for the other was manipulated in Pruitt & Carnevale's research by giving negotiators a gift prior to negotiating (expressive) or by telling negotiator-subjects that they would need to cooperate in the future (instrumental).

Trust and the social bonds of collectivist cultural patterns are probably analogous concepts. "Trusters" tended to restrict their own extractions in resource dilemma games when other parties over-exploited, rather than to match selfish behavior (Pruitt & Carnevale 1993). Parks & Vu (1994) found the same pattern in an experimental test of persons socialized in individualist (U.S.) versus collectivist (recent Vietnamese immigrant) societies. In the research reviewed by Pruitt & Carnevale, trusting was not tested for its effects on demands and concessions in negotiations, but the authors speculated that trusters would worry less about looking like suckers and be more likely to make concessions and fill the gap produced by the other party's failure to concede at a deadline. However, Parks & Vu did test this dyadic response. They found that the Vietnamese subjects were likely to cooperate longer than Anglos in the prisoner's dilemma game, even in the face of competitive moves ("defection") by the computerized other.

Negative relationships tend to perpetuate themselves by matching contentious strategies, by selective perception of the other party and inaccurate blame attributions (see Chapter Seven). Once established, changing a negative relationship pattern is difficult. Pruitt & Carnevale cite historical examples—e.g., Egyptian president Anwar Sadat's peace initiative with Israel—and research suggesting that unilateral conciliatory initiatives, gifts that have obvious costs to the giver and are irrevocable and noncontingent, are sometimes able to build trust in an historically negative intergroup relationship. Trust enhancement is especially likely if the gesture is identified, announced, and carried through by stronger parties. Mere contact with some communication is not particularly helpful, and can escalate the hostility in profoundly negative relationships, an outcome found also in some attempts to intervene in negative inter-ethnic relationships. In the absence of data, Pruitt and Carnevale theorize that past competition results in less relationship negativity if the competition was kept within normative boundaries and the other party was not perceived to be trying to gain an *unfair* advantage. Thus, theoretically, the positivity of hierarchical inter-group relations is indirect evidence of normative, or accepted hierarchy.

Trust can be considered analogous to collectivist cultural patterns of mutual dependence and generosity with insiders. Collectivist cultures might also have distinct expressive motives in bargaining situations that appear as trust but might be due to face needs. Ting-Toomey (1988) argued that "face needs" (an appearance consistent with self-identity) are particularly likely to be different for persons from collectivist, high context cultures vs. individualistic, low context cultures. Identities formed in collectivist cultures are likely to seek "positive face" (association needs) while individualistic cultures encourage an identity that values autonomy, resulting in needs for "negative face" (independence needs). Furthermore, collectivist identities would also, theoretically, be motivated to maintain the positive face of other parties, that is, to not subject them to shame.

Thus, expressive collectivist patterns might well appear as "other-concern" as discussed by Pruitt & Carnevale, but derive from very different sources and, as these things often do, obscure the difference between self and other concern.

Among New Mexican Latinos (*Nuevomexicanos*) behavior that appears as untrusting may be based in the history of Anglo exploitation. Chapter Three summarizes the ambiguous historical relationship between Anglo and *Nuevomexicanos* populations in the Southwest, especially in legal contexts. The pattern suggests a muted but conscious awareness of ethnicity-based discrimination and conflicts of interest[2]. Given the history, Latino distrust might undermine any normative status deference in Latino culture, or Latinos might avoid harmony models entirely[3]. Nader (1990) observed this as a conscious strategy in the indigenous Talean village she studied for thirty years: villagers used harmony-based justice models with other villagers but adversarial procedures to press and resist claims with the stronger Mexican state. Although Keefe & Padilla found that Chicano identity related to past discrimination, it is not clear that this identity implied a lack of trust toward Anglos. The present bargaining situation is analyzed to more clearly indicate not only whether Latinos *did* seem trusting toward Anglos, but also whether trust or distrust was warranted.

EXPLOITATION

Scholars critical of mediation are most concerned with present exploitation. Delgado et al. (1985:1400) focused this concern on the risks of prejudice in informal conflict resolution procedures: "[T]he rules and structures of formal justice tend to suppress bias, whereas informality tends to increase it." Prejudice, whether originating from psychodynamic (following Adorno), or sociohistorical scapegoating forces, or learned through group influence and socialization as stereotypes, shows "situational specificity." People express prejudice when the environment encourages it. Delgado et al. argue that justice institutions have structured procedures to encourage appropriate behavior, and unstructured and intimate environments offer less protection for women and minorities. Formality also encourages Latino disputants to pursue their rights because formality "increases the Latino group member's sense of control and . . . [thus] becomes self-fulfilling: Latino persons are encouraged to pursue their legal rights as though prejudice were unlikely and thus the possibility of prejudice is in fact lessened" (Delgado et al. 1985:1391).

Similarly, concern for outcome imbalances that result from soft bargaining when meeting an exploitative negotiator undergirds the feminist argument against mediation in divorce cases (Bryan 1992; Grillo 1991). The argument assumes that women are conciliatory and soft, and that the men are exploitative. For example, Bryan (1992:444) writes that "mediation unobtrusively reduces the threat to patriarchy by returning men to their former dominant position."

Overall, scholarship suggests that Latinos and women are vulnerable to exploitation from two sources. Delgado et al. portray ethnic minority parties as vulnerable to unconstrained and irrational majority group prejudice and therefore apt to retreat from the contest. Feminists portray women as vulnerable through an internalized relational ethic.

Culture & Negotiation

Possibly to its detriment, most of the cross-cultural research in communications, psychology, business and cognitive science, employs the cultural construct of individualism-collectivism, including ethnic and gender differences in conflict styles and behaviors. Recently, perhaps because a world that is globalizing seeks ways of understanding cross-cultural differences (Snider & Styles 2001), a startling number of studies confirm the validity and utility of the Individualism-Collectivism (IND-COL) construct (Triandis 1995), but have also revealed its limitations[4]. Researchers and theorists pursue clarity on the boundary between cultural universals and more localized patterns[5], between either of these and individual expression[6], and between objective behavior and subjective experience[7]. Despite all of these unknowns, twenty-five years of cross-cultural research, relying largely on Asian populations as "collectivists," has identified regularities in culture that can serve to deepen our understanding of others (see Chapter Two, Three and Seven).

Susan Riderle (2003), a New Mexican communications scholar, recently presented an overview of existing research on Anglo and Mexican American conflict styles. She defines the IND-COL as a "basic level of societal organization and individual orientation within cultures [where] the deepest cultural differences lie." She identifies Mexico as an undisputed collectivist culture and asserts that Mexican Americans "display collectivist tendencies."

Citing Condon (1985), Riderle describes Latino-Anglo differences in this way:

> Typical of collectivists, Mexicans see themselves as more closely interconnected than U.S. Americans, but Mexicans also value self-analysis and knowledge of their unique qualities more than Americans, which is not typically a collectivist trait. . . . the U.S. emphasizes individualism

> and Mexico values individuality. . . . Both value the individual, but U.S. Americans believe that people are basically the same barring external life influences, each person should be judged by her character or individual merit, and this merit (and one's personal worth) manifest in one's actions. Mexicans believe in the inherent, innate uniqueness of a person that is not always evident through actions or achievements. It is a concept closer to "soul" than "character" and the resulting dignity of a person, regardless of social class, must be protected and respected.

Similar to the values encoded in Anglo jurisprudence, individualists in conflict believe that they are each responsible for their own behavior; it is thus their "duty" to directly express their ideas with the right to disagree and remain unmoved by the other, in the belief that truth is found in debate. In collectivist worlds, in contrast, "the boundary between the self and others is not as defined; self-expression is often subsumed to meeting others' expectations and responsibilities, and hierarchy operates through reciprocity, not the imposition of the superior's will" (Rinderle 2003).

Power differences are often left out of the cross-cultural research. This vacancy exists even though, as Rinderle notes, the bulk of the world's population and cultures are collectivist—economically, the poor majority, adapting as humans long have through mutuality. On the other hand, trailing the United States, the most individualistic cultures are western nations—economically, the rich minority, riding modern affluence and lamenting the loss of community. This is the meeting ground of this study.

Chapter Two

Culture, Hierarchy, & Ethnicity[1]

Karst (1993:6) defines nonmaterial culture as a community of meaning and morality, "the matrix of the sense of self." Individuals, to the extent that they share a specific group identity, share conscious and unconscious *patterns* of values, meanings and taken-for-granted assumptions about proper behavior for self and others (Merry 1987; Just 1992). Culture affects people's belief or cognitive representations of what negotiation is all about, defines appropriate and inappropriate behavior, and suggests appropriate goals or what is important in the negotiation (Adair 2004). But cultures do not simply define differences, as if equal complementaries or imaginary opposites, because difference becomes a basis for constructing relations between levels in hierarchies of power (Wilden 1987). Wilden points out how dichotomization, like individualist-collectivist, obscures the way these types of opposites are organized in dependent hierarchies such that cultural identities are shaped by hierarchical status. Latino and Anglo cultures are organized not just as ethnic difference, but as minority-majority groups.

The terms "majority" and "minority," regardless of actual numbers, refer to dominant and subordinate groups.

> Ethnic groups are inherently ethnocentric, regarding their own cultural traits as natural, correct, and superior to those of other ethnic groups, who are perceived as odd, amusing, inferior or immoral. . . . a majority-minority relationship between two ethnicities will not come about unless the groups are competing for the same scarce resources and, most important, one group possesses superior power to impose its will on the other (Noel 1968 cf Yetman 1991:1–2).

Scholarship that dualizes culture as insiders and outsiders without accounting for hierarchical relationships between them, or focuses on hierarchical position without accounting for cultural content or worldviews, probably describes the vast majority of social science writing. In most of the literature used in this work, scholars have addressed *either* the two (or more) categories as if they were equals *or* have seen the categories as dominant-subordinate pairs in hierarchies without accounting for cultural differences. For example, anthropology and communications tend to explore cultural differences as horizontal and un-ranked (perhaps "nested" or concentric); but sociology tends to describe vertical relations (stratification) as if there were no specific content. The result is a tendency to ignore the way hierarchy constitutes cultural forms, or to generalize the effects of hierarchy to all subordinate groups, regardless of cultural differences. These aspects are difficult to disentangle because the stratification of cultures influences both cognitive and behavioral patterning and is notoriously divergent in response to situations (Hutchins 1995; Avruch, Black & Scimecca 1991; Baltes & Straudinger 1996; for an example see Giles & Johnson 1986).

CULTURE & STATUS

Cultural researchers borrow the distinction of *emic* and *etic* from anthropology to refer to subjective experiences of meaning and belief (emic) on the one hand; and objective, observable cultural patterns (etic) on the other (Gelfand et al 2001; Morris et al 1999). Subjective or emic culture can only be inferred; objective or etic culture is an empirical reality that can be tested and generalized across a categorical group. However, etic concepts universal enough to be applied cross-culturally have an inherent but unwarranted privilege, applying the researcher's interpretations embedded in the concepts themselves. The distinction is helpful when seeking to understand how hierarchy manifests in a specific cultural system. While it is true that individuals objectively assigned to a culture group will vary profoundly in the extent to which they personally identify with it, etic researchers have demonstrated group-level behavioral differences that suggest shared cognitive maps for understanding and acting. Although these data were not gathered with a cultural analysis in mind, and I have created variables to capture my abstract concepts, I sought regularities in Latino and Anglo objective behavior in a research strategy that might be called a "derived etic," clarified by theoretical frameworks provided by cross-cultural and negotiation scholars and their research, and the MetroCourt data itself.

This section looks at three related issues of culture and hierarchy. First, as noted in Chapter One, cultures can be described by the degree to which hierarchy is *accepted* within the society. Second, the insider-outsider distinction shown to be more critical in collectivist cultures is also a discrimination pattern, a major tool for *maintaining* hierarchy. Third, majority and minority cultures are themselves shaped by their *rank* in a society, elaborating patterns of response and resistance to oppression and privilege.

Status Acceptance and Individualism-Collectivism

Triandis & Gelfand (1998) suggested attributes of horizontal[2] (emphasizing equality) or vertical (emphasizing hierarchy) are important distinctions further defining the constructs of individualism and collectivism. Over decades of his own and others' investigations, Triandis (1995) clarified four attributes of the IND-COL "polythetic" construct: personal/independent vs. collective/interdependent definition of the self; prioritizing personal vs. group goals; emphasis on rationality and exchange relationships vs. relatedness and communal relationships; and social behavior guided by attitudes vs. norms. Combinations of these attributes give specificity to national variations in IND-COL akin to the variety of species (storks, robins) within the genus "birds" (feathers and wings). Thus, Japanese collectivism can be distinguished from Korean collectivism (Triandis & Gelfand 1998) or, as concerns us here, Latino collectivism can be distinguished from Chinese collectivism.

Triandis & Gelfand (1998) contend that the *most* important attribute that distinguishes among different kinds of individualism and collectivism is the relative emphasis on horizontal and vertical social relationships. For example, in the horizontal individualism (HI) pattern, people want to be unique and distinct from groups, are likely to say "I want to do my own thing," and are highly self-reliant (as individualists), but not especially interested in becoming distinguished or in having high status. In the vertical individualist pattern (VI), people often want to acquire status by individual competitions with others and are likely to say "I want to be the best." In the vertical collectivism (VC) pattern, according to this definition, people emphasize the integrity of the ingroup, are willing to sacrifice their personal goals for the sake of ingroup goals, and support competitions of their ingroups with outgroups. In the horizontal collectivist (HC) pattern, In HC, people see themselves as being similar to others (e.g., one person, one vote) and emphasize common goals with others, interdependence, and sociability, but they do not submit easily to authority.

The horizontal-vertical distinction can distinguish national cultures: for example, differences between individualist cultures can be identified as valuing equality and individual freedom (e.g., Sweden) or valuing market competition and freedom (e.g., the United States). Thus, in contrast to Hofstede's classification of "power distance" in which U.S. ranks as "low" power distance because we have few social forms by which authority is honored and privileged, Triandis' system would emphasize the U.S. vertical economic and social structures demanding competition to rise in rank. Triandis does not discuss the vertical-horizontal qualification in relation to Latin American cultures, but differences on this and Triandis' other dimensions may help to explain the variation in collectivism reported for Latin American countries (Oyserman, Coon & Kemmelmeier 2002).

Who is inside and does it matter?

Scholars (e.g., Triandis et al 1988; Pruitt & Carnevale 1993) consistently argue that collectivist but not individualistic cultures sharply delineate between insiders (those perceived as being within a group boundary) and outsiders (those perceived as outside a group boundary). This differentiation is presumably related to an "interdependent self construal" (Ting-Toomey et al 2001; Oetzel 1998) and a greater need for affiliation found in collectivist cultures. Specifically, collectivist cultures are likely to use generous allocation norms and harmony or conciliation models to resolve conflicts with insiders; but use equity allocation rules and adversarial processes with outsiders (Leung & Iwakwaki 1988; Nader 1990). Historical examples of insider giving and outsider resistance are commonplace. For example, until U.S. annexation of the southwest territory from Mexico, land in the current state of New Mexico could not be sold to foreigners (i.e., Anglos) but much of the land was held communally by Mexican citizens (Ebright 1994).

However, ingroups can be formed on almost any line of difference with predictable biased perception and discriminatory effects (Worchel 1999). Research cited by Pruitt & Carnevale (1993) indicated that coercion was rated as more "appropriate" with outgroup members and conciliation was seen as more appropriate with ingroup members including professional and corporate ingroups. Protectionist boundaries are not exclusive to collectivist national cultures: trade and immigration policies that exclude outsiders have been used selectively by all nations. Moreover, although ingroup dynamics are ubiquitous, the nature of the situation can readily create and disperse competitive group boundaries, primarily by prior and probable future cooperation or competition[3]. Among U.S. college students, Lawler & Yoon (1993) showed that expressive motivation, including altruistic exchange, may be generated over time through repeated instrumental exchange. Furthermore, recent research has been unable to demonstrate the more harsh and even exploitative allocation expected to apply to outsiders. Self-report research testing insider generosity has been unable to support it cross-nationally (Leung & Iwakwaki 1988) and Pruitt

& Carnevale report important qualifications in the negotiations literature. Although in several studies group boundaries did heighten trust, concession-making, and the likelihood of joint approaches with ingroup members, negotiation patterns with outgroup members were better predicted by the withingroup patterns (Pruitt & Carnevale 1993:162–63). Overall, Triandis et al. (1988; 1995) point out, the entire definition of "insider" is highly variable, ranging from family to workgroup to national group depending on the culture group and the situation.

What appears to be consistent is that cultural groups are accurately identified by the very fact of having dual boundaries that define proper insider behavior as well as defining outsiders (Royce 1982; Worchel 1999). The group identity is defined in relation to, and sometimes against, what is outside (Tajfel 1978). Barth (1969) suggested that cultural groups are best examined by the *nature* of their boundaries, their permeability and patterns of exclusion/incorporation (see also de Vos & Romanucci-Ross 1975; Royce 1982). Although ethnic boundaries are critical to this study, boundary management is a central task in all culture groups. Thus, for example, legal cultures maintain boundaries by Bar Associations and the "linguistic chauvinism" of Latin terminology (Kramarae, Schultz & O'Barr 1984). Men and women specify the behavior expected of their own and the other gender, thus defining out sexual ambiguity.

Scholars attribute the more persistent group boundaries associated with enhanced ethnic identity to historical patterns of exclusion (Banton 1983). Nieto-Phillips (2004) describes the ethnic revival of "pure blood" Spanish identity in the New Mexico territory seeking statehood (1880–1910) in reaction to prevalent views that all Mexican peoples were racially non-white and "unfit" to assume the rights and responsibilities of full U.S. citizenship. In the post-Civil Rights era, Keefe & Padilla (1987) found that enhanced ethnic loyalty among Chicanos in California was highly correlated with past individual experiences of discrimination. Banton and Keefe & Padilla noted that, theoretically and logically, resistant ethnic boundaries were caused and perpetuated by dominant culture exclusion; Banton specified that interethnic (inter-group) competition, as opposed to individual (interpersonal) level competition, builds the resistance of ethnic group boundaries. Keefe and Padilla (1987:193) specified that the ethnic enclosure (unintegrated social networks) reported by Anglos probably contributes to the persistence of Latino ethnicity: "It is striking to observe the lack of inter-group contact. . . . [and it] appears likely that as long as unequal status (majority vs. minority group) exists between Anglos and Chicanos, ethnicity will continue to be the major feature separating the two groups."

Insider-outsider relations are often vertical relationships with a power gradient across the boundary. The focus on dyadic conditions in mediation provides an inter-group relational context for questions of giving, conceding, and taking in status-imbalanced or vertical relationships on the one hand, and status-balanced or horizontal relations on the other. In vertical relationships "otherness" and "outsiders" are a basis for exclusion and discrimination. Relationships across the vertical boundary have typical patterns that can be applied to any dominant-subordinate intergroup relations (Miller 1976): men and women, majority-minority, lawyer-pro se, corporate-private individual "persons," upper-lower class.

Internalized Hierarchy

When culture and ethnicity are hierarchically ranked as majority and minority, as is the case in the United States today, the status dimension affects both the individual self-identity and the outer cultural behavior. This sort of historical experience in the life of an individual or in the "community of memory" informs ethnic identity (Bellah et al 1985; Yetman 1991) not simply as differentiation (Tajfel 1978), but as excluded, subordinated, undeserving, relatively deprived and/or angry. This individual behavior objectively carries "the mark of oppression" (cf. Emerson 1962), discouraging a sense of competence through internalized oppression and often becoming a self-fulfilling prophecy in social interaction. For example, Lipton et al. (1991) reported that when Latinos chose jobs in which they thought they would succeed from a list of neutral job descriptions, their choices tended to reflect internalized job preferences based in occupational stereotypes.

In other status dimensions, the same interactive dynamic can be found that Ridgeway (1997) argues can re-create hierarchy despite organizational and legal change. For example, members of higher class cultures may move with an ease and air of competence that encourages deference from others (Collins 1975); members of lower class cultures are often perceived as less legitimate and even less truthful than higher class culture members due to subtle differences in patterns of speech (O'Barr 1982; Kramarae, Schultz & O'Barr 1984; Nichols 1984); women, especially in tasks associated with men, are perceived as less competent by others. Prophesy fulfillment occurs when subordinates share the group assessment (Ridgeway 1993). In the last example, women participate less and lack confidence which then reaffirms the stereotype and contributes to prophesy-fulfillment (Ridgeway 1997).

All attempts to describe and explain internalized oppression, especially those linked to culture, are vulnerable to criticisms that such explanations "blame the victim," a problem that has impinged on the ability of social science to accurately investigate social problems involving poor and minority communities over the past three decades (Wilson 1987; Harvey & Reed 1996). In *Blaming the Victim* Ryan (1971) analyzed how privileged people must believe that they earned and deserve all that they have in order to maintain a positive self-concept and their belief in a just world. This bias leads to looking for differences that can be blamed for others' oppressive circumstances. Thus the distortions and compensations that *resulted* from oppression become the *cause* for social failure in the present. The charge of "blaming the victim" was leveled at the 1965 Moynihan Report use of the "culture of poverty" thesis (originally applied to a rural Mexican family) to explain persistent poverty among urban African Americans. In *The Promised Land,* Nicholas Lemann (1992:177) says of the Moynihan Report.

> Today the Moynihan Report stands as probably the most refuted document in American history (though of course its dire predictions about the poor black family all came true). . . . [T]he practical effect of the controversy over it was exactly the opposite of what Moynihan intended—all public discussions in mainstream liberal circles of issues like the state of the black family and the culture of poverty simply ceased.

In the same period, gender identities were valorized without attention to the distortions resulting from patriarchal social organization (Flax 1993). The relative silence of liberal social science has left important questions unanswered: what patterns are inherent in acculturation or socialization and which are caused by discrimination and stratification? What patterns are adaptations to hierarchical relations? Although we seem to be headed in the other direction, it is interesting to wonder what might change with increased equality[4]?

GENDER HIERARCHY

Because sex is the most conspicuous duality in our species, the relations between the sexes give insight into theories and patterns of hierarchy based on otherness (de Beauvoir 1952). But what is this otherness? Chodorow and feminists following her line of thinking (see Jordan et al. 1991) claim a gender-specific *psychodynamic development* based on relationality and empathy. Other scholars suppose that gender identity is *learned* from observation and imitation, reinforced by others' response to behavior that reflects an appropriate gender role (see Frieze et al 1978; Lorber & Farrell 1991). Scholars following Piaget and Bem (see Taylor & Bernstein Miller 1994;

Gilligan 1982; Holmbeck & Bale 1988) suggest that women and men take different paths of cognitive development patterned by gender "schema" that are more or less coordinated with biology. Although I personally lean toward the latter, cognitive explanation, all theories arrive at the same point: women and men behave *as if* they think differently, with women following a more relational logic and men following a more rule-based pattern (e.g., Lakoff 1987; Lakoff & Johnson 1980; MacCormac 1990; Rack 1991).

In terms of vertical position, it is largely undisputed that male perspectives have shaped the public social world. Feminists often extend the meaning of this empirically observed male control to contend that male perspectives carry the seeds of domination. For centuries, women have argued that if women had more power (e.g., suffrage), the public world would be different. In a more contemporary and subtle version of this argument, Keller (1985) makes the point that science has been dominated by men, and as a consequence the scientific ideologies of objectivity and dominance are largely unexamined.

Keller (1985) writes that the science establishment ignored her own and decades of prior evidence that there were no "pacemaker cells" in slime mold colonies to serve as control centers for aggregation. In fact, slime mold colonies organize themselves and maintain their survival without hierarchy, but biologists maintained belief in pacemaker cells for decades without a shred of evidence. Keller wrote that the scientific community ignored the possibility of "dynamic autonomy" because the "masculinist ideological commitments" of the scientific community are organized by a "rhetoric of mastery" or domination which selects for specific styles of thought and communication. The scientific community will exclude alternative perspectives such as Barbara McClintock's "feeling for the organism" which led to her Nobel Prize for genetic transposition. This is not to say that McClintock's approach to doing science is gendered (McClintock herself would deny a gendered association); rather because modern science has been constructed by only one kind of people, mostly white men, it lacks the self-reflection that would come from including "other" perspectives. Similar arguments are often made about the masculinist construction of adversarial justice and rationalized jurisprudence (e.g., Taub & Schneider 1990; Berg 1994; Henderson 1991; Olsen 1990; MacKinnon 1984; Menkel-Meadow & Diamond 1991) and the media-driven image of the good life patterned on upper middle class lifestyles (Pizzigato 2004; Mantsios 2004).

Flax (1993) argued that the centrality (and valorization) of motherhood in feminist theorizing obscures the complex reality of connectedness acquired in the mother-daughter relationship and the constituting effects of patriarchy on female identity ("subjectivity"). The mother-daughter relationship intermingles nurturance (food, love, feeding) and control. Theoretical maneuvers that deny and evade "bad" forms of relating (e.g., hate, envy and the desire for control) serve to suppress women's aggression and desire for separateness. Furthermore, the simplification of connectedness results in a construct of "white woman innocence" that absolves us of complicity in racial domination. The conflation of woman-equals-mother ignores the constituting effects of patriarchal power on female subjectivity, and results in the fact that relations of power and domination are rarely explored except in discussions of masculinity (but see Eichenbaum & Orbach 1987).

When applied to disputing, feminist analyses of cross-gender relationship dynamics are unambiguous. Critical scholarship has focused on mandated mediation in divorce and custody cases (e.g., Leitch 1986; Bryan 1992; Fisher, Vidmar & Ellis 1993). Grillo (1991:1603) provides a good summary of the argument:

> Whether the ethic of care is to be enshrined as a positive virtue, or criticized as a characteristic not belonging to all women and contributing to their oppression, one truth emerges: many women see themselves, and judge their own worth, primarily in terms of relationships. This perspective on themselves has consequences for how they function in mediation. . . . Some commentators have identified mediation as a way to incorporate the ethic of care into the legal system and thereby modify the harshness of the adversary process. [But] If mediation does not successfully introduce an ethic of care [and] instead sells itself on that promise while delivering something coercive in its place, the consequences will be disastrous for a woman who embraces a relational sense of self. If she is easily persuaded to be cooperative, but her partner is not, she can only lose. If it is indeed her disposition to be caring and focused on relationships, and she has been rewarded for that focus and characterized as "unfeminine" when she departs from it, the language of relationship, caring, and cooperation will be appealing to her and make her vulnerable.

RACE-ETHNIC HIERARCHY

Historical Roots

Historically, sociological theories of group difference started from implicit theories of white supremacy ("biological racism") used as a justification for slavery (Frazier 1947). By the early twentieth century, social theory explained segregation as a human instinct of hatred ("prejudice") toward strangers, leading to the mid-century reliance on contact and association ("assimilation") as a remedy for what was then conceived as a problem that would whither under the leveling force of economic progress and the inter-individual competition that presumably characterized the modern centralized state. It turned out that none of these three major theoretical explanations (biology, prejudice, or lack of contact) for race-based inequality has withstood empirical tests over time: there was no biological basis, often there is no hatred, we are far more integrated, and still there is no equality.

Psychological prejudice is unable to explain race-ethnic injustice because contact and interventions based on its premises have shown little effect. Desegregation and twenty years of research (for reviews see Hewstone & Brown 1986; Fisher 1990) has led to the relatively simple understanding that inter-group attitudes change *after* groups reach equality, not before (Tajfel 1984; Schofield 1986). Ethnic prejudice derives from stereotypes or schema (Casmir 1985) that are a fundamental cognitive shorthand for the complex sensory array that humans receive all of the time. These stereotypes are organized in early cognitive development as self and other, allies and enemies (Tajfel 1978b; Group 1987; Volkan 1990; Mayer 1984; see also Delgado et al 1985). Group identity schemas are learned early: around the age of three, children develop ally-enemy cognitive discrimination and maintain specific categorizations with relative stability after the end of adolescence.

Although coordination exists between schemas and the social world, social categorizations, belief models or hypotheses can be maintained for extended periods in the face of disconfirming evidence (Grant 1990; Arthur 1994). Even when not filtered from one's awareness by selective perception, contrary evidence will often be attributed to an exceptional individual rather than modify the group stereotype (Tajfel 1978:59; see also Gudykunst 1988). Attempts to generalize from one example to the group stereotype needed careful structuring of the situation, and even then showed mixed results (Pettigrew 1986). As with women, stereotyped group members likely share the same schema and act in accordance with it, thus fulfilling the prophecy of the stereotype (Berger & Zelditch 1985; Hegtvedt 1988; see Chapter Nine). Most researchers seeking prejudice reduction return to Allport's mid-century conclusions: contact will reduce prejudice when participants are of equal status, pursuing common goals, and are backed by social and institutional support (Hewstone & Brown 1986; Fisher 1990; see also Gudykunst 1988; Ridgeway 1993, 1997). Investigators of interethnic conflict cross-nationally (Lijphart 1990; McRae 1990) reach similar conclusions.

In the mid-twentieth century, social theorists assumed that ethnic or group level identity would decrease following economic progress and democracy in the modern state. Empirically, however, ethnically-based conflict since the 1960s has grown rather than diminished "to the surprise and disappointment of many observers, some of whom have difficulty reconciling themselves to this reality" (Esman 1990:479). Ra'anan (1990) attributes the failure of the assimilation model to the *territorial* concept of nationality held in the Western cultures. Those from the East and South, define nationality according to a *personalistic* concept—by ancestry and cultural heritage[5], and very few "nation states" have territorial state boundaries that coincide with the borders of homogenous nationalities (see also Williams & Kofman 1989). Regardless of culturally-biased theoretical fallacies, despite the Liberal notion that individualistic democracy would erode the "primitive residue" of ethnic identification, contrary to the Marxist notion that ascriptive solidarity was only a remnant of earlier historical development, and in stunning disconfirmation of Modernization theorists' assumption that economic advance and "nation building" could capture nationalist loyalties, ethnicity today is arguably the "dominant cleavage" in modern politics (Esman 1990:480; see also Barber 1992; Huntington 1993).

Overall, biological, psychological and assimilationist theories suffered from the cognitive structures that underlie inter-group problems generally: we interpret reality from our own set of working hypotheses. Our lack of clear vision is inevitable, as all cross-cultural scholars have observed (Ulin 1984; Wilson 1970 for overviews; Avruch 1991; D'Andrade 1993 [1984]; Worchel 1999; Thompson et al. 1990 for theoretical examples). According to Bourdieu (1990), our belief in objectivity is based on sympathies and antipathies formed by "affinities of habitus." We see from a certain position in social space shared by others who see as we do exactly *because* they share our "point of view" (Bourdieu 1990:130). Bourdieu (1988 [1984]) mathematically concretized this theory using prestige indicators for French academic authors, and claimed an almost perfect homology between the intellectual positions taken by faculty concerning the May 1968 student revolt and their positions in the social space of the French Academy. Bourdieu argued that a science of self-reflection, an analysis of "points of view," could free us from these "miscognitions." For the perceived other, "the low" in social space, he suggests "self-liberation" from "those internalized limits that are the social categories of perception of the social world" (1990:182).

Recent Perspectives

Since the historic defeat of colonial governments in Africa (Tinker 1977) and the legal-social revolutions in the West (Karst 1993) in the civil rights movement, critical scholars developed a sociohistorical model for construction of race-ethnic relations. Like critical race theorists in legal scholarship (Delgado et al 1985, Matsuda et al 1993), Omi & Winant (1994) argue that race-ethnic hierarchies structure competition: class stratification or core-periphery relationships are the *result* of racial formations, not the cause. Dominant race, culture and ideological groups, in this case Anglo-Americans, structure the prevailing rules of competition by sociohistorical "racial projects," thereby creating and controlling class hierarchies. At the group identity level, Omi & Winant argue, class hierarchies intersect with nation-based identities and ethnic solidarity. Thus the core's fragmenting influence is specifically a racial-ethnic one, and the falsely de-racialized core-periphery relationship merely its economic manifestation.

The civil rights movement also gave rise to the idea that ethnic identity in the developed world was strategically self-interested, politically or instrumentally motivated, situational, and symbolic. Heisler (1990) explains in political terms the argument made by many scholars (e.g., Royce 1982; Gans 1979; Hall 1979; Nagel 1986): Western (European and U.S.) ethnic identities are essentially different from those in traditional, less industrially-developed and non-Western societies. Following Coser and Simmel, Heisler argues that ethnicity in Western states is "peripheral" to the personality: some dimensions of life aim toward the center (e.g., occupational identity) while other identities, like ethnicity, remain nested, partial, local, and intermittent. Heisler writes that the political process of *centralized* democracy underlies the resurgence of this fragmented ethnic identity in two ways: ethnicity is a rationally self-interested *political* strategy in the face of the "inevitable" constraints on achievement in dominant society; ethnic identity is a *psychological* haven from the alienation of modern society (see also Rothschild 1981; Jones & Morris 1993; Worchel 1999).

Polls show perceptions of events like the Rodney King beating and the OJ trial still reflect different realities. The *two* nations we were warned about nearly four decades ago, separate and unequal[6], are now refracted into diverse ethnicities. Theorists analyze privilege more often than prejudice, cognitive schema instead of authoritarian personality. Dominant groups, white people generally, can remain comfortable with less effort and less consciousness than we could in the 1960s, unless we work in the vast correctional gulag where almost one in three black men is restrained. A backlash dismantled affirmative action because most whites think the "race problem" is solved; most people of color do not. Like economic inequalities, the divide is increasingly stark and its global reflection terrifying.

If we agree that we are not served by race-ethnic hierarchy, then it is critical to expose and dismantle the privileged side of the vertical dynamic.

Bonilla-Silva (2003) describes four strategies of the new "colorblind racism:" abstract liberalism of opportunity and meritocracy; normalized racial outcomes as somehow natural, just "the way things are"; "biologized" culture as if dysfunction were a genetic inheritance with skin color; and minimized obstacles by comparison to, for instance, the Irish more than a century ago or Asian Americans today. Wise (2005) explains how privilege is protected by privilege:

> . . . what is ultimately overlooked is that denial of one's privilege itself manifests a form of privilege: namely, the privilege of being able to deny another person's reality (a reality to which they speak regularly) and suffer no social consequence as a result . . . Whites pay no price . . . for dismissing the claims of racism so regularly launched by persons of color, seeing as how the latter have no power to punish such disbelievers at the polls, or in the office suites, or in the schools in most cases.
>
> On the other hand, people of color who refuse to buy into white reality—the "reality" of the U.S. as a "shining city on a hill," or the "reality" of never-ending progress, or the "reality" of advancement by merit—often pay a heavy toll: they are marginalized, called "professional victims," or accused of playing the race card.

CHALLENGES IN METROCOURT ANALYSES

Emerson (1962) suggested that social power is always the product of a relationship (see also Wrong 1988 [1979]). Social power, he argued, only has meaning in a relational sense because, in fact, the other's relative dependence *is* the source of power. That is, the power of party A over party B is contingent on how dependent B is on A for valued outcomes. During a civil dispute, the claimant (A) who filed the suit (provided A could serve B with a summons in the first place) always has a measure of power derived from B's (the respondent's) dependence because only A (the claimant) can terminate the suit prior to judicial ruling. Thus, in terms of dispute role, the claimant-respondent relationship is always a power dependent-relationship.

For many reasons, dyadic relations in the mediation process are not simple. All disputants are in power-dependent dispute roles as claimants or respondents and no way exists to measure dependence on the many subtle levels where it may occur. In addition, such intersected statuses as ethgender, class, and professional role, present serious challenges to dichotomized categorization. Furthermore, theoretical arguments that tend to construct culture without hierarchy or hierarchy without culture give little guidance: critical and conflict theories focus on vertical dynamics and content theories largely ignore the way both dominant and subordinate groups are shaped by hierarchical ranking. The way hierarchy shapes insider culture, and the way cultures shape the expression of hierarchy are both often neglected in this process.

Although most scholars share the notion that harmony models strengthen social cohesion and internal community, cohesion comes at the price of independence. Traditional mediation processes are critiqued and defended against the question of elite dominance. For example, Nader's (1990) study showed entrenched authority structures that supported spousal abuse by men against women. Similarly, other studies (e.g., Kidder & Hostetler 1990; Merry 1989, 1992; Edelman, Erlanger & Lande 1993) have found that popular justice and conciliatory fora are commonly introduced and utilized as a form of internal social control, benefiting the elites within the group and occurring at historical periods when state power sought to silence dissent. Similarly, the image of women's friendships with one another is often at odds with the envy, competition, fear of abandonment, and hatred that often characterize "merged attachments" (Eichenbaum & Orbach 1987:51–72). The Latino familism that is the primary expression of Latino collectivism is "stifling" (Abalos 1986) and "ambivalent" (Golding & Burnam 1990).

The hypothesis that ethnic ingroups are more giving to one another than with outsiders is difficult to test at the end of the millennia due to acculturation. Acculturation effects obscure interpretation of minority culture group behavior. For example, in their cross-cultural comparison of college students, Leung & Iwakwaki (1988) pointed out that college students in China and the Philippines, most of them business majors, had absorbed the cultural ethics associated with the West; distribution tended to follow equity allocation norms (each according to input) and flow more readily into friendship than family networks (they were more generous with friends than family or clan who were the traditional insiders). They concluded that their data reflected acculturation effects and could not accurately answer their question. Similarly, Merry (1990) argued that people at the small claims court were self-selected: they came to the city of Dorchester, MA specifically under the lure, rightly or wrongly, that more sophisticated city life, with courts and more "objective" procedures, would be better than the suffocatingly personal communities they left behind. Small claims disputants, she argued, are specifically those who left wanting to urbanize. Similarly, minority group members who proceeded to court intervention are demonstrably more willing to claim and litigate than those who chose to "lump it" (Felstiner, Abel & Sarat 1980–81; Vidmar & Schuller 1987; Black 1989; Coates & Penrod 1980–81), a stance taken more often by, for example, Dutch compared to Canadian subjects (Leung & Bond 1990) and Canadian Catholics compared to Canadian non-Catholics (Kritzer, Bogart & Vidmar 1991). Generalization of cultural patterns in hierarchy is problematic because status effects combine with structural incentives to enroll marginal group members into dominant group perspectives and patterns, including the perpetration and perpetuation of hierarchical control by the "victims."

The construct of culture itself is vague. Archer (1996) argues that the core concept of culture gives rise to theoretical problems resulting from its origins in anthropological studies of traditional "cultures"—perceived as the glue holding societies together, what Archer terms the "myth of cultural integration." The notion of culture takes no account of historical discontinuities, conflates the systemic with the individual, cannot account for cultural system change due to the individualistic notions of western observers, and remains oblivious to slow changes.

Hofstede's paradigm of cultural distinction is also problematic. It is dichotomized into "individualist" and "collectivist" but recent research has shown that the two "opposites" are more likely orthogonal (Oyserman & Kemmelmeier 2002; Triandis 1995; Triandis & Gelfand 1998; see Smith & Bond 1990 for discussion). Furthermore, most people have both independent and interdependent self-construals available and behavior consistent with either can often be elicited by "priming" (Oyserman & Kemmelmeier 2002). Finally, the Latino population in New Mexico is far from homogenous. The difference between *Nuevomexicanos* and recent Mexican immigrants is linguistically and culturally obvious to most. In addition to acculturation to Anglo patterns, it is not certain that *Nuevomexicanos* and Mexican Americans would perceive one another as members of the same ingroup.

Despite the critiques, I used these and other theoretical frameworks to shape an inquiry into what happened to women and Latinos in mediation. This book attempts to show interactive patterns of negotiating behavior based on status-ranked dimensions of culture, broadly considered. I looked for differences and similarities between dyads sharing a status ranking (insiders) and those in vertical relation (outsiders) in the context of the claimant-respondent dispute roles. A closer look at the contexts of New Mexico, small claims court, and mediation center helps to interpret bargaining patterns. The environment also suggests why the mediation situation might be considered "priming" likely to elicit identity-based Latino and female patterns.

Chapter Three

The Cultural Environment: Southwest Latinos, Bernalillo County Court, and Mediation Training

The socio-historical development of regional identity and inter-ethnic relationships, specifically the role of legal institutions and procedures, suggests reasons New Mexico Latino identities might be activated making Latinos more susceptible to the cultural message of the mediation forum. The discussion provides background for understanding the disputants in this study, the qualities of the inter-group relationships which are relevant to "principled" or problem-solving negotiations, and the worldview of mediation.

I was trained as a mediator in this court mediation program and mediated more than twenty disputes during the time of this study (none of the cases I mediated were in the MetroCourt sample). During the fifteen months of the MetroCourt project data collection, I was a daily presence in the mediation offices and the civil division usually in my role of project coordinator, but sometimes in my role as a volunteer mediator. Although mediators were intentionally kept uninformed about the ethnicity and gender focus of the study, they were cooperative and willing participants. I was one of them. In fact, as a condition of participation, the mediation center required that the coordinator of the study be also a mediator.

NEW MEXICO ETHNIC RELATIONS AND LEGAL HISTORY

New Mexico is a large state with a small population, having a population density of less than 15 people per square mile, one-fifth the U.S. average. The earth is active: volcanoes, uplifts, mountain oases and the southernmost spur of the Rockies create multiple climate zones and bioregions, lava flows and mesas, canyons and caverns. The people too are diverse: in the 2000 census, Anglos again became the numerical minority (45%); Latino

(42%) and Native American (10%) "minorities" became again the numerical majority.

The Southwest region has been the site of a layering of conquests, first religious then rational. Legal procedure was particularly central in the most recent conquest, the Anglo colonization of the *Nuevomexicano* homeland, and especially in the Spanish land grant acquisitions. Politically-oriented scholars focus on *Nuevomexicano* competition with Anglo dominance as if both were strategically poised toward self-interested goals. More culturally-oriented scholars notice a contest between individualistic and collectivistic patterns of social organization and linguistic styles. This description looks from both points of view.

Latinos[1] *in New Mexico*

Three major groupings of Latinos inhabit New Mexico and are present in this study, most are shadings of Mexican American: *Nuevomexicanos* or *Hispanos* dating ancestral residency from before the United States annexed the Mexican territory in 1848; Mexican Americans who immigrated early in the twentieth century from Mexico, often as laborers; and more recent immigrants from Latin America, mostly Mexican, sometimes undocumented and often suspected of being here illegally. The MetroCourt study did not identify disputants identifying as "Hispanic, Spanish-American, or Mexican-American" into any of these sub-categories so the analysis is unable to make these distinctions, but the socio-historical formation of Latino identities in New Mexico is important to understand not only Latino-Anglo relations, but also to appreciate possible differences from even other Mexican-based collectivist patterns.

Socio-historical identities and racial formation

Latinos in New Mexico have their own history, different in kind and especially different in place from other Latino groups in the United States. The New Mexico province of New Spain was colonized beginning in 1540 first by Conquistadors and Franciscans, then by administrators and settlers granted land by the Spanish crown and provincial governors. With the Spanish conquest, the Pueblo people retreated into greater secrecy in the kivas[2] (Naranjo 1992), while outwardly developing a religious syncretism with Christianity. Such fusion was an ambivalent adaptation usually attributed to the possibility of Spanish protection from territorial encroachment by the Navajo and harassment by Apache raids (Frank 2000). The Pueblo people who were settled in the Rio Grande Valley shared a communal lifestyle and religious forms, but neither language nor alliance. In 1680, after a century of accommodation, the Pueblos joined together in a revolt that pushed the Spanish out for 12 years. In a highly ambivalent Fiesta each year, Northern New Mexico Latinos re-enact the re-entrance which culminates in an indigenous surrender to Spanish conquerors.

Frank (2000) recounts the development of New Mexican economy and identity from 1750 to the Mexican Independence in 1820 in *From Settler to Citizen.* By the turn of eighteenth century, the Pueblo population had been reduced by 70 to 80% from disease, hardship and warfare. The Pueblos formed alliances of necessity with the Spaniards and settlers (*vecinos* meaning neighbors) against raiding Plains tribes. During the second half of the eighteenth century, the Spanish settlers took shelter in the Pueblos, intermarrying with *genízaro* (Hispanicized and de-tribalized Indians) and Pueblo Indians. A decisive defeat of Comanche raiders in 1779 allowed the New Mexico population to expand and commerce with the rest of New Spain developed rapidly. By the turn of nineteenth century, *vecinos* outnumbered *indios* for the first time and developed a vibrant and unique rural New Mexican variant of Spanish colonial arts and crafts. Intermarriage with Pueblo Indians essentially ceased and census figures began collapsing the various ethnic labels describing the progeny of Spanish- Indian *mestizaje* into categories of *vecinos* (or *Españoles*) and *Indios,* determined by culture rather than blood lineage. New Mexicans knew less than two generations as *Mexicanos* before the young United States engaged in a short war culminating in the annexation of more than one third of the newly liberated Mexican Republic. Thus the conquerors were, in turn, colonized-in-place (Barrera 1979).

In *The Language of Blood,* historian Nieto-Phillips (2004) carries the story from U.S. annexation in 1848 until shortly after statehood in 1912. Despite assurances of citizenship made in the 1848 Treaty of Guadalupe Hidalgo, late nineteenth century white America was growing uneasy with the peoples it was annexing and importing for land and labor in pursuit of its manifest destiny: At first, there was Confederate support for New Mexico statehood until New Mexico declined to enter the union as a slave state. After the American Civil War, with shared alarm[3] at darker-skinned newcomers and armed with Darwin-inspired scientific racism, white America erected boundaries by legal means: the Chinese Exclusion Act of 1882 was the first race-based immigration barrier, *Plessy* v. *Ferguson* upheld racial segregation laws in 1896, and New Mexico was denied statehood due to its "mongrel" race of superstitious Catholics of uncertain allegiance, presumed lack of industriousness, and therefore probable incompetence at governing (Nieto-Phillips 2004). Washington justified exclusion by the fact that *Nuevomexicanos* were less than unanimous about statehood: urban, commercial centers (Anglo and *Nuevomexicano*) voted in favor of the constitution aiming at statehood, while rural areas were often opposed. The difference between urban and rural *Nuevomexicanos* was the difference between merchants and peasants, both a class and culture boundary.

In this environment, *Nuevomexicano* elites deepened their identification with their Spanish colonial heritage of whiteness. Perhaps as foil to Anglo dominance and reassurance to Washington, perhaps to sell crafts to East Coast tourists, and perhaps to claim the longest-lived political identity for native-born Spanish in post-conquest New Mexico, an ethnic revival movement took hold around the turn of the twentieth century. With the European roots came creative ferment and traditions of the Spanish Golden Age including the Castilian ideal of "*limpieza de sangre*" (purity of blood). Scholars like Espinosa validated Spanish identity by demonstrating Castilian linguistic roots of Northern New Mexico Spanish; land speculators and tourism promoters used the exotic Spanish colonial heritage to attract tourism and investment. Although some *Nuevomexicanos* resisted the railroad and Anglo-European in-migration, the wealthier "Spanish Americans," *los ricos* understood that statehood would require becoming more "white" and attracting increased percentages of white Anglo Americans. Throughout the twentieth century, native New Mexican Latinos and many later generations of Mexican immigrants, at least in English, largely identified as Spanish American (Nieto-Phillips 2004)[4].

Nostrand (1992) argued that the term *Hispanos* is the most accurate descriptor for the uniquely New Mexican Latino population because they are linguistically and culturally distinct from both Anglo and Mexican cultures. Nostrand describes the *Hispanos* as having a sense of place, of "homeland"—a people, a place, and an identity with place shaped by the natural environment and cultural landscape. Nieto-Phillips argues that Nostrand accepts a somewhat static cultural content and genealogy, despite the fact that New Mexican Latino identities have changed in relation to specific moments and sociopolitical contexts. Studying Pueblo-Nuevomexicano, and Anglo boundaries in her home territory of northern New Mexico, anthropologist Rodriquez describes ethnic boundaries as "situationally defined and structurally maintained." Gonzales' close study of historical events sees ethnic identity mobilized in spontaneous protest. Nieto-Phillips (2004:9) concludes that Spanish identity was "neither genuine nor spurious—but invented. What makes it so compelling a subject is not a question of its legitimacy, but its articulation and deployment in contexts of resistance and accommodation."

New Mexican Land and Law

Legal History

Forced U.S. annexation of the region after a two year Mexican-American War (1846–48) legitimated a process by which most of the communal lands held as land grants under Spanish "customary law" and defended by oratory skill were adjudicated into private property and entered the hands of Anglos. The technical legalities of title rather than oration confiscated the land and placed the burden of defense on the resident *Nuevomexicanos* to legally "prove" their ownership rights according to Anglo jurisprudence. Only 6% of the New Mexican land-grants were confirmed, in contrast to 73% in California (Ebright 1994:37). Weighing the balance of causal influences, a leading scholar of land grant disputes in New Mexico summarized the historical record: "The evidence strongly suggests that U.S. courts and Congress did not fairly meet the obligations assumed by the United States under the Guadalupe Hidalgo treaty. The main reason for this was that the land grants were established under one legal system and adjudicated by another" (Ebright 1994:3).

Nuevomexicano resistance to Anglo colonization, like the colonization itself, also has embedded cultural meanings. According to Frank (2000), *vecinos* "resisted moving into defensible towns in the eighteenth century despite the threat of Plains Indians raids, preferring scattered villages and isolated ranches on land grants bestowed by the Spanish governors." Although activists have struggled in recent decades through formal court actions to reclaim lost land, *Nuevomexicano* resistance to land loss has involved extra-legal resistance as well. For example, in 1971 in Tierra Amarilla local people reclaimed the land with guns very much as their fathers in prior generations had cut Anglo fences during the night (Martinez 1994; Ebright 1994). Mirandé (1987) argued that these resistance activities outside the formal adjudication process account for the cultural image of the Mexican "bandito" image.

The cultural contest of collectivism and individualism permeate analyses of contemporary conflict patterns as well as land ownership patterns[5]. Abalos (1986; 2002) describes the historical Latino culture pattern, which he calls "emanation," as one in which identity is submerged in the group, notably the extended family. He argues that emanation is a kind of inertia and passivity in the Latino culture that no longer suffices in an Anglo-dominant culture. "Incoherence" is the transitional process of cultural change initiated by living the "story of capitalism." Abalos specifically identifies a dominating style of machismo as part of this incoherence (Abalos 2002). Anzaldúa (1987) argues similarly: the violence in the Latino border community results from the cultural tension between Mexican collectivism and U.S. individualism.

Procedural Implications

What effect does this historical experience have on the conflict patterns of the people in New Mexico? The pattern of collectivism and emanation logically suggests conflict avoidance and honor maintenance (Triandis et al 1988), while Anglo individualism frequently leads to direct, face-to-face, competitive conflict (Ting-Toomey 1988). Traditional Latino culture honors vertical relationships and patriarchal family organization, but Anglo culture tends to accent horizontal relationships and to resist the power-dependent relationship implied by the acceptance of hierarchy. In Spanish New Mexican towns powerful and passionate orators use their voices to persuade their fellows and maintain their stature (Briggs 1986); Anglos convince by suppressing passion, citing authorities, and controlling the flow of information.

Rinderle (2003) summarizes research on the way that Mexicans' relational focus, rather than a material or achievement-oriented focus like U.S. Americans, affects Mexican and Mexican American male cultural patterns in comparison to Anglo American men: Mexicans showed greater concern about treatment received from ingroup members than outgroup members; Mexican men appeared to trust friends and the relationship more, and were more willing to fight for a threatened friendship; Mexican men were more upset by another's denial of their personal qualities than by criticism of acquired skills, especially since only trusted intimates would be in a position to judge personal qualities. U.S. Anglo men, since their self image was more dependent on external factors, were often opposite: U.S. American men, were more willing to lose a friendship to keep other goals or self-concepts intact; were more upset by criticism coming from a stranger than Mexican men; U.S. American men's friendships were more disrupted by conflict overall. "These results suggest marked differences in how Mexican and U.S. Anglo men perceive, value and fight for their relationships, and the different impact of conflict on those relationships." (Rinderle 2003:7).

New Mexican Latinos may represent a different version of collectivism based on a cultural emic (see Chapter Two) quite different than the Asian cultures most often used in collectivism research. New Mexico has an aura of the frontier and the *Nuevomexicanos,* with the overlay of *Hispanidad* (Spanish-ness), borrow the code of chivalry from medieval Spain: horsemanship, manliness, courage, honor, loyalty and generosity. A strict code of conduct and honor suggests a conflict style that prizes fairness and disdains treachery, one that is generous in victory. Furthermore, generations of Anglicization[6] insure that New Mexico Latinos are bicultural, with independent as well as interdependent cognitive schema available: in self-construal research, Southwest Latinos were more likely to be assessed as "bi-construal" (Oetzel 1998; Ting-Toomey et al 2001; Rinderle 2002). Unlike Anglos, who are likely to have only an independent self-construal available, environmental and situational cues are likely to determine the way that New Mexico Latinos frame their conflicts (see Adair & Brett 2004; Morris & Gelfand 2004). This means that Latinos may be less prone to the "fixed pie" error common to U.S. negotiators where the contest appears as win-lose, and blame is assigned to one side rather than shared (see Chapter Seven).

The cultural conflict patterns of Latino-Anglo relations in the Southwest have an additional twist. Although Latino culture encourages an acceptance of hierarchy, native New Mexican Latinos have a long history of both covert and overt resistance to Anglo cultural domination. Anglo culture is in fact highly competitive (see Chapter Seven) but assumes an equality that masks any moral objection to unfair competition. As noted in Chapter One, Rinderle makes an important point about these differences, noting that Mexican American hierarchy operates through reciprocity, not the imposition of the superior's will.

Overall, legal procedural rituals embodied in Anglo jurisprudence have been a specific manifestation of class and cultural conquest. As a class-based formation, Anglo jurisprudence insures justice with procedures rather than by outcome. The rules of evidence and procedure that create the aura of a "fair fight" promise disputing parties equality of opportunity. However, although procedural constraints may offer protection from some forms of discrimination (Delgado et al. 1985), the justice of the fight is purchased at the cost of legal representation, thus erecting a class barrier. Furthermore, as Freeman (1990) and others (Handler 1978; Karst 1993; Scheingold 1974) note in their analysis of civil-rights law, what is given by law can be dismantled by legal interpretations—according to Freeman (1990), the change in legal interpretation from equality of results to equality of opportunity is largely responsible for dismantling anti-discrimination laws. As a cultural contest, Latino-Anglo legal relations impose limitations on the story, silencing the rural forms of orations noted by Briggs (1986) and the *resolana* (Aténcio 1988) adopted as a dialogue form by Latinos and Anglos in the city.

Note that the cultural contest may also be critical to legal outcome. For example, in a small claims court study, O'Barr & Conley (1985) concluded that narrative opportunity was more important to less advantaged litigants, accounting for a large measure of their reported satisfaction and willingness to compromise; but the "everyday talk" manner of telling the story provided few of the familiar codes that those socialized into legal culture could interpret. The narrative style of unrepresented litigants and unsophisticated witnesses lacked a deductive focus on liability and evidence; thus the court perceived them as less credible, with the logical consequences of disadvantaged outcomes.

Mediation offers this narrative opportunity without judicial consequence. Although perhaps less important in cultures more accepting of hierarchy (Brocknera et al 2001), having the freedom to speak and be heard increases all disputants' confidence in the fairness of procedures. Lind, Tyler & Huo (1997) found that this justice judgment of fairness may operate through different relational mechanisms (status recognition, intervenor neutrality, and trust in the intervenors' benevolent intent) of differing importance based on the situation, but argue that the effects of "voice" are less variable across cultures than many might assume.

ETHNIC PATTERNS IN BERNALILLO COUNTY COURT

Bernalillo County, the location of the city of Albuquerque, accounts for approximately one third of New Mexico's total population. At the time of the study, about half of the New Mexico population was Latino[7]. It is a reasonable assumption to expect the Latinos at the court will be roughly equally split between *Nuevomexicanos* (i.e., descended from the regional population as discussed above) and more recent Mexican immigrants—relatively few first generation. Adjusted for differential age structures due to the lower birthrate among Anglos, approximately 60% of the adult population in Bernalillo County was nonhispanic Anglo.

Bernalillo County is a middle income county in a state that competes with Mississippi for the dubious distinction as the poorest in the country. Incomes reported in the 1990 census show ethnic stratification similar to the rest of the country. Per capita income (rounded to nearest thousand) for the Anglo population was $17,000, while it was $9,000 for Hispanics and $8,000 for nonreservation Native Americans. Households in Bernalillo County were less often below the poverty line than in rural areas, but within the county almost one fifth (18.9%) of Latino families and one quarter (26.7%) of Native American families reported household incomes below the federal poverty line in 1989. By contrast, 5.5% of Anglo families were categorized as impoverished.

Shame and the Criminal and Civil Cultures

Triandis et al. (1988) contrast the guilt mechanism (I *did* something bad) for internal social control found in individualistic cultures with the shaming

(I *am* bad) more often encountered in collectivistic cultures. The physical and cultural overlapping of criminal and civil justice at the Bernalillo County Metropolitan Court (BCMC) created an atmosphere in which Latino shaming was more likely.

At the time of the study, the county court (BCMC) handled both civil and criminal cases. It was situated in downtown Albuquerque 300 yards away from the county detention center. To enter the court, one passed across the small plaza separating it from the jail. In 1990, Latinas were often standing in the plaza, drawing large letters in the air to communicate with the men in the upper windows of the jail. Entering the six story courthouse, one passed through a rotating door and a vestibule. On the left was a room where people stood in line to pay or plead traffic and animal control violations. To the right was a small lobby with a metal detector between the public and the elevators that led to the civil and criminal courtrooms.

The civil division was on the second floor. A high counter specified where the public should come to file a claim. At the counter, the public could obtain a form for filing and some instructions about needing proof of serving the other party who had to answer within 20 days or be subject to a default judgment based on assumed liability for the claim. The Clerk of the Civil Division, whose name appeared on each summons served on respondents from the filings, was an institution in the office. She was an attractive, intimidating, no-nonsense middle-aged woman. Although the civil records are public information, it was best to ask the Clerk's permission to access the files.

Tones of moral condemnation more appropriate to criminality saturated the civil court. Although the proper term for someone accused of a debt is "respondent," many people, including the mediation center, called them "defendants," the term for the criminally accused. Their debts were "delinquent." The first time I heard the word "judgment proof" (used as a noun, it is what a poor person *is*), it was said with tones of scorn mixed with frustration by one professional Anglo man to another. I thought the Anglo men were lawyers in the lobby of the court, discussing collection work. The term judgment proof takes the perspective of a collector who has obtained a judgment against a debtor but may be unable to collect the money owed because the debtor does not earn above minimum wage and owns no property of value. Middle-class debtors in similar circumstances might file bankruptcy, but poor people rarely do. During my year at the court, I heard the term used often and always negatively, as if respondents were getting away with something by being "so impecunious as to know that they were judgment proof" (Vidmar 1984:351).

During the data collection phase of the project, I became more aware of the punitive aspects of collections in civil justice. Each day, the secretaries in the civil division "disposed" of the civil cases concluded the prior day. They set aside the stacks of manila folders before re-shelving them so that our project and the credit bureau people could collect information from them. The credit bureau women with laptop computers and our project staff used the lunch table in the break room to gather our facts. One credit bureau woman only wanted the restitution (eviction) cases heard by judges during the first half hour of every day. Another took businesses. The third wanted all civil judgments. The MetroCourt staff were not looking at restitutions or default judgments because they were outside the criteria for the study, so whoever was there first would create more, smaller stacks as they sorted them out. The stack of default judgments always seemed to be the largest.

In the short but friendly conversations, the credit bureau women explained that judgments, both those connected with evictions and all others, stayed in the credit reports for 14 years unless there was a "satisfaction of judgment" recorded. When a judgment was satisfied and the claimant notified the court, the file would be pulled and placed on the table for the credit bureau women to see and note. This appeared to be rare.

If Latinos are more vulnerable to shame, BCMC was likely to trigger this response. As an empirical fact, both criminal convictions and civil judgments were and are disproportionately targeted against poor, and often Latino people. The pattern of civil cases through BCMC shows how the bureaucracy constructed this disparity.

Flow Patterns of Civil Cases

In civil cases, the increased rate of judgment against Spanish surnamed respondents seemed to be because Anglo and business respondents settled more cases prior to judgment (Rack 1994b). It appears likely that cultural differences, including vulnerability to shame and conflict avoidance, combined with economic marginality to create this effect. Mediation provided a mechanism to interrupt this trajectory.

Judgments and Sanctions

Similar to most if not all small claims courts in North America, collection cases filed by corporate parties against individual debtors predominate at BCMC. Approximately two thirds (69%) of the small claims cases disposed during the study period were filed by agents for businesses, usually lawyers (70%), who secured the majority (81%) of nonhearing judgments at the court. Compared to individual claimants, business agents seldom adjudicated their claims (19% business compared to 42% individuals claims). These corporate claimants were mostly Anglo men filing against diverse respondents who often appeared to be aware of the debt, seldom contested it, and often allowed default judgments to be entered against them (Hermann et al 1992).

The difference between judgment and non-judgment outcomes is the most relevant distinction in the flow of cases because mediation agreements were most often settlements without formal judgments. Judgments, whether default, voluntary (including stipulated and on the pleadings), or by court ruling, have two consequences that employ coercive powers. First, state powers can be employed to "execute" judgments for collection purposes; wages can be garnished if a convicted debtor earns above minimum wage, or the amount can be extracted from bank accounts, or the sheriff can be ordered to collect belongings such as furniture or cars from the respondent's residence. The latter measure is rarely employed. The second form of coercion is more indirect and might be called "bureaucratic justice." The process of listing all judgments is more insidious; it is longer lasting for poor people (because they are less able to pay off the judgments quickly), more amorphous because people do not usually have knowledge of their credit rating, and completely faceless. The credit effects of small claims judgments create another category of marginality used increasingly by insurance companies and other institutional entities to exclude categories of people.

Case Processing

Figure 3.1 shows the process flow of the civil small claims cases in the court. The figure reflects a random sample taken from the court records.

During the twenty-day period given the respondent served with a claim, less than half (45%) of the respondents answered. Of the unanswered claimants, more than half (59% calculated from Figure 3.1) filed for default judgments. Default judgments were the highest courts awards, routinely granted for the full amount claimed plus court costs and, for corporate claimants, legal fees and any interest noted (i.e., printed on the bill). Once determined, all judgments carried ongoing interest charges of 15% at the time of the study. Consistent with collectivist cultural conflict styles, Hispanic-surnamed men were least likely to answer a claim, that is, they tended to avoid the dispute. This resulted in a higher rate of costly default judgments than any other ethgender respondent group (Hermann et al 1992).

The remainder of the unanswered claims (41%) were administratively dismissed due to inability to serve notice to the respondent, or dismissed

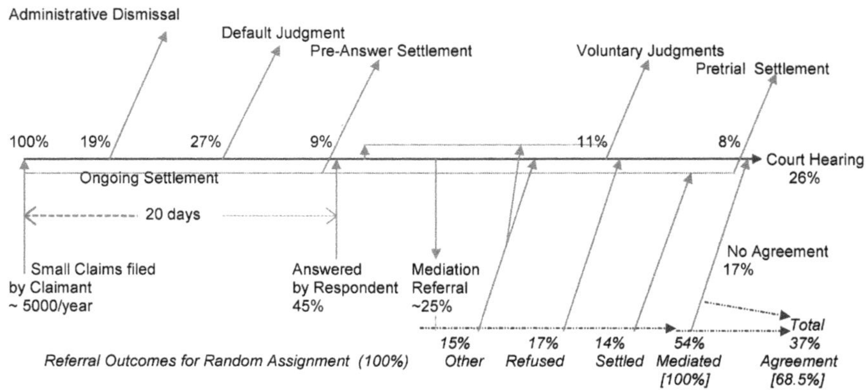

Figure 3.1 Small Claims Cases in the Metropolitan Court

after six months with no particular knowledge of what happened, or were reported to be settled privately by the claimant.

In our sample, 17% of the filed claims were reported to be settled (Figure 2.1). This was an ongoing process from the time that a case was filed until a ruling was given by a judge. Business claimants were most likely to receive settlements. However, business *respondents* settled more frequently only if the claimant was also a business. This means that horizontal business relationships reported a high prejudgment settlement rate. Consumer and tenant-landlord cases, the primary casetype in which a non-business claimant files against a business, more often proceeded to intervention. In addition, Anglo female respondents appeared to have initiated and concluded settlement negotiations more often because cases filed against them tended to be both unanswered and did not proceed to default judgment (Rack 1994b).

In the Answer, the formal response to a filed claim, respondents were required to state whether they owed all, part or none of the claimed amount. If the respondent admitted liability for a debt, the claimant could file for a judgment based on these admissions and the case was never formally heard. These judgments were most often as costly as default judgments, but occasionally the claimant would file for a judgment on a lesser degree of admitted liability. For example, a respondent might agree that she owes $500 of the $600 claimed and the claimant might file for a judgment for that amount rather than pursue a case to court hearing. Women in general, and Spanish-surnamed women in particular, were more likely to admit full liability (often, it seemed, unwittingly) and disproportionately received these judgments. In other cases, respondents signed a "stipulated judgment" admitting the debt, with similarly costly effects but involving some face-to-face negotiation of terms (Hermann et al 1992; Rack, Barnes-Anderson & Margolis 1996).

Mediation Diversion

Mediation functioned as a case diversion from the flow toward court hearing and ruling. If the respondent answered but argued that some or all of the debt was not owed, the case proceeded to third party intervention. As a routine procedure, the mediation center selected cases for mediation based on intuition and some rules of thumb. Particularly, the mediation center assumed that cases in which a pre-existing relationship existed or in which the respondent acknowledged some part of the debt, were especially appropriate for mediation. These rules of thumb reflect the logic of Anglo mediation culture: the relationship maintenance superiority of face-to-face conflict resolution processes (e.g., the assumptions underlying mandatory divorce and custody mediation) and the better negotiation process expected from cases in which some liability was already acknowledged. Figure 3.1 estimates that approximately 8% of all small claims cases filed were settled in mediation, compared to 26% decided by three judicial intervenors. Consistent with other studies (for reviews see Kressel & Pruitt 1989; Wall & Lynn 1993; Lowry 1993), mediation was not strikingly cost effective or efficient[8]. Most studies (see, for example, Merry & Milner 1993), including this one, have been unable to document better relationships in personal or recidivistic terms. In our study, mediation respondents were more often congruent with claimants than adjudication respondents about whether they expected to have contact in the future, but claimant expectation of future contact was equal between the fora (30%).

Regional Ethnic Identity & Inter-group Relationships: A Summary

Southwest and Bernalillo County patterns are distinct from many other national examples of local majority-minority relations due to the fact that *Hispanos* are historically rooted in *place* (Nostrand 1992), the New Mexican landscape. First, *Hispanos* were *dominant* before the U.S. annexation and, despite overtly racist sentiments expressed over the years, continue to have a strong voice in regional politics. New Mexico was the only state admitted to the union with an official second language—Spanish. Second, at the county level, Latino ownership in land and homes, is nearly equal to Anglos (Gonzales 1993b). However, despite the greater political and geographic power held by New Mexican Latinos, patterns at the BCMC still reflect cultural differences that contribute to the economic marginalization of Latinos.

Consider how the regional patterns might account for the historic "leitmotif" of preserving Anglo American control while providing powerful Spanish American leaders and the "gentlemen's agreement" not to openly deal with race-ethnic prejudice (cf. Gonzales 1993a:169). First, the historical layering of conquest suggests that the "minority" identity of southwest Latinos is likely to be conflicted with their historically-recent identification as the *conquistador* "majority" in relation to Native Americans. For example, Gonzales (1993b:170) cites Aténcio's 1985 study of the traditionally Latino center in the city of Albuquerque (Old Town). A recent Albuquerque ethnic conflict arose over a representational image of Latinos that might have been interpreted as referring to a Spanish rape of Native women; the *Latino* resistance to the implications of this image was effective, and an aggressive and victorious *conquistador* image was used instead.

Furthermore, Gonzales (1993a) notes high degrees of Anglo co-residence in Latino enclaves in Albuquerque. Traditionally Latino barrio populations are not as severely concentrated as, for example, African Americans in Chicago neighborhoods. Such co-residence offers the cross-cutting ties often associated with reduced inter-group conflict (Ross 1993). In addition, voluntary immigration by Mexicans has numerically diluted the more rooted Latino population: as New Mexico has Anglicized, so has it Mexicanized with similars who more clearly chose residence in the United States.

Although the distribution of economic resources in Bernalillo county reflects clear majority-minority economic patterns, the local cultural situation may explain why Hispanic voting patterns and political alliances have been conservative and non-confrontational (Gonzales 1993a; Nieto-Phillips 2004), and nationalistic ethnic identity, or instrumental political expressions, appear as relatively passing disturbances over the 140 years of U.S. Anglo control. Similarly, Hispanic-surnamed respondents were more often judged without evidence of formal resistance perhaps because they were more vulnerable to shame, were intent on face-saving, and/or avoiding conflict[9].

MEDIATION AND MICROLEGAL CULTURE

The mediation program operated with its own cultural patterns, akin to what Grillo (1993) called "microlegal" systems. Grillo (1991:1555–6) described the "informal laws" that develop in microsocial settings like mediation. These unwritten laws manifest themselves as shared expectations and "shoulds" enforced by social sanctions, such as laughing at and dismissing proscribed behavior. Grillo notes that it is "not an actor's motive or self-awareness that renders his reaction a sanction, but the effects of the reaction on those sanctioned." Grillo argues that mediation culture defined a specific version of "good" and "bad" disputing behavior, just as the civil court defined proper economic behavior.

The Training: Shared Expectations

The core experience in the Albuquerque Mediation Center (AMC) organization was the basic mediation training. At the time of the study, the AMC provided the 40-hour training for free to interested persons with the expectation that they would volunteer to co-mediate in the court program.

The training was an exciting experience. The trainers conveyed the key idea of mediation as a potential for win-win outcomes within the control of the parties themselves. The first hour of the training established the centrality of this notion. During a role play of two siblings fighting over a single orange, the trainees were invited to play the parent, asked by the children to settle the dispute. Naturally, the trainee suggested splitting the orange (a knife was conspicuously present). The trainers then established the alternative resolution, the mediation concept. They elicited from the "children" what they wanted from the orange (their "interests"), discovering that one child wanted the rind for her gerbil and the other wanted to eat the pulp. The rest of the training elaborated this idea as techniques to elicit interests (active listening, giving affirmation), and techniques to handle entrenched positions (caucusing with parties individually, reframing, restating and venting).

One communication technique was of particular interest because it provides a parallel to evidentiary rules in formal court. This was a way to handle accusations of lying called "planting a doubt." Planting a seed of doubt involves suggesting to one party that perhaps the other party is in fact telling the truth. The idea is to say: "What *if* Mr. Jones really *did* mail the check and it really *was* lost in the mail?" This kind of technique leans particularly on disputant willingness to trust the other party, to give them "the benefit of the doubt" (Bendor, Kramer & Stout 1991), a response more likely in collectivist cultures (Valenzuela et al 2005).

The charismatic trainer inspired the trainees and many left the first weekend's training with a new world view: conflict is not inevitably bad and disputes can be resolved by skillful intervention that allows parties to see their own power to end the conflict in a way that both parties can tolerate. Mediators can accomplish this by staying with the process until the disputants reveal their interests rather than *positions*. During the second weekend, trainees participated in role-plays of disputant-mediator sessions, practicing these techniques under the coaching observation of experienced mediators[10].

Mediation's Boundaries: Neutrality, Lawyers & Success

The trainings identified mediators as neutral third parties who helped individuals in conflict to craft a solution. In practice, this meant eliciting voluntary concessions in an atmosphere of respect and, preferably, of kindness. In game-negotiation terms, mediators depended on nice-nice dyads and had no training that would provide ways to identify, challenge, or disqualify disputants who were "nasty" unless the party was physically or extremely verbally abusive.

Bryan (1992:498–515) asserts that mediators refuse to acknowledge power imbalances, and their complicity in them, because it would raise fundamental conflicts with their image of neutrality. As part of this neutrality, mediators focus on procedural rather than substantive justice: mediators do not hold themselves accountable for "fair" outcomes. Neutrality meant behavior that was impersonal and distant. Mediation training considered prior acquaintance with a disputant a threat to neutrality, in contrast to indigenous mediation processes where trust (*confianza* in Costa Rica) based on personal knowledge of the disputing parties is a key component (Lederach & Kraybill 1993). Although research has indicated that disputants accept a biased mediator in "emergent" mediation (where the mediator is known to the disputants and offers him/herself as a mediator) as long as the actual process is facilitated even-handedly (Pruitt & Carnevale 1993), in this setting a mediator would commonly exclude him/her self when he/she recognized a disputant as an acquaintance.

The AMC training included no discussion of bias[11] nor did it have a cultural/gender component at the time I was trained, during the time of the study, or for several more years. In fact, the AMC director maintained that if mediators were well-trained and monitored only the process, then culture, ethnicity and class did not matter. She considered the techniques universal, the resolution in the hands of the parties, and the mediators without personal influence.

The BCMC mediation setting fostered conscious antagonism toward lawyers and adjudication[12]. Mediators often believed pursuing a case to court incurred greater costs to the disputants although once a case was filed, unless a lawyer was hired, no additional expense existed. (This study corrected that misconception.) A number of lawyers worked as volunteer mediators but they were likely to express feelings of being saved by mediation from a distasteful reliance on adversarial process. One lawyer told me proudly that he never admitted to being a lawyer in a mediation session.

The mediation center discouraged lawyers for the parties from attending the mediation session. First, the coordinator would discuss this preference with the parties during scheduling. Then, if a lawyer arrived, the non-represented party needed to give prior consent. Sometimes a lawyer would observe without participating or wait outside for consultation with his/her client during the mediation. Of course, in cases with disputants who were larger corporations, the legal representative might be the only possible representative and therefore mediated the dispute.

Mediators' negative evaluation of formal legality and their professional interests in the mediation field combined to encourage an assumption that voluntary agreements were "better" than court decisions. Thus, mediators often sought agreements in an atmosphere permeated with an unstated contradiction between seeking agreement and disputant control. Subtle competition among mediators included a usually unspoken comparison of mediators' agreement rates. Similar to Harrington & Merry's (1988) identification of an unwritten "preferred mediator" status, some mediators served in a paid role on other AMC contracts by an invisible selection process.

Pressure toward achieving agreement was at least as much a personal goal as a professional or ideological one. After investing one or two hours in a mediation session, mediators felt reassured that they made a definitive difference. Most mediators have witnessed a session in which the parties were surprised that something that had seemed so entrenched and impossible could be resolved to both parties' satisfaction. These gratifying experiences reinforced the value of bilateral consensual mediation process over the unilateral coercive process of adjudication.

Mediator Expectation and Small Claims Cases

The mediators' training led to the hope for integrative and win-win outcomes that would be "better" than the win-lose court outcomes. Neither the rigidity of adjudication nor the flexibility of mediated outcomes was as stark as mediators expected. Some cases, especially collection cases, came to mediation with their court alternatives set in stone. Some claimants arrived in mediation with judgments in their back pockets (actually, in their briefcases) based on liability admitted in the respondent's Answer[13]. On the other hand, many of the private citizens who appeared to be the logical users of mediation because they had ongoing relationships with one another, were looking for knowledge about their rights and responsibilities under the law. In fact, individual claimants (a category that includes tenants) less often reached agreement in mediation than corporate claimants.

The mediator training and general ideology aroused expectations in trainees (including myself) that differed somewhat from the reality of the cases they would be mediating. In addition to a dearth of information about power differences, nothing in the basic training addressed the routinized mechanisms of bureaucratic justice, applicable legal and procedural rules, or the predictable patterns of negotiation processes. Nor was any procedure suggested to directly address bargaining resistance. Thus, the more active mediators, predominantly men, appeared to invent their own interventions. More compliant mediators stayed wedded to an often unworkable passivity that was the prescribed process, even when disputants did not willingly engage in joint problem solving with their own interests clearly in mind.

Despite the fact that many of the cases referred to mediation involved significant disparities in resources, roles and experience, clarity about the difference between "nice" vs. "nasty" negotiators appeared nowhere in the training, the literature, or in the professional conception of mediation. Yet, reading the mediator observations, many of the more experienced mediators described disputants on quasi-moral dimensions: they were "nice people" who "appeared honest" or "seemed sincere," and perhaps "there was goodwill between them," and so on. The mediators often did not directly mention the nasty side of the same qualities, but implied them in auxiliary statements: the party was "rigid" or "wanted her day in court," or by a comparative omission.

Mediation Culture

Merry & Milner (1993) noted after a large study of a community mediation program (the San Francisco Review Boards) that the primary community in mediation programs appeared to be the community of mediators. I have described a similar situation. Like other ingroups, mediators shared and reinforced a worldview about conflict resolution that could become quite resistant to challenging information and even contradictory experience. Thus, assumptions about adjudication tended to stay intact for lack of experience. Legal professionals, who might have offered a more accurate picture of adjudication, tended to silence themselves. Mediators did not question the legitimacy of higher status claimants, but any disputant without obvious outcomes such as a collector with an admitted debtor, might be told that the court outcome was "a roll of the dice." In their minds, many mediators seemed to exaggerate the demands of formal evidentiary rules. In any case, mediators could not "give legal advice" because lawyers retain that prerogative.

Mediators did not frame their own role in the most obvious of all terms: eliciting voluntary concessions. By not articulating this goal, mediation culture privatized more assertive techniques. In the seclusion of the mediation session, mediators used a variety of techniques that Alfini (1991) called "trashing, bashing, and hashing it out," depending on their inclination. Grillo (1991:1551) asserts that an informal law of divorce mediation drives mediator biases; the image of the "good" woman (cooperative, rational, not vengeful, and willing to shoulder part of the responsibility) elicits mediator sympathies, while the "bad" woman (bitter, irrational, and unwilling to compromise) elicits subtle sanctions. In fact, experimental evidence suggests that mediator tactics are a function of the degree to which mediators value the parties' aspirations (Carnevale & Henry 1989)[14].

In sum, these interacting characteristics of mediator culture could easily influence the situation for disputants: mediators tended to be idealistic, usually sequestered from legal information and attitudes on the one hand, and critical perspectives identifying power imbalances on the other. Without knowledge of court procedures and legal constraints, mediators were largely unable to assess the BATNAs or probable alternatives for disputants. Lacking this primary datum for negotiations and untrained in the negotiation process, mediators were unlikely to identify and intervene with disputants who were resistant negotiators, especially if the disputant used more indirect strategies that tended to re-arrange the other party's perceived alternative outcome structure. Into this vacuum, mediators inserted their commitments to procedure, consciously identified as "trusting the process;" less consciously, their desires to bring about agreements, to "solve" the dispute, infused their work.

Concluding Discussion

In the Bernalillo County Metropolitan Court, the criminal and civil divisions shared location, terminology, attitudes of judgment and parallel sanctions. As in other U.S. courts, convicted debtors were economically confined with credit reports; at BCMC, this punishment was more likely for Spanish-surnamed respondents. Proximally, this increased rate of judgment resulted from an increased likelihood that Spanish-surnamed men did not answer claims and did not independently settle the cases against them, while Spanish-surnamed women more often acknowledged the debt and without independent settlement, the creditors sought judgments based on these admissions. This is partially a gendered pattern that, consistent with the collectivist culture theory, suggests a greater likelihood of conflict avoidance and conciliation. The pattern is also consistent with a conflict model of Anglo culture in which the majority group defines the rules and processes and socializes its members to understand their operations, thus gaining advantage in procedural and bureaucratic competition. Thus, the distal cause of increased rates of judgment against Latinos may well be cultural hierarchy.

The mediation case diversion at BCMC represented a contradictory influence. On the one hand, mediation offered the possibility of prejudgment settlement and relative narrative freedom. On the other, the mediators had few tools for dealing with systematic injustice or cultural hierarchies and were precluded from identifying their own competitive bias by the ideology to which they subscribed. Most of the analyses in this work, assume that mediators had a more or less consistent ideological and procedural influence on the mediation process. However, the ideology of mediation was in fact brought to bear differently by mediators of differing ethnicity and gender (Hermann et al 1992; Rack 1994a; LaFree & Rack 1996). To orient the reader to these distinctions, the effects on monetary outcomes are summarized in Chapter Six, the apparent influence on motivation, including coercion, are discussed in Chapter Eight, explicit reference to mediator ethnicity and gender influence is included in Chapter Ten.

Chapter Four

The MetroCourt Project[1]

The mediation diversion involved two critical points of choice for disputants; first, the agreement to mediate at all and, second, to jointly accept an agreement. Thus, as a voluntary process with consensual outcomes, mediation presents the unavoidable analytical and theoretical problem of sample self-selection in any comparison with adjudication. Although negotiation in mediation is the focus of this book, with adjudication only appearing as the logical BATNA, information critical to negotiations is described by analyses of exactly who agrees to mediate, who reaches agreement, and whether the agreement resulted in a monetary outcome.

To clarify this self selection I looked for patterns in case types and status conditions through the mediation diversion and final disposition. I compared the bargaining sample with cases that reached nonmonetary outcomes or settled subsequently, and finally compared the bargaining sample to cases that reached no agreement at all and presumably proceeded to adjudication. Included in this analysis is specific information about how mediator ethnicity and gender related to case disposition in mediation.

DATA COLLECTION & VARIABLE CODING

The MetroCourt data were collected under a grant from the Fund for Research in Dispute Resolution awarded to Michele Hermann and Mary Beth West with Gary Lafree (1990). The original hypotheses concerned tests of monetary outcomes for women and minorities compared to Anglo men. I was hired to collect the data in August 1990 and remained involved in the analysis and writing the final report. Some of the analyses referred to in this work are reported in Hermann, LaFree, Rack & West (1992). I have also written and presented many other analyses of these data (see bibliography). This book is drawn from my Ph.D. dissertation in Sociology at the University of New Mexico completed in 1997. I change first person pronouns according to authorship.

Selection and Description of Cases

The MetroCourt project collected data on 323 adjudicated and 280 mediated, civil, randomly-chosen small claims cases between September 1990 and October 1991. We included only non-jury cases which sought money judgments, with a single individual, business or married couple on each side, and that had been to hearing or mediation with both parties present. We also excluded cases in which either party was younger than eighteen.

We collected a random sample of adjudicated cases daily from the total dispositions entered in court the previous day; thus, the adjudication sample was collected after hearing. We randomly assigned cases within the study criteria to mediation from the pool of answered claims. After our random selection, the Albuquerque Mediation Center (AMC) selected cases that they perceived would benefit from mediation. All disputants in both groups of cases received a letter from AMC signed by the Chief Justice of the civil division "ordering" them to mediation with a second letter from AMC advising them that mediation was voluntary, with a date and time for the mediation and a request for telephone confirmation.

Slightly more than 50% of the randomly assigned cases completed mediation. Settlement with or without judgment was more likely when the respondent acknowledged the debt; admitted liability cases that proceeded to mediation reached agreement 84% of the time (compared to 66% overall). We found that Anglo male collectors, especially lawyers, were more likely to refuse mediation but often settled cases prior to court hearing. In contrast, Anglo female collectors more often agreed to mediate collection cases, even when the respondent admitted liability (Hermann et al 1992). Interestingly, collectors were far more likely to have filed against respondents of their own gender.

If a mediation case did not reach agreement during or immediately subsequent to the session, or a respondent failed to comply with an agreement made in mediation, the case was returned to court and was formally heard by one of the three Civil Court justices. Approximately 500 cases in 1990 to 91 were settled in mediation compared to approximately 1,300 cases disposed through court hearings with both parties present (see Figure 3.1).

Mediation cases were co-mediated by pairs of women, men or mixed gender pairs; and Latino, Anglo or mixed ethnicity pairs. Mediators, who were uninformed of the ethnicity/gender focus of the study, participated in data collection by completing a 52-item participant observation questionnaire after each mediation. Mediator ethnicity and gender were determined from mediator self-reports.

Interviewing and Records

Subsequent to hearing or mediation, participants were interviewed by telephone (usually within eight weeks), with a response rate of 79% for the adjudicated sample (87% for claimants and 71% for respondents) and 88% for the mediated sample (90% for claimants and 87% for respondents). In addition, we conducted eight hundred and seventeen follow-up interviews approximately three months later by mail and telephone with 81% of the parties initially interviewed (68% of the total sample). Mediators completed five hundred and seventeen participant observer questionnaire after co-mediating study cases with a return rate of 96%. Although the follow-up interviews and the mediator questionnaire data only appear in Chapter Ten, both of these data sources have informed my view of the MetroCourt mediation program and some of the questions addressed in this book.

The dataset set included a description and the final outcome of each case drawn from the original claims, answers, and total monetary outcome from court rulings or mediated agreements. Mediation agreements more often than court rulings specified payment terms (payment plans) and included nonmonetary elements.

Variable Coding[2]

Status Coding

Ethnic, gender, corporate, legal and class status variables were coded from court records and interviews. I also combined the latter three categories into "summarized structural conditions" for ease of presentation.

The participants' ethnicity was coded from the following sources, listed in order: 1) self-identification, 2) information from the other party, 3) the mediators' evaluation of ethnicity (for mediated cases only), and 4) disputants' surname.

The majority of participants in the MetroCourt sample were Anglo men, particularly in the claimant role. Minorities constituted 35% of the claimants (somewhat less than their presence in the county) and 45% of the respondents (somewhat higher than their proportionate representation in the county). Latinos (including Mexican Americans and New Mexican *Nuevomexicanos*) constituted 87.1% of minority claimants and 80.6% of minority respondents in the sample. Based on census data, the Latinos were likely to be roughly equally divided between *Nuevomexicanos* and more recent Mexican immigrants. The complete representation of claimants was Anglo (65.1%), Hispanic (30.4%), African Americans (1.8%), Native Americans (1.2%), Asian Americans (0.7%) and others (0.8%)[3]. Respondents were Anglo (55.3%), Hispanic (36.1%), African American (3.7%), Native Americans (0.8%), Asian Americans (1.8%) and others (2.3%). Anglos were assigned to higher ethnic status, minority parties to lower. Minority claimants and respondents are generalized as "Latino" except in the Case Studies (Chapter Ten).

Gender was coded for the named party. When the party was listed as a couple, gender was determined as that of the spouse who was self-identified as "most involved in the case." Men were assigned to the higher gender status, women to the lower.

Corporate parties are those listed in court records as a business, institution, landlord, professional, or "doing business as" (DBA). Consumers, tenants and private citizens were coded as noncorporate parties, or "individuals." Corporate parties (also called businesses) were assigned to the higher status, individuals (also called private citizens) to the lower.

Legal representation was coded from entries of appearance filed by lawyers in the cases. Lawyers filing on their own behalf were also coded as having legal representation. Parties with legal representation, regardless of whether the lawyers attended the mediation, were assigned to the higher legal status category and *pro se* parties (i.e., those without formal representation) were assigned to the lower legal status.

Class status was estimated by factor-scoring the responses to three questionnaire items: amount of education, household income, and occupational prestige. Factor analysis revealed a unidimensional factor structure and the standardized factor scores were then ranked as higher or lower than the median.

Cases were then characterized by the status interaction between the claimant and respondent as HILO, HIHI, LOLO, and LOHI in each of the five dimensions (ethnic, gender, corporate, legal, and class). The summarized structural conditions were formed by assigning all cases described as the first HILO condition in corporate, legal, and class dimensions to the first HILO summarized condition, all cases described as the second HIHI condition in the second summarized condition and so forth.

Outcome & Pleading Variable Coding

Monetary outcome ratio (MOR) is calculated for each case as a simple ratio of the total dollar amount of the award or settlement divided by the dollar amount of the claim. Information on the amount claimed was recorded from the original complaint filed by the claimant in the court records. The final award or settlement amount is taken from court disposition or mediated agreements.

Nonmonetary outcomes were coded from judicial ruling or mediated agreement that specified a significant material but non-dollar denominated outcome (e.g., return of personal property, repair of goods, or performance of services).

I used a global measure of disputants' reported satisfaction as an indicator of their experience. Reported satisfaction was assessed from interview questions including the entire interviewed sample of claimants and respondents in both fora. The satisfaction construct was measured by factor scoring answers to three four-point Likert-scaled questions suggested by scholars in the field of procedural preference (Lind, Thibault & Walker 1976; Lind & Tyler 1988; Lind et al 1990). The construct includes satisfaction with outcome ("Overall, how satisfied were you with the outcome of your case at the time that it ended?"), procedure ("Overall, how satisfied were you with going to court/mediation as a way to handle your dispute?"), and evaluation of fairness ("In general, did you think the decision in this case/agreement you reached was fair to both parties?"). In principal component analysis these questions were shown to be unidimensional with equal weights given to outcome satisfaction (.92 claimants; .91 respondents) and fairness (.90 claimants; .90 respondents) and slightly less weight to procedural satisfaction (.77 claimants; .71 respondents).

Admitted liability is the dollar amount admitted by the respondent in the Answer to the claim, divided by the claimed amount. This ratio measure is also the respondent's first position in the bargaining analysis (below).

Claim size was taken from court records. Larger claim sizes were common in cases between two men, two higher structural status parties, and cases falling in the fourth LOHI summarized rights-based condition. Claim sizes were lower in the LOLO insider summarized condition, and Anglo claims against Latino respondents were also somewhat lower than those in other cases.

Counterclaims filed by respondents in their Answer were recorded from the court records and refined using interview data. The ordinal measure assigned to counterclaims reflects the degree to which the counterclaim was meaningful in the case, ranging from no counterclaim in the court record nor mentioned in the interview (0), to counterclaims having direct relevance and substantive effect in the decision or negotiations (3).

Counterclaims pled by higher status respondents in the fourth LOHI structural condition and by female respondents with female claimants were more likely to be coded as effective. Counterclaims were less likely to be made or be effective lower for lower status respondents in the first HILO structural condition or for male respondents with male claimants.

Extensiveness of the prior relationship between claimant and respondent was based on claimant interviews. Claimants more often reported prior relationships when they were in the first HILO structural condition, when they were Anglos in cases with Anglo respondents, or women in cases with female respondents, but not when they were Latino claimants in cases with Anglo respondents.

Coding of Bargaining Positions

Admitted liability, taken from the respondent's Answer in the court record, was divided by the claimed amount to become the respondent's first bargaining position. In negotiations, as noted in Chapter One, early conciliation is likely to diminish the final ratio outcome for the conciliator. Thus, it is important to note that, compared to adjudication, mediation respondents reaching monetary agreements were likely to have admitted greater initial liability[4].

Claimant and respondent changes in bargaining position were reported in dollars during interviews and in mediator reports. In mediated cases, both the third and fourth positions refer to changes during mediation[5]. All bargaining positions were divided by the initial claim to return positions as ratio variables comparable to the final MOR:

> 1st Position: Recorded positions—the full claim (1.0) for claimants and the ratio of the claim recorded as admitted debt by the respondent.
>
> 2nd Position: Prior to Intervention—claimants were asked how much they "really" believed the respondent owed when they filed the claim. Respondents were asked how much they believed they "really" owed when the claim was filed.
>
> 3rd Position: During Mediation—claimants and respondents were asked whether they changed their position during the mediation but prior to the final agreement.
>
> 4th Position: For Agreement—claimants were asked whether they agreed to accept less in the final agreement and respondents were asked whether they agreed to pay more in the final agreement.

Mediators reported the duration of the mediation session and the times were converted to minutes. The mean and median duration of mediation sessions was one hour and ten minutes. Although no similar report existed in the data set for adjudicated cases, observation and the docket schedule indicated that hearings in the majority of cases lasted fifteen minutes or less. This data is discussed in Chapter Seven and is available in Rack 1997.

Bargaining Motivations Coding

I was curious whether the disputants who agreed to mediate had less materialistic goals, or recalled different goals, compared to adjudication disputants. Secondly, in order to understand how the disparate mediated outcomes were constructed in a nominally voluntary negotiation session, I wanted to discern as best I could the motivations leading to positional changes, and whether the disputants felt that the outcomes were in fact voluntary.

For dispute goal analyses comparing the fora (Chapter Five), I use claimant responses to one Likert-scaled contingency question with an open-ended clarification (N = 408) that I analyzed in 1994. Motivational variables were coded in 1996 from mediation claimant and respondent interviews reflecting the presence or absence of text indicating specific constructs. In the 1996 analysis, I selected all mediation interviews with adequate textual fields (N = 464, 79.6% of all interviewed claimants and 86.1% of all interviewed respondents).

Three primary open-ended interview questions followed the questions about positional changes (above) and a fourth asked for disputants' feelings about the agreement or lack of one[6]. The responses were coded for the presence or absence of instrumental and expressive constructs from cultural and gender arguments (rational choice motives, relational and feeling responses, and choice). Further detail on this coding and examples of text are given with the relevant analyses and in Rack 1997.

I did not have access to the numerical Likert-scale answers or to identifying references at the time of coding. However, although the text was technically coded blind, I certainly was able to recognize some of the cases due to my long familiarity with these data. In this sense, the textual variables are examples of a qualitative research process in which the researcher is more personally involved in data analysis. On the other hand, the numerical handling of the coded variables, only possible due to the large number of interviews, was also an attempt to control somewhat for the biases attending qualitative analysis, particularly in cultural and gender analyses.

Goals

Early in all interviews (N = 1009), disputants from both fora were asked, "[At the beginning of the legal case] how important was the money itself to you?" The first choice, that money "was the only important thing," I called "Cash" goals. All disputants who did not answer that money was the only important thing, i.e., answered that money was "very important," "a little important" or "not important at all," were asked "What else was important to you at that time?" In the 1994 analysis of textual responses to this open-ended question I looked for the immediate referential value: concrete or material (money, other material items, or services that could be purchased), personal (immediate reference to some aspect of the specific respondent as important in the dispute) or abstract (usually answering "the principle" or "justice") with 12 auxiliary codes.

Instrumental Bargaining Motivation

I also used reported goals (material and monetary) as a measure of instrumental bargaining. In the 1996 coding, I re-coded the same text from mediation interviews with claimants and respondents (N = 464). I used the same cash (CASH) and concrete/material (MAT) categories as in 1994 with good reproduction ($r = .46$, $p<.001$ for mediation claimants).

After each of the three times that disputants were asked if they had changed their position, they were asked "What made you change your position?" Disputants who explained their bargaining decisions in self-maximizing, rational terms were coded as strategic, "STR" negotiators. I also specified whether the disputant was reported to have said that the agreement was "better" than their alternatives (usually adjudication). Occasionally, the disputant specified that they only agreed due to some extenuating circumstance, for example, vacation plans, and these disputants were coded as strategic but not better, that is, their explanation was rationally self-interested but not in comparison with their appraisal of alternatives. Respondent statements that they were unjustly accused or were not legally liable I called "R-TUF," and claimant statements that the respondent had refused to negotiate during the mediation I labelled "C-TUF." I also noted claimant statements that indicated a preference for mediation over adjudication as a collection strategy.

Expressive Bargaining Motivation

I identified relational ("REL") answers to the questions about why the disputant had changed their position from text indicating that something about the other person was part of the disputants' motivation. I further specified whether the statements were sympathetic ("SYM") toward the other party, for example, "I could see she didn't have the money," antipathetic or hostile

("ANTI"), for example "I wanted to make it hard for her" or "I don't like him," or referred to a business relationship ("BSREL"), commonly, concern with customer relations or business reputation. A conciliatory or cooperative ("COOP") motive was attributed to statements affirming a willingness to cooperate, compromise, and/or settle the matter, for example, "I was willing to compromise."

I marked interviews for statements suggesting that the mediation had been an emotional experience ("EMO") using the full interview text, especially the text associated with questions about anger and other dimensions of psychological wellbeing; for example, "I was very upset" or "I cried during the mediation."

Choice and Coercion

I noted which interviews indicated that the disputant felt a strong sense of having been cheated, coerced or tricked into an agreement in mediation ("TRK"). The source of coercion might have been the mediators (e.g., "they pushed me too far" or "I felt I was railroaded into an agreement" [by the mediators]), or the other party (e.g., "She [female claimant] knew what to do and what to say. She was more credible.") or, more generally, the mediation situation (e.g., "I still felt I did not owe them anything. I felt totally a victim.").

Case Studies

The case studies are drawn from these textual and numerical interview data sources, including follow-up interviews, as well as from the case description, from the records and from mediator observation questionnaires.

Mediator Pairs

One-hundred and twenty-nine mediators who co-mediated cases in the MetroCourt study had each received at least 40 hours of training, usually through the process described in Chapter Three. Seventy-eight (60.5%) of the mediators in the pool were women and 92 (71.3%) were Anglos. Of the 37 minority mediators who participated in the study, 27 (73.0%) were Latino, 5 (13.5%) were African American, 2 (5.4%) were Native American, 1 (2.7%) was Asian American and 2 (5.4%) identified themselves as "other" ethnicity.

INTERSECTIONS, SAMPLE DESCRIPTIONS AND COMPARISONS

MetroCourt Status Intersections[7]

Based on the entire MetroCourt dataset, with few exceptions, Anglo women and Latinos were significantly less likely to have the achieved status of Anglo men. Anglo men were more likely to appear as corporate players, with lawyers, and with higher socioeconomic status than any other of the ethgenders. The only exceptions in the overall sample were that Anglo female claimants appeared in corporate roles, and Latina female respondents were represented by attorneys, in similar proportions as Anglo men.

Compared to other claimants, female claimants were more likely to file against corporate players. Women, especially Latina women, were likely to be respondents in cases filed by corporate entities (landlords and collectors). Latino male claimants filed more private cases against individuals, accounting for their lack of significant difference from Anglo men who also filed against individuals; yet unlike Anglo men, Latinos were rarely filing as corporate claimants. Finally, Anglo female claimants were significantly more likely than Anglo men to file suit against higher class respondents.

Overall, as shown by the correlations in Appendix Table 4.ii, hierarchical ethnic and gender relations were parallel to hierarchies in structural and class dimensions. Comparison of ethnic and gender conditions with achieved conditions in the 603 small claims cases, showed that Anglo-Latino and Latino-Latino disputes more strongly reflected (respectively) the first HILO and third LOLO conditions; male-male disputes more clearly identified the second HIHI insider condition cases in the other dimensions; and both Latino-Anglo and female-male disputes were strongly correlated with the fourth LOHI condition in structural and achieved dimensions. The anomalous condition was that women filed against women disproportionately often in power imbalanced structural roles (i.e., tenant-landlord and collections, see Hermann et al 1992).

There were critical differences in the status characteristics of Latinos and Anglo women for the two fora. Latino parties were more likely to be lower status in mediation than in adjudication; Anglo women were more likely to be lower status in adjudication than in mediation. Anglo female claimants in the mediation sample tended to be split on achieved status dimensions; almost exactly half of the Anglo women in mediation were higher status on corporate and class measures.

Analytic Samples: Monetary, Bargaining, Nonmonetary & No-Agreement Mediation

The monetary outcome sample in mediation (N = 138) and adjudication (N = 312) were cases with monetary outcomes decided during intervention. The bargaining sample is the mediation subset of cases which achieved an exclusively monetary settlement during mediation[8]. The nonmonetary samples include mediation (N = 35) and adjudication (N = 11) cases that resulted in major nonmonetary outcomes (in whole or in part)[9] and mediation cases that settled subsequent to mediation (N = 19). The No Agreement Reached (NAR) sample is comprised of mediation cases that did not reach agreement during or subsequent to mediation and presumably went on to adjudication.

Bivariate Assessment of Sample Differences

Appendix Table 4.i shows the means and frequencies of the variables used in the analyses, separated into five samples. I compared the two monetary outcome samples for forum differences and the two nonmonetary samples for forum differences (noted in the adjudication cases). For mediation cases, the nonmonetary and NAR samples are compared to the monetary sample (significance testing noted in the nonmonetary and NAR columns). Appendix Table 4.ii gives the correlation of ethnic, gender, and summarized structural status conditions with forum and the primary pleading variables for all 603 cases, and the correlations for the sample definition variables for the 280 mediated cases.

Forum Comparison of Monetary Outcome Samples

There were no significant differences between mediated and adjudicated monetary outcomes but satisfaction scores were higher in mediation, especially respondent satisfaction. Claimants reported more ongoing relationships after mediation. Respondent satisfaction and claimants' expectation for relationship were related to the payment plans[10] negotiated in mediation.

Cases involving Anglos on both sides were somewhat more frequent in the mediated sample. In contrast, cases filed by weaker parties challenging the strong (Latinos against Anglos, individuals against corporate parties), along with cases between lawyers, were more frequent in the adjudication sample.

Bargaining process changes were far greater in the mediation (see Fig 1.1). Mediation claimants reduced their claimed amounts during the session and for final agreement. Mediation respondents reported that they really felt they owed the claimant more before and during the mediation session. Total changes in the two fora were very similar, but virtually all the changed position in adjudication was in the final ruling, while in mediation, last minute movements were slight. At the end of the hearing, respondents in adjudicated cases acknowledged owing, on average, less of the debt than mediation respondents admitted in their first position.

Contrary to my cherished notions, claimants in mediated cases were *more* apt to claim a strictly monetary goal, and more often than respondents in either fora.

Comparison of the Mediation Bargaining Sample to Nonmonetary and NAR Samples.

Lower status claimants (women and especially Latinos) were likely to accept nonmonetary outcomes in their cases and are thus more often excluded from the bargaining analysis. Nonmonetary settlements accepted by Latinos from Anglo respondents were likely to be coded as additional or compensatory, meaning that they did not respond to the initial claim. LOLO mediation cases (involving two Latino disputants or two women) frequently settled for a nonmonetary outcome that responded to the original claim. Nonmonetary settlements were rarely accepted by Anglo claimants from Latino respondents, men from women, corporations from individuals, or higher class from lower class (see Appendix Table 4.ii). Cases in the nonmonetary sample often involved effective counterclaims that were less often simply strategic and respondents at all points in the bargaining process acknowledged owing less of the claim.

Compared to monetary outcome cases, nonmonetary or subsequent outcome cases were more often mediated by two Latino mediators and were less often mediated by mixed ethnicity mediators.

Individual claimants with corporate respondents and higher SES claimants with higher class respondents more often left mediation without an agreement (NAR). In contrast, cases filed by women against men or by pro se claimants against represented respondents were more often settled for monetary outcomes. Cases mediated by two women were less frequent in the NAR sample. Unsurprisingly, claimants and respondents in cases that were returned to court showed significantly less positional change in all positions, including initially admitted liability, compared to those settled for monetary outcomes.

SUMMARY OF THE METROCOURT PROJECT

By the time the case flow reached third-party intervention, approximately 70% had been disposed. Administrative dismissal and non-hearing judgments concentrated the appearance of small claims court as the lowest tier of the judicial system. In particular, as discussed in Chapter Three, corporate parties and claiming lawyers were likely to have received default judgments or judgments on pleadings. The MetroCourt sample of 603 cases was drawn from the remaining portion of the court's small claims caseload.

These were cases that bore a greater resemblance to the groups originally targeted by small claims court at the turn of the century: small businesses and private citizens seeking an accessible solution to disputes defined by small amounts of money claimed.

Data collection included 1,009 initial and 814 follow-up interviews with disputants and 517 mediator self-administered questionnaires. In addition to structured questions from interviews, questionnaires were coded for this work for bargaining positions, goals in the dispute, instrumental and expressive bargaining motivations and reports indicating that the disputant experienced a lack of choice or external coercion.

In the cases that proceeded to intervention, Latino and female disputants were highly likely to also be disadvantaged in structural (legal, corporate, and class) dimensions. Anglo women were less readily distinguished from Anglo men, especially in mediation, and especially as claimants in female-female cases. Overall, however, ascribed characteristics interlocked with structural and achieved status in a manner reflective of the stratification patterns in the larger U.S. and regional society.

Mean monetary outcomes were equivalent between mediation and adjudication, but due to higher admitted liability, respondents actually conceded less in mediation than respondents were ordered to pay in adjudication. In addition to the exclusion of cases which did not reach agreement, cases that settled subsequently or for nonmonetary exchanges are not included in the monetary outcome analytic sample used for bargaining analyses. Of the nonmonetary outcome cases in mediation, cases in the LOHI condition often settled for compensatory nonmonetary exchanges in contrast to cases in the HILO condition which were likely to have settled for cash. In the LOLO insider condition, women and Latino disputants often settled with similars for nonmonetary exchanges that responded directly to the initial claim.

Three patterns were shared by disputants and mediators. Latino claimants more often settled mediated cases for nonmonetary exchanges and Latino mediators often mediated cases resulting in nonmonetary outcomes. Anglo-Anglo cases were more frequent in the mediated monetary sample (and mediated sample overall) and the majority of mediators were Anglo. Cases filed by women against men more often reached agreement and agreements were more likely in cases mediated by two women.

Chapter Five

Forum Influence on Dispute Goals

Economist Sen (1994:385) defined rationality in economic theory: "a decision-maker is *rational* if he makes decisions consistently in pursuit of his own objectives." But Sen argues that this definition—based on intelligently maximizing a "payoff function," using all available tools, and taking account of alternatives—ignores context-dependent influences on social behavior. For example, a common choice when a fruit basket goes around is to *not* pick the last apple. Sen goes on to critique the assumption that choices must be governed by maximizing one's own well-being, including emotional preferences based on sympathy or antipathy. He argues that "action-judgments" in social interdependence can cause people to "impose restraints on their own instrumental choice[s]." Sen cites cross-cultural variation in work performance such as the emphasis in Japanese society on collective responsibility as a case in point.

In small claims mediation, three factors other than direct material self-interest may influence choices made by disputants: the mediation context, other possible non-material goals, and cultural variations derived from structural and normative constraints on instrumental choices. These may be rational choices, though not always self-interested.

Because monetary goals play such a crucial role in small claims cases and this study is based on a zero-sum monetary outcome measure, I review the relationship of materialism and self-interest to the cultural values governing giving and taking and the reasons why ethnic and gender differences might be expected. Here as elsewhere, I use the construct of individualism-collectivism for theoretical orientation in the assessment of goals, bargaining, and compromise motivation.

My suspicion is this: It seems likely that cultural individualism was birthed in the structural arrangements, especially industrialization and urbanization, of modern capitalism. Collectivism, with its communal obligations and goals, is the catchall descriptor for the myriad cultural forms that are destroyed in the triumphal march of global capitalism.

ON MATERIALISM, CALCULATION, CULTURE AND GENEROSITY

More than two centuries ago, in *A Theory of Moral Sentiments*, Adam Smith claimed that sympathy was an instinctive urge of the human race. Twelve years later, in the United States' year of birth, he published *The Wealth of Nations*, recalled as a rational theory of economic life enshrining individual self-interest as the principle of the market and social organization. Smith argued that unrestrained self-interest could operate collectively as an unregulated and ultimately benevolent guidance for the production and distribution of goods and services: the "invisible hand" of the market. In 1978, Collard observed that once Smith had firmly located generosity in an unassailable dimension, he could safely dispense with exhortation to it[1].

The Great Transformation

Economic historian Karl Polanyi claimed in 1944 that the secular belief in the "invisible hand," the self regulating market (SRM), brought a cascade of changes in social relations that were well entrenched by the middle of the nineteenth century[2]. Polanyi maintained the idea that the self-regulating market was "natural" was false, developing his argument from the work of many economic historians, historians of thought, anthropologists, and others. He argued that capitalism was a historical anomaly: previous economic relations were more often embedded in *social* relations—with rules of reciprocity, redistribution, and communal obligations—than market relations. Capitalism, as it developed through a mixture of factory production and government support in the early nineteenth century, reversed this—social relations became defined by market relations in what he saw as an irreversible change he called "the great transformation."

Polanyi echoed the early sociologists' alarm over the ascension of instrumental, individualistic social relations around the turn of the 20th century. For example, Ferdinand Töennies (1963 [1887]) distinguished "gemeinschaft" (rural and kinship-based) from "gesellschaft" (anonymous, urban) social organization more than a century ago: In the *Gesellschaft,* "there is no common will. Everyone looks after his own personal interests and does not wish to contribute anything to the community. . . . Everything in the *Gesellschaft* type of relationship is compared, weighed, and measured, so that when a person gives something away, he is sure to receive something else which he considers of equal value and/or worth" (Christodoulou 1965:61).

Émile Durkheim (1858–1917) worried whether personal self-interest could be an adequate basis for social organization. Giddens (1972) summarized Durkheim's work as an attempt to integrate two views of social reality: the Utilitarian focus on individualism with the Marxist critique of unbridled greed. According to Giddens this resulted in Durkheim's call for "the moralization of economic relationships" (Giddens 1972:14). Durkheim envisioned humans as dual beings, *Homo duplex* caught in a transitional moment of "moral mediocrity" (in Giddens 1972:244): on the one hand members of an overarching social organism with solidarity born of a collective conscience, on the other separated as individuals, vulnerable to an alienated limitless striving in a world without social support or social norms, or *anomie.*

The middle of the nineteenth century, the time according to Polanyi when the great transformation was well established—when social relations became patterned by economic relations rather than vice versa—was the heart of the industrial revolution. At about that time, Marx argued that the capitalist mode of production caused a great separation: workers, alienated from both the means and product of their work, were also estranged from their own "social being." With collective ownership of the means of production, the worker would rightfully be returned to this more communal state. Marx called his critique rational, seeking "real, positive science" (Marx 1845–46 in Tucker 1978:155) and assumed owners' greed was limitless unless it was restrained by workers' resistance. Despite Marx's renunciation of its ethical grounds, his critique of greed was profoundly moral. As Tucker (Tucker 1978:725) points out, "Value judgments resting on moral convictions abound in Marx and Engels. Thus they not only analyze exploitation and the division of labor in society, but morally condemn these phenomena as evil. Yet there is almost no abstract discussion of ethics in their voluminous writings." Marx's dialectical materialism has arguably remained the only secular critique of capitalism in western societies.

At this same juncture in history, Darwin published *Origin of Species* tracing evolution through the dual processes of competition and adaptation. The public and intellectual discourse focused on the survival value of competition over adaptation. Darwinism seemed to promote a view of nature as a competition for survival that was readily applied to humans. Self-interested competition became "natural" (see Kaye 1986 for extension into the present time), the genetic driving force of the "invisible hand."

As the genocidal "Indian Wars" were winding down in the United States, in Germany Georg Simmel related the change in social relations to urbanization and the existence of money. In 'the metropolis' people retreat into rational calculation, away from human connection, facilitated by the existence of money: "Modern life becomes an intellectual endeavor excluding emotional considerations in favor of calculability. . . . The culture of things replaces the culture of persons. [In *The Philosophy of Money* (1900) Simmel argues]. . . . Money can overcome the physical and social distance between individuals because of its capacity to be absolutely transferable, combined with a process of individualization. . . . People can be measured in an objective and absolute way according to the monetary value . . . money exerts its influence in a variety of social domains: legal rights transform into monetary claims, and labor relations become useful only inasmuch as they involve monetary gains (wages)" (Deflem 2003: 67–96).

Early in the twentieth century, the infant science of psychology also moved toward a materialistic, even mechanistic, portrait of the human being, absorbing an economic model of human nature virtually intact. The psyche, to the extent it had an autonomous reality at all, became one with the accountant blessed with double-entry bookkeeping, calculating costs (negative reinforcement) and benefits (positive reinforcement) and modifying behavior in order to acquire the most benefit. Of the less materially and behaviorally based psychologies, Freudian theory received the most acceptance. It theorized an individually-constructed psyche, of necessity patterned on the upper-class, Victorian-era men and women who sought Freud's treatment. In this psyche exists a dark space composed of animal instinct (Id) doing battle with repressed personal memories (Superego) that provided internal social control holding the animal nature in check.

In the first decades of the twentieth century, few voices were heard opposing these world views. Virtually no mention of altruism existed in sociology, despite the concerns of its founders a few decades before (Piliavin & Charng 1990).

Polyani argued that there was a dual movement in the great transformation: social welfare and regulation emerged to soothe the ravages of the capitalist system. In the early years of the twentieth century, giving became "scientific," impersonal and rational, an attitude accepted more comfortably in public health, more awkwardly in face-to-face social charities (Trattner 1994 [1974]). In the watershed year of 1935, under the distant prod of the Bolshevik revolution, the persistent effects of the Great Depression and the efforts of American labor, the U.S. government made the major leap to accept primary responsibility for giving or, rather, redistributing material benefit.

In literal and symbolic senses, public giving rose with alienation. An increase in collective responsibility can be traced to a response to the American Revolution, based on individualism, when towns created ordinances to handle increased numbers of strangers from postwar migratory movements and war widows and orphans. The Civil War brought another wave of collective responsibility for the same reasons, intensified by the legal transformation of property (former slaves) into citizens who needed help and were surely strangers. In response to immigration and urbanization, the public health movement grew in the Reform Era of the early 1900s. The unsettling fact that 25 percent of World War I troops suffered crippling psychological injuries triggered the development of personal, face-to-face social work, supported by federal funding for pre-induction testing to reduce the psychological casualties of conflict (Trattner 1994). Courts, traditionally the bastions of conflict, also moved to work in a face-to-face, personal arena in this post World War I period. After 1919 specialty courts proliferated: conciliation, juvenile, domestic, and small claims.

Overall, in the twentieth century, a large literature on the alienating social effects of capitalism proliferated and a bureaucracy of public remedies proliferated, but there was with little investigation of capitalism's relationship to human giving and restraint of taking. Although clear in the theorizing that initiated modern human sciences, including economics, the linkage between capitalism and giving/altruism is veiled through the very organization of our collective social and intellectual structures.

Material Greed and Culture

Max Weber (1958, original German publication 1904–1905) gave us the most profoundly *cultural* explanation for the rise of capitalism: the combination of asceticism—increased work with denial of hedonism or reduced consumption associated with the Protestant ethic—with a drive for moral superiority associated with material success in Calvinist theology. The two together, rationalized and systematized, Weber theorized, inspired northern European Protestant cultures to strive for the material accumulation necessary for capital formation. Though enjoying resurgence in the "prosperity gospel" delivered by protestant fundamentalist churches today, the moral motivation associating wealth with spiritual salvation was largely forgotten over the past century. Its corollary, however, that the poor are damned, is often implicit in pejorative attitudes toward the poor (for an eloquent discussion, see Devine & Wright 1993).

Our modern society is filled with strange contradictions. Nearly all theology and moral philosophies mark greed and material ambition as negative spiritual indicators; yet many of our most moralistic judgments condemn those who don't strive for more. Consumption drives the United States economy; but we criticize people and groups who don't delay gratification. Apologists for capitalism embrace the all-encompassing idea of *Homo economicus*, a human who is naturally self-interested and self-maximizing, psychologically patterned by the gains and losses that appeared to control economic behavior; the same advocates valorize women and cultural minorities who are different from this—implicitly transforming them into saintly "non-humans."

For example, in 1919 in *The Science of Power*, Benjamin Kidd drew upon the ideas of the time to indict the Darwinian "liberation." He argued that Darwin's theory equated might with right, thereby silencing all questions about the morality of the fight, thus unleashing the "aggressive and pagan western European male." Like the early Republicans (see Takaki 1979), a salvatory vision of great womanhood inspired Kidd: female compassion could save the soulless. Durkheim, in his later years (1914), equated the greater connectedness of "primitive" cultural groups to a reality of mystical participation, of being part of something which includes others. Today we speak of empathy, what is fashionably called perspective-taking, and encourage women and professional care-givers to be careful about maintaining their psychic boundaries.

Although often critiqued, the notion that women can do the caring work, thereby softening the ravages of greed and competition, has survived to the present. The idea that women have a propensity to give, whether that quality is innate or socialized, remains the core of feminist claims to excel in the task of peacemaking as well as to the feminist critique of mediation as a source of female exploitation. To this day, anthropologists and others, including myself, describe culture groups that appear to emphasize self-interest less, and group interest more, as collectivistic, often studying them with the romanticized objectivism Rosaldo (1989) called "imperialist nostalgia." The statistical likelihood that national cultures deemed collectivist are also nations categorized as less economically developed, that individualist nations and individuals are overwhelming likely to be affluent, languishes in footnotes, rarely articulated since the linkage between culture and poverty became another way to "blame the victim" (Ryan 1971; see Chapter Two).

Contemporary affluent societies have largely relegated giving to public institutions and others who are socialized differently from, in particular, white, Euro-civilized men. But the obvious corollary, that European white male culture is oriented toward taking, most often gets lost in self-interested assumptions that taking is natural survival behavior for the individual, or systemically, that profits are survival behavior for capitalism

(Hardin 2004). But hungry capital makes profits out of transforming resources into products for sale, including natural, human, and social resources. Hardin argues that, while capitalism is anti-culture, and may "bulldoze" traditional cultures, it does this . . . through the remaking of the values of individuals." I suggest that this change in values *is* the cultural invention of individualism[3].

If individualism is the culture that is, as Frankenberg (1993:228) suggested, "constructed daily practices and worldviews in complex relations with [the] material life" of industrial capitalism, then we can understand some of the qualities required. To take more than value given, required for the profits essential to capitalist survival, requires adequate protection from empathy, a sense of superiority to legitimate privilege, hoarding required for accumulation, and incessant, competitive striving. The sense of self ascribed to the independent self-construal found in cultural individualism meets these criteria: self-interest motivation unconstrained by concern for collectivities, needing to rise as an individual above others, all protected by cognitive biases that reduce any undermining information (Brett & Kopelman 2004; see Chapter Seven).

Some scholars have explored giving/taking as crucial elements in cultural formation and evolution. E. Gans in *The End of Culture* (1985) argued that constraint of taking is the formative principle of human culture. Returning to anthropological notions that representation embodied in ritual sacrifice was the "originary" point of cultural emergence, Gans claimed that self-inhibition of taking to avoid conflict was more fundamental to the development of human culture. The *justification* of this restraint, elaborated as a transcendent order and embodied in ritual sacrifice, absorbed the resentment that might otherwise have led to the conflict the restraint had avoided. Gans argued that the rise of western secular and egalitarian ethics, which offer no justification for restraint of taking, has unleashed this resentment, thus heralding the demise of culture.

Hyde, like Gans and Durkheim, linked western individualism and unrestrained taking with social fragmentation. Hyde (1979:37) argued that cohesive, lively social feeling grows from gift exchange: generalized indebtedness, gratitude, expectation, memory, and sentiment.

> Capital earns profit and the sale of a commodity turns a profit, but gifts that remain gifts do not *earn* profit, they *give* increase. The distinction lies in what we might call the vector of the increase: in gift exchange, the increase stays in motion and follows the object, while in commodity exchange it stays behind as profit. (emphasis in the original).

Hyde traced the erosion of widely accepted laws and theological prohibitions against usury into the rise of commodity exchange. Hyde claimed that charging interest (usury) is a rationalization of this natural increase, just as contract in law is the rationalization of the gift bond. "Both contract and usury imitate the structure of a gift economy," Hyde wrote (1979:86), "but both drop the feeling, the 'uneconomic' feeling." A social and expressive loss occurs when the gift portion of exchange transforms into individual profit. The last anti-usury laws, he tells us, were abolished in the 1860s.

In an incalculable irony of the twentieth century the most successful critique of capitalist need for ever-increasing exploitation, production and consumption, Marxism, denied connection with the concepts of morality—the critique of greed and the presumed roots of giving. The conceptual and behavioral merger of capitalist exchange with individualistic, Euro-American culture hides the relatively simple fact that giving often feels good and builds community; while taking often feels bad and unravels social bonds.

Is it not a coincidence that more collectively defined groups are also groups with showing relatively reduced economic power and contending with racism. Latino and female groups, clearly separable on economic indicators as disadvantaged, and targeted for majority group discrimination and domination, are also identified as more giving.

Context & Message Sensitivity & Materialism

Individualism implies a strong sense of personal identity (seeking the "true self"), Maslovian goals of self-actualization, and internal locus of control or emotional independence. In individualistic cultures, abstract principles and universalized moral reasoning are valued more than context. Compared to Mexicans, people socialized in the United States are likely to have a more field independent cognitive style, perceiving figures more than the context in which they are embedded. The United States (especially legal procedural constraints on extraneous information) is the example Hall (1976) used to describe a low context culture. Thus, applied to context sensitivity, Anglos might be expected to be less sensitive to the environment and the other disputant in mediation.

Cortese (1990) describes people from collectivist cultures as more particularistic as opposed to universalistic in their moral reasoning, that is, collectivists would be likely to make moral decisions considering the specific person in the particular context. In support of this categorization for Latinos, Mexican groups, on average, test as more field dependent (Ramirez 1983) and Mexico was the specific example used by Hall (1976) to describe a "high context" culture. Thus, applied to context sensitivity, Latinos might be expected to be specifically susceptible to environments and the specific other.

Like collectivism, the "relational psychology" at the heart of arguments for female vulnerability to exploitation assumes that women have identities and values that emphasize connectedness with others. Drawing on Chodorow's psychoanalytic model based in mother-daughter similarity and merger, scholars argue that women have developmental differences that make complete separation and individualization difficult (Stiver 1991; Flax 1993; Levenson 1984). Similar to models of high context cultures, Gilligan's (1982) cognitive model of an "ethic of care" suggests that moral decisions are based more on specific people and circumstances rather than generalizing across contexts.

Because rational and less oriented to favoritism, individualism has been associated with a greater likelihood of collaborative, goal-oriented and integrative or problem-solving approaches, certainly a central component to the message of mediation. However, researchers attempting to demonstrate this have found instead that "interdependent" people, analogous to collectivists, were more oriented to integrative problem solving conflict styles than those assessed as "independent," analogous to individualist (Oetzel 1998). Other investigators explained the lack of empirical support for individualist preference for integrative styles as poor conceptualization of what "solution orientation" actually means (Trubisky, Ting-Toomey & Lin 1991). Thus, the concept of individualism presents contrasting predictions about how Anglos might respond to the message of collaboration and problem-solving in mediation.

Collectivism is also associated with solidarity and concern for others, with psychological links between perceived obligation and behavioral intention, and favorable attitudes toward sharing burdens, material and nonmaterial resources (time and effort), and outcomes. The type of sharing associated with collectivist cultures is not sacrificial, because persons also expect group sharing of negative outcomes. In contrast to the guilt more commonly relied on for internal social control in individualist cultures, shame and religious beliefs are the more common methods for internalizing restraint in collectivist cultures. Rather than the value of ingroup harmony ascribed to collectivist cultures in the East, Latino cultures are specifically noted for the cultural value placed on respect, dignity and preservation of honor: "An ingroup member is honorable and dependable, does what the ingroup expects, and is unlikely to 'betray' the ingroup" (Triandis et al. 1988:326). Collectivistic classification is compatible with the patterns of mutual aid noted in Latino communities (Gonzales 1993; Keefe & Padilla

1987) and the increased learning through cooperative strategies that Kagan (1984) reports for Mexican American children. In the United States, *simpatía*, an attitude of easy-going friendliness, is a cultural emic for Chicano culture (Moyerman & Forman 1992). Applied to Latino sensitivity to the message of mediation, collectivist categorization suggests that Latino culture would resonate with the relational and cooperative message, but most particularly with ingroup members.

Frequently Mexicanism defines itself against Anglo materialism. In Vila's (1996) ethnographic exploration of Latino identity in the borderlands region of the Southwest, he discerned a gradient in the narrative construction Latino identity from southern Mexico to Juarez to Mexican-Americans living in El Paso. Though he focused primarily on how Catholic devotion became more "private" as Mexican identity Anglicized, he identified a tight matrix of Mexican identity: Mexican-ness, public Catholicism, and poverty were at the "conservative" pole; Anglo culture, private Protestantism, and materialism were at the "modern" pole. Vila (1996:20) writes that "the Catholic faith is a barrier that Hispanics have against the pure materialism that seems to them to characterize Anglos."

When Latinos (as well as other culture groups) look at Anglo culture, they see first the materialistic striving: "I feel that people here live better, materially, but there is more unity in Mexico, more friendship, more love towards your fellow. Here one lives on the run . . ." (Vila 1996:17, see also other interviews and text describing the frenetic pace and worship of money associated with the United States). Similarly, moving to the higher class northern suburbs where Anglos lived was perceived as an ethnic betrayal in Rubel's (1962) ethnography of a southwestern Latino community. By contrast, Anglos and dominant culture scholars rarely identify "money and work" as their own cultural trait. For example, materialism was *not* a conceptualized cultural parameter in Hofstede's index, but materialism is implied by the way researchers measure acculturation in the United States. Moyerman & Forman (1992) focused on increasing income and educational attainment as a measure of acculturation without emphasizing the cultural pattern that is being adopted and changing values are often attributed to class ascension (e.g., Malpass & Symonds 1974). In this way, circular reasoning suggests that class ascension becomes the reward and the measure of acculturation, and implicitly the goal.

From a social-psychological perspective, the process of acculturation to Anglo capitalist culture fragments minority cultures; accommodation to it is "assimilation." But nationalistic identity groups and race-ethnic scholars (Avruch 1991; Jones & Morris 1993) perceive this process as a defeat. The terms used for this defeat echo Durkheim's *anomie:* nihilism (West 1994), spirit murder (Williams 1991), and incoherence resulting from "assimilating into the story of capitalism" (Abalos 2002:55–56):

> In the story of capitalism, we agree on procedures that keep us from physically assaulting or killing eachother as we struggle with one another in the name of self-interest. To overcome our vulnerability, we seek power, which, of course, increases our anxiety. We turn this attempt to organize insecurity, without being able to name it, into a whole way of life I call incoherence. Everyone is had by this story. The powerful, the less powerful, and the powerless are all wounded but still collude with eachother to believe this is the only way to live.

Individual self-interested striving is the cultural schema for the dominating influence of market forces, structuring a culture of consumption in an "empty quest for pleasure, property & power" (West 1994).

Compared to Latinos, the theoretical and empirical evidence for women's non-materialism is scant. Though the image of the feminine includes a non-materialistic element, and females readily attribute reduced materialism to themselves (e.g., Beutel & Marini 1995), scholars seeking gender justice routinely cite income figures in order to demonstrate injustice (see England 1993). Like the contradiction discussed for Latino identity, these arguments tend to ignore the former value of non-materialism to advocate for economic justice. For example, Bryan (1992:489) argues that "Mediators often enhance the threat that women's care orientation poses to financial negotiations by appealing to emotional and relational interests. This emphasis reinforces the traditional woman's socialization and obscures that obtaining an equitable financial agreement from a reluctant husband might require the wife to sacrifice relatedness and good feeling."

Overall, cross-cultural studies show that disputing styles in the United States, especially among Anglo men, were comparatively more dominating, competitive, goal-oriented and verbally confrontational, and the resolution values more individually self-interested (e.g., Trubisky et al. 1991; Ohbachi & Takahashi 1994; Leung & Iwakwaki 1988; Leung 1988; Gire & Carment 1993; Triandis et al. 1993; Chiu & Kosinski 1994). In computerized games intended to represent social negotiation processes and resource usage, Anglo negotiators reciprocated less often and maintained reciprocity for shorter periods (Parks & Vu 1994). This cultural pattern is structurally apparent in the adversarial argument and remedies of Anglo-American jurisprudence generally, in small claims court specifically, and in the historical behavior of western European and U.S. capitalism.

RESULTS: REPORTED GOALS

The assumption of individual self-interest underlies rational choice theories, exchange/negotiation theories, and, most important here, interest-based mediation. Analyses of the characteristics of groups who are *not* Anglo men (i.e., women and other cultures) note two crucial theoretical differences: group identity and goals, and context responsiveness. Self-interest theories accommodate non-material interests as a subcategory of "valued outcomes," but largely ignore context sensitivity and conceptual distortions imposed by culture-bound and gendered assumptions of *individual self-interest* (Avruch 1991; Duryea 1992, 1994; Kolb 1994). The implicit contradiction with materialistic goals is ignored or invalidated. I wanted to explore the possibility that Latino and female goals might differ from the monetary demands that are the overt point of contention in small claims cases. In the first days of data collection, I added a question to the interview instrument. I show the results here.

All complaints in small claims court are, by procedural necessity, couched in the language of money: the act of filing a claim required a specific monetary amount claimed. For some claimants, especially collectors and lawyers, this was an obvious way to describe the dispute. But for others, especially lower status claimants, this was sometimes awkward because the monetary value of their complaint was difficult to gauge. As one claimant said, "You can't put a price on what he did" and punitive claims for "pain and suffering" were routinely disqualified from judicial consideration. The following analysis of the answers to the question asking "How important was the money itself to you?" (see Chapter Four) was intended to address the possible distortions likely to result from the imposition of a monetary definition on all disputes. The analyses use the full MetroCourt Project sample of all interviewed claimants (N = 532) who answered either the Likert-scale response question or for whom a textual response could be coded (88% of all claimants in the study sample).

Table 5.1 shows the frequency with which claimants responded that cash or material goals were primary in the dispute. Because mediation is often considered a dispute resolution forum that is more likely to serve and result in ongoing relationships, the question was aimed at clarifying the importance of relational and abstract goals held by claimants filing at the court. Appendix Table 4.i shows the results of analyzing this question for alternative goals. In the Appendix, response frequencies are given by forum and also are disaggregated by ethgender and class status[4] in both fora.

There are four levels to the analysis presented here. First, what were the expressed goals reported by claimants who brought disputes through third party intervention in this small claims court? Second, what were the differences in expressed goals for different status relationships? Third, what were the differences in the goals expressed by claimant groups after adjudication compared with mediation? Finally, and implicitly, how monetaristic and materialistic was the self presentation of the parties? The answers to these questions help to disentangle subjective culture-linked values (questions One and Four) that might be considered as a disposition of the individual, from situationally-influenced values (questions Two and Three) that might suggest situationally affected goals and therefore context sensitivity.

Cash and Material Concerns in Adjudication and Mediation

Table 5.1 shows that adjudication claimants were somewhat less likely to say that the money was the only important issue in the dispute; one fifth of adjudication claimants interviewed chose this response while more than one quarter of the mediation claimants answered that the dispute was only about money. Compared to adjudication claimants, mediation claimants more often specified that cash was the "only" issue in the dispute in seven status conditions. Claimants were significantly more likely to report that money itself was the only goal driving the dispute in the first HILO ethnic and class conditions, the third LOLO gender and legal conditions and the fourth LOHI ethnic, gender, and corporate conditions. However, none of the five HIHI insider condition cases reported a significantly greater focus on cash after mediation compared to adjudication.

Examining the text for those who responded with other issues showed that an additional 17% of adjudication claimants and 30% of the mediation claimants specified a material issue was also, or more, important than cash. Most of these textual remarks actually restated a cash issue, the claimants simply appeared to shy away from saying that money was the *only* issue. As one claimant said when asked what he meant when he said that the principle was important, "you can't really separate them, the principle and the money go hand in hand." In some cases, however, the claimants sounded aggravated; "Not the money" a woman corrected, "the *car*." Thus, having the car returned, being paid as promised, and having the original work redone are examples of non-cash issues that were coded as material. Taken together, approximately one third of adjudication claimants responded to this question with monetary or material issues as predominant; in mediation more than half of the claimants cited money or other concrete items as the most important thing.

In contrast to all other conditions, Latino claimants with Latino respondents (i.e., the third LOLO insider ethnic condition) reported material concerns *less* often after mediation compared to adjudication.

Table 5.1 Reported Goals: Frequency of Claimant Interview Responses Indicating that Money or Other Material Concerns were the Primary Goals in the Dispute in All Adjudicated and Mediated Civil Cases

	Medicated Cases				Adjudicated Cases			
	Cash Only[a]		Material[b]		Cash Only		Material	
Status Conditions	N	%	N	%	N	%	N	%
Ascriptive Status								
Anglo-Latino	76	23.7**	76	32.9***	57	42.1	57	63.2
Anglo-anglo	106	21.7	106	35.4***	109	25.7	109	56.0
Latino-Latino	54	20.4	54	48.2	54	14.8	54	38.9
Latino-anglo	43	9.3*	43	32.6***	31	25.8	31	74.2
Male-female	56	35.7	56	48.2	45	31.1	45	53.3
Male-male	123	24.4	123	42.3	102	21.6	102	51.0
Female-female	37	5.4***	37	27.0***	45	28.9	45	66.7
Female-male	65	7.7***	64	24.6***	59	32.2	59	59.3
Structural Status								
Corporate-individual	99	36.4	99	44.4***	77	37.7	77	68.8
Corporate-corporate	31	12.9*	31	29.0**	36	33.3	36	55.6
Individual-individual	63	14.3	63	34.9*	66	19.7	66	51.5
Individual-corporate	88	9.1*	88	34.1*	72	19.4	72	47.2
Lawyer-pro se	47	44.7	47	57.5	32	43.8	32	59.4
Lawyer-lawyer	29	27.6	29	37.9	12	25.0	12	41.7
Pro se-pro se	173	12.1***	173	30.6***	163	25.8	163	57.7
Pro se-lawyer	32	21.9	32	43.8	44	20.5	44	52.3

Acheived Status								
Higher class-lower	81	29.6**	81	44.4***	63	49.2	63	66.7
Higher class-higher	60	16.7	60	26.7***	58	20.7	58	50.0
Lower-lower	87	14.9	87	37.9*	83	16.9	83	50.6
Lower-higher	53	18.9	53	37.7**	47	23.4	47	59.6
Outcomes								
Monetary Outcome	274	20.1**	274	37.2***	124	29.8	124	58.1
Nonmonetary	7	28.5*	7	42.9	19	5.3	19	42.1
Additional nonmonetary		n.a.			16	6.3	16	56.3
Agreement		n.a.			173	26.6	173	57.2
Dependent Variables [c]								
CSAT	50	.020	96	-.183***	37	.297	87	.090
RSAT	33	-.445***	62	-.357***	33	.410	77	.512
MOR	55	.778†	102	.643	37	.700	72	.584†
Total [d]	281	20.3*	281	37 4***	251	27.1	251	56.2

*** p< .01; ** p< .05; * p< .10 (two-tailed tests) for differences between forums noted with adjudication percentages

† p<.10 for difference in means within forum.

Table 5.1 Notes

[a] Response of “money was the only important thing” taken from a 4-point Likert-scaled question “How important was the money itself to you?”

[b] Responses indicating that a material concern was primary coded from open-ended question asked if claimant did not answer that money was the only important thing are combined with cash only.

[c] Significance tests of mean dependent variables tested by categorical variables within the forum.

[d] Significance testing refers to chi square tests for category between adjudication and mediation.

Unsurprisingly, Table 5.1 indicates that cash concerns were more often specified by claimants who reached monetary agreements in mediation but less often by claimants who settled for nonmonetary outcomes. In adjudication, claimants who reported cash goals as the only important concern in the dispute also tended to receive more lucrative court outcomes and the respondents in these cases reported reduced satisfaction. In mediated cases, a focus on cash goals was not significantly related to monetary outcome, but claimants who reported that material concerns were primary often had negotiated agreements paying them somewhat less money.

In tests by claimant ethgender group (see Rack 1997), I found that, compared to other ethgenders, an overt cash focus was more often reported by Anglo men after adjudication and by Anglo women after mediation. Compared to all other claimants, higher class claimants were more likely to say that money was the only important issue in both fora. Compared to other ethgenders, Latino female claimants were more likely to specify concrete items were their primary concern in both fora.

In sum, although cash and material issues were cited by claimants more frequently after mediation than adjudication, men and legally represented claimants reported high and similar material interests in both fora. Latino claimants with Latino respondents were distinguished by reporting a material focus less often after mediation than similar claimants after adjudication. Gender differences among Anglos were especially strong. After adjudication, Anglo men most often stated cash interests but Anglo women rarely did; after mediation, Anglo women specified cash interests most often. Claimants who specified cash goals after adjudication had received higher monetary outcomes, considered as the ratio of their claimed amount, and the respondents in their cases reported diminished satisfaction in comparison with other adjudication respondents. Mediation claimants who did not specify cash as the only issue, but cited cash or material interests in the text, tended to leave mediation with lower outcomes compared to other mediation cases.

Nonmaterial Concerns

Two-thirds of adjudication claimants and slightly less than one-half of the mediation claimants reported that nonmaterial issues were of considerable importance to them in filing their small claims. What were these other issues? Contrary to theoretical expectation that women would tend to answer the open-ended question in relational terms, this was true only for Anglo women who responded to the question with an answer based on some aspect or issue with the respondent 40% of the time (see Rack 1997). However, the percentage of Anglo women's responses in this category was not significantly different from other claimants in either forum. Compared to other adjudication claimants, Latino women were least likely to answer the question in terms of the other party, but more often specified some sense of injury to themselves which was, ultimately, a statement assigning blame to the respondent.

Although "the principle" was the modal response to the open-ended question in both fora, adjudication claimants were far more likely to cite this or a similar philosophical point as important in their reasons for claiming (45.7% in adjudication compared to 27.3% in mediation). Interestingly, Latino women in adjudication answered in justice terms more than half the time; in mediation Latina claimants were least likely to answer the question with issues of principle or justice.

More detailed content coding of this single open-ended question showed some significant trends. In adjudication, Latino/a women more often explained the issue in terms I called "contract logic" to convey the sense of a broken agreement. In mediation, this kind of explanation for the issue was unlikely from lower class claimants and Latino men. Compared to adjudication, mediation claimants more often mentioned the avoidance pattern of the respondent as the impetus to file their claims; this was due primarily to the Anglo women in the mediation sample who more often cited this issue in relation to Anglo male respondents[5]. Of the adjudication cases, four of the six claimants who wanted to punish the respondent were Latino men; both of the mediation claimants who offered punitive statements were Latinas. Anglo men after mediation were unlikely to speak of abuse by the respondent. None of the 37 claimants suggesting the respondent had cheated them were higher class.

Compared to mediation claimants, adjudication claimants more often said that being proved right, or vindication, was important. Interestingly, this goal was most common for higher class claimants in adjudication but was never noted for a higher class claimant after mediation. Lower class claimants in adjudication and mediation claimants generally more often said that it was important to file the claim so that others would not suffer at the hands of the respondent in the future. Finally, mediation claimants, Latino men in particular, more often said that it was important to resolve the dispute.

Of the claimants who did not say the only issue was money, abstract issues of justice, primarily "the principle," were most frequently cited by all ethgenders and class extremes as the reason for filing a small claim, more often after adjudication. Higher class claimants in adjudication often specified a need to be proven right, to be vindicated. Although infrequent overall, mediation claimants were more likely to say that the case was filed for the sake of others, and more often mentioned a goal of resolution, of bringing a longstanding problem to a close.

Some aspect of the respondent was also a frequent reason for filing. Anglo women after mediation seemed to be especially focused on the way that the respondent had avoided them in the past and saw claiming as a way to insist on being dealt with. Latinas after adjudication more often conveyed a sense of personal injustice that I have called perceived abuse, and filed claims to bring the respondent to task. Using a court case to teach the respondent a lesson, usually about responsibility, was cited by all ethgenders and both class extremes in about 10% of their cases. Although punitive statements were rare, they were more frequently made by Latino claimants.

This analysis is important as well for what it does not say. Mediation claimants were *not* more likely than adjudication claimants to frame their concerns in relational terms. In both fora and in similar ratios across all ethgenders and class categories, approximately one third of all claimants who did not specify cash concerns said that something about the person of the respondent led them to file the claim. Of all interviewed claimants, an identical 22% of claimants in both mediation and adjudication described the important issue as related to the specific respondent.

DISCUSSION: GOALS AND MONEY

Although all claims were formally expressed in monetary terms, less than one quarter of the claimants in either forum said money was the only issue in the dispute. However, if the definition of the dispute was expanded to include all material concerns, more than one third of the adjudication claimants and more than half of the mediation claimants specified material goals. Claimants who settled for non-cash outcomes in mediation (nonmonetary agreements) distinguished clearly between cash and material goals; they did not seek cash but were as apt to state material concerns as other mediation claimants. The most commonly stated nonmaterial goal in both fora was "the principle."

Consistent with Marxian assumptions, higher status claimants in the HILO power dependent condition with lower status respondents were most overtly concerned about getting money, especially in the class dimensions, and this cash focus was heightened for mediation compared to adjudication claimants. Compared to other class categories, higher class claimants replied that money was the "only" issue in the dispute significantly more often in both fora (approximately one third of their cases). With higher class equals, higher class claimants cited cash concerns only half as often. Lower class claimants replied that money was "not important at all" more often in similar percentages in both fora (approximately 20% in both fora compared to a sample mean of 11%). Thus, in similar percentages in both fora, the status dimension specifically defined by having more or less monetary resources claimed interests that reflected different valuing of money. Those who already had more money were more willing to cite cash interests, and those that had less material resources, less often claimed a cash focus.

By comparing reported goals after mediation and adjudication for claimant groups, the data suggested that claimed goal structure was different under the influence of mediation culture. Statements from claimants about their goals in the dispute were assessed to determine whether ethnic and gender minorities appeared to have a different goal orientation from that of Anglo men. In adjudication, consistent with gender arguments, Latinas and Anglo women were more likely than Anglo men to eschew monetary and material goals in the interviews; Anglo men were most likely to claim monetary goals. This was not the case with mediation claimants.

Compared to adjudication claimants, mediation claimants were less abstract about their issues, and more likely to say the dispute was only about money or to give concrete versions of the problem. This trend might logically be attributed to the successful implementation of a central directive of conflict resolution and mediator training discussed in Chapter Three, which urges participants to focus on interests, not positions. Although men and legally represented claimants maintained similarly high levels of material concerns in both fora—the mediation forum appeared to have little impact on their reported concerns—Anglo women after mediation reported far more cash concerns than similar claimants in adjudication. Latino claimants with Latino respondents showed the opposite trend, reporting less material focus after mediation than adjudication.

At face value, some of this shift toward and away from reporting cash goals might be explained by structural role influence because role appearances follow the pattern of cash goals: in mediation, Latino claimants were *less* often in structurally higher status positions; Anglo women were *more* often in these roles; and Anglo men tended to be in higher status roles in both fora. Thus, a cash focus might appear to reflect the structural role influence on goals, especially as collectors. Although this issue will be clarified further in Chapter Eight, it should be noted here that Latinas, who generally did not mediate in collector roles, also reported a cash focus somewhat more often after mediation.

In sum, the mediation forum appeared to have little effect on the reported goals for most dominant group parties: men, lawyers, and corporate claimants reported cash goals with nearly equal frequency in both fora, regardless of respondent. Consistent with mediator process training emphasizing interests but contradicting mediation ideology emphasizing relationships, female claimants were generally more likely to identify specific cash and material interests in the interviews following mediation than adjudication. Consistent with collectivistic cultural arguments, the mediation forum influence diminished material focus for Latino claimants with Latino respondents. In this dyad only, claimants reported cash and material goals less frequently after mediation than adjudication.

Overall, the evidence suggests that, consistent with collectivist and relational gender theories assuming higher context sensitivity, both outsider groups (women and Latinos) were influenced by the mediation environment, but this influence worked in opposite ways. If the mediation ideology operated as a "cultural amplifier" (Group 1987), then Latino claimants took the message of mediation to mean a less materialistic and perhaps more relational goal was appropriate, especially with non-Anglo respondents. By contrast, women, especially Anglo women, more often heard the message of material interest clarification.

If material goal orientation leans toward the individualistic pole as it does in the "spirit of capitalism," and less materialistic, or at least less monetarist, goals toward the collectivistic pole, then the message of mediation, compared to adjudication, was read differently by the two outsider groups. Mediation appeared to enhance the individualist focus in women, especially Anglo women, and perhaps amplify, surely not extinguish, a collectivist orientation for ethnic minorities in the insider condition.

Chapter Six
Adjudicated & Negotiated Outcomes

INTERACTIVE STRUCTURE AND CULTURE

There are three parameters affecting outcomes that lie outside of the negotiating process: the power balance in the dispute dyad, modified by insider-outsider dynamics; negotiators' alternatives to a negotiated agreement; and the influence of intervenors. This chapter shows discrimination patterns in court and mediated outcomes, provides adjudication comparison to clarify negotiators' alternatives to a mediated agreement; and summarizes analyses designed to clarify mediators' influence based on their ethnicity and gender interaction with disputants. The relative power within the disputing dyad is encapsulated in the way we are viewing the cases.

Black argued clearly for interactive analyses in legal sociology which he called "the social structure of the case." He claimed that decision-maker discrimination favoring higher status parties is "ubiquitous" in legal systems, but biased outcomes for respondents are less likely to be statistically significant unless claimant status is controlled.

Adjudicated outcomes are the logical bargaining limits for the self-interested negotiator. In negotiations, the party who understands the alternatives inherently has the upper hand: in the dyadic power relation; lack of alternatives for one party is the most potent source of power for the other. Exchange and negotiation theories argue clearly that the dynamics of power are primarily interactive.

Most mediators construct their role as "neutral" although this appears unlikely. In adjudication, the inevitable bias is presumably limited by constraints of procedure and precedent; in mediation, by lack of mediator decision power. As Nader (1993) argued, this leaves mediation to grapple with the more subtle and psychological power of influence.

The Social Structure of the Case

Black theorized that decision-makers implicitly must balance their *support* for claimants (victims or plaintiffs) and their *protection* for respondents (perpetrators or defendants). Decision-makers, on average, weight their decisions in favor of claimants and respondents who are higher in status thus accounting for outcome variations.

Black based his theory on the ways that race affected the severity of punishment for homicide. Murder of an African American carried less penalty than murder of a white person. Thus, without controlling for the victim's race, bias in favor of white murderers was not apparent. . However, when the victim's race was taken into account, it was apparent that white defendants were penalized less than African American defendants for either the murder of an African American or a white person. Applying Black's framework to this work, the claimant is analogous to the victim.

According to Black, variation in outcomes results from social status differences between the parties. These can be organizational membership, wealth, respectability, community connection and correlated ascriptive characteristics like ethnicity and gender. In criminal cases, the relative status of the specific lawyers modifies party status in the direction of the lawyers. In small claims court, where parties can plead their own cases, the status and presentational skill of any lawyer, and their heightened similarity with judges through a shared linguistic culture, is a status category of its own. Referring to intervenor-disputant similarity, Black argues that the greater the distance in status between the parties and the decision maker, the more win-lose the decision.

Interestingly, two points critical to mediation occur in Black's thesis. First, Black argues that the magnitude of outcome variation based on the relative status of the parties will increase as the quantity of status-relevant information accumulates about the case. Thus his formulation would also predict that mediation would show increased status variation because mediation profoundly expands the quantity of status-relevant information in myriad forms (linguistic style, appearance, content of stories, encouragement of self-disclosure). Second, Black subsumes race and gender differences into other status differences based on their frequent co-occurrence. However, I was concerned that the dimensions of ethnicity and gender, compared to other status dimensions, were likely to have a *stronger* influence in mediation.

Transposed to civil cases and based on the empirically derived outcome ordering described in Chapter Two, the logic goes like this: higher status claims against lower status respondents, the power dependent HILO condition, receive the largest measure of legal support. If higher status claimants plead against higher status respondents, the HIHI insider condition, the bias toward higher status claimant support is still decisive. Thus, higher status claimants are likely to show better court outcomes regardless of respondent. This is indeed the general picture we found in analyses of monetary outcomes in these data; bias in claimant outcomes was visible and statistically significant.

Although higher status respondent outcomes are likely to be sacrificed to claimants if the claimant is higher status, they are likely to be strongly protected if the claiming party is lower status than themselves, i.e., in the LOHI rights-based condition. Similarly, a lower status respondent is better protected against a lower status claim (the LOLO insider condition) than a higher status claim (HILO condition). Thus, because respondent status exerts an influence contingent on claimant status, outcome measures based on respondent status alone are often rendered statistically insignificant.

Analytic Process

Money *is* a zero sum outcome. This is clearly expressed in the monetary outcome ratio (MOR) used in this analysis, which shows the relationship of the initial claims to monetary outcome. Claimant gain was always respondent loss. The analyses in this section are confined to mediated cases reaching strictly monetary agreements and adjudicated cases that received monetary rulings, that is, the monetary outcome samples described in Chapter Four.

Bivariate analyses describe what happened with monetary claims in court rulings and in monetary outcome mediation agreements based on ethnic, gender and structurally-defined status relationships. Multivariate analyses able to control for multiple memberships in all status dimensions clarify the predictable effects of each status position on monetary outcomes in both fora.

RESULTS: BIVARIATE & MULTIVARIATE OUTCOME COMPARISON

Bivariate Analyses of Monetary Outcomes in Adjudication and Mediation[1]

Figure 6.1 graphically displays the mean MORs for the four conditions in the summarized structural (Figure 6.1a), ethnic (Figure 6.1b) and gender (Figure 6.1c) dimensions contrasting resolutions through adjudication and mediation. Two questions were asked in this analysis: First, how consistently did the monetary outcomes in civil cases support the ordering that Black (1989) applied to criminal cases? Second, how did mean outcomes in mediation compare with adjudicated rulings in the four status conditions? Implicitly, the answer to the second question indicates the most probable court outcome for small claims cases and therefore the materially rational alternative to a mediated agreement.

Structural Status

Figure 6.1a shows that adjudicated court outcomes in the summarized structural dimension followed Black's thesis consistently, as reflected in the numbering of the status conditions: 1) Higher status claimants achieved the highest awards in HILO cases with lower status respondents; 2) higher status claimants received the second highest monetary awards in HIHI cases with higher status respondents; 3) lower structural status claimants (individuals, pro se and lower class) achieved the third highest mean amounts in adjudicated LOLO cases with status equals; and 4) lower status claimants in LOHI cases with higher status respondents received the lowest mean outcomes in adjudicated cases. Thus, Black's paradigmatic ordering of criminal outcomes was an accurate outcome ranking of monetary outcomes in adjudicated civil cases based on structurally defined and class status relationships between the parties.

Compared to their probable court alternatives predicted by similar cases in adjudication, two claimant groups and one respondent group

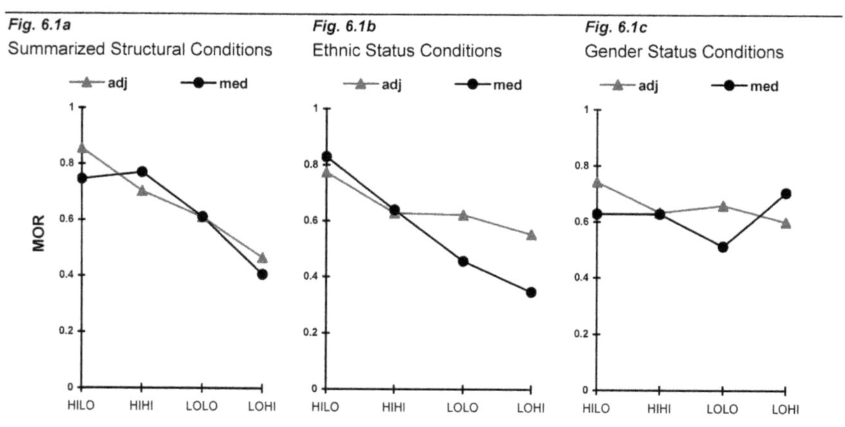

Figure 6.1 Mean Monetary Outcome Ratios in Structural, Ethnic, and Gender Status Conditions

conceded more in mediation. From the claimant perspective, the only statistically significant difference between mediated and adjudicated outcomes was observed among higher status claimants (lawyers, corporations and higher class claimants) who showed evidence of giving more in mediation, specifically in the power dependent condition. At the opposite extreme, lower status claimants appeared to give more to higher status respondents in the rights-based condition. Higher status respondents appeared to give more to status equals than their probable court alternatives.

Ethnic Status

Figure 6.1b shows mean monetary outcomes for cases disaggregated by ethnic status relationships. Outcomes in the ethnic dimension showed a stronger resemblance to Black's thesis in mediation than in adjudication. Compared to court rulings in the ethnic dimension, Anglo claimant outcomes were slightly higher in mediation with Latino respondents. The status effect predicted by Black's ranking for Latino claimants in the LOLO and LOHI conditions was unsupported in the adjudicated cases but was strongly supported in mediation. Latino claimant outcomes were significantly lower in mediation than those for similar dyads in court with Latino respondents and in 11 cases involving Anglo respondents. When combined as Latino claimant cases, the contrast with adjudicated cases was consistently significant (LaFree & Rack 1996; Hermann et al. 1992). On average, Anglo claimants appeared to take more from Latino respondents in the power dependent HILO relationship.

Gender Status

With respect to the gender dimension, adjudicated outcomes offered only partial support for the status effects predicted by Black's ordering (see Figure 6.1c): male claimants appeared to follow predictions, achieving somewhat higher outcomes with female respondents than with men or other adjudicated cases[2].

In mediation, gender status operated dissimilarly from Black's prediction in two ways. First, male claimants settled for similar mean ratios regardless of the gender of the respondent, that is, mean outcomes in the first HILO and second HIHI condition were equal. Second, women settled cases in mediation at lower mean ratios of their claims with female respondents (the third LOLO condition) than they did in cases with male respondents (the fourth LOHI condition). Thus, compared to probable court rulings, both male and female claimants appeared to give more to female respondents. Female claimants appeared to have taken more from male respondents than in similar court cases.

Multivariate Analyses of Monetary Outcomes in Mediation and Adjudication

Ethnicity and gender status was highly correlated with structural status dimensions (see Appendix Table 4.ii; Rack 1997). Specifically, Anglo men were more likely to appear as corporate players, with lawyers, and with higher socioeconomic status than any other of the ethgenders; women, especially Latino women, were likely to be respondents in cases filed by corporate claimants. In mediated compared to adjudicated cases, Latino claimants and respondents were more likely to be lower status, but Anglo female claimants were more likely to be higher status in mediation. Thus, I used multivariate analyses in which all these status differences could be simultaneously controlled to determine the status dimensions in mediation and adjudication that were the primary predictors of the mean outcomes shown above.

Table 6.1 shows the results of 3 linear regression analyses for predicting monetary outcomes in adjudicated and mediated cases. For both fora, the first equation (Eq1) includes only ethnic, gender and class status interactions; the second (Eq2) includes the variables from the first equation plus relational and initial pleading variables (prior relations, claim size, admitted liability, and counterclaims); the final equation (Eq3) includes legal and corporate status interactions in addition to those from the first and second equations. In all equations, cases in the first HILO status condition are the excluded (intercept) categories.

Overall, compared to adjudicated cases, structural variables operated quite differently in mediation. In sharp contrast to adjudication, none of the legal status conditions were distinguished in mediation from the first power dependent condition of legally represented claimants filing against pro se respondents. In fact, cases with pro se claimants are estimated with a positive coefficient compared to legally represented claimants with pro se respondents. Only the disadvantage for an individual filing against a corporation is similar to adjudication. In addition, mediation cases showed a significant disadvantage for individual claimants filing against individuals that was not found in adjudication.

Summary of Mutivariate Outcome Results

These multivariate models clarify the relevant status dimensions in adjudication and mediation. In adjudication, ethnic, gender and class differences can be reconceptualized into pleading differences and structural status relationships, primarily legal representation and an advantage for corporate respondents. In mediation, ethnic status accounted for 20% of the initial variance and the effect of being a Latino claimant was consistently significant even when the influence of pleading and structural status differences was accounted for.

In mediation, pleading differences originating with the respondent (admitted liability and counterclaims) and corporate status explained an additional 32% of variation. These influences explained the bivariate Anglo HIHI insider effects. It should be noted that the reduced outcomes shown in bivariate analyses for the claimants in the HILO power dependent condition in mediation cases, especially lawyers filing against pro se respondents and corporate parties against individuals (see Rack 1997), reduced the intercept in these models. Thus the comparative effects of structural status relationships, with the first condition as the reference group, were less significant in mediation.

Pleading differences were themselves related to both forum and structural status. Admitted liability was more common in mediated cases (see Chapter Four, Appendix Table 4.i, and the initial positions in Figure 1.1). In the full sample, compared to other status conditions in every dimension except gender, first HILO condition respondents admitted greater liability ranging from 18.8% of the claim (admitted by Latino respondents to Anglo claimants in the first ethnic HILO condition) to 24.4% of the claim (admitted by pro se respondents to legally represented claimants). In the corporate dimension, both individual and corporate respondents admitted greater liability to corporate claimants. In mediation cases, because there was no remaining enhanced outcome effect in the third equation, the multivariate model indicated that the higher liability admitted by corporate respondents in the HIHI insider relation was the probable source of the higher outcomes found in this condition in Figure 6.1a. The gender dimension was unique in this regard, with similar rates of admitted liability in all gender status conditions.

Compared to intercept categories in mediation, Latino and individual claimants gave more to respondents in both the LOLO insider dyads and the rights-based LOHI condition. Gender dynamics were difficult to see because the intercept category, theoretically modeled as the HILO male-female power dependent condition, did not show that male claimants achieved higher outcomes with female than male respondents. In fact, when male *respondents* were the comparative group (i.e., the intercept category), we found that Anglo female respondents negotiated significantly lower (i.e., monetarily advantageous) outcomes (LaFree & Rack 1996).

MEDIATOR[3] INFLUENCE ON MONETARY OUTCOMES[4]

Mediator Influence

Mediator influence is exercised primarily through narrative control and influencing disputants' perceptions of their alternatives (Cobb 1994; Garcia 1991; Kaufman & Duncan 1992). Scholars (e.g., Carnevale & Henry 1989;

Table 6.1 Regression Coefficients and Standard Errors for Predictors of Monetary Outcomes in Adjudicated and Mediated Civil Cases: Ascribed, Achieved, and Structural Status Relationships

	Adjudicated Cases						Mediated Cases					
	Eq 1		Eq 2		Eq 3		Eq 1		Eq 2		Eq 3	
Independent Variables	b	SE	b	SE	b	SE	b	SE	b	SE	b	SE
Ascriptive Status												
Anglo-anglo	-.149**	.068	-.112*	.064	-.053	.061	-.186**	.075	-.120*	.062	-.073	.065
Latino-Latino	-.094	.084	-.023	.080	-.011	.075	-.364***	.093	-.283***	.077	-.193**	.082
Latino-anglo	-.193**	.085	-.134*	.080	-.069	.077	-.495***	.129	-.400***	.108	-.322***	.111
Male-male	-.106	.071	-.093	.067	-.054	.065	.076	.090	.085	.074	.115	.076
Female-female	-.059	.096	-.045	.091	-.026	.086	-.080	.104	-.004	.087	-.028	.087
Female-male	-.143*	.083	-.130	.079	-.066	.076	.115	.094	.066	.078	.111	.080
Achieved Status												
Higher class-higher	-.079	.082	-.061	.078	-.030	.074	-.079	.091	.060	.077	.095	.081
Lower-lower	-.229***	.074	-.204***	.071	-.092	.069	-.075	.078	.027	.065	.086	.070
Lower-higher	-.118	.083	-.117	.080	.001	.078	-.090	.096	.040	.081	.123	.089

Relational Variables												
Prior relations			-.075*	.044	-.058	.042			-.054	.042	-.058	.042
Claim size			-.084***	.019	-.090***	.019			-.032*	.019	-.027	.020
Admitted liability			.370***	.122	.249**	.117			.441***	.069	.405***	.071
Counter-claim			-.083***	.029	-.060**	.028			-.058**	.027	-.060**	.027
Structural Status												
Corporate-corporate					-.021	.088					-.053	.085
Individual-individual					-.088	.070					-.173**	.075
Individual-corporate					-.248***	.067					-.216**	.089
Lawyer-lawyer					-.221**	.099					-.007	.139
Pro se-pro se					-.347***	.072					.016	.081
Pro se-lawyer					-.397***	.100					-.068	.101
N	312		312		312		138		138		138	
Y- intercept	.960***	.082	1.105***	.089	1.342***	.096	.837***	.092	.722***	.095	.720***	.110
R^2 / F	.06**	2.3	.18***	5.2	.30***	6.5	.20***	3.7	.48***	9.0	.52***	6.8

* p<.10; ** p<.05; *** p< .01 (two-tailed tests).

Carnevale et al 1989; Wittmer et al. 1991) suggest that intervenor effects may stem from psychological levels (mediators' social biases, professional investment in resolution, differential valuation of the disputant aspiration and their perception of the likelihood of resolution), from factors specific to the situation (e.g., time available and degree of common ground established in the dispute), the status of the intervenors (e.g., disputants' respect for the mediators or lack thereof), and the techniques available and employed (gains and losses that intervenors actually control). Furthermore, disputants socialized in different cultural patterns are likely to hold different values. Thus, in cross-cultural mediation, in the search for integrative agreements, mediators may encourage "trade-offs" across value domains (Bangert & Pirzada 1991) that specifically include exchanges of form for substance (Fisher & Ury 1981).

Mediator-disputant alignment is based on a mediator's similarity/dissimilarity with a disputant in particular social categories. Such alignment is the logical basis for mediator alliance reflected in consistent influence favoring aligned parties. When this alliance results in monetary advantages, it is called bias. However, alignment can be experienced as an alliance when mediators take aligned disputants more seriously and value their arguments, thereby subtly interacting with disputants' sense of psychological safety and wellbeing. This psychological support is likely to impact reported satisfaction without necessarily affecting material outcomes. Chapter Eight discusses indicators of mediator influence on satisfaction and consistent influence on disputants' bargaining motivations.

Lempert & Monsma (1994) argued that the mechanism for constructing biased outcomes in informal, quasi-legal settings is through intervenors' perception of *legitimacy* in contrast to perceived *credibility* in formal legal settings (Conley & O'Barr 1990; O'Barr 1982; Black 1989; Blalock & Wilken 1979). In "cultural discrimination," rather than truth claims, intervenors evaluate the validity of claims and excuses based on the perceived legitimacy of the parties. In mediation even more than adjudication, the argument follows, validity rests on the assumed right of the claimant to restitution and the right of the respondent to withhold, not the technical facts of the case or the structures of law. Bourdieu & Wacquant (1992) argued that the perception of legitimacy granted by others outside of the contest is a source of *symbolic power*. Thus, mediator perception of legitimacy, presumably based on familiarity and shared point of view, gives the aligned disputant additional social power in the dispute.

In sum, whether through differences in mediator tactics that allow imbalanced exchange dynamics to play out, through the search for integrative agreements (leaning on possibly different exchange values), and/or through granting disputants additional symbolic power through legitimating the claims and excuses of specific parties, mediator influence in a dispute could result in biased outcomes.

Ethnic Bias

As early as the first analyses (Hermann et al 1992) we found that Latino and Anglo mediators exerted distinct influences on monetary outcomes in mediation. Further analyses clarified that this influence was actually due to Anglo mediators particularly privileging Anglo claiming, compared to Latinos. Compared to cases mediated by two Latino mediators, Anglo claimants negotiated significantly higher monetary outcomes when one or both of the mediators were Anglo (LaFree & Rack 1996). Put another way, Latino mediators tended to influence monetary outcomes toward greater compromise regardless of claimant's ethnicity, but Anglo mediators consistently influenced only Latino claimants toward compromises of similar magnitude.

Compared to Anglo mediators, Latino mediators influenced outcomes significantly in the direction of protecting lower status respondents with higher status claimants, and supporting the claims of Latino claimants against Latino respondents. Compared to Anglo mediators (one or two) Latino mediator influence in the first HILO condition cases was strongest in the ascriptive dimensions of gender and ethnicity: mean outcomes for male claimants with female respondents and for Anglo claimants with Latino respondents, were lower in cases that had been mediated by two Latino mediators. When the claimant was Latino, Latino mediators significantly supported their claiming against Latino respondents.

The implicit message from Latino mediators was that women and Latino respondents should be protected, and Latino claiming supported. By corollary, Anglo mediators (one or two) significantly supported higher status claiming against lower status respondents, and protected Latino respondents from Latino claiming. In Lempert & Monsma's terms, the implicit message was that Anglo claims were legitimate; Latino claims were not.

Gender Bias

In multivariate models (LaFree & Rack 1996), mediator gender appeared to have particular influence in Latino female claimant cases such that, when two women were mediating, Latino female claimants tended to drop their claims significantly more often. This effect, however, was due to the use of interaction terms without controlling for other status dimensions. Multivariate analyses testing the interaction of two female mediators with cases in the third corporate condition, that is, private cases in which both parties were individuals without structural roles, showed that the diminished outcomes for Latino female claimants were part of a larger phenomenon: two female mediators consistently influenced parties without structural roles toward greater claimant compromise. When this structural condition was controlled, female mediators with Latino female claimants showed no significant ethnic or gender bias (data available from the author).

Overall, female mediators tended to privilege claimants in structural roles, but influenced claimants who were private citizens toward compromise outcomes. Compared to other mediator gender combinations, in Black's (1989) terms, two female mediators less often supported the claiming of lower structural status parties. Female mediators' enhanced ability to bring parties to agreement, particularly Latino claimants, in situations that male mediators more often returned the case to court, exacerbated the impact of this structural bias on Latino claimants. In a gender-by-ethnicity pattern, women mediating influenced Latino claimants, especially women, to settle their disputes, whether by accepting nonmonetary exchanges or by dropping their claims. The result of this pattern was that, out of 10 cases filed by Latinas and mediated by two women, nine were settled but only one of these claimants left mediation with a monetary agreement[5].

Overall, the implicit cultural message in female mediators' bias was an injunction not to claim against equals, and the lower the status of the claimant, the stronger the prohibition.

Mediator gender also exerted a significant effect on cases in the fourth LOHI gender status condition, where women claimed against male respondents. Mixed gender mediator pairs (i.e., a male and female mediator working together) appeared to particularly influence higher outcomes negotiated by Anglo female claimants with male respondents, especially Latinos (LaFree & Rack 1996).

Reception of Mediator Influence

Without controlling for alignments in the overall sample of agreement mediation cases, there were no significant differences in monetary outcome for any mediator combination. However, disputant satisfaction reports give some indication of how mediators were received. Respondents overall reported greater satisfaction with two male mediators, attributable especially to higher status respondents though the preference was a consistent trend across all ethnic and gender status conditions. Respondents reported somewhat less satisfaction with two Anglo mediators compared to two Latino or mixed ethnicity mediator pairs.

I found that Latino claimants and respondents generally reported higher satisfaction with Latino mediators regardless of the ethnicity of the other party (*direct alignment*). Only Latino claimants and respondents appeared to experience a sense of alliance with aligned mediators, and the response was bilateral, that is, both claimants and respondents in ethnic insider cases reported higher satisfaction.

Anglo and female claimants reported higher satisfaction with mediators aligned with the *other* party when the respondent was Latino and male respectively (*oppositional alignment*). In many cases, this satisfaction with opposing alignment was counterintuitive. With more favorable mean MORs, male claimants with female respondents reported below average satisfaction if both mediators were men. Anglo claimant outcomes were somewhat more favorable when both mediators were Anglo, but these claimants reported relative dissatisfaction.

Anglo claimants reported higher satisfaction after cases with Anglo respondents had been mediated by two Anglo mediators, but Anglo claimants also achieved higher monetary outcomes than with Latino mediators, and the Anglo respondents in these cases reported the strongest dissatisfaction with Anglo mediators. Thus, Anglo alignment appeared to be unilateral.

By gender, respondents tended to favor aligned mediators when all participants were male or female, but the claimants in these cases reported relative dissatisfaction. Although not as strongly unilateral/competitive as mediation with all Anglos, male and female aligned mediation sessions appeared somewhat unilateral and competitive—the party with better monetary outcomes reported higher satisfaction and the "loser" reported less satisfaction with mediation.

SUMMARY DISCUSSION OF OUTCOME STRUCTURE

Outcome Structure of MetroCourt Cases

Using the interactive status relationship in the case as the unit of analysis, this chapter compared mediation case outcomes with those that had been adjudicated. The primary goal was to distinguish the status dimensions and conditions in which mediated outcomes were distinct from the logical alternative, that is, similar case outcomes in adjudication. Secondarily, this analysis applied empirical tests to meta-theoretical questions about the relative importance of culture, structure and choice to the determination of conflict outcomes.

Mean monetary outcomes were significantly different between the two fora in two conditions, and were marginally significant in two others.

Latino claimants with Latino respondents in the LOLO ethnic condition, and structurally advantaged claimants (especially legally represented and corporate claimants) in cases with structurally disadvantaged respondents in the HILO structural condition (especially pro se and individual respondents), settled for significantly reduced outcomes in mediation compared to the adjudication alternative. Latino claimants with Anglo respondents, and female claimants with female respondents, settled for somewhat lower outcomes in mediation than court awards.

By mean outcome pattern, gender status relationships were reversed in the two fora. In adjudication, male claimants with female respondents were significantly advantaged over the opposite condition (i.e., female claimants with male respondents). In mediation, female claimants with male respondents settled at higher ratios of their claims than any other dyads.

Distinctly different monetary outcome patterns for the two fora were apparent in multivariate analyses. The reference (intercept) HILO cases settled for less in mediation compared to adjudication. Legal status relationships predicted adjudicated but not mediated outcomes. In contrast, ethnic status relationships effectively predicted mediated outcomes. In adjudication, ethnic status effects were better explained by structural status (legal and corporate). Although individual claimants were likely to conclude cases against corporate respondents with diminished outcomes in both fora, individual claimants with individual respondents in mediation were also significantly distinguished from the reference HILO category (corporate claimants with individual respondents). Class status showed consistent and significant effects in adjudication that were subsumed into legal and corporate status, but class status differences never consistently predicted mediated outcomes.

Structural status, especially legal representation, was the key determinant in adjudicated cases, subsuming all class, gender and ethnic effects. The apparent protective bias toward male respondents in adjudication can be "explained" by these structural effects. In fact, corporate respondents in adjudication, primarily Anglo men, were noteworthy for the number of claims against them that were dismissed (23%).

Ethnic and corporate status were most determinant of mediated outcomes and gender showed reversed patterns; Latino and individual claimants were clearly distinguished from Anglo and corporate claimants in the HILO condition, and women often fared better than men. Without apparent structural explanation, the mediation forum showed a protective bias toward Anglo female respondents; claims were dropped against Anglo female respondents in mediation as frequently as claims were dismissed against Anglo men in adjudication.

Mediator Bias

Mediator ethnicity was a significant factor in the reduced outcomes for Latino claimants: Anglo mediators were generally biased in favor of Anglo claimants. Mediator gender was also a significant factor in the reduced outcome for Latino claimants, especially with Anglo respondents. The mathematical effect was created by female mediators' bias in favor of claimants in higher structural roles, and their ability to influence Latino claimants, especially women, to compromise their monetary claims. Mediator gender was also a significant factor in female-male disputes: mixed gender mediators biased outcomes in favor Anglo female claimants over Latino male respondents. Compared to Anglo mediators, Latino mediators exerted a significantly protective influence in favor of lower status respondents with higher status claimants in the HILO condition at the intercept, especially Latino and female respondents with Anglo and male claimants, and supported Latino claimants in cases with Latino respondents

Overall, group alignment in ethnic dimensions tended to support claimants: for Latino disputants, mediator alignment was associated with bilateral satisfaction; for Anglo groups, mediator alignment appeared to be unilateral and operate as a win-lose dynamic. In gender dimensions, group alignments tended to favor respondents: claimants in same-sex dyads seemed to feel greater alliance from mediators of the opposite gender. Satisfaction reports by claimants and respondents suggested win-lose dynamics in gender-aligned mediation sessions.

Oppositional alignment might be preferable because it legitimates the process and outcome to the other party. This could have significant material benefit for parties concerned with compliance. It is also likely that oppositional alignment served to encourage concessions from the other party during the bargaining process itself. Apparently because oppositional alignment was preferable to Anglos with Latino respondents, Latino mediators were able to create mean outcomes appearing as win-win in any dispute involving Latino respondents.

All Latino and female claimants and respondents except female respondents with female claimants, tended to report higher satisfaction after mediation with Latino mediators. Higher status claimants only reported higher satisfaction after mediation with Latino mediators if the respondents were lower status.

Giving, Taking, and Being Taken in Mediated Cases

If court outcomes are taken as the logical BATNA, then outcomes in mediated cases that were divergent from adjudication are indicative of giving, whether willing or unwilling. Two of the instances of giving, cases involving

Latino and individual claimants, were apparently due to claimant differences because Latino and individual claimants, and most Latino claimants *were* individuals as opposed to corporate parties, conceded larger portions of their claims than reference claimants to *all* respondents. Anglo and female mediator influence apparently played a role in these concessions. In the case of Latino claimants, this pattern in mediation was significantly different from court outcomes. For individual claimants, there was no statistical evidence that their concessions represented a loss in comparison to their BATNAs.

Two other noticeable instances of claimant giving followed specific respondents: both male and female claimants gave more to female than to male respondents; and higher structural status (corporate and legally represented) claimants in the HILO power dependent condition gave more to individual and pro se respondents than comparable court awards. Although Latino mediators appeared to influence male and Anglo claimants into greater compromise with female and Latino respondents in the gender and ethnic HILO conditions, there was no evidence of a consistent mediator influence in the HILO mediated cases in structural dimensions.

In discussions of giving, it is useful to also be clear about taking. On average, female claimants took more from male than female respondents, and Anglo claimants took more from Latino than Anglo respondents. Both of these instances showed greater taking, on average, than what might be expected from comparison to court awards. I will show later in this work that these trends came together in cases where Anglo female claimants achieved remarkably high settlement outcomes in mediated cases with Latino male respondents. Although based on a small number of cases, mixed gender mediator pairs appeared to influence these outcomes in favor of Anglo women.

Conclusions

In adjudicated cases, interactive analysis strongly supported the civil application of status bias effects found in criminal justice systems. Specifically, corporate and legal status relationships in civil court received judicial rulings that were precisely ordered according to predictions based on the social structure of the case. Black argued that corporate status was the most critical status dimension but small claims cases, where *pro se* status was possible, showed that the bias in favor of lawyers over unrepresented parties was an even stronger predictor of advantage than corporate identity. In adjudication, legal representation and corporate status accounted for absolute outcome variation that disadvantaged lower class, Latino, and female parties.

Black predicted that evidence of bias would increase as more status relevant information was accumulated about the parties. However, although this kind of information was strongly increased in mediation, outcomes reflected different bias patterns. Compared to court outcomes, ethnic bias was more apparent, legal representation had no impact, and women were better supported and protected.

Black also suggested that perhaps less formal procedures would reduce bias in justice systems. These outcomes, constructed in a consensual and voluntary negotiation process, suggest that such solutions might simply replace decision-maker and structural bias with an ascriptive and/or procedural one.

Overall, only Latino claimants in the LOLO insider condition with Latino respondents presented consistent evidence that the mediation process itself may have stimulated an other than monetary or material focus in their disputes. All other conditions marked by diminished monetary outcomes were accompanied by little evidence of an alternative goal structure in the dispute. Gifting by higher status claimants in the HILO power dependent condition with lower status respondents, and Latino claimants with Anglo respondents, was accompanied by high frequencies of reported cash and material goals. Similarly, apparent concessions by male and female claimants to female respondents, and by individual claimants to individual and corporate respondents, were not accompanied by a diminished material focus.

Women, especially Anglo women, presented a reversal of the findings theorized to result from a more relational psychology; women reported cash and material goals more often after mediation than adjudication, and their mediated outcomes in comparison to men's were somewhat better than those achieved in adjudication.

Chapter Seven
Status Patterns in Bargaining

NEGOTIATION & CULTURE

Negotiations in general, and mediated negotiations in particular, take place in settings that evoke both competitive and cooperative motives in disputants. Although negotiation analyses traditionally assume negotiators maximize their own outcomes, culture and gender theories specifically suggest that Latinos and women might have more cooperative motivations. This section discusses recent developments in negotiation theory and application to ethnic and gender relations at greater length. The results section clarifies the role of the mediation forum by limiting statistical analyses to ethgender patterns *during* the mediation session (see the monetary outcome sample described in Appendix Table 4.i). The chapter concludes with a closer examination of divergent bargaining trajectories based on the ethgender of the *other* party that appeared to be empowered by the mediation situation.

Negotiation Theory

Most of what we know, or think we know, about negotiation was developed and tested in western, individualistic societies (Pruitt & Carnevale 1993). Recent experimental work in cross-cultural psychology, communications, and conflict resolution attest to the fact that "although there may be universal dimensions of conflict construals, disputants' cognitive representations are influenced by the conception of the self that is dominant in the surrounding culture (individualistic vs. collectivistic), and thus, cognitive representations of conflict vary across cultures" (Gelfand et al 2001:1059).

For example, the tendency to attribute observed behavior to internal personality characteristics rather than external situational constraints (attribution error) is a well documented judgment bias in social psychology. However, East Asian negotiators were more likely to contextualize their opponent—give the benefit of the doubt and recognize that an opponent's low offer could be due to the amount available for division (Valenzuela, Srivastava & Lee 2005). U.S. negotiators are more likely to perceive through a "win-lose" frame which means that U.S. negotiators more often compete and look to blame specific others. Gelfand at al (2001) interpreted Japanese motivation for perceiving through a "compromise" frame (seeing both parties as blameworthy and the need for both parties to compromise or find a mutually acceptable agreement) as the cognitive consequence of an interdependent sense of self whose social unit would be threatened by competition. This differential blaming tendency is apparent in other cultural indicators: content analysis of newspaper accounts of conflict indicated that Japanese newspapers more frequently made reference to mutual blame (compromise) than did U.S. newspapers (Gelfand et al 2001); Gelfand et al (2002) cite research showing that Japanese parents were more likely to focus on ways that children can improve themselves through effort (an internal attribution), whereas American parents were more likely to place blame on problematic schools and teachers (an external attribution), older Japanese professionals and Japanese students had lower self-serving tendencies, and attributions for events in Chinese newspaper articles were less self-serving compared to the United States.

Similarly, twenty years of western research have demonstrated that negotiators become more competitive when he/she represents and is accountable to others (e.g., a company agent or politician). However, Gelfand & Realo (1999) showed that this tendency changes with negotiators from collectivist cultures who are more likely to compromise when they expect to be evaluated. Wagner (1995:167) found that social psychological models of group behavior and cooperation based on free rider or social loafing constructs are limited in their applicability to collectivists, advocating "a more balanced stream of research on cooperation, perhaps one growing out of the realization that free riding and social loafing in the purest form represent individualism pursued to an extreme."

Another well-documented judgment bias in negotiation is a self-serving bias of fairness—negotiators consistently view their own behaviors as more fair than those of their counterparts. However, Gelfand et al (2002) found that Japanese negotiators were significantly less likely in the same situations to inflate their personal contribution/ performance and to discount critical appraisal. Gelfand et al (2002:833, 840) consider the implications:

> One view of judgment biases—a view which is often espoused in the literature—is that they are reflective of cognitive shortcuts that all humans use to manage information-processing demands to cope with their overtaxed cognitive systems. Viewed within this perspective, judgment biases should be universal. . . . [But] judgment biases in negotiation may be reflections of different cultural imperatives that negotiators have internalized as part of their self systems. . . . we argue more generally that much of the research on judgment biases is based primarily on an independent view of the self, and as a result, the science of negotiation does not reflect the full range of human variation. For example, our results suggest that judgment biases such as reactive devaluation, escalation of commitment, or ignoring the cognitions of others . . . should be reevaluated in light of a cultural perspective, as they may be largely applicable in cultures that cultivate independent self-construals, wherein self-enhancement is natural and expected.

Cultural Differences and Styles

As previously discussed, in comparison to U.S. culture, Latin American cultural norms are theoretically oriented toward shared benefit outcomes and a greater concern for the other party when he or she is an ingroup member. Rinderle (2003) describes how Latino-Anglo conflict can arise from differing levels of commitment to harmony due to different face-needs: Anglos tend to focus on personal concerns, or "self face," while Mexicans emphasize on the other person, or "other face," the maintenance of group harmony, and relational solidarity across levels of hierarchy. "Demonstrating *respeto*—respect of another's dignity—to all, and expressing appropriate deference or asserting appropriate superordination within the hierarchy through indirect language use that is commonly understood, is another way of maintaining harmony without being overt." (Garcia cf Ringerle 2003). The collectivist concern with saving self and other face, suggests a different motivation for conflict avoidance as well[1].

In addition, Latin American cultures are theoretically (and empirically in New Mexico, see Boyle & Coughlin 1994; Fisher, Boyle & Dresser 1995) more willing to legitimate unequal power relations. U.S. acculturation evaluated on the same scales encourages high self-concern, a willingness to challenge superiors, and a lack of ingroup preference. Indeed, cross national studies using scenario techniques have consistently found that people from collectivist cultures are more apt than those from individualistic cultures to report themselves as conciliatory, compromising, or integrating in conflict situations, if they didn't avoid the conflict altogether (e.g., Chiu

& Kosinski 1994; Donahue & Mary 1994; Gire & Carment 1993; Leung 1988; Ohbachi & Takahashi 1994; Oetzel 1998).

Rinderle (2003) summarized research showing that southwestern Latinos are fairly consistent in their values and expectations across age, gender and status. Unlike other ethnic groups, Mexican Americans do not adjust communication "rules" to fit a partner's ethnicity. They are interdependent with each other, differentiate between their inner circle of intimates and people outside that circle, and give preference to others in the circle. More than U.S. Anglos, Mexican Americans may put others' needs and dignity before their own, and a relationship before other goals or ideas. Mexican Americans appreciate individuals who are aware of and practice nuances of *respeto*. Research varies with respect to the influence of power distance on Mexican American interpersonal communication or conflict with Anglos: "[W]hile Hispanics might perceive non-Hispanics as less *simpáticos/as* for criticizing or competing too much, and therefore reject them, this perception may be moderated by power distance; superordinate behavior may be acceptable in high status persons and not necessarily lead to rejection." (Rinderle 2003:4)

Rinderle (2003: 5) summarized the somewhat complex data on ethnic vs. U.S. cultural identity and conflict styles:

> In research that examined the influence of ethnic identity on conflict style, Ting-Toomey et al. (2000) compared the effect of "ethnic identity salience," or the importance that an individual gives his or her ethnicity, and "cultural identity salience," or the importance that an individual gives his or her larger (U.S.) culture, on the conflict style of 662 respondents from four U.S. ethnic groups. Seven styles were examined: integrating, compromising, dominating, avoiding, neglecting, emotional expression and third-party intervention. . . . Those with strong U.S. cultural identity use integrating, compromising and emotionally expressive styles more and neglecting styles less than those with weak cultural identity. Those with a strong ethnic identity use integrating more, and neglecting and third party less than those with weak ethnic identity. One might expect that Mexican Americans overall showed strong ethnic identity and weak cultural identity, varying perhaps according to acculturation level. However, in the study Latinos identified with *both* groups and Anglos with only larger U.S. culture, which corroborates other research on identity (Alba, 1990; Waters, 1990). Anglos also showed weaker ethnic identity than other groups. Latinos with weak cultural identity used neglect more than other ethnic groups regardless of the other groups' cultural identity, perhaps due to the

> Latino value of *respeto* and wanting to maintain respect, dignity and positive "face" in social situations (Ting-Toomey et al., 2000) by not confronting the other party. . . . Ethnic *identity,* therefore, may impact an individual's conflict style as much as his or her actual ethnicity. (emphasis in original)

Oetzel (1998) also suggests that New Mexico Latinos' more integrative approach to conflict may be related to the fact that many US Latinos are actually bi-cultural or "bi-construal." This is an important point affecting Latino mediators as well (see Chapter Eight and Twelve).

Virtually all studies show significant gender effects, with women reporting they are more likely to conciliate than men (e.g., Hinshaw & Forbes 1993; Gire & Carment 1993; Leung & Bond 1990). Research demonstrates that men more often report dominating styles (Ting-Toomey, Oetzel & Yee-jung 2001) and women are more likely to work cooperatively (Eagly & Johnson 1990). In survey and scenario research, within the United States and cross-nationally, women self-report a greater likelihood and/or preference for using collaborative strategies in conflict situations (see Gire & Carment for review 1993). Yet, contrary to theoretical suppositions that women might take a more indirect route in conflict resolution, Ting-Toomey (1986) found that women were more likely than men to report they would directly engage their conflict partners.

As Kolb (1994) asked, are the assumptions about women's cooperation true, based on status deficiency, or valorized? As Gilligan herself and others (e.g., Larrabee 1993; Cortese 1990) have pointed out, she never argued that an ethic of care grew from biological femininity. Rather she observed that Kohlberg based his proposed stages of moral reasoning on male subjects from upper middle class environments. From studies of young, Anglo, educated women Gilligan alternatively proposed that their moral decisions ran aground on an almost paralyzing ambivalence between two assumptions: "good" means to sacrifice self for others or "good" means self-concern (see also Flax 1993).

The logical consequences of theoretical constructions of women as more relational, particularistic and giving are in question. Research has found complications in outcomes, process, and perceptual distortions. Reduced outcomes for women as a result of a preference for cooperative behavior are not well established. In divorce mediation, outcomes for women are not clearly worse than in adjudication (Pearson & Theonnes 1984, 1989). Early game research suggested that women were less likely than men to take a "tough" stance in negotiations (Bartos 1970) and more readily responded to cooperative cues (Tedeschi 1970), but exchange theory and negotiation researchers report that gender (confined to college or law students) showed no main effect on negotiation decisions. Women were as likely to "win" as men (e.g., Molm 1991). These studies as well as others (e.g., Gilligan 1982; Taylor & Miller 1994; Gaines et al 1997; Gelfand et al 2002) noted but did not answer the implicit questions about the effects of ethnicity or social status on women's self interest.

As discussed earlier, scholars debate the behavioral consequences of apparently socialized influences like gender and ethnicity compared to social structural role. In a meta-analysis of gender in leadership roles, organizational researchers Eagly & Johnson (1990) found a complex interaction between stereotypical female and organizational behavior. Women more often *self-reported* stereotypical styles such as interpersonal rather than task orientation, but the only stereotypical female pattern that Eagly & Johnson found to hold true with professional women in organizations (rather than students) was a more democratic, as opposed to autocratic, leadership style.

Where studies explicitly examined status effects on women's conflict behavior they found an interesting pattern of differences by social status. For example, Chusmir & Mills (1989) found that women abandoned less competitive conflict styles in their professional lives when they had achieved higher management positions. Similarly, women's reported higher ethical standards erode over time in professional roles (Franke et al 1997). Social psychologists (Dividio, Ellyson, Keating, Heltman & Brown 1988; Kimble & Musgrove 1988) found that *professional* women were more likely to establish visual dominance than men; O'Barr (1982) found that the powerless speech style previously attributed to women was more a matter of social class; and Bennett (1988) found that cooperative strategies were correlated with stronger power motives in women[2].

Women perceive themselves and are perceived by others as more giving than they behave. Women self-report a greater tendency for altruism (Batson 1991) but experimental research indicated that the self report measure elicited a self image, not a higher behavioral probability than men. Disputants in experimental settings judged female intervenor behavior through a stereotypical lens, rating their interventions as less controlling than male intervenors, despite independent observer ratings to the contrary (Burrell, Donohue & Allen 1988). Women are perceived as more helpful than they actually are (Beutel & Marini 1995).

Reported Positions as Indicators

Bargaining processes show how outcomes were decided within the range of possible resolution points. Pruitt & Carnevale (1993) described the theory and research showing that negotiated outcomes fall within limitations set by two motivational drives: the highest outcome in light of alternatives and the lowest outcome possible before the negotiator feels like a "sucker." For example, a respondent might be willing to pay up to $3,000 to a claimant and the claimant might be willing to accept as little as $1,500 before feeling like a sucker. Between $1,500 and $3,000 lies a range of possible resolution points in which, from a self-interested perspective, the highest ($3,000) is "best" for the claimant and the lowest ($1,500) is "best" for the respondent. Negotiating behavior, conceptualized on a continuum from *firmer to softer* depending on the negotiators' willingness to concede during negotiations, theoretically determines the balance. In the example, a softer claimant might accept an outcome near the "sucker" limit of $1,500 which would give the respondent a more optimal outcome. Conversely, a firmer claimant might negotiate an outcome nearer to the respondent's limit of $3,000.

Pruitt & Carnevale's *dual concern model* of negotiations (discussed more thoroughly in Chapter One) specifies differences in negotiation strategies as a function of the relative weights of concern for one's own outcomes vs. concern for the other party's outcomes, shortened here to "self-concern" and "other-concern." Their model as an interpretive device for examining the bargaining patterns in small claims mediation because negotiation strategies and patterns are clearly linked to self or other concern. In the problem-solving, win-win, shared-benefit ideal, where both negotiators hold an equal balance of effective self and other concern, the outcome in the above example would be $2,250.

General Framework

There are several important specifications in this analysis:

> First, reciprocal concession-making, exchanging concessions with the other party, is the essential ingredient in problem-solving negotiation processes (Pruitt & Carnevale 1993) in zero-sum bargaining, i.e., one based on a strictly monetary dispute. This means that the degree of concession *matching* is the critical behavioral dimension and the strategy involves manipulating the bargaining distance.
>
> Second, bargainers often match frequency without matching magnitude. Typically, more powerful negotiators undermatch the concessions made by weaker parties. This means that parties with good adjudication alternatives, who are thus considered to be less dependent on an agreement with the other party, may undermatch based on rationally self-interested negotiation alternatives.

> Third, early to midstage concession-making suggests a more voluntary or willing stance but later stage concessions suggest a "modified" self-interest (Pruitt & Carnevale 1993) that was elicited or leveraged by the other party's bargaining resistance.
>
> Fourth, end stage concessions, including modified self-interested concessions in point #3, are particularly decisive because these bargaining concessions make the difference in whether the session will end with an agreement or go on to court (in which case they are not examined here). This is true especially if the other party is resistant or tough, Thus, these concessions indicate an investment in reaching agreement itself. Interest in agreement, like resistant bargaining, might be rationally self-interested depending on the likely alternatives.

Overall, the group level bargaining patterns provide windows into the construction of monetary outcomes, an assessment of the party's response to the mixed-motive, facilitated negotiation process, and suggest motivational interpretations relevant to culture and gender theories. However, because alternative explanations for motivations cannot be ruled out, the next chapter pursues additional analyses of motivational indicators.

RESULTS OF BARGAINING ANALYSES

This chapter examines the way that unequal monetary outcomes, demonstrated in the last chapter, were constructed in the negotiation process. The way that the negotiation processes begun *before* mediation might change once *in* the mediation session provides insight into the effects of the mediation forum on negotiators. Shifts based on the ethnic and gender status of the other party clarify the salience of ethnic and gender boundaries. The results begin with bargaining patterns in the summarized structural, ethnic and gender status dimensions with brief descriptions of the relevant data available in Rack (1997), followed by an analysis of the divergent bargaining patterns based on the ethnicity or gender of the other party as they were reported by ethnic and gender groups.

Bargaining Sequences by Status Dimensions

The graphs (a, b, and c) that make up Figure 7.1 show the bargaining process in monetary outcome mediation cases. The graphs specify the bargaining process for dyads categorized by the summarized structural (combining legal, corporate, and measured class status), ethnic, and gender dimensions. Each set of graphs shows the bargaining process separately for higher and lower status claimants differentiated by the status of the respondent. All dollar amounts were converted to reflect a ratio of the claim in the same way that MOR was calculated (by dividing the amount by the total recorded claim), and can be accurately translated as a percentage of the initial claim.

Summarized Structural Dimension

Figure 7.1a summarizes the consistent features found for bargaining dynamics in corporate, legal and class bargaining patterns. These claimants had socially defined roles, with legal power behind their positions and, as demonstrated in Chapter Six, positive court alternatives or BATNAs. The prototype case would be a case filed brought by a business or bank with a professional collector or lawyer representing the company. Generally, they conceded little during mediation. Admitted liability was high at the outset because the respondent's obligation was often formal and legal liability was usually clear. Higher structural status claimants reported early concessions in the mediation session that changed little in the later phases. The mediation sessions were shorter than average in duration.

The additional claimed amount in the second, pre-mediation position reported during the interview represents the court costs, legal fees and interest that higher structural parties often expected to receive in addition to the dollar amount of the claim. As discussed in the last chapter and Chapter Four, these additional monies were routinely awarded to lawyers

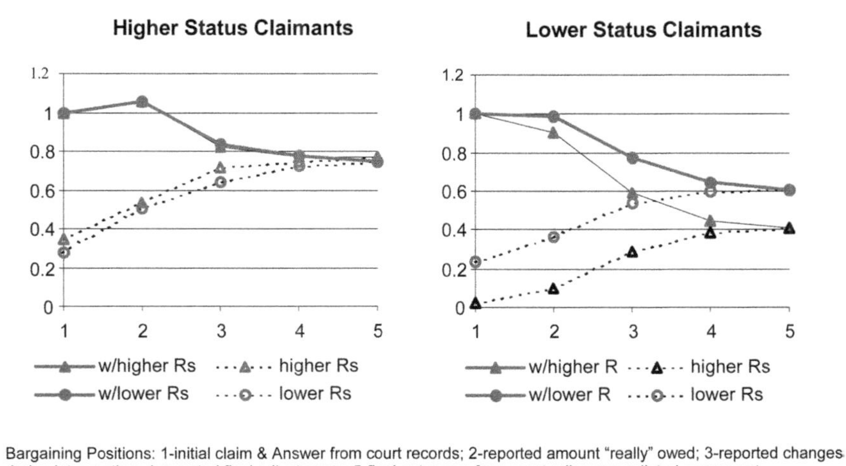

Figure 7.1a Bargaining by Summarized Structural Status: Higher and Lower Status Claimants in Horizontal or Vertical Dyads

and corporations in adjudication. Demanded at the outset of mediation, the extra costs represented a high initial demand and often became the most obvious concession during mediation.

Respondent bargaining in Figure 7.1a is somewhat misleading because it implies that all higher status respondents admitted more of the debt than lower status respondents at the outset. In fact, *legally* represented and higher *class* respondents (often the same people) actually admitted less of the debt to higher status claimants but *corporate* respondents admitted more liability at the outset to *corporate* claimants.

The pattern for lower structural status claimants shows that with higher status respondents, lower status claimants reported early concessions prior to mediation, then reported they continued to concede in early and later phases of the bargaining process. Apparently for the sake of an agreement, lower status claimants made large, late stage concessions with both respondent groups. In the final agreement, lower status claimants had conceded, on average, approximately 60% of their claim to higher status respondents, but only 40% to lower status respondents. Note that this gap in final outcomes is essentially the same magnitude as the initial gap in recorded liability admitted by the two groups of respondents to lower status claims.

For their part, higher status respondents admitted almost nothing to lower status claimants, and conceded slowly thereafter. Higher status respondents in the LOHI rights-based condition were tough bargainers. Consistent with negotiation research and theory predicting that tough bargainers would extend the negotiation session (see Pruitt & Carnevale 1993), lower status claimants with higher status respondents spent significantly longer time periods in mediation[3].

Ethnic Status Dimension

Bargaining in the ethnic status dimension shows an extreme example of patterns characteristic of power dynamics in negotiations generally. Compared to bargaining with other Anglos, Anglo claimants reported larger initial demands when the respondent was Latino. Compared to Anglo respondents, Latino respondents admitted higher liability at the outset, but reported pre-mediation concessions (position two) were similar. The gap widens during the mediation session (positions three and four), with Latino respondents conceding proportionally more than Anglo respondents to Anglo claimants.

Latino claimants conceded similar ratios of the claim in the early phases of mediation with both Anglo and Latino respondents. But Anglo respondents undermatched these concessions more during the mediation

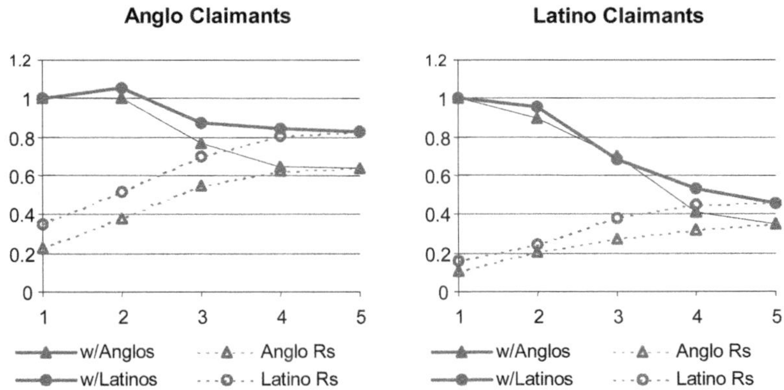

Bargaining Positions: 1 initial claim and admitted liability from court record; 2 reported amounts "really" owed; 3 reported changes during intervention; 4 reported final adjustments; 5 final outcomes taken from court rulings and mediated agreements

Figure 7.1b Bargaining by Ethnic Status: Anglo and Latino Claimants in Insider vs. Outsider Dyads

session. Apparently for the sake of agreement, Latino claimants made large concessions with Anglo respondents in the later phases of the bargaining.

Appendix Table 4.ii showed that ethnicity was strongly correlated with the other status dimensions (except gender); Latino parties were often lower status in other dimensions and Anglos were often higher. From reported pre-mediation amounts of claim and liability to the final agreements, Anglo claimants conceded less with Latino respondents and Anglo respondents conceded less liability to Latino claimants. Anglo claimants with Latino respondents spent the shortest average time in mediation (58 minutes). In contrast, Latino-Latino disputes averaged the longest mediation sessions (94 minutes).

Gender Status Dimension

Gender effects are nearly opposite of theoretical constructions in which women might be expected to be soft negotiators. Men admitted greater liability than women to female claimants making fateful early concessions, and ending with agreements paying higher ratios of the claimed amount. Female claimants reduced the amount of their claim in mediation sessions significantly more for female respondents than any other gender combination of disputants. Female respondents reported substantial upward shifts in the *premeditation* phase with female claimants but made little movement within the mediation sessions. Thus, on average, female respondents conceded more during mediation to meet men's claims than women's.

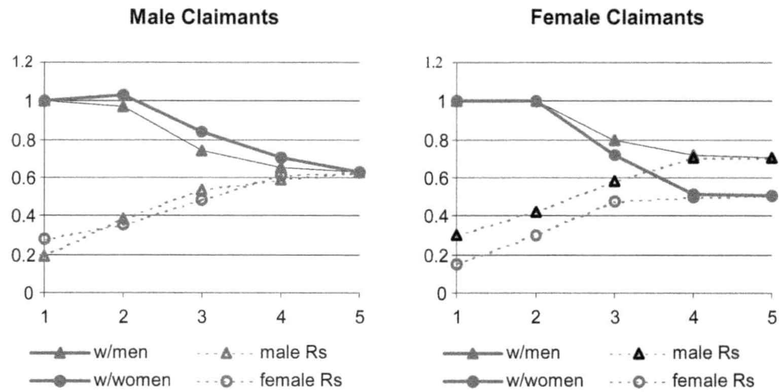

Bargaining Positions: 1 initial claim and admitted liability from court record; 2 reported amounts "really" owed; 3 reported changes during intervention; 4 reported final adjustments; 5 final outcomes taken from court rulings and mediated agreements

Figure 7.1c Bargaining by Gender Status Male and Female Claimants with Male and Female Respondents

Interestingly, women with male respondents averaged less time in mediation compared to other gender conditions (69 minutes) and male claimants with female respondents averaged the longest period in negotiations (91 minutes).

Interpreting Bargaining as Dual Concerns

Structural Status: Tacit Bargaining and Normative Power

Structural status appeared to demonstrate tacit bargaining in ways consistent with negotiation theory. Higher status claimants were firm bargainers; they entered mediation with high initial demands, resisted early concessions made by respondents in their formal answers, and undermatched concessions during mediation. Respondents appeared to believe that a negotiated settlement was better than their court alternative, continuing to concede in steady steps, overmatching claimant concessions. Typical of bargainers who share an understanding of the probable outcome, with little resistance, mediation sessions were short and settlement outcomes averaged about 80% of the claimed amount.

Lower status claimants were more firm with lower status respondents than with higher status respondents. Lower status claimants in the LOLO condition ignored early concessions but reported steady and roughly equal matching during mediation. With higher status respondents, by contrast, lower status claimants were relatively soft bargainers. Lower status claimants tracked the little initial liability admitted by higher status respondents with diminished initial positions. In the mid phases, however, lower status claimants overmatched concessions and, in the final phases, tended to mismatch in order to fill the gap. On their side, higher status respondents were firm, admitting little at the outset and resisting reciprocal concession-making. Mediation sessions took considerably longer with these higher status respondents, as negotiation theory would predict with tough bargainers. Settlement outcomes with lower status respondents averaged 60% of the claimed amount; settlements with higher status respondents averaged 40% of the claimed amount.

Thus, despite apparent differences in the negotiation process, settlement outcomes diverged by exactly the same 20% as the initial positions. Negotiating dyads disaggregated by structural status relationships showed patterns consistent with power differences described in the negotiation literature. Both graphs showed the normative tracking phenomenon by which differences in initial positions, with small differences in higher status claimant bargaining, largely determined the final outcomes.

Ethnic Status: Soft Bargaining

Anglo claimants showed patterns consistent with higher self-concerned claimants when the respondent was Latino. Anglos undermatched concessions and reporting little end stage movement. Latino respondents appeared soft with Anglo claimants; they reported high initial liability in the record and interview, and overmatched in brief mediation sessions to meet Anglo claims. In contrast, Anglo respondents with Anglo claimants were more firm: they reported lower initial concessions and a diminished rate of concession-making during mediation and at the end.

Latino claimants appeared to face tough bargainers with both Latino and Anglo respondents. The respondents recorded and reported little initial liability and consistently undermatched claimant concessions. Latino claimants appeared as soft bargainers: they reported diminished initial positions, consistently overmatched respondent concessions, and reported large end stage concessions, especially with Anglo respondents. Based on the written agreements, Latino claimants conceded even greater than the amounts acknowledged in the interview. The discrepancy between the reported final outcome and the written agreement is consistent with the idea of a negotiator making agreements outside of his/her limits; that is, Latino claimants appeared to have felt like chumps.

Gender Status: Resistance

Male claimant patterns were similar to those of higher structural status claimants except that they reported larger end stage concessions. Although they reportedly entered mediation with high initial demands, they made large midphase concessions, especially with other men. In the final phases, mean positional changes showed that men somewhat overmatched respondent concessions. Male and female respondents reported similar mean bargaining positions throughout the session and final outcomes were equal for male claimants with male and female respondents. Male claimant patterns were consistent with the idea that they were initially more open to problem-solving with male than female respondents, but modified their bargaining in later phases to meet female respondent resistance.

Male claimants, a category including Anglo and Latino men, showed indications of rather steady reciprocity that was perhaps more willing with male respondents. Because many male-male cases were also HIHI insider cases (see Appendix Table 4.ii), this pattern may reflect the tacit bargaining noted for the HIHI summarized structural condition. However, the mean duration of male-male mediation sessions was not particularly short, a characteristic of tacit bargaining. Thus it seems likely that male claimants, on average, conceded more voluntarily to male than female respondents, but modified their self-interest in response to female respondents.

Women as claimants showed mixed patterns. With male respondents, their bargaining was similar to that of higher status claimants, but with female respondents the pattern is more similar to that of lower status claimants. With male respondents, female claimants reported, on average, one major adjustment to their claims with little end stage concession-making. With female respondents, however, the claimants made greater mid and end stage concessions, indicating a modified self concern evoked by respondent resistance. Female respondents showed bargaining patterns associated with tough negotiators. In particular, they reported virtually no end stage concessions for the sake of agreement. Overall, female claimant cases were outstanding for the degree to which the final positions reported by the parties accurately reflected their final written agreements.

Exploitation: Who Started It?

Banton (1983) argued that group-level competition is the legacy and cause of ethnic stratification. He argues that ethnic stratification patterns would be eliminated by *individual* level competition but instead, *group*-level competition maintains the patterns. Keefe & Padilla (1987), in studying the network patterns of Latino and Anglo residents in four California communities showed *Anglo* social networks tended to be exclusive, not those of Latinos. They made the same suggestion as Banton: if Anglos did not maintain the boundary of exclusion, segregated sociation would probably break down. Keefe & Padilla noted that the experience of exclusion and discrimination was the largest indicator in their data of strong ethnic loyalty, a point made in more macro terms by Banton as well. Thus, both concur, historically excluded groups are likely to build ethnic identity barriers in response to dominant group exclusion.

Different patterns based on the visible social categories of ethnicity or gender suggest whether bargainers acted differently with insiders vs. outsiders[4].

Claimants

Table 7.1a and b shows tests of the positional change during the mediation session indicating which parties shifted pattern depending on the ethnicity or gender of the other party. The calculations are the reported positional change from the second, pre-mediation position to the final outcome recorded in the written agreement to determine the proportion of the claimed amount that was negotiated during the mediation. The tables show the significant differences by ethnicity or gender of the other party.

Table 7.1a shows that Latino claimants conceded larger ratios of their claims during mediation than Anglo claimants but there were not significant differences in the ratio conceded based on whether the respondent was Latino or Anglo, male or female. That is, Latino claimants appeared to concede equally large ratios regardless of the ethnicity or gender of the respondent. Anglo claimants did not appear to significantly differentiate their concession making based on the ethnicity of the respondent.

However, Anglo claimants, who conceded less overall, made significantly larger concession for female, compared to male, respondents. By gender, female claimants tended to concede significantly more of the claim for female compared to male respondents. Thus, overall, respondent gender was the significant differentiating factor in claimant concession-making; Anglo and female claimants showed preferential willingness to reduce their claims when the respondent was a woman.

Note that the bargaining process by which higher *outcomes* for Anglo claimants were achieved with Latino compared to Anglo respondents *without* affecting initial bargaining distances is due to the upward adjustment in Anglo claimants' reported pre-mediation position with Latino respondents. This tendency to claim more is discussed in greater detail in Chapter Nine.

Table 7.1a Claimant Positional Change[a] During Mediation by Respondent Ethnic or Gender Difference

	w/ All Respondents[b]		w/ R. Latino		w/ R. Anglo		w/ R. Female		w/ R. Male	
Claimants[c]	N	Mean (SD)	N	Mean (SD)	N	Mean (SD)	N	Mean (SD)	N	Mean (SD)
C. Latino	40	-.515*** (.38)	29	-.502 (.36)	11	-.549 (.37)	11	-.611 (.34)	29	-.479 (.37)
C. Anglo	97	-.312 (.38)	35	-.226 (.44)	62	-.360 (.24)	37	-.399* (.39)	60	-.257 (.37)
C. Female	61	-.376 (.41)	28	-.326 (.47)	33	-.418 (.36)	24	-.491* (.42)	37	-.301 (.39)
C. Male	77	-.362 (.38)	37	-.361 (.40)	40	-.364 (.39)	24	-.404 (.35)	53	-.343 (.38)
All Cases	138	-.368 (.39)	65	-.346 (.43)	73	-.388 (.35)	48	-.488* (.38)	90	-.326 (.38)

***p<.01; ** p<.05; * p<.10 (two-tailed tests)

[a] Positional Change calculated as final MOR minus the ratio of claim reported as position prior to mediation for claimants or respondents. See Chapter Four with notes for detailed description of data sources.

[b] Number of claimants by ethnicity add to 137 because 1 claimant could not be coded for ethnicity. Significance by t-test of means for claimant/respondent group by respondent/claimant ethnic or gender groups

[c] Significance determined by t-tests of means for claimant or respondent group compared to all others

Table 7.1b Respondent Positional Change During Mediation by Claimant Ethnic or Gender Difference

	w/ All Claimants		w/ C. Latino		w/ C. Anglo		w/ C. Female		w/ C. Male	
Respondents	N	Mean (SD)	N	Mean (SD)	N	Mean (SD)	N	Mean (SD)	N	Mean (SD)
R. Latino	65	.260 (.33)	29	.211 (.24)	35	.308 (.38)	28	.296 (.32)	37	.234 (.33)
R. Anglo	73	.239 (.25)	11	.141** (.14)	62	.256 (.26)	33	.210 (.26)	40	.263 (.25)
R. Female	48	.234 (.32)	11	.218 (.26)	37	.239 (.34)	24	.207 (.30)	24	.261 (.34)
R. Male	90	.257 (.27)	29	.181** (.21)	60	.297 (.29)	37	.276 (.28)	53	.243 (.27)
All Cases	138	.249 (.29)	40	.192* (.22)	97	.275 (.31)	61	.249 (.29)	77	.249 (.29)

***p<.01; ** p<.05; * p<.10 (two-tailed tests)

Respondents

Table 7.1b examines respondent positional changes during mediation. Anglo and Latino respondents agreed to pay similar ratios of the claimed amount during mediation, but Anglo respondents increased their offers more with Anglo than Latino claimants. There were no significant differences in Anglo or Latino respondent bargaining behavior based on the gender of the claimants, but male respondents made significantly fewer concessions for Latino claimants than they did for Anglos.

Overall, claimant ethnicity was the significant factor differentiating respondent concession-making; Anglos and men were more willing to pay Anglo than Latino claimants.

BARGAINING ANALYSIS: CONCLUSIONS

These analyses showed how changes in bargaining trajectories—a result of the mixed-motive environment—affected outcomes. By comparing mediation to likely adjudication rulings shown in the last chapter, I assessed these patterns as rational and instrumental strategies, or not.

Legally represented parties were the most powerful bargainers, apparently because they had meaningful control in the alternative of adjudicated rulings. Of the three structural dimensions (class, legal and corporate status), legal status was the most likely to show insider dynamics. However, it was difficult to distinguish the insider dynamic from tacit bargaining, apparently based on shared fairness norms, and from instrumental motives based on expectations of meaningful competition if the case proceeded to court.

Latino disputants made larger concessions during the mediation session than Anglo disputants. This greater concession-making is characteristic of soft bargainers or those who have poor BATNAs. Because, as shown in the last chapter, Latino claimant outcomes in court were actually better than in mediation, the evidence suggests that Latino bargaining reflected an *ethnically-linked negotiation style of soft bargaining* that was intensified in the mediation forum.

Concessions and investments in reaching agreement appeared to be aspects of Latino bargaining. Based on goal, outcome, and bargaining analyses, this softer bargaining style appeared to be slightly more voluntary with Latino respondents and Anglo respondents exploited it.

However, the prediction that collectivist-oriented bargainers would be more generous to insiders was not supported in these data: Latino bargaining showed no indication that this soft bargaining was differentiated by the ethnicity or gender of the other party. Regardless of the other party, in comparison to Anglos, Latino negotiators showed concession-making that was strategically disastrous. This could be due to ignorance of their alternatives, a greater investment in reaching agreement itself, and/or a higher concern for the other party than for oneself. In cross-cultural terms, this concern for the other is best described as concern for "other face": protecting the other from shame and, in Latino culture, disrespect. The lack of increased competition with outsider for collectivists is consistent with Pruitt & Carnevale's (1993) conclusion from the research literature that insider dynamics are the best predictor of dynamics with outsiders. Brett & Kopelman (2004) report research showing vertical collectivists (see Chapter Two) simply enlarging the "inner" circle, cooperating equally when outgroup members were added; vertical individualists competed with ingroup members but cooperated twice as often with insiders when outgroup members were added.

In contrast, women and Anglos as claimants, and men and Anglos as respondents, showed negotiating styles during mediation that diverged along the group boundaries of gender and ethnicity respectively. During the mediation session, female and Anglo claimants conceded more to female than male respondents and Anglo and male respondents made smaller concessions to Latino than Anglo claimants. Thus, female and Anglo claimants, and male and Anglo respondents, showed an *other-based discriminating negotiation style* by which bargaining behavior changed according to the others' visible membership in a group, maintaining an ascriptive boundary against male respondents and Latino claimants. Note that the gender pattern during mediation appeared to be more of a modified self-concern evoked by female respondent resistance.

If, as Simmel argued, conflict is part of association with others, then the Anglo boundary maintenance pattern shown so far in this work demonstrates the material dimensions of Anglo-Latino social relations. These cases show the economic expression of Keefe & Padilla's (1987) finding of greater "ethnic enclosure" for Anglos than Mexican Americans within their networks of informal social relationships: bargaining patterns showed insider dynamics for Anglos but not Latino disputants.

Communication and social psychological theory and research offer a description of prejudicial interaction that, though it does not contradict the material effect, specifies motivational and perceptual dynamics. Gudykunst (1985, 1988) uses Simmel's concept of the stranger to argue that a need to reduce anxiety (uncertainty) drives prejudicial stereotyping of someone from another culture. In an experimental study, Gudykunst (1986) matched subjects for class, education and interests (i.e., social status similars) to analyze uncertainty (attributional confidence) with intra- vs.

inter-ethnic dyads. He found that both whites and blacks were more confident with social similars, and that blacks were more confident with white similars, but whites were unable to feel confident that they understood the behavior of black people regardless of social similarity on other levels. Furthermore, gender effects were "overridden" by the effects of racial difference. Whether as cause or effect, the greater "strangeness" of Latino negotiators to Anglo negotiators is likely to have played a part in the lack of ethnically disparate bargaining by Latinos. However, Gudykunst's work does not contradict the possibility that Anglo individualist culture, not just *any* culture, misperceives others because we tend to *project* our own competitiveness on others, then justify exploitation in response.

Resistance and tough bargaining appeared as an endogenous quality of female respondent behavior able to invoke concessions from Anglo and female claimants. In cases reaching agreement, claimants confronted by female respondents appeared to choose concession (an agreement strategy) rather than matching the female respondents' resistance.

Overall, only Latino-Latino disputes gave any support for generosity as a bargaining style. All other analyses showed *ambivalent* giving: claimants to female respondents and Latino claimants to Anglos reported later phase concessions. Women in these analyses showed little direct evidence of being endangered in mediation due to the relational psychology objectively ascribed to them and often presented in self-report research data. Rather, women in mediation presented patterns strongly skewed in the *opposite* direction; women were strongly influenced by the mediation forum toward materialist goals, and female bargaining resistance grew more firm during the mediation session.

Chapter Eight

Disputant Accounts of Bargaining Motivation[1]

"The promise of mediation," according to Grillo (1991:1551), and echoed in mediation training, rests on three differences from adjudication. First, mediation relies on context rather than exclusively on abstract rules. Second, the process allows emotion to be considered in addition to self-interest. And third, self-determination takes the place of an outside decision-maker.

In this chapter, the interview text[2] shows whether mediation met the "promise." Most of the variables are coded from text in the open-ended follow-up to the same three questions that determined bargaining positions shown in the last chapter: Why did you change your position? Disputant answers show status correlates with instrumental and expressive motivations. That is, I focused on attitudes implying individualistic, rational and material self-interest contrasted with attitudes implying relational and emotional motivations (see Holmbeck & Bale 1988, Rosaldo 1993 [1984]). These analyses are confined to the same monetary outcome cases resolved during mediation shown in Chapters Six and Seven, the outcome and bargaining analyses.

What did the disputants themselves say of their bargaining patterns? What accounts did they give of concessions and/or resistance? Did the interviews suggest that the parties were coerced, that their personal motives, in fact, had little influence? Did the outcomes reflect their own choices? Did their sense of coercion reflect objective outcome? I show the results of analyses performed to answer these questions in the context of cultural and gender theories applied to the negotiation process. In addition, I report the influence of dummy-coded motivational and lack-of-choice indicators on monetary outcome analyses[3].

RESULTS: INSTRUMENTAL AND EXPRESSIVE MOTIVES

Instrumental Motives: Material Goals, Strategy, and Resistance

Table 8.1 shows the instrumental motivations cited by claimants and respondents in monetary outcome cases assessed in three ways: material motives (here confined to the monetary outcome mediation sample); responses to questions asked of mediation claimants and respondents expressing strategy[4]; and the presence of statements indicating a "tough" bargaining stance. For claimants, this last code indicated that the respondent was unwilling to negotiate; for respondents, the code indicated professed innocence—expectations of having the case against them dismissed in court because they did not believe that they were responsible or liable for the claim.

Material Goals in Monetary Outcome Mediation

In monetary outcome cases, there were no significant differences in satisfaction or monetary outcome for the claimants who specified that money was their only concern. Respondents who had agreed to pay higher ratios were more likely to say money was the "only" issue (usually because they had none), but claimant who expressed material (not cash) goals were likely to have received less money. Unsurprisingly, the expression of material concerns was related to actual monetary outcome in a reverse pattern for claimants and respondents. When claimants expressed material concerns, the monetary outcome was slightly lower than average; when respondents expressed material concerns they had actually agreed to pay more, on average, than other mediation respondents. Similar to cash concerns expressed by respondents, cases coded for respondent expressions of cash and material issues tended to be cases in which the claimants expressed somewhat higher satisfaction.

Cash and material goals specified in claimant interviews were similar after monetary agreement mediations to patterns found for the entire mediated sample shown in Chapter Five: higher status claimants were more likely to specify cash goals with lower status respondents than with high status equals; lower status claimants (Latinos, individuals and lower class) were unlikely to express cash goals in the LOLO insider condition. As in Table 5.1, the addition of textual expressions of concrete concerns alters the pattern: considering all material goals (cash and material objects) show that only male claimants with male respondents and lawyers with other lawyers in the HIHI insider condition remained relatively unlikely to assert material goals of any type. By contrast, female claimants with female respondents expressed material concerns most often of all claimants.

Respondents said that money was the only important dispute issue only half as often as claimants. In contrast to claimants, male *respondents* with male claimants chose the simple monetary description of the dispute issues more frequently than other respondents. Of all respondents, corporate respondents specified that cash issues were primary most often when the claimant was another business, but least often (N = 0) when the claimant was not. None of the lawyer-respondents in fives cases involving lawyers on both sides claimed that their primary concern was money.

When the textual responses indicating concrete concerns (usually cash shortage) were added to those acknowledging monetary primacy, the pattern is again clarified. Compared to other conditions in those dimensions, lower status respondents in the first HILO power dependent condition (ethnic, corporate, legal, and class) expressed material concerns significantly more often. Whether as businesses or individuals, respondents facing corporate claimants (often collection cases) expressed material concerns most often. In the interviews, respondents with higher status claimants often said that money was "very" important "because I don't have any" but shied away from saying that it was the *only* important thing. In general, material concerns expressed by respondents followed the patterns of admitted liability.

The converse was also true. Respondents with lower status claimants tended to report material concerns less often: Latino respondents with Latino claimants were least likely to express a material base in their disputes compared to all other ethnic status conditions; lower class respondents were unlikely to express material goals with lower class claimants; and respondents with individual claimants less often expressed a material base to the dispute whether the respondent was an individual or corporation.

Strategy: Self-maximizing Motivations

Rational and self-interested explanations were offered by approximately two thirds of the disputants reaching monetary agreements in mediation. Comparative assessments (not shown), usually based on probable court outcomes, were far less frequent overall and were twice as frequently given by respondents.

Strategic bargaining was associated with higher reported satisfaction for both claimants and respondents. Like material concerns, strategy for respondents was also related to higher monetary obligations assumed in mediation, as was respondents' comparative evaluation of "better." Debtors who understood their probable court outcomes frequently demonstrated this pattern.

Table 8.1 Instrumental Motivation: Frequency of Interview Responses Indicating Material Goals, Maximization Strategy, and Resistance by Status Condition

	Claimants						Respondents					
		CASH	MAT		STR[a]	TUF[b]		CASH	MAT		STR	TUF[c]
Conditions	N[d]	%	%	N	%	%	N	%	%	N	%	%
Ascribed Status												
Anglo-Latino	33	48.5***	66.7	31	80.7**	6.5	27	22.2	70.4**	30	63.3	20.0
Anglo-anglo	56	26.8	55.4	55	78.2***	9.1	50	14.0	54.0	53	62.3	26.4
Latino-Latino	26	15.4*	50.0	20	20.0***	20.0	22	9.1	22.7***	24	54.2	37.5
Latino-anglo	9	22.2	66.7	8	37.5*	37.5**	8	12.5	37.5	6	50.0	50.0
Male-female	21	38.1	61.9	21	66.7	9.5	20	15.0	55.0	21	42.9	28.6
Male-male	46	23.9	45.7**	40	60.0	15.0	38	23.7*	47.4	40	65.0	27.5
Female-female	24	25.0	83.3***	22	68.2	4.6	22	9.1	54.6	22	54.6	36.4*
Female-male	33	36.4	54.6	31	71.0	16.1	28	7.1	46.4	31	67.7	22.6
Structural Status												
Corporate-individual	47	40.3**	68.1*	47	80.9***	10.6	40	15.0	62.5**	42	71.1**	26.2
Corporate-corporate	22	40.9	54.6	21	81.0	4.8	19	26.3	79.0**	19	73.7	10.5*
Individual-individual	31	12.9**	51.6	25	48.0**	12.0	28	17.9	32.1**	31	29.0***	35.5
Individual-corporate	24	20.8	50.0	21	38.1***	13.8*	21	0.0**	23.8***	22	68.2*	36.4
Lawyer-pro se	20	45.0	55.0	20	90.0**	5.0	12	8.3	91.7***	15	80.0*	13.3

Lawyer-lawyer	5	20.0	20.0*	4	75.0	0.0	5	0.0	20.0	5	60.0	40.0
Pro se-pro se	80	30.0	63.8*	71	62.0	14.1	74	16.2	46.0	78	56.4	24.4
Pro se-lawyer	19	15.8	47.4	19	52.6	18.8	17	17.7	47.1	16	56.3	56.3**
Achieved Status												
Higher class-lower	40	50.0***	62.5	38	76.3*	7.9	29	17.2	69.0**	31	67.7	19.4
Higher class-higher	24	20.8	50.0	24	83.3**	8.3	22	13.6	59.1	24	75.0*	25.0
Lower-lower	41	19.5*	56.1	36	52.8**	11.1	37	16.2	35.1**	39	46.2*	33.3
Lower-higher	19	21.1	63.2	16	45.8**	31.3**	20	10.0	40.0	20	55.0	35.0
Dependent Variables												
CSAT	112	.297	.085	103	.331***	-.454*	88	.426*	.287*	94	.223	-.035
RSAT	96	.575	.606	89	.580	.601	99	.573	.550	104	.578***	.379*
MOR	124	.700	.584*	114	.745	.531	108	.869***	.748***	114	.649	.440***
% of Total	100	29.8	58.1	100	65.8	12.3	100	14.8	50.0	100	59.7	28.1
Total Coded Cases (N)	124	37	72	114	75	14	108	16	54	114	68	32

*** p< .01; ** p< .05; * p< .10 (two-tailed tests)

Table 8.1 Notes

[a] Rational self-interested strategy to get the "best" outcome for claimants and respondents.

[b] Claimant report that the respondent had been a "tough" bargainer, i.e., resistant to bargaining/concession-making.

[c] Respondent report that he/she was not responsible or liable for the claim.

[d] Monetary (CASH) and nonmonetary material (MAT) goals coded for claimants and respondents from question "how important was the money itself to you?" See variable coding Chapter Four.

Higher status claimants, regardless of the respondent's status, were most likely to offer strategic rationales for their mediation bargaining movements. As Table 8.1 shows, 90% of lawyers or represented claimants, 80% of Anglo and corporate claimants, and more than three-quarters of the higher class claimants in the first HILO power dependent condition gave self-interested, rational explanations for compromise. Large majorities of the same status groups with high status equals also expressed strategic reasoning after mediation. Comparative assessments were more likely to be offered by lawyers or represented claimants and higher class claimants after mediation with a higher class respondent. Factoring in calculated legal costs required to pursue the dispute further compared to the likely benefits in a court ruling was a common example of strategy in the HIHI condition.

Except for women, lower status claimants were unlikely to explain their bargaining movements in terms of rational self-maximization. Latino claimants with Latino respondents were coded as strategic in only 20% of their cases and in only 25% of their total (Anglo and Latino respondents) cases.

In general, strategic rationales for bargaining decisions were closely related to higher status claimants in all dimensions except gender. In monetary outcome cases, female claimants were as likely as men to express strategic motives in their bargaining decisions. When Latino and Anglo women were analyzed separately, I found that Latinas offered strategic rationales only half as often as Anglo women (36.4% to 78.6% respectively), but twice as often as Latino male claimants. Latino male claimants cited strategic reasons for bargaining decisions less often than any other ethgender (17.6%). This analysis is carried further in Chapter Nine.

By mean frequencies, respondent interviews in the structural status dimensions followed a pattern of defensive strategy with few exceptions. Regardless of their own status, respondents were more likely to express strategy when the claimant was a corporate party or higher class. Respondent comparative evaluations showed the same pattern. However, as the table shows, the same lower status respondent groups that explained their bargaining strategically with corporations and higher class claimants, were less likely to do so with status equals.

The main exception to this pattern were female respondents, especially Anglo women, who gave interview responses coded as strategic less frequently than male respondents, especially Anglo men, regardless of claimant gender.

Disputants left mediation sessions conducted by women with attitudes similar to female claimants in the overall sample of mediated cases:

more often explaining their bargaining strategically and giving rational explanations for why settlement was "better."

Tough Bargaining: Unyielding and Innocent Respondents

Negotiators who refuse to bargain or reciprocate take the risk that the other party will simply proceed to another alternative. The large majority of mediation sessions after which the claimant reported that the respondent had refused to negotiate did indeed terminate without an agreement: in the total sample, 84.4% of the cases coded for claimant reports of tough respondents ended with no agreement.

Unsurprisingly, claimant reports of tough respondents and respondent reports of innocence were associated with lower outcome satisfaction for each group. In addition, respondent explanations of a lack of liability were also associated with lower (i.e., more favorable) monetary outcomes.

Twelve percent of the claimants interviewed after monetary agreement mediation stated that the respondent had been unwilling to negotiate. Supporting the interpretation in Chapter Seven (longer session duration and bargaining patterns), lower status claimants with higher status respondents were particularly likely to indicate during the interview that they had faced a tough respondent. Latino claimants reported that Anglo respondents had refused to negotiate in 3 cases of 8; lower class claimants reported higher class respondents were unwilling negotiators in 5 cases out of 16; and individual claimants said that corporate respondents had been resistant in 5 out of 21 cases.

When each status group is examined without respect to the respondent status in their cases, Latino claimants (men somewhat more frequently than women) reported tough respondents more often than any other claimant status group and significantly more than Anglo claimants. Claimants more often reported male respondents were unwilling to negotiate, despite the evidence that female respondents apparently made fewer concessions.

Overall, interviewed respondents in more than one quarter of monetary agreement mediation cases said that their bargaining process was affected by a lack of liability. Legally represented respondents were most likely to offer this explanation, especially with *pro se* claimants. Female respondents said they were not liable for claims filed by other women somewhat more often than other gender status conditions. Respondents more often claimed themselves to be not responsible in claims filed by individuals and Latino claimants.

However, the two sides of "tough" bargaining were not correlated with each other in the cases that reached monetary agreements. Claimant interviews coded for tough respondents corresponded with respondent explanations of innocence only 3 times, only one of them with a Latino claimant[5].

Expressive Motives: Relational Bargaining

Table 8.2 shows the frequency of interviews coded for relational motivations in bargaining decisions, specifying the content as sympathetic, cooperative, business, or antipathetic, and an overall coding for an emotional tone about the dispute and/or the mediation session. Coding is described in Chapter Four and examples are available in Rack (1997).

Relational & Emotional Bargaining

The global category of relational motivations and the overall evidence of an emotional tone about the dispute and mediation are shown in the first and last columns in Table 8.2 for claimants and respondents. In the full sample, relational motivation was associated with agreement when expressed by claimants but, when expressed by respondents, had little relationship to agreement.

Relational bargaining, when not specified as to the content of the relationship, showed no effect on monetary or satisfaction outcomes for either party. Apparent emotion about the sessions reported by the disputants, on the other hand, showed a negative effect on their satisfaction, especially for claimants. An emotional experience for claimants was also associated with a significantly lower monetary outcome.

More than half of the claimant interviews (58.8%) reported relational motivations in their bargaining decisions in cases reaching monetary agreement with few significant differences by status condition. Approximately one fifth of the claimant interviews reflected an emotional experience in mediation, especially lower status claimants after mediation in the LOLO insider condition with lower status equals. Specifically, interviews with individual claimants after mediation with individual respondents were coded for an emotional tone and the percentages for the third LOLO condition were consistently higher than other conditions in the other four status dimensions. By contrast, *none* of the interviews with corporate claimant after mediation with corporate respondents and only one of 24 legally represented claimant interviews reflected an emotional mediation experience.

One third of the respondent interviews reflected a relational component in their bargaining decisions. This was especially frequent when the claimant was an individual, lower class, or pro se regardless of the status of the respondent. In contrast, an emotional tone was unlikely for respondents after mediating with professional and higher class claimants. Specifically, individual respondents related an emotional experience after mediation with individual claimants but not when the claimant was a corporation; higher class respondents sounded emotional about their mediation sessions with lower class claimants, but not in interviews after mediation with higher class claimants; legally represented respondents related an emotional experience after mediation with pro se claimants but in none of the five interviews after mediation with another lawyer or legally represented claimant.

Respondent emotional experiences were less differentiated by ascriptive status. In the ethnic dimension, although Latino respondents often related an emotional component in their bargaining with Latino claimants and Anglo respondents often spoke of Latino claimants in relational terms as motivating their bargaining, none of the six interviews with Anglo respondents recorded an emotional experience. There were no significant differences in emotional experience by gender status. Testing by respondent ethnicity, gender and ethgender showed that the frequency of emotional tone was almost identical across ascriptive statuses[6].

Sympathy, Cooperation, Business and Antipathy

The majority of relational motivations were sub-coded for harmony (sympathetic, cooperative, and business), and/or antipathetic. The coding for antipathy and sympathy tended to be mutually exclusive, for obvious reasons. Examining these qualitative distinctions gives a more accurate image of the kinds of relational and emotional dynamics that were operative in the mediation sessions.

In the overall sample, claimant expressions of sympathetic attitudes toward the respondent were more likely in cases that reached agreement but respondent expressions of cooperation were more common in cases that did not. The other relational sub-codes, for both claimants and respondents, were unrelated to whether or not the mediation resulted in an agreement.

Considering only the cases that reached monetary agreements, Table 8.2 shows that claimants expressed sympathetic relational motivations almost five times more often for respondents as respondents did for claimants but claimant and respondent interviews were coded with similar frequencies for antipathetic sentiments. More than one third of claimant interviews verbalized willingness to compromise or cooperate with the respondent and slightly less than a quarter of the respondent reported taking this stance. Respondents (primarily corporate) expressed that a business relationship was an important influence in their bargaining decisions more than twice as frequently as claimants.

Table 8.2a Expressive Motivation—Frequency of Interview Responses Indicating Relational Motivations in Bargaining: Sympathy, Cooperation, Business, Antipathy and Emotion in Monetary Outcome Mediational Cases by Status Condition

		Claimants					
Conditions	N	REL[1] %	SYM[2] %	COOP[3] %	BS[4] %	ANT[5] %	EMO[6] %
Ascribed Status							
Anglo-Latino	31	54.8	29.0	29.0	9.7	12.9	18.9
Anglo-anglo	55	56.4	25.5	36.4	7.3	20.0	16.9
Latino-Latino	20	60.0	40.0	45.0	0.0	5.0	23.1
Latino-anglo	8	87.5*	25.0	62.5	0.0	25.0	25.0
Male-female	21	52.4	28.6	42.9	4.8	14.3	15.4
Male-male	40	57.5	17.5**	40.0	12.5**	10.0	17.9
Female-female	22	72.7	40.9	22.7	4.6	27.3*	27.6
Female-male	31	54.8	35.5	41.9	0.0*	16.1	18.6
Structural Status							
Corporate-individual	47	59.6	36.2	29.8	6.4	10.6	18.9
Corporate-corporate	21	42.9*	23.8	47.6	14.3*	0.0**	0.0***
Individual-individual	25	68.0	20.0	28.0	0.0	32.0**	35.3***
Individual-corporate	21	61.9	28.6	57.1**	4.8	23.8	19.5
Lawyer-pro se	20	45.0	35.0	40.0	10.0	0.0**	4.2**
Lawyer-lawyer	4	25.0	0.0	25.0	25.0	0.0	0.0

Pro se-pro se	71	60.6	29.6	38.0	2.8*	18.3	24.0*
Pro se-lawyer	19	73.7	26.3	36.8	10.5	16.3	20.7
Acheived Status							
Higher class-lower	38	68.4	44.7***	50.0*	7.9	5.3	17.8
Higher class-higher	24	41.7*	20.8	41.7	8.3	8.3	8.8*
Lower-lower	36	55.7	22.2	22.2**	5.6	25.0*	28.6*
Lower-higher	16	68.8	18.8	37.5	0.0	31.3*	19.2
Dependent Variables							
CSAT	103	.115	.634***	.639	-.160	-.955***	-.630***
RSAT	89	.599	.718	.417**	.744	.360	.564
MOR	114	.579	.659***	.692	.627	.402***	.458**
% of Total	100	58.8	29.0	37.7	6.1	15.8	21.9
Total Coded Cases (N)	114	67	33	43	7	s18	25

*** p< .01; ** p< .05; * p(.10 (two-tailed tests) for (² or t- tests of means.

Table 8.2a Notes

[1] Reference made to the other party as a bargaining motivation for claimants and respondents.

[2] Sysmpathetic reference to the other party as a bargaining motivation for claimants and respondents.

[3] Statements indicating a willingness to cooperate or compromise for claimants and respondents.

[4] Statements indicating a business relationship was important to the bargaining for claimants or respondents.

[5] Statements indicating antipathy or hostility toward the other party for claimants and respondents.

[6] Coded from overall interview text for claimants and respondents, statements indicating that mediation had been emotionally charged for the speaker.

Table 8.2b Expressive Motivation—Frequency of Interview Responses Indicating Relational Motivations in Bargaining: Sympathy, Cooperation, Business, Antipathy and Emotion in Monetary Outcome Mediational Cases by Status Condition

		Respondents					
		REL	SYM	COOP	BS	ANT	EMO
Conditions	N	%	%	%	%	%	%
Ascribed Status							
Anglo-Latino	30	33.3	10.0	23.3	20.0	10.0	10.0
Anglo-anglo	53	30.2	5.7	26.4	17.0	13.2	18.9
Latino-Latino	24	37.5	4.2	16.7	8.3	16.7	29.2*
Latino-anglo	6	66.7*	0.0	33.3	16.7	50.0**	0.0
Male-female	21	38.1	9.5	23.8	14.3	14.3	23.8
Male-male	40	30.0	7.5	15.0	17.5	12.5	15.0
Female-female	22	27.3	0.0	31.8	9.1	9.1	13.6
Female-male	31	41.9	6.5	29.0	19.4	22.6	19.4
Structural Status							
Corporate-individual	42	21.4**	4.8	19.1	16.7	2.4***	9.5*
Corporate-corporate	19	21.1	5.3	26.3	21.1	0.0**	0.0**
Individual-individual	31	48.4*	10.0	22.6	0.0***	35.5***	35.5***
Individual-corporate	22	50.0*	4.6	31.8	31.8**	22.7	22.7
Lawyer-pro se	15	26.7	6.7	20.0	13.3	6.7	6.7
Lawyer-lawyer	5	20.0	0.0	20.0	20.0	0.0	0.0

Pro se-pro se	78	34.6	7.7	24.4	16.7	16.7	16.7
Pro se-lawyer	16	43.8	0.0	25.0	12.5	18.8	37.5**
Acheived Status							
Higher class-lower	31	32.3	12.9*	29.0	25.8*	3.2**	12.9
Higher class-higher	24	16.7**	0.0	20.8	12.5	8.3	4.2*
Lower-lower	39	35.9	5.1	20.5	5.1**	28.2***	25.6
Lower-higher	20	55.0**	5.0	25.0	25.0	15.0	25.0*
Dependent Variables							
CSAT	94	-.065	-.082	.584	.200	-.123	-.149
RSAT	104	.616	1.009**	.146	.792	.195*	.227*
MOR	114	.586	.713	.796*	.673	.518	.583
% of Total	100	34.2	6.1	23.7	15.8	14.9	17.5
Total Coded Cases (N)	114	39	7	27	18	17	20

*** p< .01; ** p< .05; * p(.10 (two-tailed tests) for (^{2} or t- tests of means.

Table 8.2 Notes

[1] Reference made to the other party as a bargaining motivation for claimants and respondents.

[2] Sysmpathetic reference to the other party as a bargaining motivation for claimants and respondents.

[3] Statements indicating a willingness to cooperate or compromise for claimants and respondents.

[4] Statements indicating a business relationship was important to the bargaining for claimants or respondents.

[5] Statements indicating antipathy or hostility toward the other party for claimants and respondents.

[6] Coded from overall interview text for claimants and respondents, statements indicating that mediation had been emotionally charged for the speaker.

Sympathetic statements about the other party were associated with higher reported satisfaction for both claimants and respondents, but had no significant relationship to monetary outcome. Similarly, cooperative statements were coded from interviews that tended to report higher claimant and respondent satisfaction without any bivariate effect on MOR. In contrast, expressions of antipathetic relations had negative effects on satisfaction for both claimants and respondents. Antipathy was associated with a reduced MOR for both parties (i.e., more favorable for respondents) though it was only statistically significant for claimants. The expression of a business relationship had no significant impact on satisfaction, though the overall effect was positive, or on monetary outcome.

Although two of the three harmony-toned relational motivations, sympathy and cooperation, were more likely to come from higher class claimants, there were significant distinctions: Higher class claimants with lower class respondents were most often sympathetic, women more than men, and Latino but not Anglo men. Cooperation was associated with higher class claimants regardless of respondents' status but appeared in more than half of the claimant interviews after mediation with corporate respondents and in exactly half of the interviews with Latino claimants. The third harmony-based relational motivation, a business relationship, was almost exclusively the language of Anglo men in structurally higher status roles.

Hostility or antipathy was most common among lower status claimants: *none* of the interviews with corporate or legally represented claimants indicated antipathy toward status equal respondents. In contrast, noncorporate claimants expressed antipathy for lower status equals in nearly one third of their cases.

If sympathy is largely a sentiment expressed by higher to lower status parties, it is not surprising that respondents, being the accused and in the weaker dispute role, were less likely to express sympathy for claimants. However, *lower* class respondents were actually more likely to express sympathetic relational motives toward higher class claimants and were less likely to express animosity than other respondents. This is probably a problem with the category: the real motivation expressed in these respondent interviews might be better understood as the generalized indebtedness and gratitude that Hyde (1979) identified as the natural increase of gift exchange (see Chapter Five). For example, a Latina respondent coded for sympathy was "given a break" for a hospital debt by the Anglo male collector (see Chapter Ten); she said that perhaps the agreement was a little unfair to the claimant because "the hospital suffers a loss," thus considered sympathetic.

Like relational motivation generally, respondents in cases filed by corporate claimants were unlikely to express either sympathy or antipathy toward claimants. Antipathetic relations were more frequently found in the interviews with noncorporate and lower class respondents after mediation with status equal claimants in the LOLO insider condition.

Note that there were no significant differences among respondent groups for expressed willingness to cooperate or compromise. I found that respondents in cases mediated by two Latino mediators more often expressed cooperative motives than those mediated by other mediator pairs.

RESULTS: CHOICE OR EXPLOITATION?

Naturally, the question of perceived choice is crucial in assessing motivation. The notion that negotiators are making choices is central to the entire paradigm of negotiated justice and voluntary mediation. Thus I coded interviews for perceived threats to free choice, implicitly indicating a lack of individual agency.

I conceptualized the challenges to the choice/consent model as a continuum from internal to external experiences of coercion but I confine myself here to only the evidence of perceived coercion that indicated a clear sense of injustice or exploitation, i.e., the sense of having been tricked or otherwise manipulated into the agreement. I do not show the results of coding for a more internal coercion (a sense of resignation) nor the sense in the interview, usually stated outright, that the disputant felt "pressured" into agreement in some way.

My reason for focusing on the most extreme sense of a lack of choice is threefold. First, bargaining implies choice and since various challenges to this assumption are found in conflict, ethnic, and gender theories, I sought clear articulations of unfairness or lack of agency in the agreements that were, in fact, signed. Second, in traditional negotiation theory, the tension between the *best* and the *worst* outcome (not feeling like a chump) is the primary bargaining motivation: a clear sense of trickery is over that edge. Third, I wanted to answer the question of whether the outcomes that appeared to result from exploitation were perceived in this way by the parties themselves.

Table 8.3 reflects a reported sense of injustice, or of having been tricked or manipulated, by parties who "voluntarily" signed an agreement despite it. Chapter Four describes the coding process (see Rack 1997 for examples).

Agreements Without Choice

Sometimes the interview showed that the disputant felt tricked or exploited but did not clearly assign blame. More often, I was able to specify whether the disputant ascribed the trickery to the other party or to the mediators. Sometimes, when the disputant felt the mediators were in cahoots with the other party, interviews were coded for both. I refer to these further specifications in this text but the results are not shown in Table 8.3

Approximately one fifth of all disputant interviews suggested that they had perceived coercion rather than making a choice. In the text, disputants seemed to blame the other party approximately twice as frequently as the mediators.

Claimants who felt tricked were likely to report strong dissatisfaction, particularly when they perceived the mediators as the culprits[7]. For claimants, reported lack of agency was associated with reduced monetary outcomes overall but claimants who blamed mediators for coercion showed no significant monetary outcome disadvantage in bivariate tests. This suggests that the perception of mediator coercion, while having a pronounced effect on satisfaction, was not systematically connected to substantive outcome effects but blame assigned to the other party had significant monetary correlation.

Respondents' reported sense of lack of agency had no significant relationship with monetary outcomes, but was associated with dissatisfaction that, like claimants, was somewhat greater when mediators were blamed.

Compared to claimants in all cases reaching agreement, those reaching monetary agreements during the mediation session (i.e., the bargaining sample) were more likely to suggest a sense of being cheated; claimant reports of trickery were unlikely in nonmonetary outcome and subsequent agreement cases. Respondents' reports of injustice did not vary by outcome categories.

Assessed by claimant status, perceived injustice or lack of agency was clearly related to lower structural status, especially pro se status: none of the 24 represented claimant interviews expressed this and individual and lower class claimants were significantly different from higher status claimants in these dimensions. Non-corporate claimants with individual respondents, the archetypal "private" disputes, reported a sense of having been tricked more than half of the time. Pro se claimants facing represented respondents were more likely to have felt cheated. By ethgender comparison, Anglo men were somewhat less likely to have felt the mediated agreement was unfair and Latino male claimants expressed a sense of coercion most frequently. These ethgender patterns for men are clearly aligned with their structural roles in mediation (see Chapter Four) but it should be noted that interviews with Latina and Anglo female claimants showed that they perceived a signed agreement as unfair in equal percentages (26.2 and 27.3) despite divergent role appearances.

Table 8.3 Choice & Coercion: Frequency of Interview Indications that the Disputant Felt Cheated, Tricked, or Exploited in the Mediation Process by Status Conditions

	Claimants		Respondents	
Conditions	N	%	N	%
Ascribed Status				
Anglo-Latino	31	19.4	30	20.0
Anglo-anglo	55	21.8	53	20.8
Latino-Latino	20	35.0	24	12.5
Latino-anglo	8	37.5	6	16.7
Male-female	21	28.6	21	33.3*
Male-male	40	20.0	40	10.0*
Female-female	22	31.8	22	9.1
Female-male	31	22.6	31	25.8
Structural Status				
Corporate-individual	47	17.0	42	11.9
Corporate-corporate	21	14.3	19	10.5
Individual-individual	25	52.0***	31	29.0*
Individual-corporate	21	19.1	22	22.7
Lawyer-pro se	20	0.0***	15	13.3
Lawyer-lawyer	4	0.0	5	0.0
Pro se-pro se	71	26.8	78	21.8
Pro se-lawyer	19	47.4**	16	12.5
Achieved Status				
Higher class-lower	38	15.8	31	9.7
Higher class-higher	24	16.7	24	16.7
Lower-lower	36	33.3	39	25.6
Lower-higher	16	37.5	20	20.0
Dependent Variables				
CSAT	103	-1.074***	94	.217
RSAT	89	.711	104	-.166***
MOR	114	.313***	114	.745
Total %	100	24.6	100	18.4
Total Coded Cases (N)	114	28	114	21

*** p< .01; ** p< .05; * p< .10 (two-tailed tests)

Overall, claimants who signed agreements that they later reported were unfair or the result of trickery tended to be unrepresented private individuals in cases with other individuals, especially when the other party was represented. Examined in bivariate tests by claimant status, without controlling for respondent status, interviews with higher status claimants were less likely to suggest a sense of being cheated: interviews suggesting injustice were less frequent when the claimant was higher class or a corporate party, both status positions in which legal representation was more likely.

In contrast to the structural/achieved dimensions that carried the variance for claimant reports of trickery, there were few significant differences in the frequency of respondent reports of feeling cheated in structural or achieved dimensions. The exceptions were primarily in the corporate dimension where perceived injustice was more common among individual respondents in cases with individual claimants (the blame was commonly ascribed to mediators) but uncommon for individual respondents with corporate claimants.

Respondent variation in the reported sense of being cheated was clustered in the gender dimension: female respondents in cases with male claimants and male respondents in cases with female claimants were both more likely to feel they had been tricked, especially by the opposite sex claimant. Female respondents in cases with male claimants also tended to blame the mediators for perceived injustice, a pattern of mediator blame that was also nonsignificantly present in cases with female claimants. A sense of coercion and lack of choice was comparatively rare in cases with same sex dyads.

Mediator Effects on Choice

Claimants and respondents expressed a sense of being cheated by the other party twice as often after mediation conducted by two women than after mediation conducted by other gender combinations of mediators. From disputant reports, female mediators seemed to have an enduring but constrained intervention style, similar to Carnevale et al.'s (1989) findings of female mediator "inaction." Disputants more often blamed female mediators for their sense of injustice but their reasons differed by gender: male claimants explained that the mediators were too passive and wouldn't give opinions; female claimants perceived or experienced this style as a pressure toward settlement. As one woman said "I gave in because I felt sorry for the mediators, they worked *so* hard." Female mediators appeared to engage relational issues in the mediation session and use rational and strategic reasoning to motivate parties for settlement: disputants left mediation sessions conducted by women with attitudes similar to female claimants in the overall sample of mediated cases—more often explaining their bargaining strategically and giving rational explanations for why settlement was "better."

Male mediators seemed to foster claimant resignation (internal coercion): disputants more often cited fatigue with fighting, "I just wanted to get it over," after mediation conducted by men.

Overall, the disputants described a female mediator pattern consistent with gender stereotypes, female mediators more often engaged relational issues between the disputants; male mediators more often focused on the money without noticing underlying issues that were readily brought out in the interview. Latino mediators appeared to generate cooperative, non-hostile explanations for disputants' negotiating decisions.

RESULTS: THE EFFECT OF MOTIVATIONAL INDICATORS ON MONETARY OUTCOMES

Model Explanation

How did motivation and choice relate to monetary outcomes? To answer this question, I tested the bargaining variables described above (instrumental, expressive, and choice) for their relationship to monetary outcome in the multivariate model developed in Chapter Six (reproduced in Table 8.4 as the "Base").

These tests involved separate assessments of each instrumental, expressive, and choice variable for claimants and respondents. I tested all bargaining variables in the base model shown using only monetary outcome cases which had interview variables for both claimants and respondents (N = 89). Instrumental motivation was a better predictor of outcome than expressive motivation, and bargaining motivation reported by claimants was a better predictor than respondents' motivational indicators. The only significant bargaining variables in this screening process were the dummy variables indicating claimant interviews suggesting strategic bargaining motivation and reporting a sense of being tricked or exploited. Thus, the sample used in this analysis was only limited by claimant interviews (N = 114) and only the claimant variables concerning strategy and lack of choice are shown in Table 8.4.

Results

Table 8.4 shows the base model developed in Table 6.1 (the final equation in mediated cases at the far left) and the second equation shows the same model when the sample was restricted to cases with coded claimant bargaining variables, a loss of twenty-four cases. Nevertheless, compared to the same model with more cases, the model predicts 57% of the outcome variance (compared to 52% in Table 6.1) and indicates only a slight loss of fit ($F = 6.6$ compared to 6.8) than the base model including more cases.

The sample of cases restricted to interviewed and coded claimants showed only one difference and two modifications in the outcome pattern. First, the variable coded from claimant interviews reporting more prior relationships becomes a significant predictor of diminished outcomes ($p<.10$)[8]. Second, there is a modest reduction in the magnitude and significance of the negative coefficient for Latino claimants with Anglo respondents[9]. Third, the base model with a smaller number of cases shows an enhanced magnitude and significance of the diminished monetary outcomes previously noted for individual claimants with individual respondents (the third LOLO insider corporate condition).

The second equation shows the effect of testing the coded variable for claimants' reported strategic rationales. The variable for strategy accounts for an estimated 16% increase in monetary outcome. Controlling for strategy eliminates the significant reduction for individual claimants who settled with corporate respondents (the LOHI rights-based corporate condition) and the disadvantaged effects for claimants reporting prior relationships. Controlling for strategy also erodes the significance of the reduction for Latino claimants with both Latino (LOLO insider) and Anglo (LOHI rights-based) respondents[10].

The third equation in Table 8.4 shows the effects of controlling for a sense of trickery or exploitation. The variable indicating a fully expressed sense of injustice accounted for a reduction in monetary outcome estimated at 20% of the claim. Compared to the base model, controlling for an expressed sense of exploitation was only able to "explain" the reduced outcome for claimants reporting more prior relationships. In fact, the reduced outcome for Latino claimants with Latino respondents, a condition reporting a sense of exploitation slightly more often than the sample mean (37.5% compared to 24.6% for the entire sample), was actually strengthened with this control. Similarly, the reduced outcome for individual claimants with individual or corporate respondents, claimants who significantly often reported a sense of injustice, was maintained. Recall that these two corporate conditions are highly correlated with Latino claimant cases.

In sum, although a strong predictor of reduced outcome itself, the reported sense of feeling cheated, tricked or exploited, did not compensate for any of the status condition patterns in monetary outcome. Claimants with objectively disadvantaged monetary outcomes (i.e., individual and Latino claimants) did not consistently report a corresponding perception.

Summary Discussion: The Effects of Strategy and Choice on Monetary Outcome

As shown in Table 8.1, strategy was the *sin qua non* of higher status claimants with lower status respondents. As shown in Table 8.4, controlling for strategic bargaining strongly affected the predicted outcomes for the (intercept) HILO condition; the intercept in the third equation was lower than the base model by an estimated 14%. This suggests that, when strategy was controlled, a significant proportion of higher status claimant outcomes in the HILO power dependent condition was statistically explained. Thus, the lack of strategy reported by Latino claimants and individual claimants with corporate respondents (see Table 8.1) explains some degree of their diminished outcomes in the LOHI rights-based condition with Anglo and corporate respondents respectively. In addition, controlling for strategic bargaining reduced the magnitude and significance of Latino claimant losses to Latino respondents. However, controlling for instrumental bargaining had no effect on the significantly diminished outcomes in the LOLO corporate condition.

Interviews with HILO condition claimants were unlikely to reflect a sense of injustice. This perception was concentrated among lower status claimants. But the reported perception was unable to neutralize any of the outcome variation for these claimants. I interpret this to mean that although lower status claimants were more likely to perceive injustice in mediated settlements, and individual respondents in cross-gender disputes more often appeared to feel the agreement was unfair, the perception was relatively uncorrelated with the pattern of monetary outcomes explored in this work. Instead, I consider the significant effect of reported injustice or exploitation in the multivariate model to be spurious because it was generated from the correlation of lower status claimants (Latino and individual claimants) with reduced outcomes. Most likely such perceptions were accurate in the individual dyad, but not related to the consistent status effects in the settlement of mediation cases. Thus, these data show that Latino and individual claimants accepted reduced outcomes without reporting injustice.

Based on interviews, overall differences in strategic bargaining statistically accounted for significant proportions of the Latino claimant disadvantage in mediation and virtually all of the status effects for individual claimants with corporate respondents (largely businesses and landlords). The model estimates imply that, if Latino claimants generally, and individual claimants in the fourth LOHI rights-based condition, had bargained more strategically, their outcomes would have been better. On the other hand, a lack of strategy offered little explanation for individual claimant

Table 8.4 Bargaining and Choice: Regression Coefficients and Standard Errors Using Bargaining Variables as Predictors of Monetary Outcomes in Mediated Civil Cases

	Base (Tbl 5.1; Eq3)		Base [CLM Vars]		CLM Strategy		CLM TRK [Exploited]	
Independent Variables	b	SE	b	SE	b	SE	b	SE
Ascriptive Status								
Anglo-anglo	-.073	.065	-.019	.063	-.035	.062	-.040	.061
Latino-Latino	-.193**	.082	-.219**	.084	-.160*	.084	-.240***	.081
Latino-anglo	-.322***	.111	-.231**	.115	-.205*	.112	-.237**	.111
Male-male	.115	.076	.057	.075	.063	.073	.048	.072
Female-female	-.028	.087	-.080	.083	-.083	.080	-.095	.079
Female-male	.111	.080	.060	.079	.051	.077	.069	.076
Structural Status								
Corporate-corporate	-.053	.085	-.041	.080	-.035	.078	-.050	.077
Individual-individual	-.173**	.075	-.252***	.074	-.228***	.072	-.202***	.073
Individual-corporate	-.216**	.089	-.180**	.089	-.132	.089	-.215**	.087
Lawyer-lawyer	-.007	.139	-.089	.147	-.097	.142	-.095	.141
Pro se-pro se	.016	.081	.020	.078	.033	.076	.053	.076

Pro se-lawyer	-.068	.101	-.057	.096	-.046	.094	.020	.097
Acheived Status								
Higher class-higher	.095	.081	.091	.074	.058	.073	.079	.072
Lower-lower	.086	.070	.100	.071	.092	.069	.097	.068
Lower-higher	.123	.089	.124	.093	.118	.091	.143	.090
Relational Variables								
Prior relations	-.058	.042	-.085*	.046	-.062	.046	-.055	.046
Claim size	-.027	.020	-.027	.019	-.019	.018	-.016	.018
Admitted liability	.405***	.071	.332***	.073	.307***	.071	.297***	.071
Counterclaim	-.060**	.027	-.065**	.026	-.060**	.025	-.053**	.025
Bargaining Variables								
CLM Strategic					.163**	.063		
CLM Tricked or Exploited							-.195***	.067
N	138		114		114		114	
Y- intercept	.720***	.110	.783***	.111	.623***	.124	.765***	.143
R^2 / F	.52***	6.8	.57***	6.6	.60***	6.9	.61***	7.2

* p<.10; ** p<.05; *** p<.01 (two-tailed tests).

outcomes with individual respondents compared to the intercept condition of corporate claimants with private respondents. The analysis further suggests that Latino and individual claimants often settled for reduced outcomes without a reported sense of trickery or injustice. That is, they perceived their lower monetary agreements were due to their own choice.

DISCUSSION: GIVING, TAKING, TRUST & STRATEGY

Instrumentality, Choice & Material Effects

Based on detailed analyses earlier in this book, two claimant groups conceded significant proportions of their claims in mediation: 1) higher status claimants in the power dependent HILO condition settled for lower outcomes in mediation than they could have expected from adjudicated rulings; 2) Latino and individual claimants settled for lower reduced outcomes relative to adjudication (Latino claimants) and to other mediation cases (Latino and individual claimants).

In the first HILO condition, higher status claimants with lower status respondents, interview data strongly suggested the operative motivation was both material and instrumental. Claimants and respondents in these cases more frequently reported cash and material goals, explained their bargaining behavior as strategically motivated to achieve the best material outcome, and rarely indicated a lack of choice in the negotiating process or a perception of injustice in the outcome. No represented claimants and few represented respondents appeared to have felt tricked in mediation.

The expressive motivation for this apparent gifting appeared to be one I interpreted as "sympathy," a stated motivation most apparent in cases involving higher class claimants with lower class respondents. Expressed sympathy was primarily a female claimant motivation, especially for Anglo women in higher status positions. I discuss this "instrumental sympathy" bargaining pattern further and explicitly highlight it in the case studies in Chapter Ten.

In contrast, higher structural status claimants with higher status equals, though they reported similar instrumental motivations, less frequently stated a cash focus outright and expressions of sympathy were less likely. Especially Anglo men framed their relational motivations in the context of a business ethic. Overall, higher status claimants reported rationally self-interested strategies for their own decisions, and the respondents in cases with higher status claimants carried the same tone. Neither higher structural and class status claimants, nor the respondents in their cases, were likely to express relational motivations for bargaining or indicate an emotional mediation process.

Compared to higher status claimants, motivational analyses showed a very different pattern in the lower status claimant conditions. Furthermore, in the apparent gifting among Latino and individual claimant cases, the motivational pattern showed similarities and differences for Latino vs. individual claimants: There were four similarities—less materialistic goals, more relational motivation, more reported resistance from higher status respondents, and a lack of choice[11]; and two differences—overt antipathy was more common among Anglo disputants than with Latinos, and Latino claimants were far less likely than Anglos to have offered strategic rationales for their bargaining decisions[12].

Reported instrumental and expressive motivations in bargaining also showed important gender differences. I interpret this as a perceptual schema effect in which women are misperceived by others and misrepresented in theory (see Chapter Five and Seven). Despite the fact that women appeared to be the most resistant of all respondents in the bargaining analysis shown in the last chapter, male respondents were more often *perceived* as resistant. In addition, in contrast to their less materialistic image, female claimants with female respondents cited material goals *most* often of all gender conditions, but the female claimants *in fact* settled these cases in mediation for less, on average, than comparable court rulings. As suggested in Chapter Seven, such generosity was ambivalent; female claimants with female respondents often gave relational meaning to their bargaining decisions, but the content of these intra-female relations was both sympathetic and antipathetic. By ethgender, Latina claimants shared a high rate of relational motivation with Anglo women, but also expressed more cooperative sentiments than Anglo women.

Claimants who settled with female respondents were slightly more likely to report they were tricked or exploited, but the female respondents were also likely to report a sense of being cheated when the claimant was male, though the actual monetary outcomes did not suggest this was the case.

Collectivistic Bargaining, Instrumental Sympathy and Status Distrust

Based on interview text, higher status claimants, especially Anglo women, conceded a significant proportion of their claims to lower status respondents in the HILO condition from instrumental motivations. They explained this with an attitude of sympathy toward the respondent. The respondents in these cases offered strategic motives toward material goals as well, primarily based on poverty. Thus, I call this claimant pattern one of "instrumental sympathy" in the power dependent condition (see Chapter Ten). It was a way of talking about bargaining and goals in a role defined by the claimant's task to maximize monetary gains and, for respondents, to resist monetary losses. The pattern is consistent with what Janeway (1980) called weaker power: concessions by the stronger party in response to the power of the have-nots to threaten the legitimacy of those with greater power. In this case, interview data suggested that lower status respondent power grew from an implicit threat of noncompliance (McEwen & Maiman 1989; Van Koppen & Malsch 1991 for research showing this implied threat was quite realistic).

Latino claimants settled at considerably lower ratios of their claims than comparable adjudicated outcomes. In the LOLO insider condition, the reduced focus on material goals and lack of animosity in both claimant and respondent interviews, and the lack of reported strategy in claimant bargaining, is consistent with the notion of a collectivistic disputing style. In this pattern, joint benefit outcomes are more valuable due to affiliation needs and a distaste for conflict and competition. I clarify this conclusion for important gender and class differences in the following two chapters.

There were few cases available for analysis in the LOHI rights-based ethnic condition (see Chapter Four) and only four included coded interview data from both claimants and respondents. However, the indicators of bargaining motivation suggested a modified collectivist style operated for Latino claimants in these cases. Compared to cases with Latino respondents, the Latino claimants were more often materialistic in their goals and more often gave strategic reasoning for their bargaining. Furthermore, the Anglo pattern of resistance shown in the prior chapter and its perception and defense reported in this chapter, together with the Anglo animosity and Latino cooperation reflected in the interviews, suggested that this modification took place in the context of Anglo engendered inter-ethnic competition.

Noncorporate parties, especially unrepresented and Anglo disputants, showed important differences from the above status conditions. They also expressed a sense of exploitation in their mediated cases and based on the adjudication alternative (see Chapter Six), claimant perceptions of diminished outcomes may have been appropriate[13]. But both claimants *and* respondents felt cheated, and the interviews frequently suggested animosity in these cases. Culturally, the relatively hostile competition implied in this pattern is clarified in these data as an *Anglo, not a male,* conflict style. Rather than collectivistic, this pattern is consistent with the "power struggle" that Pruitt & Carnevale (1993) commonly found between negotiators with relatively equal power. The pattern for these disputants suggests the lack of confidence Tutzauer & Roloff (1988) found for bargainers without perceived bargaining limits.

Inherent in mediation ideology is the attempt to balance consent and justice (Harrington & Merry 1988). If one considers diminished returns from collectivistic choices to be just, these more individualistic cases challenging assumptions of consent represent the greatest challenge to negotiated justice. Although making agreements at average rates, parties in this condition were most likely to have made these agreements under a sense of duress or, at least, later felt they had and reported it during the interview (see Table 8.3). The probable court alternatives in these cases are not clear to most people (see Fiss 1984) and the lack of corporate role and legal representation appears to have been the critical factor that made these disputants vulnerable to the sense that they might have done "better." The perception of having been tricked and the actual outcomes had no clear causal relationship to one another (see Table 8.4) but both indicators converged for noncorporate claimants with noncorporate respondents.

Furthermore, although without apparent monetary basis, male and female respondents in cross-gender disputes appeared especially vulnerable to *feeling* exploited in a pattern I associate with gender distrust in the negotiating dyad. Bryan (1992:497) reviewed similar research findings, but only for women: "There is reason to think that women are significantly more likely to regard mediation as threatening and balanced against them than are men. . . . [Women were] more likely to report a sense of being pressured into agreement, a lack of comfort in expressing their feelings, anger during mediation sessions, and a sense that mediators essentially dictated the agreement."

It should be remembered that in most cases, experiences I have called coercive were significantly more likely in cases settling for monetary outcomes during the mediation session. It appears likely that less experienced negotiators were able to compensate for a lack of knowledge about their court alternatives *either* by exchanging items that were more readily evaluated, or having the opportunity to consult with their networks after the mediation session.

Overall, the textual data support the idea that objective monetary outcomes diverged from disputants' perception of them. Disputants without structural roles and respondents in cross-gender dyads felt more exploited than objective comparison with adjudicated outcomes confirmed, while Latino disputants felt less exploited than objective outcomes suggested actually took place. Thus, inter-gender bargaining can be characterized as scarred by distrust, even in these non-divorce situations, but Latino-majority relations can be characterized as more trusting than historical and present patterns warrant.

Chapter Nine
Ethgender Bargaining and Expectations

EXPECTATION & NEGOTIATION

The previous analyses show distinctly different bargaining patterns for Latinos and women. Overall, Latino bargained less instrumentally than Anglos. Chapters Five and Eight showed some evidence that Latinos disputing with other Latinos held less monetarily-defined goals in mediation. Latino bargaining *was* "soft," involving rather massive concessions both early and late in the process. In interviews, both Latino claimants and respondents reported motivations that were often relational without being hostile. Disputants of any ethnicity but especially lower status tended to leave mediation conducted by two Latino mediators with cooperative statements about their bargaining and high satisfaction; Latino-Latino dyads reported high satisfaction on *both* sides. For Latino claimants, the absence of strategic, instrumental motivation explained statistically the majority of ethnic differences in monetary outcomes.

By contrast, the women in these cases displayed highly instrumental patterns. Women did not show other-than-monetary goals but rather identification of their material interests strengthened in the mediation environment. Female claimants consistently explained their bargaining motivations as strategic, including those who said their motivations were sympathetic. Furthermore, based on the reported pre-mediation movement, the mediation environment specifically strengthened women's resistance to concession-making so that, as respondents, they were able to elicit concessions from Anglo and female claimants. As claimants, women conceded greater portions of their claims to female than to male respondents. Disputants leaving mediation conducted by two women tended to report strategic reasons for bargaining and women especially more often felt coerced, by the other party and by the mediators.

These differences in bargaining patterns, while somewhat striking, require clarification of three confounding factors. First, because prejudice and consistent social subordination discourage aspiration (see, for example, Wilson 1987; West 1994; Merton 1968; Cook & Hegtvedt 1986) the meaning of these patterns for the disputants themselves is important to discover, as far as possible. Second, the separate-axis methodology used in the analyses over the last four chapters does an injustice to specific ethgender patterns. Third, the correlation analysis (Appendix Table 4.ii) clearly showed the way that ethgender, class and structural roles reinforced each other in these data as in the larger society. Therefore I have attempted to disentangle the alternative explanations of ethnicity and gender from what Bourdieu called cultural capital (class and professional role).

To shed more light on any differences between these four groups I examine ethgender bargaining patterns; explore the influence of class and professional role on ethgender bargaining motivations; and use an interactional theory of inequality (expectations states theory) to guide an assessment of reported expectations in relation to outcomes.

Expectation States Theory

Expectation states theorists specify the way status characteristics operate to construct power and prestige (primarily Joseph Berger and his colleagues; Berger, Cohen & Zelditch 1972; Berger, Wagner & Zelditch 1985; Berger & Zelditch 1993). Ridgeway (1993) argues that this theory explains social inequality without reliance on, but not in contradiction to, theories based on socialized disposition (i.e., instrumental-expressive differences suggested by Parsons) or related subcultural explanations such as those entertained here. Ridgeway asserts the "radically situational" nature of the theory is its primary advantage. By narrowing the scope of the explanation to goal-oriented or problem-solving groups, it supplies testable propositions.

According to expectations states theory, different status characteristics have hierarchical values: external (generalized from diffuse status characteristics like race and gender) and internal (task-specific characteristics like professional role). These hierarchical values carry with them a sense of worthiness and implicit expectations for competence. The status characteristics become salient when "activated" by contrast within the group, or in a group task clearly associated with a specific status characteristic. Through a series of normative processes, these status beliefs affect behaviors and reactions: the beliefs become self-fulfilling prophesies.

In social psychological terms, group members look to status characteristics as a way to anticipate the usefulness of their own and others' suggestions by forming "performance expectations" (usually not in awareness).

With roughly similar cultural beliefs and information, group members share performance expectations. Notably, in the pattern described by Mead, individuals construct their own identities of competence and self-worth in relation to the status value assumptions of others, especially significant others, which are then reinforced during interactional processes (Webster & Sobiezek 1974). Performance expectations become a guide for participation in group decision-making: members with lower status contribute less to the process, are less likely to maintain their own positions, and thus are less likely to influence outcomes.

In this way expectation states theory describes processes similar to those associated with the culture of poverty thesis but at a micro level. It describes the interactional processes through which lower status becomes internalized and subject to "blaming the victim" critique.

The effects of performance expectations become more coercive when a "legitimacy dynamic" develops. Ridgeway (1993:186) explains:

> people with high-status characteristics not only presume themselves more capable, they also act and often are treated as if they had a *right* to achieve high influence and respect in the encounter. Similarly, people with low-status characteristics struggle with the feeling that even if they are competent, they have no right to try for high status. A right to something implies that your possession of it is normative and legitimate . . . if you do not have a right to something, then your effort to achieve it is illegitimate and . . . may draw a negative reaction.

Increased coercion associated with a legitimacy dynamic is a backlash against "illegitimate" low-status claims to influence or rewards.

Ridgeway argues that external and activated status characteristics associated with valued positions in society evoke a legitimacy dynamic. These "referential beliefs" of status value mean the group treats low-external status claims as "a bit deviant, out of line, embarrassing, to be quickly overlooked" (Ridgeway 1993:186). Interestingly, Ridgeway suggests two successful interventions for women. The first is to improve performance expectations concerning the usefulness of their suggestions. Experimental research shows that this intervention works best if an authority figure outside the group strongly suggests that women are better at the immediate task than men. This supplies an internal status rank higher than the more diffuse and external status characteristic of female gender. The second intervention to neutralize the legitimacy effects is for women to present their suggestions as "helpful" rather than competitive. Experimental studies have shown that competent women may achieve higher influence when they include prosocial behaviors and statements of cooperation (Ridgeway 1993:187–8).

Application to Small Claims Negotiations

For a number of reasons, small claims negotiation lends itself to analysis using expectation states theory. First, male-oriented Anglo jurisprudence might logically activate external status characteristics of both gender and ethnicity (see Merry 1992; Olsen 1990; Grillo 1991; MacKinnon 1984): the normative and practiced invisibility of dominance does not make it any less real. Thus, even without mixed gender or ethnic dyads or the presence of ascriptively different mediators, ethnic and gender status characteristics are likely to be salient. Ridgeway (1993) argues that in male-controlled institutions (like courts) women often operate with a sense of gender disadvantage that encourages a shared low evaluation of group competence and a consequent emphasis on reassurance. The situation of interest-based mediation may encourage a similar socio-cognitive shift.

Second, self-fulfilling prophesies that result from identifying status with competence (noted earlier as internalized oppression) are likely to affect bargaining positions, especially the ability to articulate and maintain positions. These are precisely the behaviors examined in the many experimental tests of expectation states theory (see Berger & Zelditch 1985, 1993).

Third, enhanced initial positions, especially professional fees and interest, are evidence that higher status claimants assume legitimacy. In Chapter Seven, I interpreted these higher demands by structurally-advantaged claimants in relationship to court alternatives. Here I examine them as assumptions of status legitimacy in specific ethgender relationships.

Fourth, the analysis of the effects of professional role on ascriptive status provides insight into the way "internal" cultural disposition interacted with "external" structural role in the negotiation situation. Research in expectation states theory has shown variable results in attempts to clarify whether multiple status characteristics are combined or used as compensation (for example, nullifying diffuse and "irrelevant" characteristics like ethnicity) in favor of more immediately relevant status characteristics like legal or corporate status (see Zelditch 1985). Ridgeway (1993) claims that people in the groups cited *act as if* they had first added positive status characteristics (with each addition having a diminishing effect), then subtracted negative ones.

Finally, to the extent that ascriptively based status characteristics evoke legitimacy dynamics, the stratification patterns in the larger society are likely to be embedded in "referential beliefs." Therefore a backlash reaction to low-status claiming might be expected. As Ridgeway points out, these referential beliefs appear to operate even when participants disavow them (see also Webster & Driskell 1985; Molm et al. 1994). Although the case histories presented in Chapter Ten offer a better mode to examine backlash, I mention it here for specific ethgenders. Anglo resistance to Latino claimants is one example.

ETHGENDER BARGAINING PATTERNS

Bargaining Process Patterns

Figure 9.1 (a and b) shows the bargaining process for each ethgender as claimants and respondents using the same data and style of presentation as the preceding graphs in Chapter Seven. The number of cases is much smaller when ethgenders are examined separately. Recall that, compared to Anglo claimant cases, fewer Latino cases are included in these analyses because they more often settled, in whole or in part, for nonmonetary exchanges. In addition, Latino claimants were significantly more likely to adjudicate their cases with Anglo female respondents: there were 16 Latino-Anglo female cases in adjudication but only three cases in the full mediation sample. Of these three, only one reached a monetary outcome (MOR = 0.0) and is excluded from the graph (this case is discussed in Chapter Ten). Especially for Latino claimant cases, the patterns offer insight but can not be generalized.

Anglo Claimants

Figure 9.1a concentrates on Anglo male and female claimant cases. The upper and lower graphs on the left show that both Anglo men (upper) and women (lower) conceded larger ratios of their claim with Anglo female respondents than with Latinas. In the nine cases with Anglo men, Latina respondents had conceded large proportions (averaging 64%) of the claimed amount prior to mediation.

Note that the actual settlement amount was lower, on average, than either the claimants or respondents reported in the interview. This was caused by a bargaining pattern in which both parties acknowledged greater amounts "really" owed, but the Anglo men agreed to take less from the Latinas, that is, they "gave her a break." This was not an uncommon occurrence in mediation, especially with lower income female respondents, though it is not as clear anywhere else by mean ratios in bargaining patterns. Claimants sometimes reported that they dropped the amount because the respondents didn't resist: a pattern that was significantly less likely if the respondent was male.

Compared to Latinas, Anglo female respondents admitted far less liability for Anglo male claims prior to mediation. In nine cases, Anglo women admitted, on average, only eleven percent in their formal answers in the court records. However, Anglo female respondents steadily conceded greater proportions of the claim prior to and during mediation.

The lower left graph of Figure 9.1a shows Anglo female claimants with female respondents. Anglo female claimants entered mediation with similar ratios of their claims admitted by Anglo women (N = 13) and Latinas (N = 6). But Latinas reported substantial increases of the amount they were willing to

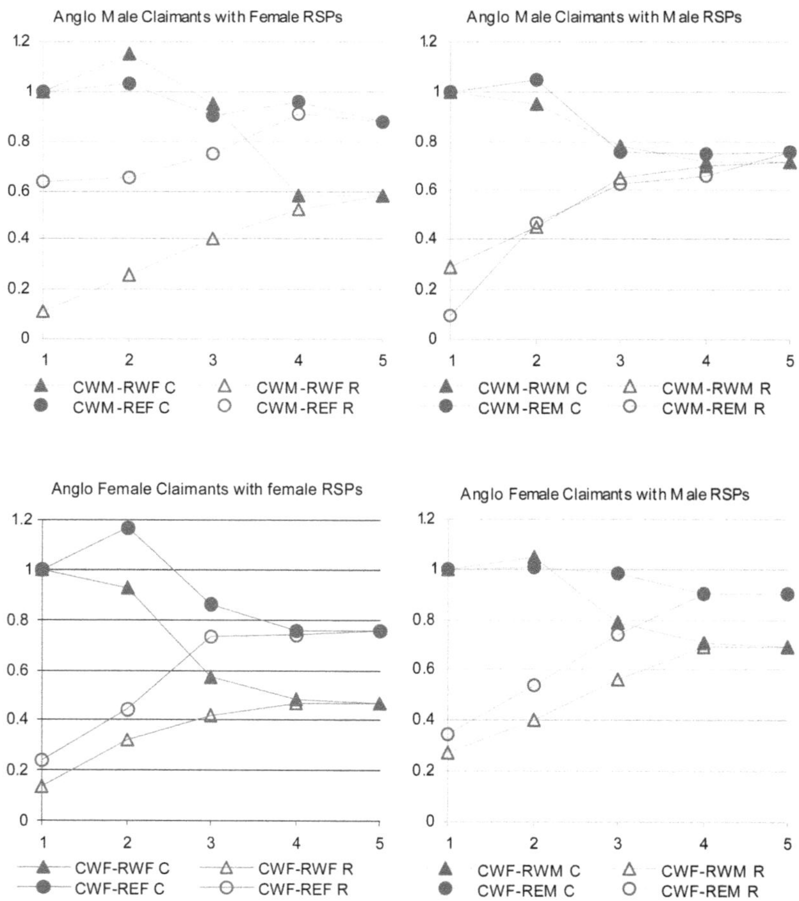

Bargaining Positions: 1 initial claim and admitted liability from court record; 2 reported amounts "really" owed; 3 reported changes during intervention; 4 reported final adjustments; 5 final outcomes taken from court rulings and mediated agreements

Figure 9.1a Anglo Claimant Bargaining by Ethgender

pay to Anglo women claimants in early phases of the mediation session. In contrast, Anglo female respondents reported slowing their average concession-rate during the mediation session with Anglo female claimants.

Anglo female claimants reported early phase concessions with Anglo female respondents. Anglo male claimants, on the other hand, reported large end stage concessions. Based on the dual concern negotiation theory, this pattern suggests Anglo female claimants were concerned about female respondents' outcomes, but Anglo male claimants modified their bargaining more often in response to respondent resistance. Further evidence for this distinction is discussed below.

The two charts on the right of Figure 9.1a show Anglo claimants with male respondents. In the court record, Latino respondents admitted smaller proportions of Anglo men's claims, Compared to Latino male respondents (N = 10), Anglo male respondents (N = 24) conceded greater liability in the record to Anglo male claimants, but male respondents of both ethnicities reported owing, on average, identical ratios (42%) when the mediation began. During the interview, Anglo and Latino male respondents cited similar settlement ratios. However, the final agreement signed by Latino male respondents was actually somewhat higher than they reported. Both Anglo and Latino respondents tended to report near-final concessions at the mid-phase of the bargaining with Anglo male claimants, the tacit bargaining pattern consistent with higher structural status bargainers (see Chapter Seven). The pattern between two Anglo men shows matched reciprocity settling at about 75% of the claim, suggesting a shared equity fairness norm.

Anglo female claimants with male respondents, shown in the lower right graph of Figure 9.1a, entered mediation with Latino male respondents (N = 11) already, by record and by report, acknowledging somewhat larger proportions of the debt than Anglo male respondents (N = 16). Anglo female claimants conceded larger ratios of their claims to Anglo men, including later phase adjustments on both sides for the sake of agreement. Latino respondents in these 11 cases reported consistently overmatching Anglo female claimants' concessions.

Compared to Anglo respondents, Latino respondents conceded larger proportions of the debt to both male and female Anglo claimants in three situations out of four. In the exception, Latino men reported more strategic bargaining: initial concessions were low and later concessions tracked Anglo male claimant concessions.

Latino Claimants

Figure 9.1b shows Latino claimant bargaining patterns. Latino male claimant bargaining was outstanding in two respects. In the first pattern,

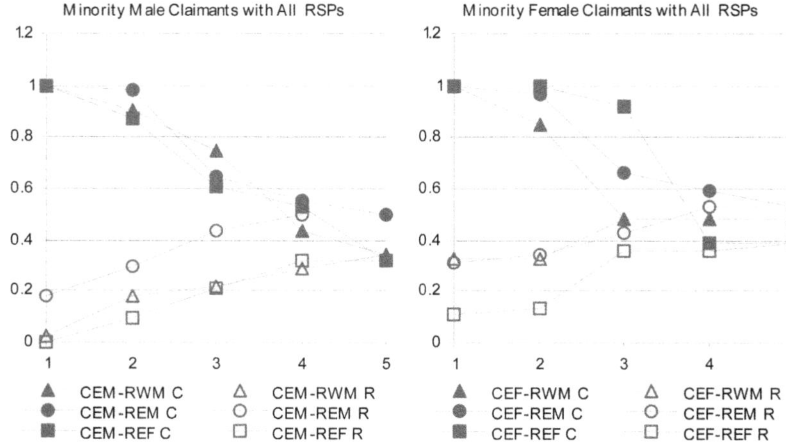

Bargaining Positions: 1 initial claim and admitted liability from court record; 2 reported amounts "really" owed; 3 reported changes during intervention; 4 reported final adjustments; 5 final outcomes taken from court rulings and mediated agreements

Figure 9.1b Latino Claimant Bargaining by Ethgender

with Anglo men and Latinas as respondents, Latino male claimants made late stage concessions and overestimated the final settlement (i.e., reporting better outcomes). Anglo male respondents (N = 7) and Latina respondents (N = 6) both appeared to have been tough bargainers; from their answers to the final agreement, these respondents adjusted their positions in roughly 10 percent increments to arrive at final agreements paying Latino men, on average, one third of their claims. Latino male claimants reported an initial ten percent concession, but then overmatched to achieve an end-stage settlement which was, on average, substantially lower than Latino claimants reported in the interview.

The second outstanding pattern is the more reciprocal pattern shown in 12 cases with other Latino men as respondents. Latino male respondents acknowledged greater liability at the outset, and both parties traded concessions in roughly equal proportions at a steady rate. In fact, the mean outcome in these 12 cases was exactly 50% of the original claim. Furthermore, Latino men in cases with one another reported the final settlement accurately, though with other ethgenders they often did not. Like Anglo men together, the Latino male pattern is the balanced reciprocity possible between negotiators who share fairness norms, in this case, 50–50 or equality matching.

Latina claimants reported consistent overmatching but in different phase structures with different ethgender respondents. With Anglo male respondents, Latina claimants reported early phase agreement (N = 3). In cases with Latino male respondents (N = 7), Latina claimants reported mid-phase overmatching, and otherwise a more typical negotiation pattern in which concession-making appeared to proceed throughout the mediation session. With Latina respondents, Latina claimants reported no initial and few midphase concessions. However, in the end stage, Latina claimants reported sudden and precipitous concessions with Latina respondents (N = 4). In three of these four cases, the claimant eventually dropped her claim, but reported that she maintained her full demand throughout the mediation session.

Latina respondents with Latino claimants were similar to Anglo female respondents with Anglo claimants; they were tough bargainers who conceded little and elicited late stage concessions from the claimants who settled. Latina respondents in cases filed by Latino claimants (N = 10) conceded little initially, and undermatched concessions throughout, thus ending cases with mean settlements that were equal to or less than those of Anglo men.

INDICATORS OF DESERVING AND PRIVILEGE

Early in the interview, we asked disputants the question estimating the claimant's second position: "At the time you filed the complaint, did you feel that the respondent *really* owed you all, part or none of the money you were asking for?" On average, neither male nor female Latino claimants reported an initial position higher than their claim. By contrast, Anglo claimants typically reported that they were owed more than the claim. Most often, these extra amounts were a reflection of professional status privilege granted by law to lawyers and corporations as interest and legal fees[1]. I noted, however, that lawyers and corporate representatives who would have received these extra amounts in court, did not always include them in the amount they felt they were "really" owed. Nearly all Anglo male claimants with Latina respondents were corporate collectors[2], often lawyers, who would have been routinely granted court costs, legal fees, and often interest in adjudicated cases. But, as shown in mean positions, these Anglo men rarely mentioned these additional monies during the interview. For example, in the hospital collection case (M023) described in Chapter Ten, the Anglo male lawyer never mentioned these additional monies as part of the concessions he made to a Latina respondent. Overall, the question seemed to elicit answers reflecting a subjective sense of *feeling* owed.

If these mean positions are understood as a rough estimate of a claimant's sense of deserving, of competence and confidence, then Latino male claimants would appear to have felt the least deserving of all ethgenders. On average, Latino male claimants only reported that they were "really owed" the full claim with Latino male respondents. Latina claimants appeared to feel less deserving with Anglo male respondents but they maintained their original claimed amount with all other ethgenders. Anglo claimants appear to have felt less deserving with their ethgender equals: Anglo men maintained that they were "really owed" the full claim or more when dealing with all but Anglo male respondents and Anglo women held to the full claim or more with all but Anglo female respondents. Anglo women appeared to feel that Latinas "really" owed them the most. Anglo men appeared to feel that Anglo women owed them the most.

The analysis of ethnic and gender boundary maintenance during mediation (Table 7.1a and b) was based on the difference between *reported* pre-mediation positions and *recorded* final outcomes. The analysis thus reflected concessions during the mediation process that were experienced in comparison to a reported initial sense of deserving, the amounts claimants reported they *felt* they were owed.

Compared to Anglo men, Anglo female claimants made larger sacrifices for Anglo female respondents and both Anglo claimant gender groups conceded more to Anglo than Latina respondents. However, if the interview responses to what claimants felt they were "really" owed indicates a subjective appraisal, the experience appears quite differently. Specifically, Anglo female claimants conceded, on average, more than half of their claim (53%) with Anglo women compared to only a quarter (24%) with Latina respondents. However, the drop from the reported initial demand in mediation, the amount "really owed," was quite similar with the two groups of female respondents; 46% of what was "really owed" was conceded to Anglo female respondents and 41% was conceded to Latina respondents. Furthermore, Anglo male claimants conceded approximately 42% of their claim with Anglo female respondents. However, compared to what they reported was "really owed," Anglo male claimants conceded more (57%) than Anglo female claimants (46%) to Anglo female respondents. Similarly, although Anglo men made slightly greater concessions, on average, with Anglo male respondents compared with Latino men (dropping 28% of the claim with Anglo compared to 24% with Latino male respondents), calculations based on Anglo male claimants' sense of deserving shows that the sacrifice with Latino men was greater (29% conceded to Latino men compared to 23% with Anglo men).

Two points have been made in this discussion of experienced privilege and deserving. First, on average, only Anglo claimants reported feeling owed more than their claimed amounts. I have interpreted this as an experience of feeling privileged that makes concessions seem larger, to the interviewer and statistically, than they numerically were. Anglo men reported feeling that Anglo female respondents owed them more than their claims; Anglo women reported feeling that Latinas really owed them considerably more than their original claims. Second, Latino male claimants reported feeling "really owed" less than their claimed amounts with all ethgenders except Latino male respondents. I have interpreted this as a tendency to feel less deserving with other ethgenders than their own. It also makes concessions appear smaller, to the interviewer and statistically, than they were.

The Effects of Structural Status on Ethnic and Gender Instrumental Bargaining

The pattern for higher structural social status parties was more overt monetary claims, strategic rationales, and relational patterns of sympathy for lower status respondents, cooperation with higher status respondents, and the affirmation of customer relations with business parties. However, Latino claimants tended to report their bargaining motivations more often as sympathetic and cooperative, like higher structural status parties, but few of the interviews with these claimants were coded as strategic and their presence in higher status roles was minimal.

This section describes the patterns of structural status with outsider groups. I conducted trivariate analyses for the frequency of instrumental motivation, comparative strategies, and sympathy reported by Anglo men, Anglo women and Latino disputants when they were, and were not, in structurally dominant roles. I discuss the significant differences below (see Rack 1997 for significance testing).

Anglo Claimants: Structural Materialism & Female Strategy

Anglo female claimants showed the most pronounced effect of dominant roles on their reported goals and relational bargaining motivations. Compared to lower class Anglo women, higher class Anglo women more often reported that money and material goals were most important in their dispute. When representing a business, Anglo women more often responded that cash or material goals motivated them than did Anglo women who pursued claims as individuals. Anglo women more often explained their bargaining decisions as sympathetic to the respondent when higher class or in corporate roles, compared to Anglo female claimants who were ranked as lower status.

However, Anglo women expressed *strategic* reasoning regardless of status: lower corporate (66.7%), legal (72.1%) and socio-economic (70.0%)

status made little difference in Anglo women's strategic explanations in compared to their overall mean of 78.6% (equal to Anglo men). In contrast, Anglo male claimants significantly more often offered strategic explanations for their bargaining when acting in a corporate capacity, or when they were lawyers or represented by one.

The role (structural status) effects in Anglo women's reports of material goals were more marked than equivalent comparisons for Anglo men. Though tending in the same direction, the difference in claimed monetary goals between role-dominant Anglo men and role-subordinate Anglo male claimants was only marginally significant in the class dimension: higher class Anglo male claimants specified that money was "the only important thing" more often and were somewhat more likely to express sympathy for the respondent than lower class Anglo men.

Overall, the material goals associated with Anglo men appeared to be structurally acquired by Anglo women. In contrast, the strategic rationales were particular to Anglo women regardless of structural role.

Latino Claimants: Need-based Materialism & Lack of Strategy

Reports from Latino claimants were less affected by role position than Anglos, and in the case of class and corporate status, the effects of role were often reversed: higher class Latino claimants, both men and women, were significantly *less* likely to cite material interests (36.8% of 19 higher class claimants compared to 60.7% of lower class claimants) and none of the five Latinos expressing sympathy for respondents were corporate parties.

Similar to Anglos, Latinas *did* report sympathetic rationales more often when in corporate roles and legally represented Latinos reported strategic and comparative bargaining motivations more frequently than *pro se* Latinos. However, legal status did *not* increase the likelihood that cash or material concerns would be reported as primary.

Overall, in all status dimensions, higher status significantly *decreased* the reported primacy of cash and material concern for Latino claimants. Higher status Latinos were less likely than Anglos to cite cash as the goal and material concerns were cited slightly *more* frequently by lower status Latinos. Only legal representation appeared to increase Latino use of instrumental bargaining.

ANALYSIS: INTERNALIZED OPPRESSION OR ALTERNATIVE VALUES?

This analysis uses subjective outcome evaluation to explore participants' sense of deserving. First, mean reported evaluations are contrasted with mean monetary outcomes. Second, a correlation analysis suggests whether or not ethgender variation in evaluation is due to the influence of alternative dispute values.

The most parsimonious explanation for an enhanced evaluation of outcomes is that the experience of mediation added some value to the negotiated outcomes that, in response to an open-ended question, influenced disputants' comparative evaluation of them. This explanation is consistent with the overwhelming bulk of research in mediation (see Lowry 1993; Wall & Lynn 1993 for reviews) showing enhanced reported satisfaction from mediation compared to adjudication disputants. Furthermore, as Wissler (1995) concludes in her small claims mediation study, this enhanced satisfaction transcends "case characteristics" (called structural status and case factors in this work).

On the other hand, expectation states theory describes how reduced expectations might be constructed, reinforced, and even required in small group interaction. Cohen (1986) described the way that reduced expectations, a diminished sense of deserving, could cause a heightened evaluation of outcome. In this explanation, consistent with exchange and expectation states theory, a lack of complaint is the result of choosing a reference group against which the outcome appears more normative.

These data were not collected with these questions in mind. Indeed, it would be a significant task to construct an objective research process that *could* distinguish between subjective, or emic, values and, as Goffman (1959) called it, people's self-presentation in everyday life. Cultural differences complicated this problem even further. Thus, the analysis presented is an attempt to explore rather than determine which of these theoretically likely alternative explanations for bargaining differences, alternative values or reduced expectations, is best supported in this cross-sectional, existing dataset.

Ethgender Comparison of Mean Reported Evaluations of Outcome

Figure 9.2 shows graphically the mean ethgender responses to an interview question posed as, "Altogether, how did the outcome compare with what you expected when the case was originally filed?" Disputants were offered choices from a five point scale (re-ordered for this analysis) ranging from "much worse than expected" (1) to "much better than expected" (5) with the midpoint being "just about as expected" (3). Ethgender responses after adjudication or mediation are shown as bar graphs to evaluate the difference in forum. Mean monetary outcome ratios (MORs) in the two fora are indicated as connected points in squares (adjudication) and circles (mediation). The MOR scale for respondents is inverted so that better respondent

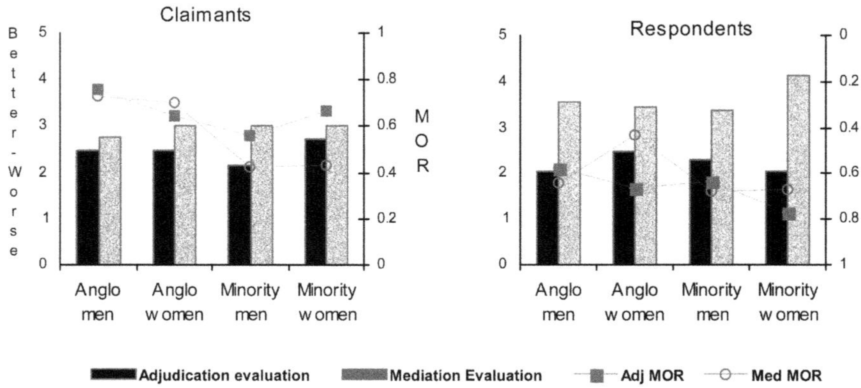

Figure 9.2 Mean Outcome Evaluations Reported by Ethgender Groups by Forum with Mean MORs

outcomes read visually high although "better" is a lower monetary ratio for respondents. All mean values for reported comparative assessments and monetary outcomes were derived from monetary outcome cases in which the parties were interviewed and answered the question.

Forum Comparison

As the graphs in Figure 9.2 show, all claimants groups and, especially, all respondent groups, rated mediated outcomes more highly than adjudicated rulings in comparison to their initial expectations. The mean difference between the fora was highly significant for both claimants (N = 386) and respondents (N = 330), despite the fact that mean monetary outcome ratios were essentially equal in the two fora. In comparison to adjudication, all claimant ethgenders except Latinas reported that their mediated outcomes were significantly better ($p<.10$ for male and female Anglo claimants and $p<.05$ for Latino men) in relation to their expectations compared to Latina claimants in adjudication. However, the graph shown in Figure 9.2 implies ethgender differences in these assessments when forum differences in monetary outcomes are considered.

Claimants

For claimants, the graph shows that Anglo men (N = 158) and Latinas (N = 45) reported the smallest increase in mean comparative assessments between adjudication and mediation. However, for Anglo men this assessment was reported in the face of equivalent mean outcomes in the two fora (73% in mediation and 76% in adjudication) while Latinas reported more equal assessments between fora in the face of severely reduced outcomes in mediation compared to adjudication (43% and 67%). Thus, Anglo men indicated the highest sense of deserving in both fora and reported little evidence of additional value in mediation. Latina claimants appeared to have reported outcome assessments indicating a strong forum influence: either their sense of deserving was less in mediated cases, or they included some additional (nonmonetary) gains in mediation in their appraisals.

In comparison to Latinas, Anglo women (N = 101) showed only slight evidence of diminished deserving or added value. Compared to adjudication, Anglo female claimants in mediation reported a moderately higher assessment of mediated outcomes, and their monetary outcomes were also slightly better.

On average, compared to other ethgenders, Latino male claimants (N = 81) showed the strongest forum difference in their assessments of outcome in comparison to expectations, largely because they reported adjudicated outcomes as particularly lower than expectations: Latino male claimant outcomes in adjudicated cases averaged the lowest of the four ethgenders. However, like Latinas, Latino men reported that their mediated outcomes were, on average, about what they expected, despite the fact that they settled for considerably less in mediation than they were awarded in court cases (42% in mediation and 56% in adjudication).

Overall, both Latino claimant genders reported evaluations suggesting either nonmaterial dispute goals were better met in mediation, or a diminished sense of deserving in mediated cases. Anglo claimant responses showed little of this forum-based effect.

Respondents

Respondents reported that mediated outcomes were far better than adjudicated outcomes. In reversal of their claimant evaluations, Anglo men and Latinas reported the greatest difference between the fora in their assessments, and Anglo women and Latino men showed the least forum difference, when these groups appeared as respondents.

Latina respondents, on average, evaluated their adjudicated outcomes (averaging 77% of the claims) as "somewhat worse than expected" and mediated outcomes (averaging 67%) as "somewhat better than expected." Anglo male respondents, consistent with their sense of deserving in adjudication as claimants, assessed their advantaged court outcomes (paying an average of 57% of the claims against them) as "somewhat worse" than expected. However, the same ethgender group of Anglo men evaluated their outcomes as slightly better than expected in mediation, where they settled for slightly higher ratios of the claim (an average of 64%).

Latino male respondents, with slightly worse outcomes in mediation (63% in adjudication and 67% in mediation) reported better evaluations in mediation.

Of respondent ethgenders, Anglo women presented the greatest paradox in this analysis. Despite dramatically better outcomes in mediation (from 70% of adjudicated claims to 43% of mediated claims), Anglo women reported the least forum effect in their comparative assessments.

Overall, compared to adjudication respondents, mediation respondents evaluated their outcomes in comparison to their initial expectations more highly. For male respondents, these better evaluations were reported in the face of outcomes that were, on average, objectively worse. Female respondents, on average, negotiated somewhat better outcomes in mediation than in court rulings, but were differentiated by ethnicity. Latina respondents reported vastly higher evaluations of their mediated outcomes, which were minimally better. By contrast, Anglo female respondents reported minimally better evaluations of their mediated outcomes, though they were vastly better.

Interactive Ethgender Effects

I clarified the specific ethgender interactive patterns in disputants' evaluations (data not shown) and found that higher claimant evaluations of mediated outcomes were almost entirely due to enhanced ratings in cases with male respondents. Court rulings with male respondents were rated significantly poorer than mediated outcomes by every claimant ethgender group with both Anglo and Latino male respondents.

In contrast, mediated outcomes with female respondents were rated more equally with court outcomes. In fact, only Anglo female claimants reported (nonsignificantly) higher mean evaluations of their mediated settlements than adjudicated rulings in cases with female respondents, both Anglo and Latino. The fact that Anglo female claimants reported an evaluation of their mediated outcomes with Anglo and Latina female respondents more highly than similar claimants in adjudication with the same respondent ethgenders supports the notion that the concessions shown in the ethgender bargaining analysis were experienced as voluntary, and contradicts the analysis of deserving implied in Anglo female claimants' average pre-mediation position in their cases with Latina respondents.

The effects of the other party's gender were reversed for respondents. In every case but one, respondents in all four ethgender groups rated mediated outcomes with all four claimant ethgenders more highly in relation to their expectations than similar respondents in court cases. The single exception to this was Anglo female respondents in cases with Anglo male claimants who, on average, reported that adjudicated outcomes were slightly better than expectations (N = 10) and mediated outcomes were slightly worse (2.86, N = 7), despite the fact that their outcomes with Anglo male claimants were somewhat more advantageous in mediation.

Within the mediation forum, male claimants rated mediated outcomes with women in their ethnic status category (Anglo or Latino) as more disappointing than mediated cases with other respondent ethgenders.

Correlation of Outcome Evaluations with Monetary Outcomes

Table 9.1 shows the simple correlation of the monetary outcome ratio with the five point reported evaluation of outcome in light of expectations for the four ethgender groups of claimants and respondents in the two fora. The MOR reflects a ratio of the claimed amount that might have widely varying dollar amounts but is a specific measure of winning and losing in a zero-sum conflict. As a percentage of the claim, MOR is an inherently competitive outcome measure. Thus, correlation with evaluation suggests a keen association between monetary win and expectations for winning.

Table 9.1 Correlation of Monetary Outcome with Evaluations[a] by Ethgender and Forum

	Claimants				Respondents			
	Adjudicated		Mediated		Adjudicated		Mediated	
Ethgenders	N	r	N	r	N	r	N	r
Anglo men	115	.610****	44	.278*	87	-.281***	40	-.196
Anglo women	60	.526****	41	.390**	34	-.223	20	-.548**
Latino men	61	.561****	20	.529**	40	-.461***	21	-.158
Latina women	33	.508***	12	.271	57	-.534****	31	-.208
Total	269	.559****	117	.319****	218	-.360****	112	-.219**

**** p< .001; *** p< .01; ** p< .05; * p<.10

[a] Interview Responses to question "Altogether, how did the outcome [from mediation] compare with what you expected when the case was originally filed? Five pint Likert scale responses re-ordered so that 5="much better than expected"; 3="just about as expected"; 1="much worse than expected."

After adjudication, the answer to the question, "how did the outcome in this case compare with what you initially expected [when the legal case began]?" was highly responsive to the MOR for both claimants and respondents. Furthermore, after adjudication, claimant and respondent evaluations were strongly and negatively correlated with one another as well ($r = -.419$, $p = .0001$, $N = 189$); that is, both parties evaluated their outcomes competitively in relation to the claim and with one another. In contrast, mediation claimant and respondent evaluations were somewhat less sharply tied to monetary outcomes and evaluations were not negatively correlated with one another ($r = .048$, $N = 97$). Thus, parties in mediated cases appeared to answer the question with monetary outcomes in mind, but there was no indication that in a case where one party evaluated the outcome as better than expected, the other party would report the outcome as worse than expected.

After mediation, Anglo male and Latina claimants' evaluations were less clearly related to monetary outcomes than those of Anglo female and Latino male claimants. Notably, Latino male claimants' evaluations were more precisely responsive to monetary outcome than those of any other mediation claimant ethgender. The smaller number of Latina claimant evaluations ($N = 12$) were not significantly correlated with outcomes.

As respondents in adjudication, all ethgender groups except Anglo female respondents reported evaluations that were negatively correlated with monetary outcomes. After mediation, in complete reversal, only Anglo female respondents reported evaluations that were significantly correlated with monetary outcome.

If a lack of correlation is interpreted as an indicator that some expressive values were involved in the disputants' evaluations, then Anglo female respondents were the only ethgender group to evaluate adjudication expressively. After mediation, Latina claimants and respondents, along with male respondents generally, responded to the question expressively. As an ethgender, Anglo women in mediation showed the least indication of expressive values at play.

Summary Discussion: Inflated Evaluation, Particularism, and Inflated Expectations

These analyses suggest that while Latino claimants of both genders reported higher evaluations of mediated than adjudicated outcomes, Latino male claimants responses were largely the result of an inflated evaluation. This pattern is consistent with reduced expectations, a diminished sense of deserving, a shifting of reference group or over-reporting, all of which amount to the same idea. Implicitly, Latino male claimants reported their evaluations with the percentage of their claims in mind, but expected less.

Latina claimants, on the other hand, reported evaluations implying that alternative values entered into their assessments. These might result from high variation of expectations among the women or responses that were more specifically (particularistically) linked to the specific experiences in each negotiation session. Particularism seems more likely because, compared to other claimant ethgenders, Latina claimant interviews more frequently indicated harmony motivations, respondent evaluations in their cases were more positive, and their bargaining patterns showed distinctive phase structures with different ethgender respondents (suggesting highly variable processes, at least as reported in the interview). The point here is that evidence suggests clear differences between Latino male and female claimants in mediation. Note, however, that Latina claimants also demonstrated reduced expectations in both fora.

Anglo male claimants, compared to other claimant ethgenders, reported evaluations suggesting higher expectations in adjudication. In mediation, Anglo male claimants reported evaluations of their mediated outcomes that were less closely related to the negotiated outcome ratios of their monetary claims. This was due to a more consistent response pattern; Anglo male claimants evaluated almost two-thirds (63.6%) of their mediated outcomes as "just about as expected," an evaluation chosen by other ethgender claimants far less often, especially Latino male claimants (who chose this response in only 10% of their cases)[3].

As respondents, Latinas appeared to have the lowest expectations for claim reductions, Anglo women the highest, and male respondents of both ethnic statuses in between. In general, mediation respondents' appraisals of their outcomes were unresponsive to outcomes calculated as a ratio of the claim and it is this lack of monetary anchoring that is responsible for the fact that mediation disputants did not report evaluations that were inversely related to one another[4].

PATTERNS AND IMPLICATIONS

Patterns in Ethgender Bargaining Behavior

The ethgender bargaining patterns showed the precise way in which differential bargaining described in Chapter Seven actually played out for each ethgender group of claimants and respondents.

Latino Bargaining

Latino claimants consistently overmatched the concessions of Anglos and Latina respondents. Latinas overmatched Anglo male respondent concessions early and reported massive concessions with Latina respondents only in the final stage, that is, they maintained during the interview that they were actually owed close to the full amount[5]. Latino claimants in particular showed a pattern of exuberant and steady overmatching, ending with the lowest MORs of all ethgenders in cases with Anglo male and Latina respondents (about one third of their claims). With these two respondent groups, Latino men consistently reported final agreement amounts better than those recorded in the written agreement, consistently near 50% of their claims regardless of respondent ethgender. Latino male claimants achieved their highest mean outcomes, averaging exactly 50–50, with other Latino men. For Latino male respondents, this outcome with Latino male claimants were the lowest (i.e., most advantageous). On average, compared to bargaining partners of any other ethgender, Latino men as claimants and respondents provided the most advantageous outcomes to one another. Viewed in light of negotiation research, it seems that Latino men, as soft bargainers, were best paired with each other, a statement that is true theoretically and experimentally of all soft bargainers.

Gender Differences in Bargaining

Contrary to all theories suggesting that women might be more likely to concede too much in mediation, women were highly resistant bargainers during mediation. With the exception of Latina respondents with Anglo male claimants, female respondents reported little concession-making during mediation and no end stage mismatching. These cases typically were imbalanced on structural levels as well and Latina respondents showed strong indicators of deference. Within Anglos and Latinos, *all* claimants tended to make greater concessions with women than with men. In their cases with female claimants, female respondents tended to report a single concession in mediation that remained unchanged through later phases, and which accurately reflected the final agreement. With male claimants of their own ethnicity, female respondents appeared to steadily undermatch male claimant concessions. Women were more likely to overmatch as claimants than as respondents, but primarily with female respondents.

Cross-gender Anglo-Latino dyads involved few claimant gifts but high respondent deference. The Anglo claimants with Latino respondents of the other gender achieved the highest outcomes of all ethgender groups without later recalling additional costs in their claims. Anglo men conceded almost nothing to Latinas and Anglo women conceded almost nothing to Latino male respondents.

Of all claimant ethgenders, Anglo male cases with male respondents showed the least ethnically-biased outcome variation, apparently because

Latino male respondents used more bargaining strategy (i.e., lower admitted liability and smaller concessions than in cases with other claimant ethgenders). In contrast, Anglo claimant cases with female respondents and Anglo female cases with male respondents consistently showed the greatest ethnic disparity in outcomes (approximately 20–25% difference between Anglo and Latino respondents). Overall, Anglo women were involved in all of these biased outcomes, a point I will further discuss in the final chapter.

Structural Status Effects on Bargaining

Higher status, especially socio-economic status, had the paradoxical effect of encouraging materialism and instrumentality for Anglo claimants, especially women, but perhaps *de*-legitimized overt monetary claims for Latinos, especially men. This observation is based on a composite and comparative image: Anglo claimants reported they were "owed" more than their claims while Latino claimants did not. Latino claimants focused more on material goals when they were lower class and were less likely to claim cash goals or strategize instrumentally when they were in structurally more powerful roles. For Anglo and Latina women, instrumental sympathy was a way to soften their highly instrumental task when in structurally powerful roles; but for Latino male claimants, concern for the other apparently had no relationship to role appearances of this type. Case studies in Chapter Ten show further evidence for this interpretation of cultural differences in status legitimation of materialism.

Ethgender Expectations

Considering their outcomes, Latino claimants of both genders reported better assessments of their mediated outcomes than Anglo claimants. Correlation analysis showed that Latino male claimants' reports tracked monetary outcome but Latinas' reports did not. I interpreted this to indicate that Latina claimants incorporated other than monetary values into their expectations and assessments in particularistic response to the situation, but suggested Latino male claimants quite accurately assessed mediation outcomes using a lowered standard of comparison. Combined with analyses of the sense of deserving and bargaining, the data indicate that Latino men internalized oppression through a lower expectation for material rewards. In Chapter Ten, I show how the equality fairness norm associated with collectivist bargaining (see Chapter Seven) and found for Latino male bargaining, combined with a vigilance toward the other party. This combination became the mechanism through which Latino men were constructed in mediation as less competent negotiators.

I compared mediation ethgender groups' evaluations to those of the same ethgender groups in adjudication. These analyses suggested that claimants preferred mediation with male respondents and, less significantly, respondents preferred mediation with female claimants. The respondent-gender preference, though perhaps over-stated and containing expressive elements, relates logically to the monetary outcome patterns that showed female respondents faring better than men in mediation, and male respondents faring better in adjudication (see Chapter Six). Male claimants' reaction to women's power in resistance was clear: within Anglos and Latinos, male claimants rated their outcomes with female respondents as lower than outcomes with other respondent ethgenders. The men particularly seemed to expect better outcomes with female respondents of their own ethnicity.

Anglo female respondents were the exception to other respondent patterns in both fora. Compared to other respondent ethgenders, Anglo women's evaluations of adjudicated outcomes were higher than monetary outcomes would predict and were not correlated with gains and losses implied in the ratio outcome measure; Anglo female respondents reported evaluations in mediation closely tied to monetary outcome, and indicators of additional forum values were relatively absent.

Theoretical Implications

Ethnic & Gender Status Activation

What do these findings say in terms of expectation states theory? First, these results support the proposition that these disputes activated gender status. As Ridgeway (1993, 1997) suggested, women appeared to operate with a sense of gender disadvantage in the court setting even without men present. Anglo women, in their gifting to other women and especially to Anglo women, appeared to operate from an emphasis on reassurance that Ridgeway hypothesized grew from a sense of shared disadvantage and threatened competence identities.

Ridgeway suggested that in all-male task-groups where the task assumed greater male competence, the men would more productively settle down to competitive problem-solving work with confidence they could solve the problem. This is a possible explanation for the noticeable *lack* of ethnic bias in the outcomes with Anglo male claimant cases with Anglo and Latino male respondents: possibly ethnicity was not activated, or it was neutralized in the shared male competence-identity. However, most of these cases imply that ethnic status became a factor in all cases[6]. For example, in the male-male condition discussed above, note that outcomes for Anglo men were much higher (approximately 75%) than the 50% that appeared to be Latino men's normative settlement point, or fairness rule.

Legitimacy & Backlash

The pattern of claimant outcomes can be best understood through legitimacy dynamics, where external status appears to confer or deny certain rights to money. Bourdieu uses the term symbolic capital for the power passively acquired from the others who habitually associate certain kinds of people and roles with legitimate authority. Privilege is another way to describe this dynamic. The assumption that only Anglo men are perceived and perceive themselves as legitimate claimants to money is a good way to describe the pattern of Anglo male vs. female and Latino claiming. The backlash against individuals of non-legitimated status who attempted to claim is apparent for all *claimants* who were not Anglo men[7]. The reduced outcomes in female-female and Latino-Latino disputes can be interpreted as the interactional effects predicted for individuals of illegitimate external status trying to claim.

Latino claimants without structurally powerful roles were vulnerable to backlash effects, especially from Anglo male respondents, for which they appeared to construct little defense. In a manner suggested by Ridgeway, Anglo respondents often disparaged Latino male claimants and patronized Latina claimants. The only claiming role in which Latino men appeared comfortable was a family dispute. Supported by Latino patriarchal assumptions and claiming against other men in the extended family, the claimants conducted the disputes with dignity and settled at the 50% mark, regardless of socio-economic status (see Chapter Ten).

One female claiming strategy was largely based on what Ridgeway proposed as an intervention: women who had achieved otherwise threatening status roles constructed instrumental sympathy. Another evident strategy was the invocation of motherhood status: women were fierce and often successful when their claims related to their children (see Chapter Ten). Also, women more often claimed in landlord and tenant roles (see Chapter Four): they asserted rights in an arena that is more female than male and in which they appeared to feel confident. The defensive rationality found in interviews with female claimants could be explained by this as well.

Overall, both gender and ethnic status appeared to be activated in a task that was legitimated for Anglo men. In the few cases where women pursued Anglo male respondents, the negotiation process suggested that Anglo men had different responses if the women were in professional roles. Anglo male respondents appeared to accept the legitimacy of these roles. In Ridgeway's terms, the structural role compensated or nullified their more diffuse status role as women and/or Latinos. Concessions from Anglo male respondents could be elicited by Anglo female claimants as consumers, but the men's compliance was deeply shaded by their patronizing attitudes (see Chapter Ten).

What of female respondents? Lipman-Blumer (1984) called women's micromanipulation the "poaching of power," a good description of female bargaining power, especially as respondents, in these data. Respondents were in subordinate dispute roles, not assertive ones. Women appeared to be more comfortable in these roles, and an "innocent victim" status was their most effective strategy. Although female bargaining resistance appeared to offend male claimants who settled with female respondents despite their annoyance, mediation gave women the opportunity to refuse. Although it was ineffective in some cases, refusal often worked to women's material advantage. However, based on the mosaic of results more thoroughly discussed in the following chapters, little evidence exists to believe female respondents generally perceived poaching in mediation as an empowering experience.

Chapter Ten
Case Studies

In all the cases included in this study the narratives from questionnaires and interviews enriched, expanded, and humanized the quantitative analysis. After all, the ultimate reason for both the civil court system and a mediation alternative is to resolve disputes between *people*. In a basic but abstract way, we are all "equal before the law." Clearly, however, this study and others like it reveal inequalities of such a complex nature that articulating them stretches the tools we have available. I have separated the disputants into overlapping groups, and analyzed mediation dyads as if the individuals fully represented those groups and categories. This methodology has a logic and legitimacy that reveals real group patterns. Yet this study would not be complete without including more of the actual cases, with the voices and idiosyncratic stories of individual humans at the forefront.

This chapter relates fifteen of the cases from the project. Each case includes a brief description of the disputants, the case, and the outcomes; a narrative synopsis of the questionnaires and interviews[1]; and several paragraphs fitting the case into the bargaining patterns analyzed earlier in the book.

The case studies show collectivistic bargaining by Latino disputants and informal female power to negotiate beneficial outcomes. Legitimacy dynamics are at the forefront of interpretation even though the cases show the nexus of multiple influences. The "backlash" described by Ridgeway (1993) is easy to see in the more complete story: it is more likely when external status became a referential position, facilitated by the mediators, implying greater rights. In different processes, these cases illustrate how discrimination clues suggested exploitation of Latino bargainers, and the way women both presented themselves and were perceived as more legitimate in their resistance to concession-making.

The cases show soft bargaining for Latino men in three conditions: with other Latino men, with Latinas, and with Anglo respondents. The stories suggest what expectations states theory calls "prophesy fulfillment through disempowering performance expectations," and how it was expressed in cultural patterns understood as collectivistic. Particular status affected these negotiation processes is different ways: especially when the respondent was Anglo, the mediators' status deference and ethic of "neutrality" became a means through which the mediation environment served to support exploitation of soft bargaining.

Women approached their bargaining task with constructions of instrumental sympathy, closely related to the gender status of claimants and respondents in these negotiation processes. I also show Anglo female skills, or "informal power" (Elshtain 1992), could evoke moral legitimacy with male respondents when structural roles were absent.

COLLECTIVISTIC AND OPPORTUNISTIC BARGAINING

Intra-Latino Disputes: Other-Vigilance, Equality Norms, Status Effects, and Mediator Influence

In the dual concern negotiation model, Latino men appeared to be the most concerned with the outcome of the negotiation process for the other party. This pattern of other concern is consistent with collectivist culture expectations, particularly face and affiliation needs (Ting-Toomey 1985, 1988; see also Tutzauer & Roloff 1988). If the other party was also a Latino man, the negotiation process appeared to be matched, reciprocal, and organized around patriarchal family status and an implicitly shared equality (50–50) fairness norm.

The following cases illustrate equality-based fairness norms and soft bargaining, and suggest *other* face-saving (Ting-Toomey 1985). The case also suggests what appeared to be primary mediator patterns in these cases: Anglo mediators leaned on external status characteristics to grant legitimacy in the absence of cultural understanding, a pattern that perhaps reinforced hierarchy acceptance within the Latino culture[2].

Structural Status

In this case, the mediator granted symbolic power to the lawyer. This case also suggests mediator gender differences in perceiving the focus for resolution. As noted elsewhere, male mediators often appeared to "zero in" on solvable problems.

> *[M053] The claimant was a 57 yr. old Latino claiming $200 he had paid the lawyer-respondent as a retainer to arrange for an adoption of the claimant's stepchildren. The 41 yr. old Latino respondent answered*

that he was not liable. The two men agreed in mediation to settle for $100 giving a calculated MOR of .500.

Status in Latino-Latino Bargaining

The claimant, a restaurant owner, said the money was "very" important because of the principle: "service was not delivered." He said he changed his position in mediation because "He [the respondent] was going to hold his stand. [I] did not want to bicker over a small amount." In later stages, in order to reach agreement, the claimant said he conceded more because "I did not want to put him into a trauma for a small amount." The claimant said he had control over the case "because right is right and wrong is wrong." The claimant liked mediation, saying "There is power in mediation. In the court system it is up to the judge." In answer to the question about power, he said he felt "normal." He said he was only angry at the late mediator. When asked how satisfied he was with the mediators, the interviewer transcribed the claimant to have said "I had to wait an hour for one mediator? So I only had one mediator. . . . since the mediator was late, it had caused a problem." He said his feelings didn't change at all from the beginning of the case until its resolution. He noted at the end of the interview that "I would like to see the mediators be more professional. Possibly law students so they can learn."

The respondent said the money was only "a little" important: "it was more of an emotional thing . . . breach of friendship." The respondent said that he has control over the case because "I am a lawyer by trade." In order to reach an agreement, the respondent said "I accepted less." In response to the fairness question, the respondent explained that his evaluation was affected by "the emotional issue, getting sued by a friend."

Although there was no counterclaim according to court records, the Anglo female mediator noted the respondent counterclaimed in mediation $309 more (additional to the original $200 he was paid) for his services. The mediator's perspective of the dispute was "claimant made downpayment on adoption service—adoption not successful." She described the claimant as "well groomed but work clothes stained, moderately articulate," the respondent as "well dressed, very articulate," and the disputants' ongoing relationship as "many years, social clubs, military clubs."

The mediator clearly perceived the respondent as having more legitimacy. She described the claimant as "somewhat willing" to mediate because he "immediately agreed to reduce claim by 50%." She wrote

> that the respondent was "very willing" to mediate because he "ignored completely his legitimate claim for consultation," i.e., the unrecorded counterclaim. In answer to a question about motivating the disputants, she wrote "after determining claimant was seeking other means to adopt three children, focused on monetary compromise." She wrote that the claimant was only a "little bit" creative because he had "willingness to negotiate but no recognition of obligation for services provided by lawyer. However, he did ignore 50% of [the claim]." The respondent, she wrote, was "very" creative because he "offered alternatives to continue adoption process. Offered $75—but when refused, immediately increased offer to $100."
>
> She thought the claimant had the greater psychological power: "Claimant was dominant in my opinion because he refused to acknowledge any obligation for services rendered or provide information about needed documents to continue process. Respondent humored him throughout mediation." She wrote that agreement was reached because "respondent wanted to maintain friendship." She herself felt the agreement was "a little unfair" because "Lawyer received $100 for 3 1/2 hrs service—plus many phone calls. Claimant refused to provide documentation needed to process adoption papers so the lawyer *could not* provide this service."
>
> The mediator who completed the questionnaire (the second mediator refused) said that her male co-mediator "zeroed in on need to resolve the money issue before I did—but I appreciated his insight and would like to work with him again." She did not mention which of the mediators was late, writing that the session lasted 40 minutes.

In terms of bargaining, this case shows an early concession by the Latino male claimant. He attributed this to his understanding that the respondent was going to resist, but the concession, in the eyes of the Anglo female mediator, was "immediate." This seems to be a case of a common perceptual bias (reactive evaluation) that occurs when an objectively positive offer is undervalued because of who made it (Thompson, Neale & Sinaceur 2004). To Anglo negotiators, such concessions were often an opportunity[3].

The Latino respondent reported his motivation as "emotional" but he came into the session with an unrecorded counterclaim that he strategically dropped. The mediator obviously found the respondent's counterclaim more legitimate than the claimant's original claim. The claimant mentioned the discourtesy of the late mediator at least twice in the interview, but the mediator never mentioned it and probably had no idea that it was such an important part of the claimant's experience.

After reading all of the records associated with this case, it seems fair to say the claimant was fundamentally arguing a consumer complaint; the work was not successful, and therefore the lawyer should not be paid. The fact that the mediator appeared oblivious to this, interpreting the claimant as stubborn, suggests that the claimant never directly criticized the respondent's professional competence, though it was eventually clear the claimant had taken his business elsewhere.

Patriarchal Family Status

The Latino family is, arguably (see Mirandé 1985), a patriarchal structure. The older Latino male claimant in the case below exemplified this tradition and the Latino respondent and mediators reveal the generational conflict noticeable in other disputes. This case was one of the few in which the outcome was *not* 50–50. The claimant was an older man pursuing a younger one who had divorced a woman in his family. The mediators did not, at the end of the session, ask the disputants for their cooperation in the study and they both refused the interview when contacted. Thus, the story is only told from the eyes of the mediators and the court records.

> *[M270] The claimant, an approximately 60 year old Latino man, claimed $545 for the balance owed on a vehicle purchased from him by the respondent, an approximately 30 yr. old Latino. In his answer, the respondent said he knows nothing about the vehicle and that the claimant was retaliating because he had divorced someone in the claimant's family. The two men settled in mediation for the full amount of the claim, without additional costs giving a calculated MOR of 1.0. Neither party was interviewed*

> Traditional Latino Family

> In describing the dispute, the Latino male mediator reported that "the claimant wanted to be paid for an unpaid bill from a broken marriage." He described the claimant as coming from an "old Spanish family; conservative/private—afraid to share information" and the respondent as "30ish, Spanish; more willing to be open." He described the claimant as "somewhat" willing to mediate, the respondent was "very" willing. The Latina mediator had the opposite impression, saying the respondent was "just here because he had to [be]." The male Latino mediator thought that the claimant had the greater psychological power and was most uncomfortable with the dispute. The Latina thought power was equal; "lots of determination, quiet but strong willed." The male mediator said that the parties were only "a little" hostile toward one another, but the

> Latina said they were "very" hostile, "angry but quiet." The Latina concluded "It seemed R. was decided beforehand to pay off the debt that he owed." The mediation session lasted 30 minutes.

The claimant in this example appears to embody the dignified performance of *Latino* men who have resisted acculturation. Note that the younger man, the more "open" and, implicitly, acculturated Latino, shows a resistant style more in keeping with *machismo*. However, although the younger Latino answered resistantly in the court records, he appeared to have bowed to the patriarch (from the Latina mediator's perspective, the decision was made beforehand). Mirandé argues that "authentic" *machismo* is a cultural style that embodies the female-protective (paternalistic) qualities of historical patriarchy. This case implies there might be a worthwhile distinction between elder, conservative patriarchal style and that of younger Latinos.

Latino Men and the Fifty-Fifty Fairness Norm

Another example of *machismo* or patriarchal status is one of the cases included in Figure 8.1 showing Latinas' late stage claim collapse with Latina respondents. The men were, in fact, not the listed principals in the case but actually determined the outcome between themselves. The named parties were two Latinas, claimant and respondent in an auto accident case. According to the interview, the respondent had been cited in the accident and was legally liable. While the two women spent the time of the session waiting in the mediation room with the two women mediators, the claimant's husband and the respondent's brother negotiated a settlement in the hall. The men discovered at mediation that they were acquainted with one another. The respondent in this case had a higher income than the claimant. The outcome negotiated by the men was for *both* women to apologize for their part in the accident, evoking again a 50–50 outcome structure. However, the monetary outcome was zero and the claimant was ambivalent about the outcome: "It was okay. . . . My husband was in charge. She (the respondent) offered me a job at the end [But] I really should have gotten something for my car."

Nonmonetary outcomes that responded directly to the claim were more frequent in Latino-Latino cases and were excluded from the bargaining analyses. The case below, however, shows how the 50–50 fairness rule operated in these cases as well. In addition, the interview with the respondent shows how a monetary focus was justified by economic need. The Latina mediator perceived the informal power of the wife, but the male mediator perceived the sophistication of the claimant in regard to contract.

[M306] The claimant was a 23 yr. old Latino claiming $625 for his furniture which was held by a 53 yr. old Latino respondent who was the uncle of the claimant. The claim states that R is demanding that C pay for storage. The respondent answered that the furniture would be released when the claimant paid back the $300 previously loaned by the R to the claimant. The parties settled in mediation: the claimant agreed to pay back the $300 and the respondent agreed to allow the claimant to collect his furniture. In monetary terms, the settlement was .520 for the claimant and .570 on the respondent's counterclaim.

Latino Family and Equality Norms

The claimant, a "resin handler," said he felt very powerful and in control during mediation. He said that money wasn't important; "money was not involved. I wanted my furniture back and they wanted $300 for rent and $225 for storing my furniture." The respondent said that money was "very" important; "I had just had surgery and I had to pay the doctor." He compromised his counterclaim; "I decided not to charge him storage, just the personal loan."

Both parties agreed that the claimant was in better control of the case. They agreed that the outcome was "much better" than expected. At the follow-up, the respondent said "If he [his nephew, the claimant] would have just talked to us we could have avoided the whole ordeal."

The Latino male mediator described the claimant as "average dress (very long hair), good grammar and knowledge of contract, male 23, Hispanic" and the respondents (a couple) as "average dress, good, male and female late 40's/early 50's, Hispanic." He wrote that the claimant was "somewhat" willing to mediate; "at first he stated that he thought court would be the place to resolve the conflict." When asked what motivational techniques he had used to encourage negotiation, this mediator wrote that his tactic was to "avoid litigation. They own the agreement. (It's theirs.)." He said that agreement was reached because "They solved the dispute on very 'contract' type grounds." Of his own satisfaction, the mediator wrote "The dispute was resolved, however, I believe that the parties lost out on a continued relationship."

The second mediator, a Latina, noted the fact that the respondents were the aunt and uncle of the claimant. She credited the aunt with the fact that the case reached resolution; "I give her most of the credit for settling this dispute. She was the catalyst between the two men . . . the key player. Also, the claimant was reasonable."

Gender in Latino Disputes

The following case demonstrates the defensive female rationality and the greater legitimacy women appeared to sense in disputes relating to the home. The case also suggests the role of the family as audience and social network in Latino bargaining[4].

> *[M057] The claimant was a 30 year old, lower class Latino (probably Nuevomexicano) man acting as an agent for landlords (who were his parents) claiming $1,464 from a former tenant for back rent, damages and interest. The respondents, a lower class Latino couple (perhaps Nuevomexicano), denied the claim. Both parties were represented but lawyers did not attend the mediation, conducted by two Anglo women, where they agreed to settle for $650 (MOR calculated at .444*

> Gender in Latino-Latino Dispute
>
> The claimant said that money was "somewhat" important but did not specify other issues. He said he compromised because "they had receipts we weren't aware of. Poor bookkeeping on our part" and because "something is better than nothing." About fairness, he said "It's a pretty fair method to take payments." The agreement was "pretty good." He said control over the case was "equal" because "both sides came in with points that were basically true. The other side couldn't disprove them." His feelings in the dispute didn't change: it was "something I had to do."
>
> The 29 year old wife in the couple was interviewed for the respondent. She expected contact with the claimant "until paid in full." Money was "very" important, but also "they were claiming there were damages to the apartment that wasn't there. It made me mad." She attributed the agreement to "the fact that we were able to talk to the owners face-to-face instead of their son who is the manager. In fact, it was the owners who came up with the lower amount." About fairness, the respondent said "I think mediation is a great way of settling." "I dreaded going to court so it worked out well." In response to the question about anger, she said she felt "bugged." She said she had more control over the case because "we were more prepared than they were." "They went in with no proof. They couldn't find receipts and their records were a mess." At the conclusion of the interview, she said "The way things were handled in mediation was great. The two women mediators did a great job. I was real pleased because at first I went in ready to fight. I had my notebook ready."

> The mediators also noted that the arrival of C.'s parents was critical; "C. was very slow, couldn't back up his claim, seemed confused and out of his depth. His parents came and made the difference." One of the Anglo women mediating described the parties as "very" willing to mediate because "the parents (owners of the apt) wanted it settled and the respondent made the first offer (had receipts, etc.)." Agreement was reached because "All were honest, friendly people who wanted to get along rather than win." She considered the agreement "very" fair because "tenants owed money, but landlord didn't have records. It could have gone either way. I felt their agreement was better than a court outcome would have been." The second mediator (a novice) wrote that agreement was reached because "they were all well-meaning people who saw the other side."

Inter-ethnic Disputes: Anglo Resistance, Opportunism and Reducing Expectation

Bargaining resistance (high demands, lack of reciprocity, and undermatching) usually resulted in a lack of agreement or leveraging later-stage concessions from a party intent on agreement. The case studies that follow illustrate how Anglo respondents resisted Latino claims, and how mediators worked to leverage concessions, thus showing the consequences of mediator training that did not acknowledge settlement pressure, leaving it necessary but veiled (see Chapter Three).

Anglo Resistance to Latino Claims

Anglo respondents grew significantly resistant to Latino claims during the mediation sessions. The following case study illustrates how this resistance was constructed in a neighborhood dispute as an intersection of respondent and mediator perceptions, especially by Anglo female mediators in the absence of clear structural status markers.

This case clearly shows the legitimacy dynamic in mediation through which discrimination clues became the basis of bargaining resistance. It suggests that Anglos were protected from Latino claims by a perception that a Latino claimant was not to be taken seriously. This case was chosen because, unlike many, the Latino claimant was higher class himself and clearly "had a good case," (i.e., held the power in terms of legal adequacy). The respondent constructed her legitimacy from her role as mother, a consistent basis for women's legitimacy in these cases. This case also illustrates the quality of endurance that female mediators appeared to bring to mediation, especially in private disputes.

[M173] The claimant was a 41 yr. old higher class, unrepresented Hispanic man claiming $1,426 in full restitution for items taken and damaged in vandalism act from the parents of two Anglo males in the neighborhood. The respondent-mother said her sons had returned the only item (radar detector) that they took. The disputants reached an agreement in mediation that the respondents would pay $450, some of which may have been a compensatory nonmonetary exchange, calculated as an MOR of .316.

Anglo Resistance to a Latino Claimant

A higher class Latino man filed against Anglo boys in the neighborhood for damaging his car and stealing a radar detector. The boys admitted to stealing the radar detector but denied they did "all" of the damage to the car. There were witnesses and a pending criminal charge was part of the negotiation process. The mediation lasted for a total of four hours and 15 minutes in two sessions with two Anglo women conducting the mediation. The Anglo mother (a psychologist who attended the first session) wrote a letter of complaint between the two sessions stating that the process was unfair to her sons.

According to the mediator questionnaires, the mediators saw the claimant as "unyielding" and "authoritarian-seeming." One mediator wrote "It was hard to empathize with this C. because he was so judgmental and accusatory." Perhaps especially after the respondents' mother complained, the mediators went to considerable lengths to make the Anglo boys feel powerful, establishing secret gestures (putting sunglasses on the table) that the boys could use to alert the mediators when they felt "overpowered" by the claimant. One mediator wrote, "[we caucused] several times, mostly to help the boys clarify what they wanted—and once to let the claimant vent." The other mediator wrote: "Without becoming advocates for the kids, we worked hard to let them participate as equals in the process." To encourage agreement "[we] reframed their statements to one another to show conciliation." One mediator noted that "there was also some issue concerning truth-telling between [the respondent] mom and her son." The second mediation session with the boys' father attending went better.

The respondent interview with the older son (18) was sparse. He said that threats by the claimant's son (who also attended mediation) was an additional issue beyond the money itself. He said that the caucuses were "not helpful" but didn't elaborate. He said that he agreed to pay approximately one third of the claim "because the claimant came down in his demand."

> The claimant agreed to settle for minimal cash (it is unclear how much of the settlement was actually a nonmonetary work exchange), and to drop the criminal charges, because "the boys acknowledged that they had learned their lesson and asked for forgiveness." The claimant was "disappointed because I expected the boys to come prepared with estimates for repair." In response to the question about anger, the claimant said he felt "resentment [because I] expected cost estimates." He was appreciative of the caucuses because "some items can't be said in the presence of the other party without heating up the issues." He said that he filed the claim because he was "very angry because their mother had been very adversarial." During the mediation "I was impressed with the attitude of the young men [and] didn't want them to have a court record so young." However, the respondents "never showed up on Saturday as planned and I had to track them down for payment."

The mediators in this case implied that the "boys" (aged 17 and 18) had not admitted fully their culpability in the vandalism, but the mediators were unable to challenge them, perhaps especially because they were defensive about the respondent-mother's allegation of bias against her sons. However, even subtracting for this defensiveness, it seemed that the mediators' interpretation of the claimant as "unyielding" and "authoritarian-seeming" contributed to an Anglo-protective bias. The mediators' painstaking work to coach the admitted vandals in conciliatory statements was successful in eliciting concessions from the Latino claimant. However, the beneficiaries, who avoided criminal prosecution, constructed themselves as victims in the interview and did not feel particularly positive about it. Note that the interviewed adolescent attributed agreement to the fact that the claimant conceded. The subtext of violence between the sons was not addressed and played no part in the way that the Anglo respondents explained their bargaining; however, the image fit conveniently well with a Latino male stereotype of threat.

Anglo resistance to giving Latino claimants money was implicit in their bargaining resistance, the likelihood of settlement for compensatory nonmonetary exchange, and was also expressed outright[5]. In the above case note that this resistance to paying money, which may have extended to a compensatory nonmonetary, began prior to mediation; the Anglo respondents did not attempt to assess their monetary obligation for an admitted theft before or during mediation. This stance is particularly notable when viewed in contrast to the opposite interethnic dyad; Anglo claimants defined their goals with Latino respondents as strictly monetary and virtually never substituted a nonmonetary exchange.

Discrimination Clues & Reduced Expectations

How did Latino male claimants come to reduce their expectations in mediation? The meaning of Latino male cases coded for strategy appeared to be largely based on the reasoning that something is better than nothing. The following case described a Latino claimant who was coded for both a sense of trickery and reported strategy.

> *[M209] the claimant was a 31 yr. old Latino male claiming $5,000 in bodily and vehicle damages after a traffic accident from a white North African respondent of similar age and class status. The respondent answered that a third vehicle caused the accident. Neither party was represented. The parties settled in mediation for $450 (covering medical bills to date) for an MOR of 0.090*
>
> Latino-White Men
>
> The Latino male claimant settled this traffic accident case in mediation for less than 10% of his claim. Both respondent and claimant were without liability insurance, the claimant was physically injured, his motorcycle was "totaled," and the respondent had left the scene of the accident. The mediated settlement amount was calculated to be a portion of his already incurred hospital bills, nothing for his motorcycle, nothing for lost wages, and nothing for future medical expenses. The interview with the claimant was coded for a sense of having been tricked ("I didn't get a fair shake") but his interview was also coded for the presence of strategic reasoning ("It was better than nothing").
>
> Both mediators (a Latino male and an Anglo female) expressed relative dissatisfaction with the mediation process but were instrumental, according to the claimant interview text, in convincing the claimant (during a caucus) that he didn't have the money or the legal power to win in court: according to the Anglo female mediator, the effect of the caucus was "C. decided to pursue medical costs only—instead of vehicle damage and [future] medical costs." According to the claimant, the settlement encouragement from the mediators was that "they spelled out what I was likely to get in court," and the effect of the caucus: "It helped me understand what would happen if I went to court."
>
> The mediator wrote that the white respondent had greater psychological power because he had "better education—more experience—R. from North Africa, world-wide traveler. C.—blue collar local Hispanic. . . . [the claimant was more uncomfortable with the dispute because he was] not able to express anger—needs. . . . He only saw that he was hurt—seemingly no conception of the whole situation—police cited R.

for leaving scene of accident but not for accident responsibility. Citation dismissed in court." She wrote that she motivated the parties toward agreement with the technique of "Caught and made C aware of R's 'hidden' change from his bottom line stance of 'I will give nothing, even though I feel sorry for the guy' to a willingness to pay part of C.'s medical costs." The Anglo female mediator wrote "I feel C. could have pushed for more money—he has future medicals . . ." She said she was able to remain neutral but "It was hard. . . . [I was] 'somewhat' dissatisfied with the outcome, not the process." The Latino mediator wrote nearly nothing except that he was "not at all" satisfied with the mediation process.

The irony in this case was apparent in others: the mediators might have felt the party received an unjust outcome but felt powerless to intervene; the mediators in essence blamed the disputant for not fighting harder. Also note the Latino mediator reported strong dissatisfaction but did not textually participate in reporting on the case and that the Anglo female mediator did not mention her co-mediator's participation in the session[6].

Overt Prejudice

Overt prejudice was rarely acknowledged by disputants or recognized by mediators although the effects were apparent in the outcomes. The following case is an exception to this pattern. The two Latino mediators, a woman and a man, reported themselves to be "very" satisfied by the mediation process and evaluated the outcome as "very" fair.

[M261] The claimant was a forty-one yr. old, unrepresented, middle class Hispanic man claiming $600 in repair costs for his parked vehicle that had been damaged by a truck belonging to the respondent, a higher class Anglo businessman. The respondent claimed that only the taillight was damaged and counter-claimed $1,999 in damages from the claimant for harassment. The parties settled in a 90 minute mediation session for $181 giving an MOR of .302.

Latino-Anglo Men

The claimant, a meatcutter, offered little unsolicited comment during the interview. He claimed that money was the "only" issue in the dispute and that the agreement was "a little" unfair: "I didn't get what I deserved." He reported being "somewhat satisfied" with the outcome in the initial and follow-up interviews and "very satisfied" with the process. The claimant thought that control over the case was "equal."

> He said that he changed his position because the respondent "was going bankrupt and was having financial distress" and thought the agreement was "OK. I felt sorry for him." At the follow-up he said that mediation "was fair and I liked the way it was handled. I just resent the loss I took on my truck." If he had to do his case over, the claimant said "I would have held out for more money. I jumped at not having to go to court."
>
> The respondent never mentioned any financial distress. He reported that money was "not at all" important in the dispute: "[It was] the principle of it. R felt like society owed something to him." He reported that he felt "very" powerful, in control, and that he, the respondent, had the most control over the case. The caucus was "helpful:" "That's when I let them know about this weasel's antics." Although he didn't mention his counterclaim, he maintained that he really owed the claimant none of the claim: "I paid $100 [sic] to get it over with so this goofball would stop bothering me." The agreement "sucked but this guy was one of society's losers." He didn't think that the mediators took sides; "on the surface they had to be fair until they heard my side." In the future, he would go to mediation again because 'it was safest, going to trial in America is a roll of the dice. Mediation is good. Our court system is bad.' In final comments in the follow-up interview he said "Your system is ok but the average man feels that society is in debt to him. We have to change this socialism by reeducating the educators."
>
> The college-educated Latino (age 35) and Latina (age 46) mediators described the claimant as a casually-dressed "working man" who was "mild-mannered yet persistent," "calm, rational, firm." The claimant "was willing to resolve 50–50." The mediators described the respondent as also casually dressed, "aggressive" and (the Latino mediator wrote) "could be perceived to be slightly prejudiced." Both mediators found the respondent more psychologically powerful than the claimant; "aggressive to the point of borderline overpowering," "much more aggressive, opinionated and intimidating." The Latino mediator wrote that during the caucus (requested by the respondent), the respondent made an offer "after suggestions and ideas were provided by the mediators." The case was resolved because "both wanted a resolution and to avoid court."

This case is an extreme example of Anglo male respondent exploitation of Latino male claimant collectivist bargaining because it is so overt. But the case reflects many of the patterns described in previous chapters.

Note that the mediators, despite recognizing prejudice and intimidation, were satisfied with the mediation process and outcome. In fact, in cases mediated by Latino mediators, higher Latino claimant concessions were not significantly different from those made by Anglo claimants (LaFree & Rack 1996). The procedural satisfaction reported by the claimant in this case was also a consistent pattern: Latino claimants reported significantly higher *process* satisfaction in mediation than either Anglo mediation claimants or Latino claimants in adjudication (Hermann et al. 1992).

Doing Anglo Woman: Resistance & Lack of Proof

As respondents, both Anglos with Latino claimants, and women with female and Latino claimants, appeared to get tougher during mediation than their initial bargaining positions might indicate. The following case shows some of these patterns.

Although this case was *not* included in the graph presented in Figure 8.1b, the bargaining pattern was similar: the Latino female claimant never lowered the amount she felt she was "really" owed, but at the end stage she dropped her full claim. Like the previous cases, respondent resistance appeared to prevail when the tough party was also higher status. Although Latina claimant cases were infrequent in the court, class status appeared especially critical to determining outcomes[7].

This case also shows the ambiguity of ethnicity. Because the respondent identified herself to the interviewer as Anglo, but was perceived by the mediators as Latina, it shows a particularly evocative portrait of how a woman chose not simply to "do gender" (West & Zimmerman 1991) but more specifically, to "do Anglo woman." She explained during the interview how this works.

> *[M008] The claimant was an unrepresented Latina claiming $190 in repair costs for a windshield she claims was broken by the respondent, an unrepresented Anglo woman who was her neighbor. She settled in mediation for no money, with an understanding that the parties would have no contact for the remaining time until the R completed her move to another residence. MOR calculated as 0.0 with only a minor nonmonetary.*
>
> Gender Resistance, Status & Rationality
>
> The claimant, a seamstress, said in the interview, "no one saw her break the window but they saw her throwing rocks on my porch then a few minutes later the windshield was broken and the rocks were in my car." The women were both in their early forties, divorced with

children. The violence followed a long dispute that the apartment manager had tried to mediate in which the self-identified Anglo female respondent complained repeatedly about the noise from the claimant's radio. In mediation, the claimant dropped all claims because "I didn't have proof. . . . [But] I didn't feel comfortable. People can go around breaking things . . . I felt like something could have been done." She said that the respondent had more control because she simply denied doing the damage: "she said she didn't break my windshield or bang in my door with a crowbar."

The respondent, a "research analyst in the library for [newspaper companies]" said that what was important to her was the fact that she didn't do it[8]. She described the claimant as "a volatile person, lashing out." She felt powerful and in control because "I just go in and expect the best. . . . I feel I was able to express myself better. That really counts in life, how you can express yourself, present yourself."

The mediators noted that the claimant was not happy with the outcome but that they "explained again that mediation did not mean she would get everything she wanted but that it would result in a compromise that each felt they could live with." The compromise that was constructed was that, since the respondent was "moving to a house," she would incur moving expenses which the mediators placed against the claimant's damages.

Interestingly, both mediators (Anglo women who appeared to have answered the questionnaires together) identified the respondent as "Spanish" but the respondent identified herself as Anglo, specifying "French, Irish, some Hispanic."

The respondent, like many Anglo female respondents, exemplifies a kind of tough bargaining that verges on withdrawal, basically denying all responsibility for the debt. Respondent denial of responsibility was phrased by higher status respondents, especially if they had or were lawyers, as not being "liable." This is an important distinction, since lower status parties appeared to be in pursuit of a justice based on guilt and innocence, not liability. In these mediated cases when the respondent resisted, rather than error being ascribed to the respondent, the terms of the argument appeared to shift toward blaming the Latino claimant for failing to have evidence.

Overall, failure to provide evidence was a common way of de-legitimating Latino claiming. The tactic appeared to be common. In its most extreme form, all pretense of liability was dropped. The Latino female claimant was convinced, by the police and the mediators, that her case would not hold up in court because she lacked "proof." As an earlier case suggested, middle status parties, perhaps especially women, and the other party in disputes with them, tended to emphasize "record-keeping." Both words (proof and record keeping) carry the same meaning of evidence. Higher status disputants collapsed these issues of evidence into "having a case" which usually meant a legal contract or bill of sale. Legally valid proof and record-keeping are assumed in the bureaucratic ordering of structurally advantaged parties. These are by far not the only cases in which lower status, especially minority, claimants were discouraged from pursuing court judgments for lack of proof. As one African American man said after dropping his claim in mediation because he had no evidence: "I didn't keep words. I didn't know I had a problem so I didn't have words."

WOMEN POACHING POWER: INSTRUMENTAL SYMPATHY AND MORAL LEGITIMACY

Of the 22.3% of the total collection actions in the MetroCourt sample that involved lower income respondents, more of the cases were brought to mediation than adjudication: 16.3% of adjudicated collection cases involved lower income respondents compared to 29.4% of mediated collection cases. Claimant gender was a highly relevant variable in these decisions.

Male collectors were less likely than female collectors to agree to mediate collection cases (Hermann et al. 1992) and their forum choice was not significantly related to respondent economic status. In contrast, female collectors, mostly Anglo women, were *not* more likely than men to file against lower income respondents in the overall dataset. However, they *were* especially likely to mediate such cases: only 6% of adjudicated collections filed by women involved low income respondents compared to 32% of female claimant collection cases that were mediated. Thus it is female collectors who were responsible for the somewhat higher frequency of collection actions brought to mediation against lower income respondents. The tendency for female claimants to agree to mediate collection cases extended to cases in which respondents admitted full liability, a situation in which male collectors often settled without third party intervention (Hermann et al. 1992).

Instrumental Sympathy and Gender

Male Collectors

As shown in the bargaining analysis, Latina respondents with Anglo male claimants tended to admit large portions of the debt, and the claimants often responded with gifting.

The claimant was a 42 yr. old Anglo male lawyer claiming $1,408 for unpaid hospital bills against a 43 yr. old, unrepresented, lower class Hispanic woman. In mediation, the claimant agreed to accept $500 if the amount was paid within 30 days resulting in an MOR of .356

Medical Collections-Male Claimant

The respondent had signed documents at the hospital for maternity expenses for her daughter who was under 18 years old and unmarried at the time of delivery. The father of the child, now married to her daughter, had accepted responsibility for the debt and both mother and new husband attended mediation, conducted by mixed ethnicity, mixed gender mediators. In the interview, the claimant explained his compromise as 'no sense in putting these people into bankruptcy . . . I thought it was fair, the financial situation of these people . . . ' He said that he had the most control over the case 'purely from a legal standpoint. I wanted to do something that was fair. The client's [the hospital] position was to do what was fair. If there had been a problem, we could have proceeded with the court case.' At the conclusion of the interview, he said 'I liked mediation, this was the first time. I would continue to use it.'

The respondent (the mother of the patient) explained in the interview that the debt 'was owed but I wasn't the real liable one . . . I signed the papers but I told them her boyfriend (now husband) was responsible.' In response to questions about the agreement and fairness, the respondent said 'we liked it.' "[F]or us, very fair and I don't know about them . . . the hospital suffers a loss." 'It's very important that it got settled.' On the process questions, the respondent said "I wasn't overpowering or anything." She said she was "a little bit" angry because her deceased husband was also named on the claim but "he [the claimant] apologized for that right away." She said that both parties had equal control over the case because "he understood me and I understood him." When asked for additional comments, the respondent offered "I was so glad to go to mediation, I don't know what I would have done going to court." 'When he [the claimant] said "one third of the bill," I just felt this big relief. [My son-in-law] too. A big weight off his back. He isn't one to try to avoid paying bills[9], but they are just starting out . . . sometimes you have to not pay some bills to pay another. It's not easy for young people to get started these days.'

In another case (M276) with an African American female respondent, the Anglo male attorney collecting for medical debt did not negotiate the amount, included court costs, and obtained a stipulated judgment which would have had the same coercive power and credit effects as an adjudicatory ruling. The gifts in this case were a lack of legal fees and a relatively generous payment plan: the stipulated judgment for the claimed $766 and court costs (MOR = 1.057) was to be paid over two years. During the interview, the claimant said that "to collect the money" was the important issue, explaining that he dropped legal fees and interest "to settle the matter and because of her [the respondent's] statement that she didn't have very much money." The agreement was "reasonable under the circumstances." At the end of the interview, the claimant commented, "In general, I think Metro Court is a quick way to handle disputes. However, in a case [like this], it is time consuming and costly for my client to go through such a lengthy process. In situations like this, creditors do not sue if the money is not owed." In response to the question about what was important besides money, the respondent said, "my name and reputation—I told them I couldn't pay before they performed the surgery." Concerning the agreement, she said, "I had no choice. I guess it was fair." In response to the fairness question, she said, "I guess they just expect you to pay no matter what." At the end of the interview, the respondent offered, "I was happy with it because it didn't have to go in front of a judge."

In both cases, Anglo male attorneys worked as collectors and, to a greater or lesser extent, compromised their probable court outcomes. There is no way of knowing from these data whether these men were working on a contingency basis, but it was unlikely in both cases. Thus, the men appeared to have the authority to negotiate the claims for their clients, without cost to themselves.

Female Collectors

Structurally dominant Anglo women who claimed in these data appeared to specifically construct an instrumental sympathy in mediation more comfortable to them, and perhaps to respondents. The Anglo women often observed mediation was a better way to do collecting; in the auxiliary coding discussed in chapters 4 and 8, one fifth (21.2%) of claimants reaching monetary agreements made statements that mediation was a preferred strategy for collecting. Most of these claimants were Anglo women, usually professional collectors but also landlords and attorneys in private collection actions. Of 24 claimants making statements that mediation was a preferred collection forum, 11 (45.8%) were also coded for sympathetic statements.

Thus it is fair to say that Anglo female claimants in structurally dominant roles chose mediation to pursue monetary goals with lower income respondents. These women found a way to do collecting while doing gender. That is, they combined what Gilligan (1982) has termed an ethic of care with instrumental motives.

However, instrumental sympathy was more likely if the respondent was female compared to male respondents. As indicated in Table 8.2, male claimants extended sympathy toward male respondents about half as often as female claimants did. Not only in interview statements, but in substantive negotiations, male respondents were less often recipients of gifts in negotiations guided by instrumental sympathy.

Gender Effects with Latino Respondents

These two cases are matched for status relationships on all dimensions except the respondents' gender. The excuses offered by the two respondents are also gendered, though there are other cases in which Latino male respondents where abandoned by women, without any evidence that this excuse increased their legitimacy.

> *[M265] Claimant was a 40 yr. old Anglo female lawyer claiming $3,466 for unpaid medical bills from a lower class, unrepresented, 42 yr. old Hispanic woman. The respondent admitted the debt in her answer but said she only made enough money to get by day-to-day. The agreement in mediation, conducted by two minority, mixed gender mediators, was to leave the case pending (coded as an additional nonmonetary agreement).*
>
> Medical Collections-Female Claimant
>
> In the interview the claimant said "we did not agree on any amount. We are going to look at this case later when she gets on her feet." Explaining her motivation to compromise in mediation, the claimant said "on behalf of the hospital, we are giving her time to get on her feet. I think this is a wonderful way to help people get through bad credit times without ruining their whole credit history." Although the claimant said she was "very much" in control, she said that control over the case was "equal" because "this was not an adversarial situation." At the conclusion of the interview, the claimant said "the mediation service is just great. Most of the people served with a suit are scared to death. This process enables people to talk to us without going to court. Helps the hospital communicate with people."
>
> In the interview, the respondent said "the hospital is willing to wait until I can get on my feet. I really appreciate them letting me pay later." The agreement was "very fair to me," control over the case was

"equal" because "I do owe the money but they were very understanding." At the conclusion of the interview, the respondent offered, "mediation makes owing money alot easier, let's you talk to the people and work out a deal." She said she was "very" satisfied with the procedure and, in the follow-up interview, said she would change "nothing" if she had to do it over.

The Latino male mediator described the respondent as "desperate:" "R was unable to make payments because of unemployment, husband left. It was a mess." He wrote that "the attorney for [the hospital] was very kind and understanding, so it was more like she (the lawyer), [the female co-mediator] and I were trying to help the R. find options to her problem. R. was not even aware of the kinds of aid available to someone with her financial problems."

In contrast to the above case in which the claimant agreed to wait to pursue the case against the Latina respondent (coded as a nonmonetary outcome and thus excluded from the bargaining analysis), the Anglo female lawyer in another medical collection case (M277) drove a harder bargain against the Latino *male* respondent, probably under the influence of her client, the hospital collecting agency.

[M277] Claimant was a 37 yr. old Anglo female lawyer claiming $1,656 for unpaid medical bills from a 25 yr. old lower income, unrepresented, Hispanic male, who admitted the debt. The agreement in mediation, conducted by two female minority mediators was for the full amount to give an MOR of 1.000 with along term payment plan. Within days of the mediation, the claimant demanded a steeper payment schedule.

In contrast to abandonment by a husband as in the case above, he based his poverty defense on a demotion and costs for rehabilitation for a drug problem. In this case, the agreement signed by the parties was for the full amount without additional monies for court costs, legal fees, or interest (MOR = 1.0). As suggested in Figure 9.1a, the claimant did not mention being "really owed" the usual additional adjudicatory charges. In the interview she said she had the most control because "the respondent admitted to the debt." At the end of the interview, the claimant offered, "Mediation is wonderful. It has been tremendous. It would be nice if we could go directly to mediation without first having to go to the judge to ask for the case to be referred to mediation[10]."

However, the payment plan negotiated during mediation was rescinded after the session. The respondent said "I knew I owed the money . . . really it was my fault, but they [initially] agreed to payments and then didn't agree." The respondent explained the original payment plan involved small monthly payments but the claimant had since specified a much steeper pay plan that would complete payment within six months. The respondent said the claimant had "all the reasons" to be in control; "I owed the money. I needed the time to pay." When asked how powerful he felt during the mediation, this respondent said he felt "very" powerful, noting, "I knew I should keep quiet."

Gender Effects with Anglo Respondents

I have specifically limited my examples to medical debt collection for ease of comparison, because these cases were so frequent, and because the construction of sympathetic instrumentality in mediation takes place in the larger context of an irrational blame[11]. However, two non-medical collection cases offered a serendipitous view of how gifts moved more easily to female respondents than to men. The claimant in both cases was the same Anglo woman. She had filed very similar complaints against an unrelated man and woman that were settled in separate mediation sessions.

Though this claimant was an example of what Carnevale & Pruitt discussed as an insecure representative who tended to be a more firm negotiator than her employers demanded, I also present these cases to show the more subtle status aspects of Anglo gender relations in bargaining motivation. The claimant blamed the Anglo male respondent for being a failure, repeatedly saying "he probably shouldn't be in the business" as a realtor. The Anglo female respondent was constructed as a victim with hurt feelings. Thus, the cases demonstrate the expressive dimension of instrumental sympathy, its gendered quality, and the unconscious nature of the pattern.

It is likely that mediator gender also contributed to the construction of these outcomes. Pruitt & Carnevale (1993:60) cited research showing that male compared to female audiences, (which can be analogous to mediators), affected negotiations by increasing contention and decreasing concessions.

[M117 & M119] The claimant was the same 47 yr. old higher class Anglo woman claiming $788/$407 respectively for delinquent homeowner association fees. Both respondents were lower class, unrepresented and Anglo. In mediation, the claimant settled for $456 in the first case giving a calculated MOR of .579. In the second, she settled for $287 calculated as an MOR of .705. The respondent and both

mediators in the first case were women. In the second, the respondent and both mediators were male.

Respondent Gender in Collections

During the interview, the claimant noted the similarity in the two cases filed against two otherwise unrelated former owners who had moved. She was seeking association fees, including their pro-rated portion of the utility charges, for the time after they had moved but before they were able to sell their condos. In mediation with the female respondent, conducted by two women, the claimant agreed to drop the utility charges because "after all, she didn't even live there at the time." The claimants said "the mediators shared that [the respondent] felt no one had understood her over the years. They showed me that the respondent needed to have her situation recognized, needed verbal reassurance from me." She said that she had made prior arrangements with the Board of Directors to drop the utility charges for her "bottom line."

The 68 yr. old respondent in this case said during the interview "They are a large company with alot of money, and if I had gone to court I would have got the wrong end of the stick. . . . I'm glad its over." The two women, claimant and respondent, went to lunch after mediation. The respondent paid the check.

In the other case (M119), the respondent had bought the condo as an investment. According to the claimant, he had rented it at a loss (less than he needed to pay the mortgage). The bank foreclosed on his mortgage. The disputants compared notes about the actual foreclosure date which was earlier than the claimant had calculated, so the real debt was less. This reduction was the only concession the claimant made.

During the interview, the claimant said in response to the fairness question: "Maybe unfair to him. He really had the same situation as the other respondent where he was charged for utilities and didn't live there. I didn't drop it in his case. . . . I'm the representative of other people's money." The claimant said she "felt powerful because no one else knew what was going on, including the respondent." She said the agreement was "Fine. I'm surprised he agreed to it." She said she had control over the case: "he came in overalls, said he was pulling nails out of boards. . . . he rented the condo for less than he needed—he's had a hard time. . . . it wasn't my money. . . . he seemed defeated as it was. He probably shouldn't be in real estate . . . as a realtor, I had less sympathy till I saw him. . . . He probably shouldn't be in the business."

The claimant overstated the amount of her original claim by 20% early in the interview (an otherwise unlikely event for Anglo female

> claimants, see Figure 9.1a). Later she said she "hated to add to his hard times but it wasn't my place to make a deal." Asked if her feelings had changed from the beginning to the end of the case, the claimant said "I had more empathy but I guess the answer would be no because I didn't change my position."
>
> This respondent said "I hoped she wouldn't show but then I found out that it wouldn't matter and I understood it was hopeless to pursue it. It would cost me more." He was glad to have arranged a payment plan in mediation; "I didn't want another judgment against me. But it really wouldn't matter. She didn't do anything to me, she was just doing her job."
>
> Both respondents had paid in full by the time of the follow-up interview and all parties said they would not change anything about the way they handled their cases went if they had to do it over.

These cases show the use of a lack of agency as a bargaining tactic but also suggest the more profound influence of structural role on Anglo women's bargaining. The claimant continued to explain her decisions, almost reflexively, as carried out for the sake of her employers, "the association." But in this situation, unlike the Anglo female lawyer collecting for the hospital described above, it was clear that the agent was empowered to negotiate more flexibly. Thus, as Kolb (1994) suggested, her explanation can be instrumentally considered a negotiation tactic rather than an actual lack of agency.

The second case also demonstrates Anglo men's acceptance of female claiming when in structural roles or internal status overcoming gender distrust leading to resentment: she was "just doing her job."

Finally, the Anglo women's responses in both cases with male respondents describe an apparently unconscious bias against male respondents who appear incompetent in their gender roles: the male respondents may receive a distanced sympathy, but they do not earn substantive consideration.

Invoking Moral Legitimacy: Anglo Female Claimants Without Structural Role

Anglo women were particularly likely to pursue cases to intervention against higher class Anglo men (see Chapter Four) and achieved their highest outcomes in cases with Latino male respondents. I argue that the mediation forum empowered Anglo women to pursue material goals at least in part because Anglo women could frame their claiming in less threatening ways, thus deflecting backlash effects.

However, approximately half the Anglo female claimants who settled in mediation were *not* in structurally dominant roles though they frequently reported strategic rationales for their bargaining (see Chapter Eight). The following cases show how lower status Anglo women succeeded in achieving higher outcomes in private roles. The first two cases also show a pattern suggesting the gendered gift-giving of Anglo disputants in cases with one another; the third shows a cross-ethnic, cross-gender dispute. All three cases show how lower status Anglo women constructed moral legitimacy for themselves in claiming money from men.

Anglo Women with Anglo Men: Case #1

> *[M167] The claimant was a 25 yr. old, low income Anglo woman claiming $400 refund for her deposit on a used car purchased and then returned to the respondent's used car lot. The respondent answered that the car was sold "as is" and that the claimant owed a $200 payment on the sales contract. The parties settled in mediation for the full claim without court costs, a calculated MOR of 1.0*
>
> Anglo female consumer #1
>
> The claimant, a clerical worker and student, said that she filed the claim because "I felt the car lot did me over and I was concerned that that would happen to someone else." She said she "felt a little nervous at first because I didn't know what was going on and what mediation was all about." She was "very" satisfied with the outcome, procedure and remained very satisfied at the time of the follow-up. She said that control over the case was "equal—we were both working with each other and neither tried to be stronger than the other." She said that "mediation was a good factor in settling this dispute" and would change "nothing" about the way she handled it.
>
> The respondent, owner of the used car lot, said that though he felt he really owed "none" of the money claimed, he "agreed to pay what she asked for [because it was] the difference between business and morals. She didn't do my business no harm. I felt good about the decision that I made. She treated me with respect, and hadn't hassled me and I appreciate that." He said "I just felt bad for the girl from the beginning. She was a student, and a single mother." He also said that control was "equal because nobody tried to gain control—after the mediators made their initial statement, we both felt better and knew we could try to work it out." He said that the agreement was "very" fair, explaining "it depends on whether you're looking at it from a business or a moral standpoint."

The Anglo male mediator (age 59, graduate education) described the claimant as attractive, articulate and well-dressed and the respondent as "casual dress, one day's growth, 40 years old, aggressive, talkative, articulate." He wrote that the respondent had greater psychological power because "he was older—knowledgeable—and felt he could be generous with a young person." The mediator said that "the respondent was rather verbose and I interrupted his dialogue to ask him to make an offer to settle." He attributed settlement to "R. was wanting to help out a young person."

The Latina co-mediator (age 41, graduate education) wrote that the claimant was "quite well dressed . . . wasn't terribly articulate. She just wanted her money back." She also thought the respondent had more psychological power in the dispute "He was more self-assured, he spoke more easily," the claimant was more uncomfortable "she was unsure of herself, spoke haltingly." In her final comments, the mediator wrote "The used car salesman tried to come off as a nice guy for returning her money, but he in the meantime had resold the car. Legally, I'm unsure what effect, if any, this has on her contractual obligation. They are both on rather shaky ground. I'm glad it worked out the way it did."

Anglo Women with Anglo Men: Case #2

[M283] The claimant was a 39 yr. old unrepresented Anglo woman claiming $1,098 for breach of implied warranty on repairs to her Volkswagen engine. The respondent, an Anglo male owner of the auto repair shop, answered that there was no breach of warranty. The parties settled in mediation for $475 giving a calculated MOR of .433

Anglo female consumer #2

The claimant, who apparently brought her husband or significant other to mediation, said she reduced her demand because "to compromise was an important goal . . . [I took] less [because] the next step would have been court and I didn't feel it was necessary." In answer to the fairness question, she explained that "Luke said compromise is important." She reported maximal satisfaction, commenting "It was very satisfying to meet with someone face to face and work out differences—I didn't really want to win, just talk things over." In the follow-up interview she said "I think going to court would have been a real pain . . . I thought it was very efficient and the people were very helpful." Asked what she would do differently if she had it to do over, she voiced a single regret: "I wish I would have asked him to pay the filing fees."

The 57 yr. old respondent said that he really owed "none" of the claim but "I paid the $475 just to get it over with. Legally they had no point, morally they did." Money "is always important when you are in a business" but he thought the agreement was "very" fair because "legally they had no claim but I felt morally that I had an obligation to them." He reported maximal satisfaction, commenting "It was a very satisfying experience. Everybody left with a much better taste in their mouths than if they had gone to court." In the follow-up, the respondent said that if he were to do it over, "I wouldn't have paid so much." Still, "Mediation is 1,000 times better than court. It should be the wave of the future."

The two Latino mediators had little comment on the 35 minute mediation. The claimant was described as "proper" and "middle class" and the respondent was described as a businessman with "business-like" attire. The relatively less educated Latino (age 30 with some college education) wrote that he thought the respondent had more psychological power, but the other (age 27 with graduate education) thought power was equal. The second mediator thought the respondent was more uncomfortable with the dispute because "business—no time to be away." The agreement was fair because "strong compromising w/both parties" and agreement was reached because both parties "came in with cooperative attitudes." Overall, it was "a good case for mediation."

Anglo Woman with a Latino Man: Ethgender Status Extremes

Of the 11 cases involving Anglo female claimants with Latino male respondents diagrammed in Figure 9.1a, casetypes and admitted liability had normal distribution for Anglo-Latino disputes. The exception is that if Anglo female landlords filed a claim against a male tenant, it was more likely to be against a minority male tenant. A statistical pattern of higher outcomes in these cases appeared to reflect higher cash expectations. For example, a great-aunt by marriage filed against her Latino nephew for a debt that he apparently owed and agreed to pay in full (M302). But in the interview, the lower class Anglo woman regretted the payment plan she had granted her nephew ("I should have been firmer. I need more money per month"). An Anglo businesswoman settled for immediate payment of her total claim from an Ethiopian businessman (M195), but in the interview expressed dissatisfaction because she had not asked for court costs saying "I was too nice."

The following example describes a somewhat extreme case for female power. The Anglo woman (she brought her husband, but she was clearly the central party) claimed in her role as a mother with an injured daughter. It was also extreme in its outcomes, because the settlement amount actually exceeded the jurisdictional limits of the court (more than $5,000) and was more than double the amount of the original claim. The complexity of ethnicity and gender was also extreme (though not as rare) because the mediators were an Anglo man and a Latina woman. Thus all four ethgenders are represented in the mediation session.

> *[M178] The claimant, a 35 yr. old, lower income and unrepresented Anglo woman filed for $2,600 in damages resulting from a hit and run accident that injured her 15 yr. old daughter. The owner of the truck, a Spanish-only speaking 49 yr. old Mexican man answered that a neighbor had borrowed his truck and he thinks the man might have returned to Mexico. In 1.5 hours of mediation, without bilingual mediators but using the respondent's 11 yr. old daughter to translate, the parties settled for $5,400 to be paid as $100 per month for 54 months. MOR was calculated as 2.077. As of March 1996, only $500 remained to be paid on the agreement*
>
> Anglo woman-Latino man
>
> The claimant and respondent brought their daughters, the Anglo daughter the victim and the Latina daughter of the respondent who served as the translator. The respondent immediately conceded in mediation, though he never, in mediation nor during the interview, said that he was driving the car. The claimant raised her claim more than 100%, arguing that the hospital bills were higher than when she originally filed. The respondent agreed to everything. In the interview, the claimant, a cashier, said that money was not important, she was more concerned with her "daughter's health and getting my car fixed so I can go to work" (coded as material goal). The extra amount was because "we got my daughter's medical bills." The outcome was "much better than expected." In the follow-up interview she said she would change "nothing." She added the comment: "A friend of mine had her car hit . . . driver took off. . . . my friend caught him, he had no insurance . . . she took him to court and has not received any money for damage. I feel mediation works better than the court system."
>
> The respondent, an insulation installer, said that money was the "only" important thing, and that only "part" was really owed. He said he changed position because of "the language barrier. I didn't have a

choice; it happened that the truck was mine." The outcome was "much worse" than expected. He didn't feel understood at all because "they didn't speak Spanish." The agreement was "somewhat" fair; "I didn't have a choice." He reiterated in the interview that "my word is my bond." In the follow-up he said he was only "a little" satisfied "because I still have to pay her." If he were to do it over? "I don't know, perhaps get a really good lawyer."

The Anglo male mediator described the claimant as "mad, fearful for daughter's future health resulting from accident, casual clothes, clear about what she wanted, Caucasian/Anglo" and her daughter as "15, quiet." The claimant's husband, who also attended the mediation was wearing "work clothes, really angry/verbal, cooperative" and "a little" willing to mediate, "but [he] didn't have to since R agreed." The mediator described the respondent as "emphatic about his willingness to pay and 'his word is his bond.'" This mediator noted that the claimant had threatened the respondent with other legal actions and explained the respondent's eagerness to settle as "My guess—he felt he had more to lose." He implied that reciprocity was accomplished when he evaluated the psychological power as "equal" between the disputants and his explanation of why agreement was reached: "R immediately accepted responsibility and said he would pay. He then agreed to pay larger amount. C. [was] willing to take risk that payments will continue for 54 months." He did not mention the respondent's daughter as attending the mediation, only appending a note: "One party did not speak English. All were patient about explanation."

The second mediator, a 43 yr. old Latina (less educated but reporting a higher income than the Anglo male mediator) described the claimant as "casual clothes, 35–40, female, got her point across" but didn't mention the claimant's husband or daughter. She described the respondent as "Mexican male, about 45, very casually dressed. Daughter, about 11 years old, shy. Both were limited in expression. Daughter was helpful in interpreting some." She evaluated the claimant as having greater psychological power "because they were able to express themselves better and had a valid claim." She thought the respondent was most uncomfortable with the dispute because he was "at a disadvantage because of the crime committed."

Both mediators wrote about the caucus that they convened with one another: The Latina wrote "[Anglo male mediator's first name] and I discussed whether we felt it was a just settlement. We agreed and continued." The Anglo male mediator wrote "Mediators held a brief conf. to check out fairness of agreement. I was comfortable about agreement."

This case provides a wealth of information about the status ranking in mediation. The Anglo woman was "clear about what she wanted" and "got her point across." She was primary to all observers. The ranking in these data is Anglo woman, Anglo man, Latina woman, Latino male.

Latino men, by mean and multivariate analyses by ethgenders (LaFree & Rack 1996), achieved the lowest outcomes in mediation. This respondent was further handicapped by a language barrier and an unacculturated moral code that could only be interpreted as self-interest by the Anglo man, and shame by the Latina. We don't know, but have no reason to doubt that the respondent was *not* the driver of the vehicle. Nor do we know if the claimant's medical bills were paid by insurance. We don't know the respondent's immigration status. We do know that elements combined in this case to result in one of the most extreme monetary outcomes in the MetroCourt data, though removing the case as an outlier does not affect any of the results. Follow-up interviews and the mediation center confirmed regular payments up to the last time I checked in 1996.

Summary

Case studies show the way outcomes were constructed through the facilitated negotiation process in mediation. The interactive process helps in understanding how cultural, structural, individual and environmental influences combined.

Apparently soft bargaining was often leveraged by mediators and exploited by opportunistic parties into greater concessions. The appearance of soft bargaining often resulted from equality fairness norms invisible to others, especially Anglo mediators, because the initial concessions were elicited rapidly from Latino male disputants who anticipated resistance and their value reactively discounted. The mediation process itself seemed to suggest to Latino bargainers that the equality norm was appropriate.

Patriarchal and generational status hierarchies were relevant bases for invoking legitimacy in intra-Latino disputes. These hierarchies often became decisive for outcome distributions, but were regularly contested, even if only in the record or interview, by the lower status party.

Mediators, especially Anglos, tended to leverage concessions from the weaker party defined by class and legal status. Latinos may have had nearly opposite assumptions about the legitimacy bases for consideration. Generally, Latino bargainers seemed to use equality norms and family status first for deciding outcome distribution, with secondary bases such as moral claims to justice as guilt/innocence (which could be maneuvered into record-keeping) or need (including defense of children). The Latina claimants who settled in favor of higher class parties resented the class bias and only agreed, it seemed, because mediators convinced them that their cases lacked legal adequacy. Mediator influence was critical in these intra-Latino disputes, and the cases here demonstrate the process through which mediators bestowed symbolic power on higher class Latinos and Anglos. Less acculturated, lower class disputants accepted mediator bias as authoritative. Thus mediators, often unknowingly, translated immediate status deference toward *mediators themselves* into outcomes following their own biases. Latino negotiators appeared to accept market-defined equity rules only when in the respondent role of debtors or other "shameful" positions.

If class and structural status are analogous to "input," then Latino bargaining fits the rationalized description of collectivistic "generous allocators" (Leung & Iwakwaki 1988): without mediator influence, higher input/status bargainers used equality distribution norms but lower input/status bargainers agreed to equity rules.

Women, regardless of ethnicity, used highly gendered legitimatizing strategies to stalk and snare power in the negotiation process. Protection of home and defense of children, abandonment by men and hurt feelings, an air of sympathy and/or cooperation in the interests of their employers, and better house and record-keeping were some of the more common approaches. Except for Anglo women with one another, these strategies worked best with men. All these strategies aroused a moral sense critical to conflict and justice narratives (Wilson 1993; Cobb 1994; Mather & Yngvesson 1980/81). Anglo women were noteworthy for their ability to translate their claims into dilemmas which men perceived, or at least articulated, as questions pitting profit against morality.

Chapter Eleven

Summary of MetroCourt Findings

At the start of this book about the data in the MetroCourt Project, I asked: is everyone equally capable and equally situated to negotiate resolutions to their public disputes? Are some people, by virtue of their socialization, more likely to choose cooperation in the mediation situation? Does the ethgender of the other party make a difference? Did their structural role determine their behavior? What does the MetroCourt data say about ethnic and gender relations? Along the way I became intrigued with what choices the different ethgenders made when faced with the power and privilege to give and to take.

I've used several theoretical frameworks to analyze the data, searching for patterns in an admittedly complex situation. Any real-world environment would be equally complex, but the MetroCourt Project offered several specific elements that helped structure the study and the findings. First, the cases all concerned monetary claims, offering a way to quantify process and outcomes. Second, New Mexico's long-established Anglo and Latino populations provided a well-balanced sampling of both cultural groups. I believe this dichotomy is valid, despite the diversity of Latinos in Bernalillo County.

What follows is a summary of findings from the MetroCourt Project. I refer the reader to earlier relevant chapters for more extensive discussions.

STRUCTURE, CULTURE AND CHOICE

Overall, in contrast to adjudication, where structural and correlated pleading factors largely explained outcomes, mediation outcomes were influenced by ethnic socialization, interpreted both as soft bargaining and a tendency to exploit it, by disputants and mediators alike. These were largely equal to structural effects in adjudication. Furthermore, in mediation individual choices influenced by ethgender socialization modified structural patterns.

Cases at the Metropolitan Court reflected the stratification patterns in the State of New Mexico, the United States, and internationally: class, gender, and ethnicity correlated strongly with achieved categories. In adjudication, as shown in Table 6.1, status relationships in ascribed categories of ethnicity, gender and class, contributed 6% to the explanation of outcomes, pleading differences accounted for an additional 12%, and structural status relationships accounted for 22%. In adjudication, ethnic, gender and class categories were subsumed into structural advantages (legal and corporate status) that completely "explained" the ascriptively-based discrepancies in outcomes: corporate and legal representation, more likely for Anglo and higher class litigants, were the significant predictors of adjudication outcome. Thus, for adjudication, structural sociological models including pleading differences were able to explain nearly one third of the outcome variance in formally adjudicated small claims cases. Furthermore, considering all filed claims at the court, nearly two thirds of the small claims filed (all those receiving formal judgments, see Figure 3.1) were likely to have outcomes with enhanced proportions predicted by structural factors because default and voluntary judgments depend exclusively on the pleadings. These pleadings, in turn, related strongly to structural positions (see Chapter Four).

In mediation, by contrast, ascribed status relationships, specifically ethnicity, exerted a definitive influence on outcome. In fact, cultural factors appeared to explain a similar proportion of mediated outcomes (20%) as structural roles had predicted in adjudication (22%). Ethnicity alone predicted 20% of the outcomes, pleading differences predicted an additional 28%, and structural role relationships predicted only an additional 4%.

The analyses in this work have shown that ethnically disparate outcomes were largely the result of bargaining differences consistent with theories of ethnic but *not* stereotypical gender socialization, facilitated by Anglo and female mediators' differential support for higher status parties. The bargaining and related analyses indicated that Latino claimants, especially men, negotiated under the influence of a different value structure than Anglos. Latino claimants valued nonmaterial goals, showed reduced self-maximization strategies, displayed other-vigilance, relied on equality norms, and demonstrated greater trust by continued concession in the face of bargaining resistance. This difference is consistent with the paradigm of collectivism as an internalized Latino cultural pattern. If the relevant Anglo cultural pattern includes individually self-maximizing motives and opportunism, the corresponding Anglo exploitation of soft bargainers would explain virtually all the variance associated with ethnic status. Latino co-mediators apparently influenced *all* claimants away from privileged, self-maximizing outcomes resulting in similar outcomes for both Anglo and Latino claimants.

Legal representation was not a significant predictor of mediation outcomes; therefore structural status had a diminished influence on mediated outcomes. Although legal representation was a structural advantage in the rational choice negotiation model as the court alternative, structural position did not operate in a classically maximizing way: claimants who were most advantaged in adjudication, i.e., corporate lawyers, settled for significantly reduced outcomes in mediation with lower status respondents. Higher structural status disputants were clearly aware of their court alternatives, often refusing to mediate at all and refusing agreement as corporate respondents. However, higher structural claimants, specifically Anglo women, more often mediated cases with lower income respondents who were likely to be "judgment proof" (see Chapter Three and Four) in a strategy I have called instrumental sympathy.

This pattern was apparently due to claimant choices based on sentiment and strategy interacting in the HILO condition with respondents' "weaker power" (Janeway 1980). These claimant choices were rational, discretionary, were reported as self-maximizing, and were clearly related to the structural relationship between claimants and respondents (legal and corporate). Using structural models, the explanation further reflects that choosing mediation and making bargaining concessions was significantly related to the class status of the respondent. This demonstrates the influence of weaker power, that, as Janeway described it, is the power to give or withdraw the recognition of legitimacy required by dominant parties. In small claims court, these tokens of legitimacy had a material focus in the form of payment plan negotiations and compliance.

Although a structural model reducing behavioral differences to social role might account for the outcomes in HILO cases specifically coded for these dimensions, it could not explain the fact that Anglo female claimants and not others were more likely to make these choices (see Chapter Four, Chapter Ten, and Hermann et al. 1992). Similarly, individual choice models would be hard pressed to explain the systematic patterning of these choices by gender and structural roles. Thus, the concept of "role equivalence" does not apply here, and gender theories conceptualizing women as less advantaged or actors with less agency could not explain this pattern without structural theories. The behavior of higher structural status claimants in the HILO condition in mediated cases appeared to be an instance of individual action modifying role behavior, patterned and perhaps impelled by Anglo female socialization toward other-concern.

Compared to ethnicity and gender, the corporate status dimension had greater similarity in the way it influenced outcomes in both fora. As predicted by Black's model of the social structure of the case, reduced outcomes for individuals (usually consumers or tenants) filing against corporate respondents (businesses and landlords) were apparent in both adjudication and mediation. Without legal representation, corporate parties showed no consistent strategy of concession-making in mediation, although interpersonal factors, especially within the Anglo-to-Anglo dyad, were apparent in some consumer cases (see Chapter Ten). More often than in other cases, corporate respondents settled for nonmonetary outcomes or were unable to reach agreement (see Appendix Tables 4.i and 4.ii). The lack of settlement, judging from respondent interview text, clearly related to knowledge of probable court dismissal due to prior containment of legal liability. By comparison to these corporate advantages, outcomes were diminished for claimants when both parties lacked corporate status[1]. Thus, primarily because the adjudication alternative constrained mediated outcomes, corporate status relationships defined outcomes similarly in both fora and across conditions.

EQUALLY CAPABLE AND EQUALLY SITUATED?

At the outset of the MetroCourt Project, we intended to explore differences first suggested by conflict and feminist critiques of mediation. We found predicted outcome discrepancies for Latino claimants before the first word of the report was written (Hermann et al. 1992). But we could not easily identify the reasons for these discrepancies in mediation cases, because, after all, mediation was a consensual process and the disputants chose to settle. The court system presented mediation as a voluntary procedure to disputants. In theory and practice, disputants were free to refuse the mediation alternative and, if mediating, they were free to leave without an agreement. But only half of the disputants in randomly assigned mediation cases refused mediation, and only one third of these left mediation without an agreement. This agreement rate is amazingly consistent across myriad studies in multiple situations (Lowry 1991; Wall 1990).

Were the disputants in these cases equally situated and equally capable in the negotiation process? I used four questions to address this central concern: 1) Were Latinos and women more vulnerable to contextual influence and/or specifically vulnerable to the ideology of mediation? 2) Were Latinos and women more willing to concede due to internalized values scholars identify as collectivist or relational? 3) Did disputants experience themselves as making rationally self-interested bargaining choices? 4) Were bargainers vulnerable to nonmaterial motivations then substantively disadvantaged due to exploitation by the other party? I will address these questions in order.

Context Sensitivity and Message Vulnerability

Chapter Five analyzed reported goals to clarify context sensitivity and vulnerability to the message of the mediation forum. Anglo men and legally represented parties appeared to be relatively unaffected by the mediation environment. But, compared to adjudication, the mediation forum affected the reported goal orientation of both women and Latino claimants. Latino claimants with Latino respondents in the LOLO insider condition reported strict monetary definitions of their goals *less* often after mediation than similar claimants after adjudication; both Anglo women and Latinas reported goals *more* often monetary and material.

These data supported theoretical formulations proposing that collectivistic Latino and women are particularly sensitive to environmental and contextual influences, but different messages affected the two groups. The reported goal structure of Latino claimants with Latino respondents largely conformed to mediation ideology emphasizing cooperation and relationality; the reported goal structure of women, especially Anglo women, more closely approximated Anglo men and the negotiation paradigm stressing strategic bargaining for material interests. The greater likelihood of professional and higher class Anglo women appearing in mediation, two status categories who consistently emphasized monetary goals, confounds supporting data here.

Participants' Bargaining Behavior: Goals, Concessions, Rationales, and Evaluations

With their heightened response to the mediation environment, women and Latinos made specific bargaining choices. I assessed these choices in light of alternatives and outcomes (Chapter Six) as bargaining behavior (Chapter Seven), reported motivation (Chapter Eight), and outcome evaluations (Chapter Nine).

For Anglo women, the outcomes from negotiation relative to court alternatives were improved. Women were notably resistant to concession-making during mediation, especially as respondents, and they presented their motivations as highly rational. For Anglo women, I interpreted this highly-accented rationality as forum defensiveness, that is, the harmony ideology of mediation aroused a defensive response in women. Anglo women gave calculated rationales for bargaining decisions, appeared highly distrustful of male claimants, and were consistently discriminating in their evaluations of their outcomes. Anglo women, but not Latinas, accurately reported evaluations on a win-lose and inherently competitive monetary measure. Interestingly, disputants more often reported strategic motivations for bargaining decisions after mediation sessions conducted by female co-mediators.

For Latino disputants, concessions in mediation were less readily defined as variations on the rational choice model because their final monetary outcomes were diminished. Compared to Anglos, Latino claimants reported goals less often monetary and motivations less often strategically self-maximizing. Compared to Anglos and consistent with cultural explanations, Latino bargaining choices suggested that they held greater concern for the other party's outcomes. Latino claimant bargaining and outcomes clustered around an equality rather than the equity distribution norm that characterized Anglo expectations and outcomes. Latino male claimants accurately perceived and evaluated reduced monetary outcomes, but the reference standard was apparently lower. Alternative dispute values, including distaste for court, other-vigilance and equality distribution norms, and perhaps the affiliation and other-face needs associated with collectivistic cultures, played an *adjacent* role in their bargaining, but these nonmaterial goals did not subsume or overwhelm monetary goals. Latina claimants, on the other hand, more particularisticly bargained, conceding in different phases depending on the other party, and apparently evaluated outcomes in light of these interactional distinctions.

Agency and Rational Choice

The most overt examples of disputant agency and choice were the "refusal choice" not to mediate at all or to refuse agreement in mediation. In cases reaching agreement, I developed a measure for the subjective experience of choice from interview text showing that the negotiator did *not* experience themselves as making choices: they felt coerced, exploited, tricked or otherwise non-consenting to what seemed like an unjust outcome. I defined instrumentally rational choices by comparison to adjudication outcomes in comparable cases, the rational bargaining limit for negotiators.

The refusal choice was illustrated in forum frequencies, NAR cases, and many of the subsequent agreement cases (see Appendix Table 4.i and Rack 1997). Using this indicator, legally represented claimants more often chose against the mediation alternative (Hermann et al. 1992), and dyads composed of individual claimants with business respondents, or male claimants with female respondents, showed a significant likelihood of refusing agreement (NAR). In addition, cases with Latino male claimants and Anglo female respondents appeared to have used a combination of refusal to mediate and lack of agreement so that these cases were significantly infrequent in the mediated monetary outcome sample[2].

In all of these situations, the refusal choice can be easily understood as rationally self-interested because these disputants were likely to achieve better monetary outcomes in adjudication than mediation. Legally represented claimants routinely achieved higher awards in court, the cases against corporate respondents were routinely dismissed, and outcomes for Latino claimants and cases against Anglo female respondents were higher in adjudication than mediation.

One quarter of the claimant interviews recorded a sense of injustice. Claimants who articulated this were often those who had bargained without the rational bargaining limits provided by knowledge of alternatives. Although these claimants had indeed agreed to diminished outcomes in comparison to higher status claimants who rarely suffered from a sense of injustice, and the variable was significant in the multivariate model, it did not alter any of the outcome patterns found for ethnic or corporate status relationships. Thus, Latino and noncorporate (individual) claimants who received reduced outcomes did not consistently report a sense of being exploited.

Trends were contradictory among respondents, so a sense of exploitation had no statistical relationship with outcomes. Lower status respondents in the HILO condition who agreed to pay most, especially Latino respondents with Anglo claimants, were specifically unlikely to report a sense of coercion; but higher status respondents who paid less appeared to feel exploited more often. Notably, the tendency to have felt tricked without apparent material basis was most common for Anglo female respondents, who settled at a significant advantage, and for respondents generally in cross-gender disputes. Consistent with the increased contention between negotiators of relatively equal status reported by Pruitt & Carnevale, the sense of injustice for individual noncorporate respondents in the LOLO structural status dyads, like claimants, was related to the lack of a meaningful grasp on probable alternatives and/or the status-related costs of pursuing the dispute.

Because the perception of exploitation was not statistically related to respondent outcome disadvantage and, for claimants, did not explain the disparate outcome pattern for any of the status conditions, the vulnerability to feeling exploited appeared to refer to a *rights-consciousness* that was ultimately more psychological than material. This psychological injustice represented the greatest threat to assumptions of voluntariness (agency and choice) and was concentrated in cases that settled without the guidance and claiming support provided by structural roles. Lower structural status parties, perhaps especially in cross-gender disputes, who had neither clear awareness of probable court outcomes *nor* the advantage of paid participation in the dispute, were likely to have felt they made agreements in mediation against their own interests. Thus, these cases challenged the assumption of negotiation theory that negotiators make informed choices *and* also reflected differences in disputant situations. Private cases, often assumed to be likely candidates for mediation, were the most vulnerable to psychological injustice.

Latino parties, who were often in private disputes, appeared to report a sense of exploitation based on a lack of bargaining reciprocity. A Latino landlord clearly articulated the panic of bargaining without limits in the face of a non-reciprocating partner when the Latina tenant-respondent (M129) resisted reciprocal bargaining:

> I gave away the store. I said she didn't have to pay me for cleaning and damages. I wanted to compromise. I thought they would give some. I just kept going on and on and I thought they would be willing to compromise. They say there are no losers but I was a loser. One side gives and the other is supposed to give. The more I thought about it, the worse I felt. The lady was lying blatantly. She continued to do this and the mediators allowed it.

Substantive Exploitation of Cultural and Ethnic Difference

Perceived exploitation related to gender and structural status, but substantive exploitation strongly related to ethnicity. The cases showed the material bases of inter-ethnic relationships.

Cases with Latino claimants showed one pattern. The analyses presented in chapters 7 and 9 as well as some of the case studies in Chapter Ten showed the way Latino claimant concession-making was substantively exploited during the mediation session, especially and significantly by Anglo and male respondents. Anglo male respondents[3] bargained differentially with Latino claimants, developing resistances during mediation not apparent in premediation positioning or with an Anglo claimant. These Anglo men tended to report antipathy toward the claimants, sometimes overt prejudice. They were more likely to report a lack of liability for Latino claims, but the case studies showed little legal adequacy in these arguments. Consequently, their denial of liability seemed to be strategic opportunism. Adjudicated outcomes in comparable cases were higher and, in more than one instance, Latino claimants had considerable case documentation. The mediation forum itself, with mediators seeking agreement and encouraging Latino claimants to believe that their court alternatives were poor, often because they had no "proof," appeared to collude in protecting Anglo male respondents.

The cash-specificity of Anglo resistance was apparent in the negotiation process and the outcomes that were constructed, including the non-monetary outcome cases that were excluded from the bargaining analysis (see Chapter Ten). By contrast, cases with Anglo claimants showed the opposite pattern. With Latino respondents (the HILO condition) these cases tended to be monetarily defined from start to finish. Anglo claimants strategically raised their initial demands to maintain similar bargaining distances with Anglo and Latino respondents, but the Latino respondents had admitted greater liability and conceded rapidly during the mediation session. This echoed the quick concessions of Latino claimants.

Anglos maintained an ethnic boundary relatively impermeable to reciprocal cash flow: they resisted giving cash to Latino claimants and resisted accepting anything *but* cash from Latino respondents.

Intersections and Interactions

My analysis necessarily examined the intersections of structural status with ethnicity and gender, and ethgender interactions in the dispute dyad. This section reviews some of the more important findings that complicated ethnic and gender analyses.

Status Intersections

Structural and dispute roles affected the agreement to mediate, the court alternatives, the bargaining processes, and the outcomes. However, I found little evidence that the class dimension exerted an independent influence on outcomes in either forum outside of the correlated structural roles in adjudication, or of ethnicity in mediation. Nevertheless, class was critical to attitudes and influenced ethgender patterns. Class status appeared to have a more pronounced effect on women. Between Latinas, relative class position was apparently the major determining influence in mediation; with Anglo women it strongly shaped bargaining patterns. As the most reliable indicator of acculturation, higher class allowed more acculturated Latino disputants who knew "how to present themselves" (see Chapter Ten) to sway mediators' perceptions of their legitimacy. Compared to the same ethgenders of lower class, higher class Anglo claimants reported more focused monetary goals and instrumental strategies in cases with lower class respondents. In contrast, higher class Latino claimants *less often* reported monetary goals and instrumental strategies in a similar situation.

Status Definers: Anglo Men

Using the analytic focus in this work, the self-presentation of Anglo men corresponds to the schema and possible stereotype of their social-structural status. Anglo men seemed comfortable in higher status roles, believed themselves deserving of privileged outcomes (see Chapter Nine), and felt competent to negotiate outcomes "just about as expected." Anglo men were the least affected by the mediation forum, possibly because Anglo male socialization accounts for the model and strategies of negotiation enacted in Anglo jurisprudence.

When Anglo men negotiated for themselves in mediation in dominant dispute roles or with higher structural status partners, they were courteous and apparently fair when calculating their positions. Neither Anglo male claimants nor adjudicated outcomes showed ethnic discrimination patterns not better expressed as institutionalized biases. As Thibault, Walker & Allen (1972) found with French male law students, explicit rules constrained "irrational" bias. Thus, higher status Anglo male patterns reflect the ideal of Liberal philosophical and political traditions that stress equal and "color blind" opportunity.

Anglo men were more actively competitive and opportunistic when the situation or a person threatened their privilege or the structure supporting it. For example, Anglo men reported a negative reaction to the resistance of Anglo female respondents, but made willing agreements with Anglo and Latina women who were corporate debt collectors. On average, Anglo male respondents were the only respondent ethgender to comply more frequently with adjudicated rulings than mediated agreements (Hermann et al. 1992). This also suggests a pattern of commitment to structural privilege. In the dependent role of respondent, Anglo men were the primary contributors to ethnic, not gender, negotiation outcome disparities.

In general, Anglo men were comfortably committed to structural privilege, but resentful and competitive with gender and ethnic challenges.

Women's Status Deference

Anglo women with higher class, corporate and professional status showed statistical pattern of deference to their structural roles. This schema included disputing patterns of defensive rationality, and, especially, instrumental sympathy. Similarly, female mediators' influence favored parties with higher structural status: the pattern of reduced outcomes found in Latino claimant cases (LaFree & Rack 1996) were part of a consistent reduction of lower *structural* status claimant outcomes. This apparent deference to structural status has implications for gender identity studies more generally.

Defensive rationality is a speculative concept that links a relational psychology to rational choice bargaining in the context of mediation culture. Based on multiple analyses, women in this study used a kind of hyper-rational explanation of their bargaining stance. This evidence includes the qualitative sense derived from reading the cases. Even with instrumental sympathy, consistent with Pruitt & Carnevale's (1993) "insecure representative," Anglo women in dominant roles were likely to present themselves as "good" agents who made maximizing decisions for cash and material goals. Organizational researchers (Eagly & Johnson 1990) found a possibly parallel pattern for female leadership styles: female managers did *not* have gender stereotypical interpersonal styles but rather were as task-oriented as men. Interestingly, disputants reported strategic and maximizing bargaining rationales more often after mediation conducted by two women.

The Anglo female schema presented no certain relationship to either self-service or self-sacrifice. On the one hand, role deference combined with a cooperative image is consistent with multiple studies reviewed in Chapter Seven and the strategy for avoiding backlash discussed in Chapter Nine, where interpersonal styles of cooperation and sympathy could be presented as a mask for self-interest. On the other hand, Anglo women's status deference could provide a role-defended and therefore safe outlet for the expression of empathy. An Anglo male mediator observed that a professional Anglo female disputant was "clearly raised in the western civilization (maybe midwest) model—able to empathize but didn't feel responsible for [the claimant]." But this pattern could also be interpreted as easily in the opposite way: maybe she was even more obdurate in refusing responsibility for the other party *because* she empathized and felt related and responsible, but still wanted to maintain a conflict stance. The latter interpretation suggests women had to justify their choices against internalized patriarchal injunctions to operate in rationally goal-oriented ways.

With rational explanations overlaying relational *and* self-interested motivations, the bargaining for Anglo women had important and probably unintended consequences. Stated succinctly, the evidence suggested that the relational pattern observed for Anglo female claimants resulted in preferential treatment for other Anglo women. Anglo women did not discriminate *against* men and Latino disputants, but their substantive bargaining followed a relational conflict resolution psychology that tended to include greater "other-concern" for negotiators similar to themselves, i.e., other Anglo women. From positions of power, Anglo women were gracious and generous, showing similar "insider" dynamics to those scholars associate with collectivists[4].

Latinas often reported a preference for judicial decision-making[5]—that is, a choice not to decide. This can be considered a culturally distinct variant of Tyler's (1994; see also Sarat 1993) argument that many litigants seek the dignity of court procedure and intervenors of higher stature. Although Tyler maintains that such respect for legal process crosses ethnic, gender and class lines, the Latina cases seem to show a unique respect for law and authoritative decision. This respect is consistent with cultural theory and research suggesting many collectivist cultures also have a higher acceptance and respect for hierarchical relationships than Anglo culture. In addition, Latinas' reliance on court decision-making may reflect the patriarchal influence that arguably orders traditional Latino cultures (Orozco 1990; Segura 1990; Mirandé 1985; Barrera 1979; Blea 1992; Hinshaw & Forbes 1993).

Although the Anglo women presented themselves as legally innocent in mediation, it is also plausible that Anglo female respondents' lack of enthusiasm for mediation similarly reflected a preference for judicial decision-making. Anglo female respondents were the only respondent ethgender to evaluate their adjudicated outcomes more highly than mediated ones, despite far better monetary outcomes in mediation. I combined this pattern with a lack of correlation between monetary outcome and the women's evaluations and concluded that Anglo female respondents derived some expressive gains from the adjudicatory procedure, perhaps especially with male claimants. In another expression of preference for higher status intervenors, Anglo women in this study clearly preferred male mediators. This interpretation is also consistent with Leung & Lind's (1986) scenario-based study showing that female college students in the United States preferred adversarial procedures when the non-adversarial alternative featured a low-status investigator.

Thus it is possible to interpret the evidence for both types of strategic resistance (innocence and court preference) as coming from a similar source. Anglo cultural patterns include a need to appear autonomous and self-referencing: perhaps Anglo women were unwilling to *articulate* their resistance as a preference for judicial decision-making. Note also that Anglo women tend to hold higher ethical standards in business (Franke, Crown & Spake 1997) and were able, at least in some cases, to inspire Anglo men to negotiate in a *moral* framework—perhaps the possible adjudication preference implicit in these data is based on seeking moral judgment.

These data showed one consistent pattern: women often justified resistance through commitments to others. Kolb (1994) noted similar patterns from anecdotal reports in her own narrative-based research: women appeared to negotiate more firmly if they were bargaining for someone else's interests rather than their own (see also Zur 1989).

Status Intersections for Latino Disputants

For Latino disputants, class and higher structural status had nearly opposite patterns, especially for men. Compared to Anglos and lower class Latinos claimants, higher status Latino claimants reported themselves less strategically goal directed and less interested in money. It was as if material self-interest was *less* justified when Latino disputants were *not* poor.

Latinos are culturally defined as much by Catholicism as familism (see Chapter Five and also Rodriguez 1994). At the turn of the twentieth century, Weber attributed the "spirit of capitalism," especially its acquisitiveness, to Protestant (Calvinist) cultural influence as opposed to Catholicism. He noted that Catholics in the early 20th century remained "traditional," content with living rather than striving, while Protestants more often took it as their "calling" to amass greater material power than they needed. These data and links in other research (Vila 1996; Kritzer, Bogart & Vidmar 1991) suggest Weber's religious distinction remains relevant.

Rubel (1962) offers another interpretation for Mexican-American modesty. Based on his fieldwork in a southwest Mexican American community, Rubel describes an ethos that fears material success because it would arouse *invidia,* the envy and hostility of their neighbors. Written four decades ago, Rubel cites parables and statements he heard frequently that would not be uncommon today.

Ethgender Insiders and Outsiders

These data suggested an insider bargaining dynamic associated with collectivist cultures in various ways, but not in monetary outcomes. Latino parties were likely to concede earlier with Latino than Anglo respondents, a pattern associated with higher other-concern; the analysis of reported goals (Chapter Five) showed more frequent materialistic goals with outsiders than insiders and bargaining rationales with insiders were often emotional and sympathetic without hostility. However, in contradiction to insider theories, neither Latino claimants nor respondents appeared to significantly alter their bargaining positions in relation to the ethnicity of the other party. This is consistent with research results reviewed by Pruitt & Carnevale that problem-solving negotiations with outsiders more often reflected the same pattern established within the group.

Similarly, Latinos' generous allocation pattern showed no insider bias. Latino disputants agreed to outcomes allowing higher status negotiators greater proportions, an equity distribution, but used equality as the basis of their own rewards. This is the distribution pattern associated with generous allocators (see Chapter Nine and Leung & Iwakwaki 1988) but *without* insider bias. In contrast, as discussed above, Anglo women showed a clear expression of insider bargaining with other Anglo women.

Overall, little evidence emerged that Latino disputants of either gender resisted concessions across an ethnic boundary. In contrast, there was considerable evidence that Anglo disputants of both genders did. However, *gender* boundaries *within* ethnic groups were often consciously antagonistic on both sides, and defensively maintained.

Chapter Twelve

Implications & Future Directions

IMPLICATIONS FOR JUSTICE AND THEORY

Court-annexed mediation creates the dilemma of negotiating justice because negotiation and justice operate on different principles. Justice is a moral demand with equality at its core: something is just, theorists say, because it would appear fair from any position, from any perspective. Negotiation assumes self-interest, trusting in the power of Smith's invisible hand to optimize both rewards and fairness. Unsurprisingly, many people resist negotiation processes for resource allocation decisions. Tyler & Blader (2004:298) ask the question: Why have principles of distributive justice not received more attention in negotiation contexts? They offer this answer:

> Because negotiations are typically viewed as a market transaction, in which the role of social factors is minimized. Markets are highly prized by economists as situations in which the forces of supply and demand operate more or less unrestricted by societal norms. As such, they are not an arena in which we might think of issues of social justice as being key factors shaping people's judgments and behaviors. In negotiation settings, people typically believe it is acceptable to exploit dependence and power differences. Those possessing desirable or needed resources feel justified in extracting concessions from their less powerful negotiating partner. But in the real world, the general public often regards such behavior as inappropriate.

Court-annexed mediation leaves allocation decisions in the hands of disputants, substituting consent for legal decision-making.

This analysis specified where the contradictions between negotiation consent and justice would most likely occur: in cross-gender disputes, in non-reciprocal bargaining with Latino claimants, and with disputants lacking knowledge of alternatives. In all these situations, the mediation environment presented conflicting messages of justice and fairness that are the nexus of consent-coercion implicit in negotiated justice. In this study, bargaining resistance and soft bargaining, as well as the perceived coercion coded from lower structural status parties' interviews, appeared to have roots in these conflicts.

Negotiation & Justice

The psychological injustice revealed in the interview text and the economic injustice revealed in the monetary outcomes challenged assumptions of consensus-based mediation. The interest-based negotiation process and the mediators' influence (often unexamined, unintended, or lacking altogether) involved many possibilities for betrayals of justice. These data support legal feminist scholars who have perceived a gender-specific psychological danger, but do not support expectations of substantive gender injustice in mediation[1]. Latino disputants rather than Anglo women manifested bargaining patterns implying their socialization was substantively exploited by more dominant parties.

Women appeared to be more dominant in mediation than they were in adjudication but, in nonprofessional roles, were likely to undervalue their outcomes. The complex picture of female negotiation included strategic use of a more caring persona, not lack of choice-making. Social science documents that women report themselves to be less materialistic than men, and are often perceived this way (see Chapter Five and Seven). From this self-image, they constructed a maximizing defense more often than generous action. The overall pattern for Anglo women suggested an underlying role conflict similar to that found in women's moral dilemmas reported by Gilligan (1982): women were defended against their own relational "ethic of care" by their role commitments and fears of exploitation. Although it rarely appears in women's self-presentation or in feminist theory, female bargaining control by resistance appeared to be an embedded defense, perhaps developed as informal power over the millennia of patriarchal control.

In her study of white women's racial and cultural identity, Frankenburg (1993:228) argues that "culture is [best] viewed as constructing daily practices and worldviews in complex relations with material life." She writes that the normative nature of Anglo culture provides a rationalized social behavior that makes material domination both possible and invisible. In the micro situations of mediation, it appears likely that Anglo women's psycho-cultural skill in "poaching power" combined with market-based equity assumptions for status rewards. This combination facilitated a power evasion with an enhanced impact on Latinos. A similar connection between "neutrality" and Anglo female mediators' status deference resulted in ethnically disparate outcomes. Wise (1998) examined the decisive role of white women's vote in the rollback of affirmative action California's 1996 Proposition 209 interpreting it through a combination of not wanting to admit the role of affirmative action played in women's changed status and protecting "their" white men's privilege. Interestingly, Wise points out that electoral strategies to win the white female vote based on *self-interest* had backfired: white women would have been more readily moved by appeals to their sense of justice.

Latino men held adjacent, perhaps bi-cultural, awareness of their instrumental and expressive negotiation processes, but the data suggested that the combination of mediation culture and ethnic prejudice led them to bargain outside their limits. Even when they had convincingly positive adjudication alternatives, they began a disastrous downhill slide with early concessions that targeted the equality fairness norm, then, in the cases that settled, they lost even more due to mediator blindness and respondent resistance that leveraged greater concessions. On the other hand, without the fateful early concessions, Latinas arrived at a similar outcome when they reached monetary agreements, and through similar means. Mediator influence appeared to be critical in these cases of Latina respondent resistance. As described elsewhere (LaFree & Rack 1996), Anglo and female mediators were able to influence these cases toward settlement with tactics that often took the form of altering disputant perceptions of their alternatives, especially by challenging Latinas on the issue of evidence (see Chapter Ten).

Most clearly for Latino men, but also for Latinas, monetary and non-monetary values represented different, or adjacent, continuums. Unlike the Anglo claimant who often explained the principle and the money were synonymous, Latino disputants did not seem to collapse all dispute values into the metaphor of money.

In terms of economic justice, these data raise important and politically treacherous questions for social science investigators generally and mediation scholars in particular. Higher status claimants most often sought money and appeared to get it; Latino claimants less often claimed a goal of money and they did not receive it. Do these outcomes reflect only an exploitation of the trade-offs inherent in the interest-based model? Or, as discussed in Chapter Five, are there also rationally justifiable nonmaterial interests that are projected on to, and expressed by non-dominant groups?

Culture & Justice

A more telling measure of justice for Latino disputants is *reciprocity*. Indeed, Gouldner (1960) argued that the essential definition of exploitation *is* a lack of reciprocity. Oyserman, Coon & Kemmelmeier (2002) review studies finding that Hindus (a collectivist group), but not Americans, viewed reciprocating help as a moral obligation. Hui (1988) points out that collectivist cultural patterns are best understood in terms of reciprocity: giving is not done as a personal sacrifice, but with the understanding others will give in return. Latino disputants expected matched reciprocity, and often experienced the procedure as balanced and fair due to the matched "talking" time, even though it did not conclude with a balanced outcome. We simply cannot know, from *post hoc* cross-sectional data, to what degree their interview responses stressing less material goals, reduced monetary expectations, and positive evaluations based on procedural reciprocity were emic styles of *sympátia* (easy-going friendliness) and/or compensations for the challenges to negotiating competence detailed in the bargaining analyses. Nor do we know the degree to which Latinos responded to interviewers with a face saving presentation of self[2]. We *do* know Anglo disputants in the same uncertain and challenged situations were *less* likely to voice nonmaterial goals and unstrategic identities, and were *more* likely to express antipathy and instrumentally competitive motivation.

If reciprocity was the underlying justice value for Latinos, opportunism seemed to be the central fall-back position for Anglos. As the quotes in the beginning of this chapter pointed out, this invitation to exploit power is embedded in the western negotiation model and thus would be readily available in the framing of the process for Anglo negotiators. Without higher status structural roles, Anglos often presented themselves as innocent or cheated, but appeared to have little cultural support for seeing generosity as anything other than foolish. The Anglo culture of competitive individualism and lower acceptance of authority left Anglos with identities that assumed competence for negotiating their own outcomes, but without any real basis for rational decision-making and evaluation. In effect, mediation appeared to challenge Anglos who lacked structural roles to use a negotiation model for which they were culturally prepared to be self-maximizing when they did not know what the maximum was.

I suggested (see Chapter Two and Five) that progressive social scientists may be blinded by the Marxian ethic that imposes a consistent analytic focus toward *economic* value at the expense of *cultural* value. Dominant group scholarship may misrepresent Latino and female resistance, both conscious and unconscious, by perceiving and thereby constructing resistance as static, traditional, residual, and failing to achieve, or as rationally self-interested and strategic (but also losing). Group loyalty intended as justice-seeking is commonly diverted toward—and often judiciously resolved by—the materialist metric. In this picture, economic injustice is perceived as the only grievance and monetary compensation the only remedy: poor people just want more money. But perhaps *defense,* not material desire or envy, has a more profound effect on the attitudes and actions of outsider groups.

Perhaps the deeper contest is not "relative deprivation," one that implies that satisfaction is to be achieved through having more, but is a cultural argument against the game itself: *against* striving so hard and *against* exploiting every opportunity. Weber & Messick (2004) discuss the "might vs. morality" effect in which pro-social negotiators (cooperators) framed the cooperation-competition choice as a *moral* decision but pro-self (competitors) framed the same choice in terms of *power.* Pro-self negotiators saw cooperation as *weak* and unintelligent; pro-social saw competition as *wrong* and unintelligent. In a "loss frame" in which the game is set up as an attempt to minimize loss, pro-social subjects were more likely to cooperate and pro-self subjects more likely to compete more strenuously. Over time, with consistent exploitation, pro-social negotiators *became* competitive, resulting in misperception of reactive/defensive competition by observers who don't have a grasp on the antecedents.

Over the past century, and especially the past two decades of a winner-take-all economic restructuring, the game has grown less visible, more normalized, and ever more vicious in the penalties exacted against those who opt out: "losers" are responsible for their own exploitation. In addition to increased competition by cooperators with experience of becoming a sucker, Latino and female negotiators might see another contradiction between two aspects of group loyalty: on the one hand, a member is loyal by seeking distributional justice for one's group; on the other, a member is loyal by maintaining *less* materialistic values. Contradictions of this type are likely to consistently produce incongruence in expressed identity (Burke 1991). These manifestations may well appear to others, and even to the individual and group, as "situational" or episodic but grow from deep ambivalence about which loyalty to honor.

I don't argue that competition and relative deprivation do not exist in the cultural periphery, but rather that an equally valid perception exists. The schematic contest can be more accurately characterized as between the *value* of the materialist striving associated with dominant culture achievement ("success" in the core) and alternative social goals often relegated to the "other" world: the private sphere of home, relationship, family and community. A century ago, social scholarship saw the problem more clearly than we do today, although recent African American intellectual discourse has dared to name it (e.g., West 1994; Dalton 1995) as central to our current social emergency. Abalos (2002:56–57) calls for radical transformation:

> It is not enough to break with European American male domination: Latino men need to experience a deeper breaking. They need to empty their souls of the archetypal story of capitalism . . . that gave mysterious power to their white or brown bosses . . . [the bosses] are not the enemy; they are also victims of a story that destroys their humanity when people become obsessed with greed and power.

If we say that we lose important values in striving, if we say we don't want *more,* must we imply we choose to have *less?* Such a question becomes a societal query: how much economic inequality can we tolerate, given its proven destructiveness for social relations and democracy (for review, see Pizzigati 2004)? The question ought to concern those who answer the charge of global inequality with recommendations for economic development. And this question troubles all of us who seek greater social justice for the same reason it affects the image and identity expression of Latinos and women. Without clarifying the value and social costs of pursuing material goals, the contest remains obscure.

Overall, by avoiding the relatively simple equation proffered a century ago by Weber—that the dominant culture schema is primarily characterized by materialistic striving—we evade a critical justice questions at the turn of the millennium. Dominant values impose an "entirely transcendental and absolutely irrational" (Weber 1958:53) way of life:

> The peculiarity of this philosophy of avarice appears to be the ideal of the honest man of recognized credit, and above all the idea of a duty of the individual toward increase of his capital, which is assumed as an end in itself.

MEDIATION POLICY & PRACTICE

There is no absolute reason that economic justice must be traded for nonmaterial goals. Both Latino and Anglo disputants evaluated their outcomes more highly and reported greater satisfaction (including fairness) with mediated justice than court rulings. This was particularly true with respondents and disputants who settled subsequently or settled with nonmonetary outcomes[3]. In the following sections, I discuss the implications for negotiated justice based on the ideal that economic (distributive), psychological (procedural), *and* cultural justice is the goal.

Procedural Discrimination

According to Lempert & Monsma (1994) in their Hawaiian Housing Board study, bias in an informal setting cannot be called legal discrimination because there is no apparent conscious intent. They offer the term "cultural discrimination" to capture the set of dominant culture assumptions about legitimate claiming and excuses that resulted in ethnically divergent pardoning. In Bernalillo County small claims cases, where disputants themselves made decisions, assumptions inherent to the interest-based mediation model enabled discrimination.

I call this pattern procedural discrimination. In the MetroCourt data, the culture-boundedness of U.S. mediation procedures is clearest in the analyses of strategy. The bargaining variable coded to indicate strategically self-interested motivation was able to "explain" virtually all of the ethnic disparity in outcome. Although this mathematical explanation cannot be considered conclusive because many other indicators statistically linked to Anglo-Latino claimant differences might have similar effects, the bargaining patterns show that Anglo claimants limited their concession-making in ways Latino claimants did not[4]. Strategic reasoning seems a good descriptor to generalize how this happened.

A clear sense of limits, derived from comparison with alternatives, is a pre-requisite for Anglo-defined, rational negotiations. I have identified intertwined loci in negotiated justice where procedural discrimination became explicit: the variable knowledge of court alternatives, fairness as reciprocity vs. legitimated opportunism, and the inability of the mediation model to address bargaining inequities. This discussion logically extends to policy issues in mediation.

Poor Alternatives

Although court outcomes are critical to understanding the workings of court-annexed mediation, most critics of mediation ignore the fact that the alternative to mediation is not a good one for lower status claimants and, especially, respondents. In terms borrowed from "principled negotiations," this is the problem of poor BATNAs. Adjudicated civil outcomes showed the ordering that Black described as the "ubiquitous" status discrimination in criminal justice systems. The class-based (see Table 6.1) and ultimately rationalized structural bias in favor of lawyers and corporations in adjudication *is* the BATNA in court-annexed mediation, the referential alternative.

When disputants understood the way structural bias operated, as they most often did in the structural HILO condition, mediation appeared to function well. In monetary and psychological terms, the settlements in the structural HILO condition appeared to further justice: poor respondents knowingly made agreements in mediation to pay less than court rulings would probably have required. Judging from the interview responses from lower class respondents in the HILO condition in this study, the mediation process probably did have the effect of building the legitimacy of the more powerful claimants. The intent and probable effect of mediating collection cases was actually to further economic imbalance through increased compliance by poor respondents[5]. Thus, "gifting" in HILO mediated cases was beneficial to dominant claimants through economic and social returns.

Nevertheless, HILO cases appeared as the most obvious example of win-win outcomes to the disputants. There was little evidence in these cases that the "victims" did not perceive themselves as winners. But these cases are and should be unsettling to mediators. In a paper delivered in 1996 concerning this conundrum, we (Rack, Barnes-Anderson & Margolin 1996) proposed that mediators design a specific form of case settlement in HILO cases that could enhance respondent's strategic awareness of their "weaker power" and require that collectors agree before mediation that recorded judgments (the coercive force behind consent) be open to negotiation. This approach, pending further research, might at least minimally contribute to more balanced negotiations and address the unpleasant use of volunteer mediators as unwitting (and unpaid!) partners in the work of collecting.

Unknown Alternatives

Interest-based bargaining *without* knowledge of alternatives, which are theoretically synonymous with bargaining limits, is a more complicated problem in negotiated justice although less consciously challenging for mediators. Lower structural status parties could be strategically manipulated into thinking that they did not have a legally adequate case. Disputants who had no grip on their alternatives were psychologically disadvantaged even with no economic disparity because they were unable to evaluate their own outcomes, thus leaving them vulnerable to the most negative outcome in negotiations, feeling like a sucker.

In small claims court, disputants are unlikely to obtain this information[6]. The immediate constraint was the apparent competition between lawyers and mediators (see Chapter Three and Menkle-Meadow 1991). Legal advice is too costly for lower status parties in monetarily small disputes, and the legal profession has constrained advice not their own. Unlike criminal justice, the state does not guarantee representation in civil court, despite economic sanctions that are arguably equivalent to criminal punishments. Mediators were proscribed from providing objective legal advice concerning probable court outcomes for a variety of reasons: legal constraint, ignorance, professional settlement goals, or the nonadversarial ideology of the mediators.

The distal constraints on legal knowledge are perhaps more insidious. Legal scholars (e.g., Bryan 1992) have argued in the case of divorce mediation that policy should encourage "lawyer-assisted mediation." The women without structural roles might agree, just as lower income Latina respondents apparently used legal representation defensively in adjudication. However, the encouragement of legal representation as a policy involves less apparent problems for disadvantage lower-status parties. The Latinas and other represented noncorporate parties in adjudication ultimately suffered net financial losses, because the cost of representation was usually excluded from rulings for private citizens and was even less likely in mediation agreements. As a policy, as Black (1989) noted, relying on lawyers frequently invites more discrimination rather than eliminating it.

A more workable solution might be a return to the initial ideals of small claims courts to exclude all lawyers categorically. This means that corporate parties who use small claims for collection would necessarily represent themselves. Although it is unclear that lower status respondents would fare any better, this change would tend to close the gap between individuals and faceless bureaucratic justice, and return debtors and creditors to a more direct and perhaps more human relationship.

Mediation Practice

The negotiation model, as noted at the beginning of the chapter and in Chapter Three, invites mediators to de-link issues of justice, encouraging a quick disregard of challenges to practice stemming from outcome examination. Mediators often define class, race-ethnicity, and (still sometimes) gender issues out of mediation practice. They don't feel it is their place to intervene, make judgments, in the seemingly infinite layers of social hierarchy. Mediators are likely to think, as in my training 17 years ago, if we just follow the process, the disputants themselves will work through the communication structures we help to create to reach their own solutions. It is unnerving to see that our own social identity influences outcomes for others. For mediators who want to improve their practice *and* respond to justice issues, the data presented here suggest where corrective measures might be taken.

In practice the most imbalanced outcomes resulted from settlement pressure through constructing non-monetary *substitutes* for monetary claims[7], and by invoking, even misrepresenting, evidentiary rules to discourage disputants from adjudication. In both cases, a solution is for mediators to embrace more openly the court alternative. Whether or not policies regarding lawyers in small claims courts are modified, the right of private citizens to judicial review of their disputes should be maintained and mediation should readily withdraw from intervention in these disputes. Merry (1990) pointed out that many of the working class users in the Dorchester Massachusetts Court, like users of the court in Bernalillo County, were at the outset seeking a more rational and "better" conflict resolution device than violence. The diversion to nonadversarial process appeared to skip a step, jumping from violence to negotiation without defining "fair" and "unfair" in the intermediate phase, constructing a conflict frame inviting opportunism, and with neither the identification nor processual tactics for intervening with exploitative bargainers. The problem requires creative thought and articulation about ways a mediator might intervene, but therein lies the problem. Intervention, even making a judgment about what *is* exploitation, crosses the boundary of neutrality (Chapter Three) and takes a step closer to social justice commitments. But really, in a world that presents overwhelming needs for cross-cultural cooperation, we *need* to be having the conversation about values and justice.

Conflict resolution theory, and particularly interest-based mediation, usually leaves value conflicts unmentioned, despite their strategic position in negotiations (see Bangert & Pirzada 1991; Fisher & Ury 1981). But direct questioning about the values underlying disputants' interests is not only possible but is probably useful. In simulated international disputes (Druckman, Broome & Korper 1988), conscious attention to cultural value issues resulted in higher resolution rates, more trust of the other party, greater tolerance and optimism, and significantly more symmetrical resolutions compared to randomly-assigned other dyads who put value issues aside, or "de-linked" them from negotiation issues.

In cross-ethnic disputes, mediators were apparently unable to challenge Anglo exploitation and sometimes appeared to contribute to it. Mediators seemed to substitute class and ethnic biases most easily when disputants were least knowledgeable and, perhaps, prone to following what appeared to be authoritative judgments about their disputes. Mediators need to acquire awareness of how culture groups are also dominant-subordinate groups and to understand the impossibility of our own "neutrality:" our social biases are inherent in U.S. culture but are also a hazard to the *impartiality* we can aspire to (see Chene 2001; 2004). Increasing awareness would also help to recognize exploitation but mediators will also need to develop intervention strategies for interrupting it. Until mediator training and ideology can find a place for these concerns, these data suggest that mediation should not construct itself as culturally competent to intervene in cross-cultural disputes. After years of analysis, I see no evidence that mediation served Latino claimants with Anglo respondents except possibly as consumer-provider cases[8].

Female mediators might avoid biased effects by *restraint* of their power, even though agreements constitute a common measure of mediator success. Women apparently have special capacities for reaching agreements using "soft power" of influence and persuasion. Without reviewing all the possible historical and socialized reasons for this, suffice to say that female mediators motivated parties to reach agreement significantly more often than men (78.2% compared to 63.2% for male mediators) and female claimants reached agreement more often than male claimants (78.4% compared to 62.1%). This soft power advantage appears to function unconsciously and through the projections of others at least as much as it is consciously wielded by women. These data showed, in claimants and mediators, an undertow of race-ethnic and structural status bias in women's soft power. One useful technique that is now more often used in the Metro Court setting, partially as a consequence of this study, is to strongly encourage disputants to take a few days to review the agreement *before* signing it.

Kritek (1994) suggests a more compelling and deeper approach in her book, *Negotiating at an Uneven Table.* After discussions of the complex and ultimately inevitable ways that a negotiating table is uneven, including the manipulations by the less powerful that ultimately maintain victim-victimizer roles and the social metaphors that normalize it, Kritek proposes working in concert with the paradigm shift affecting our current social evolution to undermine our distorting U.S. obsession with "dominance power." Her strategies are "ways of being" based on developing and using moral courage: find and inhabit the deepest human space that capabilities permit, speak truth about unbalanced power, honor our own integrity enough to refuse complicity, be ready to forgive oneself and others, notice co-optation, pay increased attention to context, dare to innovate, remember our own knowledge limits, stay in the dialogue but be ready to leave the table if the process compromises our own self-worth. All of these ways of being involve risk, but Kritek has found that people are more often relieved and empowered to hear someone articulate the realities usually left unsaid, sexism and racism being among the most frequent examples.

In intra-ethnic cases, *in comparison to adjudication,* Latino men reported surprisingly positive evaluations, satisfaction, and comfort. Unlike the LOHI condition with Anglo respondents, Latino claimants with Latino respondents did not often specify monetary goals and only relatively infrequently gave indications in the interview that they themselves perceived the outcomes as unfair[9]. It is possible that the preference for mediation implied in this pattern actually results from adjudication distaste, perhaps a legacy of Nuevomexicano-Anglo historical legal relations. Alternatively or concurrently, the importance of narration in the *Latino* culture might be at least partially responsible for this pattern.

Most scholars (e.g., O'Barr & Conley 1985; Cobb 1994; Lind, Tyler & Huo 1997) understand that the higher satisfaction from mediation than adjudication stems from the relative narrative freedom ("voice") permitted and encouraged in mediation. The data presented here suggest that the rituals, not necessarily substance, of reciprocity and cooperation were central for Latino disputants. This impression coincides with detailed research in educational environments finding that Mexican Americans learned more in cooperative environments than in competitive situations (Knight & Kagan 1977; Kagan 1984). Interestingly, Kagan's work also showed that, over time, Anglo children were more able to dismantle their prejudice in the same learning processes, a longer range outcome that was not apparent in the mediation situation studied here.

Mediation practitioners and researchers might do well to examine Latino mediators (and possibly other bicultural groups) because, in comparison to all other gender and ethnicity combinations, they appeared to have most successfully balanced justice and consent. In correlation research Oetzel (1998) found people assessed with interdependent self-construal (collectivist), *not* independents (individualist), were far more likely to choose integrative conflict styles. In the MetroCourt data, *both* disputants in cases mediated by Latinos were more likely to be satisfied with the outcome. Also supported in the MetroCourt data, Ramirez (1983) argued that the cognitive differences associated with Mexican American context sensitivity could enhance cross-cultural conflict intervention showing experimental results to support this hypothesis. In the MetroCourt study, higher status Anglo claimants preferred Latino mediators when the respondent was Latino, even though, on average, they had compromised their claims more than with Anglo mediators. Cases mediated by Latinos showed no discernible difference in Anglo vs. Latino outcomes. In fact, *all* Latino and female claimant and respondent groups (except female respondents with female claimants) tended to report higher satisfaction after mediation with Latino mediators. Latino mediators were the only common denominator for respondent reports of cooperative motivation in their bargaining decisions; Latino mediators themselves (especially men) explained their own settlement techniques as describing the benefits of mediation and the possibilities for nonmonetary types of agreements.

PEACE, JUSTICE, AND CULTURAL KNOWLEDGE

Over the last decade, cognitive approaches to understanding the role of culture in negotiation and justice have moved to the forefront of knowledge creation (Morris & Leung 2004; Thompson, Neale & Sinaceur 2004). This approach offers a dynamic "constructivist" model for how accessible and situationally-activated cultural knowledge structures guide judgment (Morris & Gelfand 2004). A major area of research, briefly reviewed in Chapter Seven, concerns our understanding of negotiator biases heretofore assumed to be universal but stunningly revealed as culturally influenced. What is hopeful in revealing this blindness, besides the greater awareness that can be applied to cross-cultural negotiations, is to realize that all of the world is *not* as obsessed with what Kritek called "dominance power."

The usual situational ethnicity argument shares this blindness: interethnic conflict behavior is motivated by Hobbesian instrumental, rational and self-interested striving that we associate with public capitalist life, assuming the same materialistic power goals that propel Weber's "spirit of capitalism" must underlie both sides of the conflict. This potential "miscognition" was discussed in Chapter Seven but should be re-stated here: evidence suggests that "competitors," not cooperators, mis-attribute competitive motivation to noncompetitive behavior;[10] individualists, not collectivists, more often hold self-serving biases that they are more "fair" than others. Stated simply and thereby over-generalizing, untrustworthy people tend to distrust the other, mis-perceiving their motives; cooperative people are likely to trust others for longer periods in the face of exploitation.

Unfortunately, like the Anglo disputants' emphasis on money at MetroCourt, the obsession with dominance correlates with actual dominance, protected by judgment biases that blind the privileged from seeing contradictory evidence. Nevertheless, I find it deeply encouraging that researchers are unmasking these distortions in our worldview. My hope is more research will expand our knowledge of the cognitive limitations suffered by all of us captured in what Abalos called the archetypal "story of capitalism." In our own multiethnic society and in our dealings with the world, we need to learn these cognitive limitations and how to adjust our perceptions to account for the resulting miscognitions.

This study described the economic injustice that resulted in part from intercultural dynamics. Latinos, in general, valued reciprocity and equality fairness norms combined with a trust through which these become socially cohesive. Anglos, in general, valued the "ideal of the honest man of recognized credit, and above all the idea of a duty of the individual toward increase of his capital, which is assumed as an end in itself" combined with the competitive instrumentality that make this value tangible. With our history of racialized relationships and a cognitive tendency to privilege our own worthiness, Anglos easily moved toward opportunistic exploitation of Latinos. Expectations (internal and external) supported this performance. Was this a function of location, ethnic groups, type of court? Further research is important to replicate or refute, and to validate or further specify these results.

Whether from adjudication distaste or a preference for the narrative and reciprocal style in mediation, these data clearly suggest that Latino disputants found values in mediation that were not reducible to the material. Kritek (1994) makes this argument as well: non-privileged groups are likely to have developed values outside the "dominance power" framework that so pervasively structures life in the United States. Further research might clarify what these values are, and how a less culturally-bounded intervention process might eliminate the *unstated* trade-off between these values and economic ones.

It is less obvious that mediation held alternative values for women, despite its traditional connection with women in origin and practice, in this setting as well as many others. Women appeared to be sensitive to the context of mediation culture without strongly indicating much comfort with it. For Latinas, this appeared to be a subset of the problem of a missing BATNA combined with a preference for the authority of the court's decision-making. For Anglo women, the harmony model appeared to arouse a defensiveness that contributed to an extreme rationality. In both cases, the women's resistance was often able to limit the substantive effects of gender disadvantage that might have followed. Further research could clarify this effect, particularly as it related to cross-gender disputes in contrast to intra-gender disputing.

Such research might also explore Duryea's (1994) hypothesis that cultural differences account for the variation in a mediator evaluation instrument tested in a Hawaii mediation program. Duryea argued that the lack of validation should perhaps be seen as a positive finding in a mediation program. In this study, Latino claimants and mediators appeared to re-shape the mediation process toward a more diverse, and possibly more meaningful, form of dispute resolution. And Kritek's model of moral courage would be difficult to standardize, rooted as it is in self-awareness and personal integrity. However, the questionnaire data allowed an indirect measure of mediators' ability to influence win-win outcomes by the relatively simple correlation measure of satisfaction on both sides.

Although requiring further research support, these cases suggested specific Anglo reluctance to give cash to Latinos, despite apparently having easier access to it. We can see similar patterns in our social welfare and foreign aid policies. Deflem (2003) traces theorizing about money through the classical sociology literature, arguing that the study of money deserves to be a specialization within the discipline: Marx' argument that money represents the epitome of man's alienation as congealed labor; Simmel's treatise on money written in 1900 that money was central to gesellschaft replacement of gemeinschaft community; Weber's attention to the centrality of rational profit calculation made possible by double-entry bookkeeping in the capitalist ethic. But money—what James Buchan (2001) calls "frozen desire"—is a broadly interdisciplinary study of the ultimate abstraction. We are currently living in a world where, since eliminating the gold standard, global *currency* speculation grew from 20% in 1975 to 97% of global investment today—money is now radically independent of the "real" economy (Lietaer 1997). Hardin (2004) points out that transactions enumerated in cash make the producer's rewards increasingly generalized and abstract even as production is increasingly specialized and impersonal—craftsmanship and barter both play ever decreasing roles in a developing capitalist world. In these cases, nonmonetary but material outcomes were evaluated very differently by different people. What are the differences in valuation? Further research and theorizing might explicate the meaning of money cross-culturally, and explore the implications of such abstraction to "materialism" in our cross-culture relationships.

The cultural meaning of materialism is worthy of study. Many international observers and scholars within different frames (e.g., Barber 1992; Huntington 1993) enumerate western materialism as the primary element underlying deadly "cultural" disputes in Iraq and elsewhere. Recent voter polls on the most important national problems put excessive materialism at the top of the list but I see little critical study of the meaning, effects, consequences, and alternatives. Echoing scholars reviewed here referring to acculturation, William Pfaff is eloquent in a column in the International Tribune (July 21, 2005) concerning Islamist terrorism:

> There is a crucial factor . . . that few in the West understand. Modern Western civilization is the product of Western history and culture. The West is what it is because of its past. Nobody imposed foreign ideas on the West. Hence the West is at home in the modern world. The modern world was created by, and belongs to, the West.
>
> But the West is trying to impose not only foreign ideas on everyone else, but ideas that contradict and would destroy the fundamental values and assumptions of non-Western societies.

> It says: This is progress. Our progress is your destabilization, the destruction of your cultures, the creation of millions of culturally alienated, deracinated, displaced persons, ripped from their own past to become integrated into a radically materialistic ethic.
>
> It should hardly be surprising that the reaction to this is nihilistic violence.

Reducing this conflict to "envy," as our president does today, takes the kind of blinding projection cognitive researchers found more likely in individualistic cultures. Similarly, the construction of politically and materially self-interested "subjectivities" (see Best & Kellner 1991; Nicholson 1990; Weedon 1987) is an insidious (and probably inaccurate) capitulation to dominant cultural values of self-maximization through acquisition and opportunism. The perception of ethnic and gender differences as "instrumental" identities motivated solely by materialistic striving represents a *de facto* discursive and cultural defeat.

Merry (Li & Merry 1987) wrote that the guiding metaphor of U.S. mediation was the contract. Perhaps that is the reason mediation made the most positive contributions to the public in cases involving corporations. For those who had no knowledge of their alternatives, mediation presented a procedure that encouraged rational bargaining but was a process that would not or could not assist them in the fundamental precondition of knowing their limits. Higher status Anglos appeared to utilize the procedure most effectively. As an antidote to the hyper-individualism and self-interest that permeates the dominant culture, mediation offered a progressive cultural influence to these constituents. But, as researchers argue (e.g., Folger & Jones 1994), the mediation profession, researchers, and local practice requires greater cross-fertilization to evolve more self-reflective justice strategies and less culturally biased procedures before mediation is imposed on less-experienced disputants.

Rinderle (2003) points out that there is little research on Anglo-Latino conflict patterns, despite the fact that Latinos rival African Americans as the largest minority group in the country. These data could not tell us anything about differences among Latinos, whether Anglo-Latino negotiations would be different for non-Mexican derived Latinos, or how unique Southwestern Latinos might be. We would likely benefit from both etic and emic approaches to clarifying different values and conflict styles in Latino-Anglo grouping. The more emic or ethnographic investigation could perhaps enrich our understanding of what a Latino small businessman (M330) meant when he said that the outcome in mediation was "very" fair because it was "able to get spiders out of the attic."

Afterwords and Thoughts

Dualisms invite the either-or and win-lose thinking that plagues the modern era. In 1990, when data collection began, the MetroCourt investigators made the decision to include only two-party cases and to exclude multi-party disputes. I made a similar choice in this analysis when I chose to approach intersected status as multiple dualisms that were amenable to mathematical analysis. One of the results of this binary approach and the answers I found is to encourage the notion that one answer, one conclusion, must be more true than the other. But the ideal of mediation practice, in this setting as many others, seeks to integrate these kinds of conflicts.

Both-and answers are messier, but they are more accurate. Latino disputants were exploited by Anglos who failed to match reciprocity *and* collectivistic cultural socialization encouraged behaviors and attitudes that were more readily exploited. Women in the MetroCourt often constructed a gender expression that worked to their own and their employer's advantage *and* they defensively sought to relieve their empathic distress, most clearly through altruistic gifts to other Anglo women. The negotiation process used in this setting was constructed by and for the individualistic, self-maximizing pattern associated with the dominant Anglo culture, creating less competent and/or defensive identities for outsider negotiators, *and* outsider disputants in mediation often valued their outcomes more highly than adjudicated rulings that might have returned greater monetary benefits.

These paradoxes leave small claims mediation with its greatest challenge: to articulate the conflicts between negotiation and justice, between cultural justice—including narration, reciprocity, and peace-making—and economic justice. Otherwise, mediation will indeed substitute a non-material harmony for substantive justice. Perhaps, for many of us, the value of harmony is held more highly than any monetary returns, and we would choose it, despite the shame of being seen as a sucker, if the choice were clear. More in image and in hope than in practice, mediation stands as an emergent cultural form that might articulate and announce this alternative set of choices: living with one another in an inevitably grumpy and patchy peace, or locked in the competitive struggle of acquisitive striving.

I leave with new questions: Is individualism, arguably synonymous with westernized, economically-developed countries and, at the individual level, higher class individuals, *inherently* exploitative? What cultural accommodations have been invented? Like Benson's (1985) white collar criminals' accounts of their crime, has the American dominant culture twisted itself around its need to deny criminal intent? What self-serving, self-securing, self-sustaining identities are evoked and elaborated by unequal accumulation? What privilege is protected, what unfair aggression is justified, by our projections?

Where you stand determines what you see. Invisibility distorts not only the perceptions of mediators, but theoretical work on race-ethnic and gender justice as well. Dominant Anglo emphasis on striving for material reward, accumulation, and the exploitation of opportunity is *culturally* hegemonic. I have argued in concert with many earlier social theorists and some contemporary ones, that acquisitive materialism is the *substance* of cultural conflicts in the modern state, and a source of many problems attributed to social fragmentation. I think it is likely that outsider individuals and groups, and many who live in the iron cage of a successful life, construct instrumental identities and behaviors to defend themselves against the mathematical certainty of failure to be the "best."

Since these analyses were completed, I have been teaching peace studies and more frequently use a macro frame for seeing conflict, culture, and justice issues. The micro-macro parallels are haunting. The war metaphor is pervasive in our culture, we are pre-set to find enemies and a short scan of the horizon tells us that we identify them by color. Protected by our cognitive judgment biases, it seems obvious that they warrant attack. Like Benson's (1985) white collar criminals' accounts of their crime, has the American dominant culture twisted itself around its need to deny criminal intent? What self-serving, self-securing, self-sustaining identities are evoked and elaborated by unequal accumulation? What privilege do we protect with our projection?

I don't think we really have any positive choices if not to become aware of the avarice and complacency in many of our cultural practices. But I am not arguing that our world situation is just a matter of few faulty perceptions. I suspect our perception, behaviors and material world are in fact interwoven in the mysterious way of creation. In the material world, we really *are* running out of cheap oil and we really *do* need it because we really *are* addicted. Only a willingness to share will change our current trajectory toward lose-lose outcomes.

Sharing and generosity are relegated to tightly circumscribed welfare systems and the private, peripheral domain in modern society. We shade our rational and Western intellectual eyes in the face of communal interdependence, where one gives because it is needed. Since the ascent of the Protestant reformation and the materialism of capitalism, Hyde argued (1979:139), survival depends on the detached style of the "alien" who lives in the spirit of usury, the spirit of boundaries and divisions: "The 'bleeding heart' [of the Christian era] is now the man of dubious mettle with an embarrassing inability to limit his compassion." We associated this kind compassion with pre-industrial, traditional and "primitive" social organization and female care-giving. Triandis & Gelfand (1998) associate this structure with collectivism.

We need to encourage sharing where possible and re-invent it where necessary within our society. I am an idealist: I firmly believe that human nature is miraculously mutable: I think we would all do better—physically, emotionally, culturally, economically, and socially—if we encouraged people and institutional arrangements toward greater generosity and equality of outcome. Generosity and reciprocity are actually contagious and grow more sincere as the benefits of mutuality are realized (Schlicht 2001; Lawler & Yoon 1993; see also Peet & Peet 2002). We individualists need to strengthen the nascent alternative paradigms, the metaphors of interdependence, ones that demands courage, integrity and compassion, and shameless generosity. As I noted in the introduction, I think the jig is up, the party's over. Without a paradigm shift, a cultural transformation, we are really in a pickle.

Glossary

BATNA (Best Alternative to a Negotiated Agreement): the best possible estimate of one's alternative options. The BATNA, for a rational negotiator, is the standard against which all offers for settlement are measured. In small claims court assuming strictly monetary interests, this is usually the probable court ruling.

CLAIMANT: (syn. complainant) In civil court, the party who files the complaint against the other party (the respondent). In civil courts, the complaint is couched in monetary terms and the claimant must assure that the respondent is adequately identified so that the respondent may be notified that a complaint has been filed against him/her. In criminal court, and often in civil courts as well, the claimant is called the "plaintiff," the one who suffered injury or the state in the victims behalf.

CONDITION(S): Claimant-Respondent status relationship based on dualized ranks in five dimensions for all cases thus generating for each cases one of four possibilities in all five dimensions: HILO, HIHI, LOLO, LOHI.

CORPORATE STATUS (syn "business"): Dualized as corporate, landlord or business entity (including self-employed) v. private individual citizens.

CULTURE: the shared conscious and unconscious *pattern* of values, meanings and taken-for-granted assumptions about proper behavior for self and others (Merry 1987). "Culture is a community of meaning and morality, the matrix of the sense of self" (Karst 1993:6). This definition applies to ethnic, gender, corporate, legal, and class cultures. It also describes the culture of mediation.

DIMENSIONS: Group-level memberships that are status indicators and are also cultural influences. In this work, the status/cultural dimensions examined are ascriptive (ethnicity and gender), structural (corporate and legal) and achieved (SES).

DISPUTE ROLE: refers to position in the dispute dyad as the claiming or responding party.

EMIC AND ETIC ANALYSIS: A distinction borrowed by anthropologists from linguistics. Emicists concentrate on describing the indigenous values of a particular society while eticists apply broader theoretical models across a number of societies. The emic approach became popular in the late 1960s as part of the movement towards cultural relativism. In practice, anthropological research has always entailed a mixture of emic and etic approaches. (*A Dictionary of Sociology*. Ed. Gordon Marshall. Oxford University Press, 1998. *Oxford Reference Online*. Oxford University Press)

ETHNIC STATUS: dualized as majority-minority ethnicities where the majority possesses superior power to impose its will on the other.

HIGHER STATUS INSIDER CONDITION (syn HIHI; second condition): cases in which the claimant respondent status relationship is HIHI status balanced, that is, the claimant is higher in status (specified dimension) and the respondent is also higher in status (same dimension). Also one of the two horizontal or balanced power relationship conditions.

INTEREST-BASED MEDIATION: a common style of mediation practice adapted from the form popularized by Fisher & Ury (1981) as "principled negotiation" in which mediators elicit the "interests" of the parties, discourage positional bargaining, and attempt to initiate a problem-solving process in which both parties interests might be met, leading to a win-win outcome. Interest-based mediation depends on parties having differing interests. A common example in small claims mediation is where the money claimed is admitted owed by the respondent. During mediation of admitted liability cases, the claimant may sacrifice immediate payment by negotiating a payment plan that suits the respondent's ability to pay and the amounts associated with court costs and interest are commonly "on the table" (i.e., negotiable). Another fruitful interest-based negotiation tactic is to substitute "nonmonetary" solutions to monetary claims, commonly, credit at the respondent's store, repairing or re-doing the job, etc. Many mediators in this study used the value of a good future relationship as an interest possibility. Other differences that might expand the agreement probabilities suggested by Fisher & Ury include trading form for substance, economic for political interests, symbolic for practical concessions, interests in precedent with interests in this case only, interests in progress with interests in tradition.

LEGAL STATUS: In small claims participants, dualized as represented by an attorney or acting *pro se,* that is, without representation.

LOWER STATUS INSIDER CONDITION (syn LOLO; third condition): cases in which the claimant respondent status relationship is LOLO status balanced, that is, the claimant is lower in status (specified dimension) and the respondent is also lower in status (same dimension). Also one of the two horizontal or balanced power relationship conditions.

OBJECTIVE CULTURE: behavior that reflects the conscious and/or unconscious individual choice from the variety of options that cultural socialization provides. Cultural behavior is strongly affected by the situation and the specific other people in it.

ORDERING OF CONDITIONS: Anticipated variation of outcomes based on the relative status of the claimant-respondent dyad in the case. Claimants with higher status are anticipated to achieve higher outcomes due to their advantage of being in the claimant role as well as being higher status and respondents of higher status are anticipated to achieve better (i.e., lower) outcomes than lower status respondents. Thus the order of outcomes predicted from Black's analysis of criminal court outcomes is HILO, HIHI, LOLO, LOHI (see table below).

Anticipated Ordering of Outcomes by Claimant-Respondent Status Relationships (Conditions)

Respondent Status	Claimant Status	
	Higher	**Lower**
Lower	1 HILO	3 LOLO
Higher	2 HIHI	4 LOHI

POWER DEPENDENT CONDITION (syn HILO; first condition): cases in which the claimant respondent status relationship is HILO status imbalanced, i.e., the claimant is higher in status (specified dimension) and the respondent is lower in status (same dimension). Also, one of the two vertical or imbalanced power relationship conditions.

PRINCIPLED NEGOTIATION: The form of negotiation suggested by Fisher & Ury in which the negotiation process focuses on interests, the negotiation is "soft on people, hard on merits," negotiation is reasonable not willful, uses objective criteria, and is careful to ascertain the BATNA beforehand.

RESPONDENT: In civil court, the party who is named in the complaint as owing the claimant. The respondent is legally obligated to respond to the complaint (file an Answer) within a certain period of time. If the respondent was served (a "proof of service" was entered) and did not file an answer, a default judgment may be requested in which the complaint is presumed to be valid and a judgment may be entered against the respondent for the full amount plus court costs. If the respondent files an Answers, any admission of liability may be used to file for a judgment based on this admission without need for a court hearing.

RIGHTS-BASED CONDITION (syn LOHI; fourth condition): cases in which the claimant respondent status relationship is LOHI status imbalanced, that is, the claimant is lower in status (specified dimension) and the respondent is higher in status (same dimension). Also, one of the two vertical or imbalanced power relationship conditions.

CLASS STATUS: dualized measure of socioeconomic status derived from factor scoring reported educational attainment, profession (ranked as prestige), and household income. Missing data was replaced by the means for the three variables for the forum. "Higher" refers to SES scores falling above the sample median and "lower" refers to SES scores below the sample median, where the sample is all 603 small claims cases (including adjudicated and mediated cases.

STATUS: dualized ranking of "higher" and "lower" in ethnic, gender, SES, legal, and corporate status dimensions where "higher" is majority, men, higher SES, represented, and business party; "lower" is minority, women, lower SES, pro se, and individual (private) party.

SUBJECTIVE CULTURE: individually internalized patterns of values, meanings and taken-for-granted assumptions about proper behavior for self and others (Merry 1987). The internalized or subjective culture acts like a perceptual screen through which events are enacted, experienced and interpreted (Thompson Ellis & Wildavsky 1990). Experience is thus ordered by resemblances, or metaphorical translations, patterned by prior cultural experience (Lakoff 1987; Lakoff & Johnson 1980; Rosaldo 1993). Cultural patterns are modified by individual variations in degree of internalization or identification, and commitment or loyalty to the group identity (D'Andrade 1993). Individual and group level differences are also found to be related to the shape of historical group experience (Li & Merry 1987), and in the cognitive rigidity or flexibility with which cultural patterns are actually used for perceptual ordering and behavioral response to experience (Casmir 1985; Ramirez 1987; Rack 1991).

SUMMARIZED STRUCTURAL CONDITIONS: All cases ranked as HILO, HIHI, LOLO, LOHI in legal or corporate dimensions with cases ranked in those conditions using SES conditions determined without replacing mean variables are included in the corresponding summarized structural condition. Cases in corresponding ethnic and gender conditions were not included.

Appendix

Appendix Table 4.i Variables, Coding, Means and Frequencies[a]

All Cases N=603		Adjudication N=323				Mediation N=280					
		Monetary Outcome		Nonmonetary		Monetary Outcome		Nonmonetary & Subsequent[b]		Mediation w/o Agreement	
Variable	Coding	N	% or Mean (SD)	N	% or Mean	N	% or Mean	N	% or Mean	N	% or Mean
Dependent Variables											
Monetary Outcome Ratio (MOR)	outcome in $ / claim in $	312	.653 (.49)	11	.474 (.46)	138	.628 (.38)	54	n.a.	88	n.a.
Claimant Satisfaction (CSAT)	standardized factor scores	248	-.096** (1.02)	6	-.596 (1.31)	112	.163 (.96)	40	.273 (.82)	5	-.378* (.53)
Respondent Satisfaction (RSAT)	standardized factor scores	201	-.385*** (.99)	7	.194 (1.14)	106	.589 (.71)	36	.571 (.68)	9	-.770*** (.53)
Independent Variables											
Ethnic Status[c]	1 = Anglo-Latino	85	27.2	2	18.2	35	25.4	8	14.8	19	21.6
	2 = Anglo-Anglo	114	36.5*	4	36.4	62	44.9	19	35.2	40	45.5
	3 = Latino-Latino	55	17.6	3	27.3	29	21.0	13	24.1	18	20.5

	4 = Latino-Anglo	52	16.7**	2	18.2	11	8.0	14	25.9***	11	12.5
	0 = uncoded	6	1.9	0	0.0	1	0.7	1	1.9	0	0.0
Gender Status	1 = male-female	70	22.4	2	18.2	24	17.4	6	11.1	21	23.9
	2 = male-male	136	43.6	5	45.5	53	38.4	22	40.7	43	48.9
	3 = female-female	39	12.5	1	9.1	24	17.4	9	16.7	12	13.6
	4 = female-male	67	21.5	3	27.3	37	26.8	17	31.5	12	13.6**
Corporate Status[d]	1 = corporate-individual	106	34.0	4	36.4	52	37.7	10	18.5**	24	27.3
	2 = corporate-corporate	34	10.9	1	9.1	22	15.9	6	11.1	10	11.4
	3 = individual-individual	74	23.7	1	9.1	36	26.1	13	24.1	25	28.4
	4 = individual-corporate	98	31.4**	5	45.5	28	20.3	25	46.3***	29	33.0**
Legal status	1 = lawyer-pro se	49	15.7	2	18.2	21	15.2	5	9.3	9	10.2

(continued)

Appendix Table 4.i—*(continued)*

All Cases N=603		Adjudication N=323				Mediation N=280					
		Monetary Outcome		Nonmonetary		Monetary Outcome		Nonmonetary & Subsequent[b]		Mediation w/o Agreement	
Variable	Coding	N	% or Mean (SD)	N	% or Mean	N	% or Mean	N	% or Mean	N	% or Mean
	2 = lawyer-lawyer	33	10.6**	1	9.1	6	4.3	3	5.6	8	9.1
	3 = pro se-pro se	196	62.8	5	45.5	90	65.2	35	64.8	54	61.4
	4 = pro se-lawyer	34	10.9	3	27.3	21	15.2	11	20.4	17	19.3
Class status	1 = higher SES-lower SES	77	24.7	5	45.5**	42	30.4	9	16.7*	16	18.2**
	2 = higher-higher	62	19.9	1	9.1	24	17.4	11	20.4	24	27.3*
	3 = lower-lower	108	34.6	3	27.3	50	36.2	21	38.9	28	31.8
	4 = lower-higher	65	20.8	2	18.2	22	15.9	13	24.1	20	22.7

Relational Variables											
Prior relationships (C)	0 = No ongoing relations	105	33.7**	4	36.4	31	22.5	13	24.1	27	30.7
	1 = 1 ongoing relation	181	58.0	6	54.5	85	61.6	32	59.3	50	56.8
	2 = 2 or more	26	8.3**	1	9.1	22	15.9	9	16.7	11	12.5
Intervenors[e]											
By ethnicity	Both mediators or judge minority	62	19.9	1	9.1	37	26.8	23	42.6**	27	30.7
	One mediator minority		n.a.			43	31.2	10	18.5*	20	22.7
	Both mediators or judge Anglo	250	80.1	10	90.9	58	42.0	21	38.9	41	46.6
By gender	Both mediators or judge female		n.a.			42	30.4	19	35.2	17	19.3*
	One mediator female		n.a.			59	42.8	24	44.4	43	48.9
	Bothe mediators or judge male		n.a.			37	26.8	11	20.4	28	31.8

(continued)

Appendix Table 4.i—*(continued)*

All Cases N=603		Adjudication N=323				Mediation N=280					
		Monetary Outcome		Nonmonetary		Monetary Outcome		Nonmonetary & Subsequent[b]		Mediation w/o Agreement	
Variable	Coding	N	% or Mean (SD)	N	% or Mean	N	% or Mean	N	% or Mean	N	% or Mean
Bargaining Variables[f]											
Claim size control	Claim/1000	312	1.397 (1.38)	10	1.540 (.87)	138	1.326 (1.38)	54	1.489 (1.48)	88	1.390 (1.46)
Counterclaims	0 = no counter-claim	193	61.9**	5	45.5**	100	72.5	38	70.4	59	67.0
	1 = present in record only	60	19.2*	2	18.2	10	7.2	3	5.6	7	8.0
	2 = apparent strategy (interview)	42	13.5	2	18.2	12	8.7	1	1.9*	7	8.0
	3 = substantive in ruling/ bargaining	17	5.4**	2	18.2	16	11.6	12	22.2*	15	17.0
Claimant Positions (CR)	Position in $/Claim in $	312		11		138		54		88	

CR1	position on record		1.000				1.000		1.000		1.000
			(0)				(0)		(0)		(0)
CR2	position before intervention		1.039				.996		.976		1.117*
			(.64)				(.28)		(.26)		(.63)
CR3	position during intervention		1.032***				.771		.757		.973***
			(.65)				(.34)		(.34)		(.44)
CR4	position at end of intervention		1.021***				.657		.558		1.010***
			(.67)				(.39)		(.40)		(.50)
Respondent Positions (RR)	Admitted Liability in $/ Claim in $	312		11		138		54		88	
RR1	admission in record		.061***				.232		.092***		.036***
			(.22)				(.40)		(.27)		(.16)
RR2	admitted prior to intervention		.134***				.379		.227**		.096***
			(.31)				(.40)		(.36)		(.21)
RR3	position during intervention		.151***				.531		.309***		.147***
			(.32)				(.37)		(.37)		(.24)
RR4	position at end of intervention		.156***				.611		.375***		.140***
			(.33)				(.39)		(.38)		(.25)
C.-Importance of money	mean of 4 pt scale	270	2.70***			120	2.98				
			(.94)				(.91)				

(continued)

Appendix Table 4.i—*(continued)*

All Cases N=603		Adjudication N=323				Mediation N=280					
		Monetary Outcome		Nonmonetary		Monetary Outcome		Nonmonetary & Subsequent[b]		Mediation w/o Agreement	
Variable	Coding	N	% or Mean (SD)	N	% or Mean	N	% or Mean	N	% or Mean	N	% or Mean
R.-Importance of money	mean of 4 pt scale	211	2.36 (1.05)			108	2.49 (.96)				
Payment Plans	1 = reported or recorded	63	20.2	3	27.3	70	50.7	12	22.2***		n.a.

* p <.10; ** p <.05; *** p <.01

Appendix Table 4.i Notes

a. Significance testing by t-test of means or x2 test of distribution using two-tailed tests. Testing between adjudicated and mediated cases in monetary and nonmonetary outcome analysis are beside adjudication cases; significance in mediated nonmonetary/subsequent agreement cases refers to differences with monetary outcome sample; significance noted in mediation cases without agreement refers to difference from mediated monetary cases.

b. The mediated nonmonetary sample includes 19 cases that reported settlement after the mediation session and prior to court hearing (4 of these involved nonmonetary elements) and 35 cases settled in mediation with substantive nonmonetary elements. Twenty-one of the nonmonetary outcome cases involved no monetary exchange but are converted to dollar amounts where equivalence could be determined and 18 outcomes in which nonmonetary obligations were accepted by the respondent in addition to a monetary obligation. In the latter case, no monetary equivalence is attempted.

c. In the total sample, 182 Hispanics (30.4%), 11 African-Americans (1.8%), 4 Asians (0.7%), 7 Native Americans (1.2%), and 5 "others" (0.8%) were coded as "minority claimants" and 216 Hispanics (36.1%), 22 African-Americans (3.7%), 11 Asians (1.8%), 5 Native Americans (0.8%) and 14 "others" (2.3%) were coded as "minority respondents" for the purposes of analysis.

d. In the overall sample, "individual claimants" (55.4%) include 307 individuals and 27 married couples. "Corporate claimants" include 96 claimants (15.9%) filing as "Doing Business As" (DBA) or landlords, 23 professionals (3.8%), 98 small businesses with less than 100 employees (16.7%), 13 large businesses (2.5%), 19 institutions (3.2%) and 18 collection agencies (3.0%). "Individual respondents" (57.2%) include 286 individuals and 59 married couples. "Corporate respondents" include 126 DBAs (20.9%), 8 professionals (1.3%), 106 small businesses (17.6%), 14 large businesses (2.3%), 3 insitutions (0.5%) and 1 collection agency (0.2%).

e. Three judges heard all but five adjudicated cases. One was African-American (63 cases, 19.8%), another Hispanic (116 cases, 36.5%) and the third was white (133 cases, 41.8%). All three were male. A total of 129 mediators mediated in the study. Seventy-eight (61.5%) were female and 92 (71.3%) were white. For the purposes of analysis, 27 Hispanic mediators (21.0%), 5 African-Americans (3.9%), 2 Native Americans (1.6%), 1 Asian (0.8%) and 2 "others" (1.6%) were coded as "minorities". No significance levels between adjudication and mediation are given because samples are not comparable.

f. In adjudication, position is coded as unchanged from the prior position when party was not interviewed or question was not answered. In mediation cases, the positions recorded by the mediators are used in the second, third and fourth positions when the party was not interviewed. Statements in the record that admitted some liability but without a specific amount were assigned a value of 0. In one case where the claim for a an amount "to be determined at trial," interview data was used to assign a dollar amount.

Appendix Table 4.ii Correlation of Conditions, Casetypes, Forum, Pleading and Outcomes with Ethnic, Gender and Summarized[a] Status Conditions

Condition	ETH1	ETH2	ETH3	ETH4	GND1	GND2	GND3	GND4	SUM1	SUM2	SUM3	SUM4
All Cases N=603												
Conditions												
GND1	.05	-.05	.07*	-.07*								
GND2	-.04	.06	-.06	.02								
GND3	-.01	.03	.00	-.04								
GND4	.00	-.06	.00	.07*								
SUM1	.21****	-.04	-.04	-.16****	.16****	-.10**	.08*	-.11***				
SUM2	.05	.07*	-.11***	-.03	-.05	.09**	-.03	-.03				
SUM3	-.08**	-.05	.16****	-.01	.00	-.02***	.10**	.06				
SUM4	-.13***	.04	-.02	.14****	-.09	-.00	-.05	.14****				
SES1	.15****	.05	-.10**	-.12***	.06	.02	-.03	-.06				
SES2	.04	.16****	-.18****	-.05	-.04	.09**	-.01	-.05				
SES3	-.08*	-.17****	.30****	-.04	.06	-.08*	.06	-.02				
SES4	-.11***	-.01	-.07*	.23****	-.10**	-.02	-.03	.14****				
CORP1	.21****	.00	-.10**	-.15***	.17****	-.12***	.13***	-.12***				

CORP2	.05	.05	-.11***	.00	-.07**	.07*	-.05	.04				
CORP3	-.11***	-.07*	.24****	-.05	.04	.03	-.01	-.07*				
CORP4	-.14****	.03	-.05	.20****	-.15****	.05	-.08**	.16****				
LAW1	.14****	-.02	-.04	-.10**	.10**	.02	-.08**	-.05				
LAW2	.01	-.03	-.01	.04	-.02	.07*	-.02	-.05				
LAW3	-.05	-.03	.06	.02	-.06	-.08*	.08**	.08*				
LAW4	-.08*	.08*	-.03	.04	-.01	.03	-.02	-.02				
Casetypes												
Collect	.15****	.04	-.14****	-.09**	.07*	.06	.00	-.14****				
Consumer	-.08*	-.01	-.00	.13***	-.19****	.16****	-.15****	.13***				
Private	-.11***	-.05	.15****	.01	-.00	.03	.04	-.06				
LLT	.03	.03	-.01	-.08*	.11***	-.14****	.06	.00				
TLL	-.00	.05	-.06	.02	.03	-.19****	.09**	.12***				
Forum & Pleading												
Mediated	-.06	.07*	.04	-.05	-.05	-.02	.05	.02	-.06	-.01	.02	-.00
Prior Relationships	-.03	.08*	.05	-.09**	.00	-.06	.07*	.01	.07*	-.03	-.01	.01

(continued)

Appendix Table 4.ii—*(continued)*

Condition	ETH1	ETH2	ETH3	ETH4	GND1	GND2	GND3	GND4	SUM1	SUM2	SUM3	SUM4
Claim Size	-.07*	.01	.04	.05	.05	.11***	-.06	-.07	-.04	.13***	-.25****	.08**
Admitted Liability	.09**	.04	-.07*	-.09**	.04	-.03	-.01	.00	.17****	.06	-.06	-.24****
Counterclaim	-.03	.00	.03	.01	.02	-.07*	.10**	-.02	-.07*	-.06	.06	.10**
Mediation Cases N=280												
Monetary Outcome	.08	.03	-.01	-.14**	-.02	-.07	.04	.08	.17***	.02	-.00	-.17***
Agreement	.01	-.03	.02	.01	-.10*	-.09	.04	.16**	.06	-.03	.00	-.04
Subsequent	.03	.02	-.11*	.07	-.02	-.03	.08	-.02	-.02	-.01	.05	.05
Nonmonetary	-.15**	-.06	.18***	.05	-.10*	.03	-.01	.08	-.10*	.00	.06	.02
Add Nonmonetary	.04	-.11*	-.03	.16***	-.05	-.02	.00	.06	-.11*	-.08	-.03	.12**

*p<.10; **p<.05; ***p<.01; ****p<.001

a SUM is summarized structural conditions composed of cases in corresponding conditions in SES, CORP (corporate), and LAW (legal status). See variable description in Chapter Four.

Notes

NOTES TO THE INTRODUCTION

1. More than 80% of the small claims disputants categorized as race-ethnic minorities were of Hispanic origin. I discuss this in more detail at numerous points but I want to clarify here that I use the designation "Latino" to refer to the entire group of minority disputants. In most cases, I use the term "Latino" to designate persons of Spanish descent. However, when describing others' scholarship, I often use the term that they have used. In the Southwest region, "Anglo" is the common term for non-Hispanic whites.
2. All interview schedules (see Chapter Four) were finalized before I began work on the project, though I did add 3–4 questions early in data collection.
3. The MetroCourt research was supported by a grant from the Fund for Research in Dispute Resolution to UNM Professors Michelle Hermann and Mary Beth West with Gary LaFree. The final report (Hermann et al 1992 and subsequent analyses (Rack 1994a; LaFree & Rack 1996) showed significant ethnic and gender differences in monetary outcomes in mediated disputes compared to those adjudicated in small claims court In Chapter Six, these analyses are repeated with the same results using the relational case variables designed for this analysis.
4. Chapters Six and Eight provide summaries of many analyses specifying mediators' ethnicity and gender effects on monetary and satisfaction outcomes, and the apparent messages to which disputants responded. Mediators are again discussed in Chapter Twelve.
5. Intersection terminology is necessary. I read an article in the criminology literature suggesting the term "ethgender" to describe intersections of ethnicity and gender akin to the term "ethclass" Gordon proposed to specify a different intersection. I cannot find the reference so I take responsibility for initiating use of this term in this book.
6. Harding (1991) proposed a three dimensional conceptual tool she called a "matrix of privilege" using race, gender and class. This is a conceptual advance from Gordon's "ethclasses" but is unwieldy in analytic practice because ascriptive and achieved statuses are conflated and analytic categories are, at a minimum, increased to eight. Used interactively, this would result in 64 possible disputant variables.

7. *Pro se* is the Latin term used in legal settings to specify a party without legal counsel, thus acting "for oneself."

NOTES TO CHAPTER ONE

1. Peace Studies grew from pacifist Christian traditions and Ghandian nonviolence. The key notion is the unity of means and ends: scrupulous moral consistency.
2. For example, Gonzales (1993) reports scholarly and anecdotal evidence suggesting that, through 1930s and 1940s the Anglo-*Hispano* leadership observed a "gentlemen's agreement" not to openly deal with prejudice. At that time, New Mexicans were motivated to avert ethnic conflict to avoid charges of a lack of loyalty during World War II and avoided mention of regional prejudice issues when debating national ones in, for example, the Fair Employment Practices Act 1944. A member of the debate was quoted as saying, "Not once did we question or challenge the powerful interests in our homeland, nor did we dare mention words like racism . . . for fear we would be chastised and accused of being ungrateful Mexicans" (Gonzales 1993:169–70).
3. Although complicated with gender intersections, there is evidence (see Chapter Ten) that Latino men and Anglo women avoided meeting in mediation.
4. IND-COL research demonstrates variability in individual expression and content across national cultures and by ethnic groups within national cultures. Oyserman, Coon & Kemmelmeier (2002:42) concluded their meta-analysis of the research of individualism-collectivism: "On the basis of our integration of the available data, we propose that the most basic way of defining and assessing IND is the extent to which personal uniqueness and independence is valued. Likewise, the most basic way of defining and assessing COL is the extent to which duty to ingroup (and in cross-national comparisons, group harmony) is valued."
5. Michele Gelfand and her colleagues (Gelfand et al 2001) have launched a highly productive research program to determine how various taken-for-granted negotiation truisms (e.g., self-serving bias, attribution error, etc) are culture-bound. At the conclusion of their study of conflict construal (conflict framing), they write:

   "This research illustrates that there are both universal and culture-specific dimensions of conflict construal. Theoretically speaking, this study illustrates that culture is intricately tied to cognition in conflict situations, which suggests that research on cognition in the dominant paradigm in negotiation research may be laden with cultural elements and should be further examined to explicate universal and culture-specific elements. Practically speaking, this study illustrates that people from different cultures can perceive identical conflicts differently, which may ultimately relate to intercultural difficulties." (Gelfand et al 2001)
6. Unsurprisingly, the correlation between IND-COL and various behavioral indices like conflict styles is more significant when individual orientation

is measured (Oetzel 1998; Ting Toomey, Oetzel & Yee-jung 2001), an impossibility in this study. Nevertheless, as discussed in the following chapters, significant behavioral differences between populations socialized in individualist vs. collectivist cultures exist when investigators use ethnicity and/or nationality as a proxy.

7. Cross-cultural researchers usually seek cultural "etics" that can be used for comparison across cultures–like the IND-COL construct—but are aware that the various components of culture manifest in unique ways within interconnected cultural wholes. See Triandi et al 1993; Gelfand et al 2001, 2002; Morris et al (1999); Morris & Leung (2000).

NOTES TO CHAPTER TWO

1. Cohen (1978) traced the term "ethnicity" to 1971, finding that it represented a paradigm shift in anthropology and sociology away from an idea of discrete cultures (because few were homogenous) and Parsonian models of static cultural influence, and toward cultural multiplicity and change. Anthropology began to see nesting dichotomizations of we/they characterized by boundaries; sociology began to define ethnic identities with a more open-ended "sense of common descent" that was unstable and discontinuous. Cohen concluded that the essence of the paradigm shift was that culture (anthropology) and stratification categories (sociology) could have no salience without a context of "when, where, and who." Omi & Winant (1994) argue that the term "ethnicity" usually downplays racial structuring. However, because ethnic (not racial) differences are an increasingly salient basis for describing group conflict internationally, and "race" categorization for Southwestern group differences are arguably invalid, I use the term "ethnicity" for categorical difference.
2. Note that I use these same terms (horizontal and vertical) to describe the power gradient in the dispute dyads in this study but I am not using the terms as Triandis does here.
3. In often-cited research conducted four decades ago, Sherif & Sherif manipulated competitive and hostile group boundaries into existence among otherwise similar young boys, and dispersed them through engagement in cooperative tasks, a "superordinate goal." Numerous studies since then have shown the strength and reliability of the cooperative and competitive effect on inter-group relations (Fisher 1990; Pruitt & Carnevale 1993).
4. It is increasingly clear in the U.S. that inequality, even more than deprivation, is a key variable in a myriad of social dysfunctions including crime, physical and mental illness, alienation, political corruption and ecological degradation (Pizzigati 2004).
5. This point is interesting for clarifying domain differences in identity; the turf and ethnic dimensions of gang affiliation comes to mind.
6. Conclusion reached by 1968 National Advisory Commission on Civil Disorders (see Hacker 1992).

NOTES TO CHAPTER THREE

1. Latinos in the New Mexico identify with a variety of ethnic labels, almost *never* as "Latinos." However, most of the country uses this term and so it is used here.
2. Kivas are round ceremonial chambers common to a diverse group of tribes linked by other cultural similarities as "pueblo" Indians.
3. Non-protestant and often non-Christian, darker skinned immigrants in the northeast; newly emancipated black citizens entering the political and professional classes the south; Chinese men now idle with completion of the railroad in the west; and in the southwest, Indians and Spanish-speaking Catholics.
4. In the 1990 census, at the time of the study, about half of Bernalillo County residents "of Hispanic descent" answered the race question as "white" and half as "other" race, presumably Mestizo.
5. Today, the reclaimed land is home to Tierra Wools, a weaving collective using the grant for grazing sheep. The legacy of communal ownership in New Mexico is still apparent; approximately one third of the total land in the state is owned by the U.S. Government, another form of collective ownership.
6. In a meta-analysis of research findings on Latino acculturation in the United States, Moyerman & Forman (1992) find a transitional moment in culture-linked attitudes for Latino respondents. Traditionally, Latino cultural values (like collectivist cultures generally) emphasize good relationships, especially vertical ones with superiors and patriarchs. In the middle phases of acculturation, this binding respect for authority is lost. In middle class attainment, the studies showed that the prior pattern of respectful vertical relationships was re-established. This is not co-optation and assent to domination, Moyerman & Forman argued, but rather a return to a traditional cultural pattern. In a meta-analysis of 111 studies, increased field independence or perceptual context independence (see Witkin et al 1979) was the most consistent indicator of acculturation of all psychological dimensions assessed (Moyerman & Forman 1992).
7. In the 1990 census, 38% of the population in Bernalillo County identified as "of Hispanic origin;" of these, approximately half identified as "Mexican" and the other half as "other" Hispanic, and 10% reported being born out of state. The non-Hispanic county population in 1990 was reported as 55% Anglo and 7% other minorities, primarily Native American. In the 2000 census, 42% of Bernalillo County (similar to the entire state) identified as Hispanic or Latino, 48% as non-Hispanic White or "Anglo," and 10% other minorities, mostly Native American.
8. The mediation contract was roughly equal to one judicial salary and the disposition rate roughly the same. However, there were obvious bureaucratic benefits for mediation over one judge: space allocated to the mediation service was about half that of a courtroom and chambers, costs were added to filing charges to recoup and the court was relieved of one clerk

position. In addition, the mediation service operated evenings and weekends at no further cost to the court.

9. Ting-Toomey points out that the greater use of avoidance as a conflict style by collectivist groups comes from a different root than avoidance in individualist cultures: avoidance is a face-saving strategy that rests on respectful avoidance of overt conflict for self *and* others.
10. The trainees and subsequent mediators tended to be over 35 years old, well-educated and idealistic. The mediators' income was often lower than what might be expected from their educational status. Mediators commonly remarked on the fact that, as a group, we tended to be people who were uncomfortable with conflict in our own lives and sought out mediation as an opportunity for personal development. As observers often note (e.g., Harrington & Merry 1988; Merry 1987), mediators tended to be "nice," well meaning people. As in other mediation settings (Wahrfatig 1982; Rifkin 1989), Anglo women comprised most of the volunteer mediator group. In fact, the gendered quality of mediation is cautiously discussed as a "feminization" of law (see Kolb & Rubin 1989), although this assessment is vulnerable to gender-based ghettoization and increased gender stratification. A fair to large proportion of the mediators aspired to a paid profession in the mediation field.
11. Interestingly, the little research done suggests that disputants in power imbalanced dyads accept mediator attempts to balance power by supporting weaker parties more strongly. The researchers note that the question, of course, is how much weaker party support is acceptable (Pruitt & Carnevale 1993).
12. Legal scholars often question the institutional relationship between adjudication and mediation. Resnick (1986) for example, identifies the growth of mediation as a social response fueled by dissatisfaction with adjudication, what she called a "default" preference for mediation. Menkle-Meadow (1991) attempted to clarify whether mediation was a competitive or complementary forum, concluding that it was both. Nader (1993) is adamant that harmony ideology in the legal profession is an instrument of coercive pacification. Nader (1991; 1993) argues that, historically, the rise of harmony based justice models correlates with times when dominant groups fear insurgence (e.g., Spanish colonial rulers and after the Civil War). She reports on Supreme Court Justice Warren Berger's 1974 call for alternative dispute resolution (ADR) fora because "healing [is] more civilized than contentiousness" (cf. Nader 1993) as another example of suppression, this time of rights-based litigation resulting from the 1964 Civil Rights Act. Various researchers (e.g., Merry 1982; Nader 1990; Kidder & Hostetler 1990) have found historical and contemporary evidence that conciliation-based dispute resolution models serve to maintain existing hierarchical social relations. The second justification for legal informality, over-crowding in the justice system, is (arguably) spurious. Gallanter (1983) gathered data showing that the "litigation explosion" used to justify ADR innovations was significantly overstated.

13. Sometimes, this appeared to be unwitting. For example, an Answer might have said "yes, we bought the couch but my husband took the debt in the divorce agreement" but the respondent didn't realize that she could be nevertheless legally liable for the entire debt. More often, the Answers were simply excuses of poverty, a defense that also held no legal merit.
14. It is important to note that the court mediation program where this study was conducted has changed in various ways since 1991. Sensitivity to ethnicity became part of the basic training process, extreme care is taken to avoid scheduling monolingual mediators with Spanish-speaking disputants, a more overt process for mediator evaluation is planned, and the mediation program has been more institutionalized as part of the court rather than contracted out.

NOTES TO CHAPTER FOUR

1. The MetroCourt Project dataset (#6487 Metro Court Project: A Study of Mediation and Adjudication in Bernalillo County [Albuquerque], New Mexico, Small Claims Court, 1990–1992 Investigator: LaFree, Gary & Rack, Christine) is available from the Inter-University Consortium for Political and Social Research: ICPSR, University of Michigan, Institute for Social Research, P.O. Box 1248, Ann Arbor, MI 48106–1248 or on-line at http://www.icpsr.umich.edu.
2. See Hermann et al (1992), LaFree and Rack (1996), and Rack (1997) for detailed description of coding decisions.
3. Middle Eastern disputants were coded as "others" and assigned to the lower ethnic status category because the study took place during the first Gulf War. Various disputants mentioned the high level of public animosity during this time.
4. Of the ethnic, gender, and summarized structural condition, greater liability was initially admitted by lower status and Latino respondents in the first HILO conditions but was unlikely from higher status and Anglo respondents in the fourth LOHI structural and ethnic conditions. Latino respondents with Latino claimants were also unlikely to admit initial liability.
5. To determine bargaining positions, I carefully screened a document I compiled from all disputant and mediator questionnaires with responses to questions about positional changes. Disputants were asked, "[When the case was filed] How much did you feel you were really owed [or owed]" (position 2); "During the mediation but before the final agreement, if any, did you change your position about how much you [were owed/owed]?" If they answered affirmatively, they were presented with a request for the amount (position 3). Disputants were asked, "In the final agreement, did you agree to [accept less/pay more] than you wanted to in your final position?" again followed by a query for the amount (position 4). Missing data was substituted from mediator reports answering the following questions for claimants: "What was the initial claim sought by the claimant

from the respondent," (substituted for position 2), "If there was an initial modification, how much was the claimant seeking at that time?" (substituted for position 3), and "Later, in joint session or caucus, how much was the claimant willing to accept?" (substituted for position 4). Missing data about respondent bargaining was provided from mediator responses to these questions: "Liability admitted at the start of mediation" (position 2), "Later, in joint session or caucus, how much was the respondent willing to pay?" (position 3) and "How much did the respondent agree to pay in the final agreement, if any?" (position 4). In some cases, I clarified disputants' intermediate positions using this process, but for the most part, the bargaining variables were coded directly from interviews when they were available.

6. In 1994, I also coded mediation claimant bargaining rationales from the same open-ended questions used in the 1996 coding. In 1994, these fields were assessed for inter-coder reliability. Other than one problematic code, independent coding agreed in approximately 85% of all cases. The coding structure used in 1996 was adjusted somewhat to account for the problematic code, to incorporate the learning from the 1994 analysis (Rack 1994c and 1995), and to more clearly address the theoretical constructs of interest in the present analyses.
7. See Rack (1997) for maximum likelihood estimates of ethgender intersections with structural (achieved) status.
8. Subsequent agreement cases were also linked to nonmonetary outcome cases according to the logic that subsequent settlement, even if for money, was a nonmonetary benefit from mediation. In interviews, these settlements were often linked to the mediation session for the disputants. Quite possibly, the study itself created this linkage, directly by the research process chosen and the questions asked, and indirectly by our repeated efforts to ask people questions about their experience, and thus to define it.
9. Most often, the nonmonetary outcome was coded as "minor;" e.g., a small act of reciprocity such as that the claimant would drop the suit, or a process agreement such as future avoidance between the disputants. Payment plans specified in the agreement were specifically coded into the dataset as present (1) or absent (0). Other nonmonetary elements that could be translated into a material value were coded as "major" nonmonetaries (e.g., return of a car or other personal belongings, specific work to be done, or additional warranties or credit at stores). A subset of major nonmonetaries were coded as "additional" or "compensatory" because they were exchanges in which a material item that was not a part of the original claim, had been substituted for part (additional) or all (compensatory) of a cash obligation. All cases including major nonmonetary outcomes (whether additional or compensatory) are excluded from the bargaining analyses.
10. Because payment plans were coded from different sources for the two fora, no statistical comparison is made in Appendix Table 4.i

NOTES TO CHAPTER FIVE

1. Other economists (see Walsh 1994) point out various fallacious understandings associated with classical and neoclassical theory that are attributed to Adam Smith but take little account of his actual writings and the context in which he wrote them. Walsh (1994:404) argues for a "morally nontrivial" economic theory that might acknowledge responsibility to other persons and to the community on the one hand, and malevolence on the other, without recourse to altruism—"something that makes self-interest's pursuit worthy of being called rational . . . self-interest is a component, not the sole or dominant principle of human rationality." Korten (2001[1995]) argues that the corporate capitalism currently holding sway violates a number of Smith's assumptions and should not be considered capitalism at all.
2. Polanyi describes how, in spite of the threat to social order, the philosophy that came to be called "laissez faire" was "[b]orn as a mere penchant for non-bureaucratic methods . . . [and] evolved into a veritable faith in man's secular salvation through a self-regulating market" (p. 135). Polanyi describes this evolution of British thought from the humanistic approach of Adam Smith, who wrote in a time of "peaceful progress," through Malthus' acceptance of poverty as part of the natural order, and on to the triumphant liberalism of the more prosperous 1830s. What is important is that a set of recommendations about public policy was transformed into widespread acceptance as the laws of a natural order (Mayhew 2001).
3. Triandis (1995:26–29) makes this association of individualism with modernity and industrialization. He associates collectivism with agriculture and theorizes that hunter-gatherer societies would have leaned toward individualism.
4. Note that the class categories of high and low are defined more exclusively than the status variable: only the extremes of the factor-scored measure were used for classification and the classification was restricted to interviewed parties who answered the three questions that are the basis of the class measure.
5. I clarified this charge of avoidance from Anglo women because theoretical expectations would hypothesize that persons from collectivist cultures and men might avoid disputes. The patterns in larger dispute processing implied that Latino respondents did not answer claims as often as other ethgenders. However, the respondents in the cases in which Anglo women stated this reason for claiming were likely to be Anglo men.

NOTES TO CHAPTER SIX

1. Rack (1997) presents the numerical data with significance testing included in the three dimensions summarized in the first figure.
2. Female claimants with female respondents (the third LOLO insider relation) showed slightly higher mean monetary outcomes than the HIHI

insider relation. The unexpectedly higher outcomes for female claimants with female respondents can be understood by recalling that female-female cases were significantly likely to be HILO cases in structural dimensions, primarily as collection cases (see Chapter Four).

3. In order to achieve a near equal number of cases mediated by the three combinations of mediator gender pairs (2 women, 2 men, or mixed) and ethnicity (2 Anglo, 2 Latino, or mixed), individual male and Latino mediators were called to mediate study cases more often than individual Anglo women (see Chapter Four). As a result, individual men and/or Latino mediators could have a strong influence on the patterns found in these analyses. In this analysis, all non-Anglo mediators are called "Latino."
4. This summary is not intended to describe the full analysis which is published elsewhere (LaFree & Rack 1996; Rack 1994a; Rack 1995) or is available from the author.
5. Of 22 Latino claimant cases mediated by two women, 19 were settled during mediation resulting in a higher agreement rate, especially compared to male mediators (86.4% to 54.8%). However, nearly one third were resolved for nonmonetary exchanges and another quarter were settled by the Latino claimants dropping their claims. This Latino claimant outcome pattern with female mediators was significantly different than either Anglo claimants with female mediators or Latino claimants with other mediator gender combinations. Furthermore, compared to Latino male claimants, Latino female claimants dropped their claims most frequently with female mediators. Of 10 cases filed by Latino women that were mediated by women, nine reached agreement during the mediation session (the tenth reached agreement the following day); three were settled for nonmonetary outcomes, and the Latinas dropped their claims without substantial nonmonetary exchange in 5 cases.

NOTES TO CHAPTER SEVEN

1. Boulding (1962) suggested three over-arching forms of conflict behavior: approachers, avoiders, and absorbers. Of these, avoidance was specified as the most frustrating pattern for conflict resolvers. Theory and research results are contradictory about conflict avoidance, primarily because avoidance requires both motive and opportunity, and may depend heavily on the specific situation. Conflict avoidance is a covert conflict style, often related to a harmony motivation to spare feelings that is theoretically and empirically related to a collectivistic pattern, especially with ingroup members (Leung 1988; Ohbachi & Takahashi 1994; but see Chiu & Kosinski Jr. 1994). Abalos (1986) sees avoidance among Latinos as one expression of the submerged identity pattern of "emanation." However, conflict avoidance has been found in other situations where a harmony or collectivistic motive is less clear. For example, Ting Toomey (1986) found that black and white men were more likely than women to avoid relational conflict or tension (black women preferred to confront and white women

to compromise); avoidance is predicted to be a form of weaker party resistance and refusal (Donahue & Bresnahan 1994; Janeway 1980) especially when the options for action are poor (Delgado et al. 1985); and, interestingly, avoidance of direct conflict might also be a defense mechanism in the face of discomfort caused by intercultural contact (Kim & Ruben 1988) especially among dominant group members (Keefe & Padilla 1987; Schofield, 1986). What all of these theories and research have in common is the idea that conflict avoidance is an ambivalent behavior, stemming from psychological motivations that especially include shame, guilt, and passive-aggression. Legal scholarship is more clear about avoiding claims vs. avoiding claim-making (a stance also called "lumping it"). This scholarship stresses the opportunity side: Felstiner (1974, 1975) argued, conflict avoidance (for the respondent) is *more* likely in technologically complex and rich societies like the United States where exit costs are low, and *less* likely in technologically simple, poor societies (likely to be "collectivist") where exit costs are higher. On the claim-making side, even when opportunity exists, Vidmar & Schuller (1987) note that some of their Canadian respondents who did not initiate a formal complaint, appeared to have chosen a path of non-action ("lumping it") not because they didn't think a claim was likely to succeed (a primary motive given and an expectation of the researchers), but because they simply would rather not expend energy in conflict.

2. Other scholars have investigated negotiation behavior under different names. For example, Tutzauer & Roloff (1988) examined the ability to reach integrative agreements as a function of high limits and "interpersonal orientation." Forsyth (1990[1983]) reviewed the literature on interpersonal conflict resolution styles as cooperator or competitors. The former research indicated that high interpersonal orientation with high limits increased satisfaction directly but the research was unable to find that the outcomes were more integrative. In the latter review, Forsyth summarized that men used more jointly cooperative strategies but women negotiated with more jointly competitive styles. Forsyth suggests that results are mixed because motives were different for the two genders; men may have been more cooperative because those choices would maximize their outcomes, but women chose strategies based on the characteristics of the other party and the nature of the interpersonal setting.
3. As indicated in the graph, higher structural status claimants bargained relatively equally with higher and lower status respondents. If one examines the disaggregated components summarized here, only the legally represented claimants showed a different bargaining pattern based on whether the respondent was also legally represented. Similarly, *pro se* claimants conceded more of their claimed amount to legally represented respondents than to *pro se* respondents, and reported more substantial concessions during mediation. The graphs in Figure 7.1a minimize the divergent patterns found in legal status conditions because the number of cases was relatively small.

4. Bargaining Distances: analysis of pre-mediation distances taken from the second bargaining position showed frequent differences among conditions in structural/achieved dimensions but there were no significant differences in pre-mediation dispute distance between claimants and respondents for ethnic or gender status conditions. For example, structural HILO cases, due to higher admitted liability entered negotiations with *smaller* initial bargaining distance. In the fourth LOHI structural conditions, despite initial concessions made by claimants in position 2, the low rate of initial liability by the higher status respondents showed significantly *larger* mean distances between the parties in comparison with other status conditions. Ethnic HILO cases had *average* mean pre-mediation bargaining distances because, although Latino respondents admitted more of the debt, Anglo claimants raised their claimed amount above 100% to leave a 60% gap, similar to the other ethnic status conditions. Reported pre-mediation positions show the "tracking" phenomena in which initial positions tended to keep a proportional distance from one another.

NOTES TO CHAPTER EIGHT

1. I report many statistically significant patterns in this analysis that are not shown in the tables. For precise percentages and significance testing, see Rack (1997).
2. I described the coding used in this analysis in detail in Chapter Four but briefly remind the reader here. Instrumental variables are coded from 1) reported goals (material and monetary) taken from the same questions used in Table 5.1 with three differences—I coded the open-ended question for mediation claimants and respondents at the same time; the analysis is restricted to monetary outcome mediation cases rather than the full sample shown in Table 5.1; the focus of this analysis is a comparison of each status condition with all other disputants in the mediation monetary outcome sample; 2) interview text recording disputant responses to a question asked three times: "What made you change your position?" I interpreted disputants' instrumental explanation for their bargaining decisions as strategic (STR) if self-maximizing and rational; as better (BET) if their decision was perceived as better than alternatives; if the respondent claimed they were unjustly accused (R-TUF) or were not legally liable or the claimant reported that the respondent had refused to negotiate (C-TUF). I interpreted expressive motivations (from the same text as #2 above) indicating that something about the other person was part of the disputants' motivation (REL). I further specified whether the statements were sympathetic (SYM) toward the other party, antipathetic or hostile ("ANTI"), referred to a business relationship (BSREL), and/or affirmed a willingness to cooperate, compromise, and/or settle the matter (COOP). I marked interviews for statements suggesting that the mediation had been an emotional experience (EMO) using the full interview text, especially text associated with questions about anger and other

dimensions of psychological wellbeing. I noted which interviews indicated that the disputant felt a strong sense of having been cheated, coerced or tricked into an agreement in mediation (TRK). The source of coercion might have been the mediators, the other party, or the mediation situation. See Chapter Four for more detailed descriptions and Rack (1997) for examples of coding.

3. Note that the categories for motivation, unlike the coding for goal orientation used in Chapter Five, were not mutually exclusive. For example, claimants in the first HILO structural condition were likely to be both rational and relational; that is, they were likely to say that they thought they would get more (instrumental strategy) by negotiating, considering the poverty of the specific respondent (relational and often sympathetic).
4. Disputants may have settled for strategic reasons, that is, their explanation was rational and self-interested, but not in comparison with their appraisal of alternatives—for example, the dispute was settled because prolonging it interfered with vacation plans. I discuss my analysis of these comparative responses although they are not shown in Table 8.1
5. Claimant reports of unwilling respondents and respondent explanations of a lack of liability *were* strongly correlated with failure to reach agreement. Including all cases that went to mediation with interviews coded, nearly one third of the claimant interviews mentioned that the respondent had been unwilling to negotiate; Latino claimants reported this significantly more often than Anglo claimants. Cases with represented respondents, showing a lower monetary settlement rate overall (36.7%), were equally likely to settle regardless of interviews coded for a lack of liability. Thus, it appears likely that represented respondents who settled in mediation were reflecting a *style* of resistance when they noted a lack of liability rather than an expectation that they were not legally liable.
6. Emotional mediation experiences appeared to stem from two different sources- feeling ripped off or feeling emotional about the conflict-and therefore showed inconsistent patterns in subsequent analyses. When the sense of injustice was controlled in multivariate analyses, reports of an emotional experience from claimants indicated a higher monetary outcome. Despite this problem, I include these data here because emotion is theoretically a key factor to gender differences.
7. When intervenors enter a dispute, research suggests that the relational needs shift from wanting recognition (in the dispute dyad) to assurance that the intervenor is neutral and can be trusted to be generally benevolent or at least not harmful (Lind, Tyler & Huo 1997).
8. The significantly reduced outcomes for claimants reporting more prior relationships appears to be an effect of more precise interview data, and thus accurate. Missing interview data in Table 6.1 had been replaced with a prior relationship indicator of "1" (the modal response).
9. The weakened coefficient in this condition probably indicates that some or all of the 3 uncoded cases were ones that had the lowest monetary outcomes.

10. When the cases used are confined to those with both claimant and respondent coded bargaining variables, the outcome for Latino claimants with Anglo respondents shows only a marginally significant effect in the base model (-.272, $p<.10$) which was eliminated with the addition of claimant strategy.
11. First, cash and material concerns were less often cited by claimants and respondents in the LOLO insider condition in the ethnic, corporate and class dimensions. Second, interviews with both claimants and respondents in cases filed by lower structural status claimants more often offered relational bargaining rationales. Thus, relational motivations in bargaining tended to be a distinct pattern of lower status claimants in a pattern similar to strategy for higher status claims; respondents tended to match claimants. Third, lower status claimants (Latino, lower class, and individual claimants), especially in the LOHI rights-based condition reported bargaining resistance more frequently. Finally, interviews with lower status claimants more often reflected a sense of injustice in the process or outcome.
12. Compared to lower status Anglo claimants, lower structural status Latino claimants more often expressed sympathetic bargaining rationales ($p<.05$), cooperative intentions ($p<.05$) and less often expressed antipathy for the other party ($p<.10$): claimants in cases with two Anglo parties who were both individuals, showed antipathy in 41.7% of their interviews, sympathy in 8.3%, and cooperative statements in 16.7%. By contrast, claimants in intra-Latino disputes that were also individual-individual expressed antipathy in 12.5% of their interviews, sympathy in more than one third (37.5%) and cooperative statements in exactly one half (50%). Generally, patterns for antipathy were similar to reportage of emotional experiences except that recounting emotional interactions was less frequently associated with antipathy for Latino claimant interviews after mediation with Latino respondents. Overall, as a corollary, interviews with Latino disputants were responsible for the average frequency of harmony motives in lower structural status claimant disputes.
13. Outcomes for individual claimants with corporate respondents, although they appear disadvantaged and unstrategic, may well have been rational in light of the alternatives. Perhaps because liability is legally controlled by corporate parties, court outcomes showed a strong likelihood that the cases against corporate respondents would be dismissed. Individual claimants who settled with corporate respondents in mediation expressed significantly higher satisfaction, especially after nonmonetary outcomes were negotiated (data available from author), a trend suggested in the case studies offered in Chapter Ten.

NOTES TO CHAPTER NINE

1. Court costs were additions that all claimants would normally receive in a winning court case. Like interest and legal fees, these extra costs were

often major points of negotiation. On a small claim, they could be a significant factor in the ratios calculated here. Either the effect of these sums was balanced by diminished deserving, or most lower status claimants did not feel they were actually owed for court costs.

2. Maximum likelihood estimates demonstrating this can be seen in LaFree & Rack (1996) or Rack (1997).
3. The interview response that the outcome was "just about as expected" was interesting to examine in relation to structural status differences. Anglo male claimants chose this response most often when in corporate roles (76.7% to 35.7% when not corporate). Anglo and Latina women also chose this response more often when in structurally dominant positions, a pattern that was particularly extreme for Latinas who chose it in all cases in which they were in corporate roles (2 of 2, $p<.05$ compared to 2 of 10 individual appearances) or higher class (3 of 3, compared to 1 of 9 Latina claimants who were lower class). By contrast, none of the higher class Latino male claimants reported that their mediated outcomes were what they expected and their appearances as businessmen did not affect their likelihood of choosing this response.
4. This was a major forum distinction: by both satisfaction and evaluation responses: subjective evaluations in adjudication showed win-lose patterns where in mediation they did not. I clarified the source of this discrepancy to be in cases where payment plans had been negotiated. When payment plan cases were excluded, claimant and respondent satisfaction *was* inversely related, albeit less strongly than adjudication. This could be due to a more determinant value placed on payment plans or the fact that payment plan negotiations were most likely in cases where the respondent was lower incomes and often had poor alternatives. The latter explanation is consistent with motivational analyses in Chapter Eight and my overall interpretation stated in Chapter Eleven.
5. The mean positions obscure the fact that, of the four cases with respondents of similar ethgender, Latinas dropped their full claim in three of them. Of the three cases with Anglo male respondents, Latinas dropped their claim in 2 of them. Class and professional status appeared to determine the outcomes in both of these ethgender conditions.
6. In their experimental study of ethnic status activation, Rosenholtz & Cohen (1985) found that the Anglo and Hispanic junior high school student groups reported differentials in initiation and influence that were consistent with the idea that "distinctive" looks (i.e., darker complexion, hair and eyes) were the salient "discrimination clues" that activated stereotypes resulting in Anglo domination in mixed groups, a pattern they associated with a color-based discrimination in the United States. Because Latinos did not initiate less and weren't perceived by themselves or Anglos as less competent when their ethnic status was defined by Spanish surname (ethnic groups were similar in attitudes toward school), the authors ruled out cultural differences in cooperation. Class differences were not significant. The authors noted that similar studies with various Middle Eastern

group members found ethnic identity (by name and an introduction that included mention of ethnicity), not color, activated group power and prestige orders. Thus they concluded that the cues needed for discrimination of a status difference are culturally relative, determined empirically within "the mediating context of social reality. . . . the critical cue for discrimination of a status difference varies with time and place." In New Mexico, future research might clarify whether the disputants who identified themselves as Latino, but were identified by the mediators or the other party as Anglo, showed the same bargaining pattern as those who were perceived by all participants as Latinos.

7. In adjudication, the backlash against female claimants was even more severe. Respondents, regardless of gender, reported significant discomfort, dissatisfaction and poor evaluations after litigating with female claimants, despite unremarkable outcomes. Combined with the ethgender by forum analyses discussed in this chapter, it seems that the preference for mediating rather than adjudicating with female claimants is due to the way that the mediation forum allowed women to construct a cooperative rather than competitive style, thereby constraining backlash effects.

NOTES TO CHAPTER TEN

1. Single quotes indicate the interviewer is slightly paraphrasing; double quotes indicated verbatim transcription.
2. My opinion is that the same patterns would *not* be found in research with other minority group members. African American claimant patterns suggested a pro-active claiming stance; for example, one African American woman *claimed* against the moving company that held her furniture because she had refused to pay the bill (it was higher than the estimate). Interestingly, African Americans as a group scored more highly on individualism than any other U.S. ethnic group, even whites, in Oyserman's et al. 2002 meta-analysis. Native American claimants were more firm bargainers than Latinos; for example, an adjudication claimant who achieved the highest ratio outcome was a Native American female tenant who had refused agreement in mediation and taken the legal knowledge she gained from her respondent-landlord to hire a lawyer who successfully pled penalties. Asian claimants preferred rationality in mediation. This opinion can be readily critiqued because the patterns are consistent with stereotypical schema and the number of cases was too small for assessment. However, the relationship of stereotype to both empirical generalization and internalized schema complicates any quick disregard.
3. One Anglo claimant was explicit about a Haitian respondent: "He could have done better. He came in saying 'I know I owe,'" at the beginning of the mediation
4. The need for network input may be a major part of the reason that disputants who settled after the mediation session were less likely to later regret their outcomes. For less experienced bargainers, the pressure to

individually decide outcomes was a recipe for uninformed bargaining. Higher status parties were hardly without a similar network. Many of the cases involving lawyers and insurance companies included phone calls and private caucuses to include more people, especially people with greater decision-making power, in the bargaining.

5. For example, one Latina claimant who settled for a nonmonetary exchange (M305) said of her Anglo male respondent, "I knew he wouldn't come up with any money, but I did not feel comfortable confronting him in this situation." Another woman, Guatemalan and Spanish-only speaking (M211), who settled for a nonmonetary outcome said, "I expected that there would be justice. He said he wouldn't pay and he didn't." In one case (M159), a Latino woman claimed in concert with three other tenants against an Anglo male landlord. Of the lack of agreement in mediation (she settled subsequently) she said, "he wouldn't agree to pay . . . I deserved the money." The much higher class landlord in this case said that what was important to him was "Not to pay if I could help it." Anglo respondents were sometimes willing to go to extreme lengths to avoid monetary exchange: in one case (M243), the Anglo male respondent agreed in mediation to *undo* the repair work done on cars for a Latino couple, and return the cars in the original condition, rather than simply release the cars for which the final bill exceeded the estimated amount. The single mediator (an Anglo women) wrote "I felt that the [Anglo] respondent gave more than the claimants, but he seemed satisfied with his decision." In fact, he didn't follow through on this rather cumbersome solution and the case was returned to court. Between Latino disputants, nonmonetary agreements often answered the precise claim (e.g., returning items), a type of outcome that was associated throughout these analyses with more positive indicators. However, cases filed by Latino claimants against Anglo respondents resulted in "compensatory" nonmonetary agreements, that is, the Anglo respondents substituted a noncash exchange for a monetary claim.
6. In earlier analyses of mediator influence, we found that mixed ethnicity mediators showed the same privileging of Anglo claims as two Anglo mediators (LaFree & Rack 1996).
7. Competition between Latino women was often overt, and class status appeared determinant when cases were resolved. The only two cases between self-identified Latinas where class status was confirmed by interview as being a lower class claimant with a higher class respondent, like this case in which the respondent identified as Anglo, resulted in the claimants dropping their claims. The first case (M180, discussed above) was settled by the claimant's husband and the respondent's brother in the hall. The other case (M168) bore a striking resemblance to this one (M007): the lower income (household income below $20,000) claimant was discouraged by two Anglo mediators from pursuing her case based on a lack of evidence: "I thought it was like a court hearing. If I had known what the process was like I wouldn't have gone." The claimant reported

strong dissatisfaction: "I feel this way because they said I had to *see* the stupid kid throw rocks at my windows. Even though I know it was him." The claimant felt that the mediators took the respondent's side: "I would not even think of doing it this way again. I didn't like the people who handled the case." The claimant identified a class bias: "I wouldn't even advise anyone I know to go through mediation. I think these people go with people who have more money. Middle class people [sic] don't count with them. But one thing they like is my taxes." The respondent also felt that the mediators were biased, but toward the claimant's side; she said she had control because "I was not going to agree with her. The mediators kept trying to talk me into paying. I kept saying no." Class intimidation was obvious from the respondent's interview as well: the respondent was "upset" and said she felt this dispute was more of a "personal thing" noting that "The other party would not speak while everyone was there. When they caucused she talked alot. They were in the room for a long time." Even the respondent, who appeared to have been defending her 14 year old son out of loyalty (but effectively avoided paying the claimed $113 for the claimant's broken window) seemed to have preferred the idea of adjudication; "I expected it to be more like a court . . . It was too easy. It should be more like a court hearing, i.e., People's Court . . . [it] should scare kids. They might not respect [mediated] decisions. [It should be] more professional." In contrast, the agreements hovered at the 50% point in two matching LOHI class Latino cases that were *not* also female-female.

8. I interviewed this respondent. At a specific point in the interview, she started to use language that acknowledged breaking the windshield, then caught herself and changed the wording to a more hypothetical phrasing.
9. Conflict avoidance is a specific pattern associated with collectivist cultures and debt avoidance was a primary assumption of the morally pejorative term "judgment proof" discussed in Chapter Three. Chapter Five discussed earlier analyses showing Anglo women were particularly likely to explain their claiming as in response to Anglo male avoidance of them in the past. In the more extensive coding in 1996, using the full interview text, I found that 17.5% of the claimant interviews, more often female claimants with male respondents, discussed respondent avoidance as a dispute issue. On the other hand, I also coded respondent interviews which, like the one here, specifically responded to this implicit criticism: twelve percent of all respondent interviews contained a moral disavowal of intentional avoidance, primarily lower status respondents in the first HILO power dependent condition, significantly more often Latino respondents with Anglo claimants (30.4%) and pro se respondents with legally represented claimants (34.6%). However, claimants in these conditions were unlikely to suggest in the interview that the respondent was avoiding them.
10. This case was randomly assigned to adjudication but was referred to mediation by the judge in compliance with the claimant's request.

11. In the rare cases in which respondents tried to argue that charges were unfair because tests were unnecessary or because the care was incompetent or unsolicited, I found that collectors ended up making slight adjustments to their claims, usually in subsequent agreements. In adjudication, respondents who argued various consumer counterclaims were regularly told by the judge to file a new case and were ordered to pay the full claim with all additional charges.

NOTES TO CHAPTER ELEVEN

1. Recall that Latino-Latino disputes in the third LOLO insider condition were correlated with the LOLO corporate condition, that is, intra-Latino disputes often involved two private, noncorporate individuals (see Rack 1997). Thus, according to the logic of regression analyses, the disadvantaged effect for these claimants was additive; both effects were of similar magnitude and significance in the multivariate model.
2. Of twelve cases, only 3 cases were brought to mediation and only one of these cases reached agreement. This one case settled after the mediation session so that there were no cases in the bargaining analysis.
3. Because there was only one Latino claimant cases settled with an Anglo female respondent, and this respondent was perceived by mediators and the claimant as Latina, these data cannot speak for Anglo female respondent exploitation of Latino claimant bargaining.
4. Anglo female claimants made greater concessions to Anglo female respondents and were the defining cases responsible for significantly advantaged (i.e., reduced) outcomes for Anglo female respondents reported earlier (Rack 1994; LaFree & Rack 1996). In goal analyses, female claimants with female respondents cited material goals most often but settled in mediation for less than comparable adjudicated outcomes. In contrast to all other claimant ethgenders, Anglo women reported little disappointment with their reduced outcome with Anglo female respondents. Though female claimants were likely to express antipathy toward female respondents, their interviews were rarely coded as indicating that they felt cheated. Although often sympathetic in cases with both female and male respondents, Anglo female claimants made fewer substantive concessions with men than they did with female respondents of the same ethnic status. This material effect was specific to higher status Anglo women: Unlike all other claimant ethgender groups, where higher class status resulted in higher mean outcomes, higher class Anglo female claimants (N=20) settled for mean outcomes than were 8% *lower* than lower class Anglo female claimants (N = 21).
5. An overt preference for judicial decision-making was common for Latina disputants. As one young Latino teenager said in an interview (M147) concerning the mediation he had attended with his mother who was the respondent: " . . . my mom wanted to wait for court. Then she'd know if it was fair." Among the NAR cases, the preference for court decisions was

often articulated during the interview but, interestingly, was readily misperceived by mediators. For example, a 24 year old higher class Latina claimed $275 as a return for her damage deposit from her 61 year old lower class Latina landlady (M160). The Latina respondent was described by the more experienced Anglo male mediator as an "older Hispanic very conservative woman" and by the inexperienced Latino male mediator as "non-accommodating, unwilling to compromise, hostile" who didn't want to mediate "except to be vindicated." The mediators agreed that "animosity between the parties never dissipated." However, this respondent in the interview explained her resistance as wanting legal guidance: "I needed to know my rights as a landlord . . . I didn't feel as much in control . . . she came out right away lying and that upsets me and then I can't talk." About the lack of agreement she said, "These people are very aggressive and young. They try to overpower people and that's why I'm going to court." In the follow-up interview the claimant reported that the ruling was "the same" as the final position in mediation but the respondent said it was "much better." The respondent-landlady would prefer mediation in the future "because I'm an understanding person. But if I wasn't satisfied, I would take it another step."

NOTES TO CHAPTER TWELVE

1. Respondents in cross-gender disputes reported a sense of injustice in their mediated outcomes three times more often than respondents in same-sex dispute dyads. This psychological vulnerability gives support for the various arguments against divorce mediation (e.g., Bryan 1992; Grillo 1991) but makes three important distinctions: 1) men as well as women were vulnerable to gender distrust; 2) gender distrust had a potent psychological content but no apparent substantive basis; 3) gender distrust was most visible in a dependent role relationship with a member of the opposite gender.
2. I examined answers to the question "how satisfied were you with the outcome of this case?" controlling for *interviewer* ethnicity. I did find that Latino men expressed less satisfaction to other Spanish-surnamed male interviewers.
3. In analyses that are not included in this work, I found the higher claimant reported satisfaction in mediation than adjudication specifically resulted from procedural comfort and the presence of nonmonetary elements in the agreements, including payment plans. Claimant satisfaction was reduced by feeling tricked. Respondents' higher satisfaction was explained in part by procedural comfort, but residual respondent satisfaction could not be explained in terms of subjective interview questions or objective outcome measures. In my opinion, increased respondent satisfaction in mediation is due to respectful treatment rather than shaming, and a greater sense of outcome control for HILO respondents.
4. I found that Anglo male claimants were more likely than other claimant ethgenders to explain their bargaining positions with itemized calculations,

e.g., "Agreed to discount 20% if paid now" (M106), "80% was sort of like the deductible in an insurance claim" (M036); "I wanted interest and court costs if I had to go to court" (M021). These rational calculations effectively provided limits to their bargaining concessions and numerical definition for their demands (Rack 1994b; 1995), By way of contrast, one mediator noted that a Latino male claimant (M220) "had no bottom line that he was willing to share." In the interview, this claimant described the respondent's offer "an insult," responding to bargaining positions but not calculating.

5. In adjudication, compliance in the HILO corporate and legal condition measured in the follow-up was significantly worse than in other conditions, and improved significantly in the mediated cases. This improvement was due to a significant shift in Latina compliance: Latina respondents were *least* likely to comply with adjudicated rulings and *most* often complied with mediated agreements.
6. This may be changing. A "pro se office" now exists at the Bernalillo County Court. Someone from this office now assists with filing and navigating and offers a "legal facts" night once a week for means-tested disputants to consult with a pro-bono lawyer.
7. Nonmonetary outcomes that *directly* responded to the claim (e.g., returning the car, repairing the damage) were likely to be evaluated more highly by disputants than any other outcomes, but constructed nonmonetary tradeoffs or substitutions for clearly monetary claims had the opposite effect.
8. Within the zero-sum constraints of small claims mediation bargaining, businesses confronted with a consumer complaint were the one rights-based dispute category that was able to achieve somewhat integrative agreements by expanding the pie: businessmen could add value by offering products and services that represented little loss to themselves and had higher value for the customer; the counterpart relationship added other-concern bargaining incentives.
9. Latino respondents tended not to comply with agreements they considered unfair. The pattern of "agreement breakdown" (early failure of an agreement) was more common in Latino respondent cases, most often Latino men. Exploration of these cases showed a focused pattern in exactly which agreements Latino men did not fulfill. For example, a lower class ironworker sued by a higher class Latino schoolteacher for $700 "consumer/fraud." The $700 was stolen by a third party claiming to represent the respondent and the claimant had written a check in the third party's name. The respondent agreed in mediation to give the teacher a new estimate with the disputed $700 subtracted. According to the respondent's wife, her husband had felt pressured by all the talk in the mediation session, particularly by the claimant's wife. The respondent, in an interview dotted with long and largely impenetrable silences, explained that his lawyer had threatened to drop his case if he accepted liability for the stolen check in mediation. The respondent, though he delivered the new

estimate, had simply inflated it. The claimant returned the case to court where it was dismissed.

10. Citing foundational experiments in 1970 by Kelley & Stahelski, and others subsequently, Forsyth (1990:351–357) reports this phenomenon: nearly half—47%—of competitors mis-perceived cooperators as competitive. See also Weber & Messick (2004).

Bibliography

Abalos, David T. (1986). *Latinos in the United States: The sacred and the political.* Notre Dame: University of Notre Dame Press.

——. (2002). *The Latino Male: A radical redefinition.* Boulder: Lynne Rienner Publishers.

Abel, Richard L. (1982) Introduction. In Abel, Richard L. (Ed.). *The politics of informal justice,* Vol 1 (The American experience). New York: Academic Press.

Adair, Wendi Lyn & Jeanne M. Brett (2004). Culture and negotiation processes. In Gelfand, Michele J. & Jeanne M. Brett (Eds.) (2004). *The Handbook of Negotiation and Culture.* Stanford CA: Stanford University Press.

Albert, Rosita Daskal (1986). Communication and attributional differences between Hispanics and Anglo-Americans. In Kim, Young Yun (Ed.) (1986). *Interethnic communication: Current research.* Newbury Park: Sage.

Alfini, James J. (1991). Trashing, bashing and hashing it out: Is this the end of "good mediation"? *Florida State University Law Review* 19(1):47–75.

Anzaldúa, Gloria (1987). *Borderlands/la frontera: The new mestiza.* San Francisco: Spinsters.

Archer, Margaret S. (1995). *Realist social theory: The morphogenetic approach.* Cambridge: Cambridge University Press.

——. (1996). *Culture and agency* (revised edition). Cambridge: Cambridge University Press (first edition 1988).

Arthur, W. Brian (1994). Inductive reasoning and bounded rationality. *American Economic Review* 84(2):406–411.

Atencio, Tomás (1988). "Resolana: A Chicano pathway to knowledge." Ernesto Galarza Commemorative Lecture, Stanford Center for Chicano Research, Stanford University.

Avruch, Kevin, Peter W. Black (1991). Introduction: Culture and Conflict Resolution. In Avruch, Kevin, Peter W. (1991), Black & Joseph A. Scimecca (Eds.) (1991). *Conflict resolution: Cross cultural perspectives.* New York: Greenwood Press.

Avruch, Kevin, Peter W. Black & Joseph A. Scimecca (Eds.) (1991). *Conflict resolution: Cross cultural perspectives.* New York: Greenwood Press.

Axelrod, Robert (1984). *The evolution of cooperation.* New York: Basic Books.

Baca Zinn, Maxinne (1989). Family, race, and poverty in the eighties. *Signs: A Journal of Women in Culture and Society,* 14(4): 856–874. Reprinted in Yetman, Norman R. (Ed.) (1991). *Majority and minority.* Boston: Allyn and Bacon.

Baltes, Paul B. & Ursula M. Straudinger (1996). Interactive minds in a life span perspective: Prologue. In Baltes, Paul B. & Ursula M. Straudinger (Eds.) (1996: 1–32). *Interactive minds.* Cambridge: Cambridge University Press.

Bangert, David C. and Kahkashan Pirzada (1991). Culture and negotiation. *Program on Conflict Resolution Working Paper Series,* 1991–1994, University of Hawaii at Manoa.

Banton, Michael (1983). *Racial and ethnic competition.* Cambridge: Oxford University Press.

Barber, Benjamin R. (1992). Jihad vs. McWorld. *The Atlantic Monthly* 269(3) March 1992.

Barrera, Mario (1979). *Race and class in the southwest.* Notre Dame, IN: University of Notre Dame Press.

Barth, Fredrik (Ed.) (1969). Introduction. In Barth, Fredrik (Ed.) (1969) *Ethnic groups and boundaries: The social organization of cultural difference.* Boston: Little Brown & Co.

Bartos, Otomar J. (1970). Determinants and consequences of toughness. In Swingle, Paul (Ed.) (1970). *The structure of conflict.* New York: Academic Press.

Baruch Bush, Robert A. & Joseph P. Folger (1994). *The promise of mediation: Responding to conflict through empowerment and recognition.* San Francisco: Jossey-Bass.

Batson, C. Daniel (1993). Communal and exchange relationships: What is the difference? *Personality and Social Psychology Bulletin* 19:677–683.

——. (1991). *The altruism question: Toward a social-psychological answer.* Hillsdale, N.J.: Lawrence Erlbaum Associates, 1991.

Beauvoir, Simone de (1952). *The second sex.* New York: Vintage.

Bellah, Robert N., Madsen, Richard, Sullivan, William M., Swidler, Ann and Tipton, Steven M. (1985). *Habits of the heart.* New York: Harper & Row.

Bendor, Jonathan, Kramer, Roderick M. & Stout, Suzanne (1991). When in doubt . . . Cooperation in a noisy prisoner's dilemma. *Journal of Conflict Resolution* 35(4): 691–719.

Bennett, Joel B. (1988). Power and influence as distinct personality traits: Development and validation of a psychometric measure. *Journal of Research in Personality* 22:361–394.

Benson, Michael L. (1985). Denying the guilty mind: Accounting for criminal involvement in a white-collar crime. *Criminology* 23(4):590–599.

Berg, Ellen Ziskind (1994). Gendering conflict resolution. *Peace & Change* 19(4):325–348.

Berger, Joseph & Morris Zelditch (Eds.) (1985). *Status, rewards, and influence: How expectations organize behavior.* San Francisco: Jossey-Bass.

Berger, Joseph, Bernard P. Cohen & Morris Zelditch, Jr. (1972). Status characteristics and social interaction. *American Sociological Review* 37:241–55.

Berger, Joseph, David G. Wagner & Morris Zelditch (1985). Introduction. In Berger, Joseph & Morris Zelditch (Eds.) (1985). *Status, rewards, and influence: How expectations organize behavior.* San Francisco: Jossey-Bass.

Berreman, Gerald D. (1972). Race, caste and other invidious distinctions in social stratification. *Race* XIII:4.

Best, Steven & Douglas Kellner (1991). *Postmodern theory: Critical interrogations.* New York: Guilford Press.

Beutel, Ann M. & Margaret Mooney Marini (1995). Gender and values. *American Sociological Review* 60:436–448.

Black, Donald (1989). *Sociological justice.* New York: Oxford University Press.

Blalock, Hubert M. & Paul H. Wilken (1979). *Intergroup processes: A micro-macro perspective.* New York: Free Press.

Blau, Peter M. (1987). Microprocess and macrostructure. In Cook, Karen S. (Ed.) (1987) *Social exchange theory.* Newbury Park: Sage.

Blauner, Robert (1972). *Racial oppression in America.* New York: Harper & Row.

Blea, Irene I. (1992). *La Chicana and the intersection of race, class, and gender.* New York: Praeger.

Bonacich, Edna (1980). Class approaches to ethnicity and race. *Insurgent Sociologist* 10:2.

Bonilla-Silva, Eduardo (2003). *Racism without racists: Color-blind racism and the persistence of racial inequality in the United States.* New York: Rowman & Littlefield.

Boulding, Kenneth (1962). *Conflict and defense.* New York: Harper & Row.

Bourdieu, Pierre & Loic J.D. Wacquant (1992). *An invitation to reflexive sociology.* Chicago: University of Chicago Press.

Bourdieu, Pierre (1988[1984]). *Homo academicus.* Stanford: Stanford University Press.

——. (1990). *In other words.* Palo Alto:Stanford University Press.

Boyle, Richard & Richard Coughlin (1994). Conceptualizing and operationalizing Cultural Theory variables: Survey research results. In D. Coyle & R. Ellis (Eds.) *Politics, Policy and Culture* (1994) Boulder: Westview Press.

Brett, Jeanne & Shirli Kopelman (2004). Cross-cultural perspectives on cooperation in social dilemmas. In Gelfand, Michele J. & Jeanne M. Brett (Eds.) (2004). *The handbook of negotiation and culture.* Stanford CA: Stanford University Press.

Briggs, Charles L. (1986). *Learning how to ask.* Cambridge & New York: Cambridge University Press.

Briley, Donnel A. & Robert S. Wyer, Jr. (2001). Transitory determinants of values and decisions: The utility (or nonutility) of individualism and collectivism in understanding cultural differences. *Social Cognition* 19(3):197–227.

Brockner, Joel, Grant Ackerman, Jerald Greenberg, Michele J. Gelfand, Anne Marie Francesco, Zhen Xiong Chene, Kwok Leung, Gunter Bierbrauer, Carolina Gomez, Bradley L. Kirkman & Debra Shapiro (2001) Culture and procedural justice: The influence of power distance on reactions to voice. *Journal of Experimental Social Psychology* 37(4):300–315.

Bryan, Penelope E. (1992) Killing us softly: Divorce mediation and the politics of power. *Buffalo Law Review* 40:441.

Buchan, James (2001). *Frozen desire: The meaning of money.* New York: Welcome Rain Publishers.

Buldoc, D.S. (1990). "Mediator style perspectives: An innovative look at mediator behavior." (unpublished Master's in Science thesis, Arizona State University).

Burke, Peter J. (1991). Identity processes and social stress. *American Sociological Review* 56:836–849.

Burrell, N.A., Donohue, W.A., & Allen, M. (1988). Gender-based perceptual bias in mediation. *Communication Research* (Special Issue: Communication, conflict and dispute resolution) 15:447–469.

Burton, John (1990). *Conflict: Resolution and prevention.* New York: St. Martin's Press.

Canary, D.J., Cunningham, E.M., & Cody, M.J. (1988). Goal types, gender, and locus of control in managing interpersonal conflict. *Communication Research* (Special Issue: Communication, conflict and dispute resolution) 15:426–446.

Cannon, Lynn Weber, Elizabeth Higgenbotham & Marianne Leung (1991). Race and class bias in qualitative research on women. In Lorber, Judith & Susan A. Farrell (Eds.) (1991). *The social construction of gender.* Newbury Park: Sage.

Carnevale, P.D. & Henry, R.A. (1989) Determinants of mediator behavior: A test of the strategic choice model. *Journal of Applied Social Psychology* 19(6):481–498.

Carnevale, P.J.D., Conlon, D.E., Hanisch, K.A., & Harris, K.L. (1989). Experimental research on the strategic choice model. In Kressel, K. & Pruitt, D.G. (Eds.), *Mediation research: The process and effectiveness of third-party intervention* (344–367). San Francisco: Jossey-Bass.

Casmir, Fred L. (1985). Stereotypes and schemata. In Gudykunst, William B., Lea P. Stewart & Stella Ting-Toomey (Eds.) (1985). *Communication, culture & organizational processes.* Beverly Hills: Sage.

Chene, Roberto (2001). Reconciling an intercultural world. *Conciliation Quarterly* 20(1).

——. (2004). Effective intercultural facilitation: A critical need. *Conciliation Quarterly* 23(4):5–6.

Chiu, Randy K. & Frederick A Kosinski Jr. (1994). Is Chinese conflict-handling behavior influenced by Chinese values? *Social Behavior and Personality* 22(1):81–90.

Christodoulou, Stavroula (1965) *19th-Century Sociologists.* New York: Monarch Press.

Chusmir, L.H. & Mills, J. (1989). Gender differences in conflict resolution styles of managers: At work and at home. *Sex Roles* 20(3/4):149–163.

Clark, M. S. & Mills, J. (1993). The difference between communal and exchange relationships: What is and is not. *Personality and Social Psychology Bulletin* 19:684–691.

Coates, Dan & Steven Penrod (1980–81). Social psychology and the emergence of disputes. *Law & Society Review* 15(3–4):655–680.

Cobb, Sarah (1994). A narrative perspective on mediation: Toward the materialization of the story-telling metaphor. In Folger, Joseph P. & Tricia S. Jones (Eds.) (1994). *New directions in mediation: Communication research and perspectives.* Thousand Oaks CA: Sage.

Cohen, Ronald (1978). Ethnicity: Problem & focus in Anthropology. *Annual Review of Anthropology* 7:379–403.

——. (1986). Power & justice in intergroup relations. In Bierhoff, Hans W., Ronald L. Cohen, & Jerald Greenberg (Eds.) (1986). *Justice in social relations.* New York: Plenum Press.

Collard, David (1978). *Altruism and economy: A study in non-selfish economics.* New York: Oxford University Press.

Collins, Randall (1975). *Conflict sociology: Toward an explanatory science.* New York: Academic Press.

——. (1981). The micro foundations of macro-sociology. *American Journal of Sociology* 86:984–1014.

Conley, John and William O'Barr (1990). *Rules versus relationships: The ethnography of legal discourse.* Chicago: University of Chicago Press.

Cook, Karen S. & Karen Hegtvedt (1986). Justice and power: An exchange analysis. In Bierhoff, Hans W., Ronald L. Cohen, & Jerald Greenberg (Eds.) (1986). *Justice in social relations.* New York: Plenum Press.

Cook, Karen S. (Ed.) (1987) *Social exchange theory.* Newbury Park: Sage.

Cortese, Anthony (1990). *Ethnic ethics: The restructuring of moral theory.* New York: State University of New York Press.

Covert, Michelle Vowell & Deborah Hill Barlow (1998). Are shame & guilt related to distinct self-discrepancies? A test of Higgin's (1987) hypotheses. *Journal of Personality & Social Psychology* 75(1): 256–268.

Crenshaw, Kimberle (1990). A black feminist's critique of antidiscrimination law and politics. In Kairys, David (Ed.) (1990). *The politics of law: A progressive critique.* New York: Pantheon.

Dalton, Harlon L. (1995). *Racial healing.* New York: Doubleday.

D'Andrade Roy G. (1993[1984]). Cultural meaning systems. In Shweder, Richard A. & Robert A. LeVine (Eds.) (1993[1984]). *Culture theory: Essays on mind, self, and emotion.* Cambridge: Cambridge University Press.

Darwin, Charles (1979[1859]). *On the origin of species by means of natural selection.* New York: Avenel Books.

Davis, Kingsley & Wilbert Moore (1945). A functional theory of stratification. *American Sociological Review* 10(2):242–249.

de Vos, George & Lola Romanucci-Ross (1975). Ethnicity: Vessel of meaning and emblem of contrast. In de Vos, George & Lola Romanucci-Ross (Eds.) (1975), *Ethnic identity.* Palo Alto: Mayfield Publishing Co.

Deflem, Mathieu (2003). The sociology of the sociology of money: Simmel and the contemporary battle of the classics. *Journal of Classical Sociology* 3(1):67–96.

Delgado, Richard, Dunn, Chris, Brown, Pamela, Lee, Helena, and Hubbert, David (1985). Fairness and formality: Minimizing the risk of prejudice in alternative dispute resolution. *Wisconsin Law Review* 6:1359–1403.

Devine, Joel A. & James D. Wright (1993). *The greatest of evils: Urban poverty and the American underclass*. New York: Aldine de Gruyter.

Dividio, John F., Steve L. Ellyson, Caroline F. Keating, Karen Heltman & Clifford E. Brown (1988). The relationship of social power to visual displays of dominance between men and women. *Journal of Personality and Social Psychology* 54(2):233–242.

Donahue, William A. & Mary I. Bresnahan (1994). Communication issues in mediating cultural conflict. In Folger, Joseph P. & Tricia S. Jones (Eds.) (1994). *New directions in mediation: Communication research and perspectives*. Thousand Oaks CA: Sage.

Druckman, D., Broome, B.J., & Korper, S.H. (1988). Value differences and conflict resolution: Facilitation or delinking? *Journal of Conflict Resolution* 32(3):489–510.

Duryea, Michelle LeBaron (1992). *Conflict and culture: A literature review and bibliography*. Victoria BC: UVic Institute for Dispute Resolution.

——. (1994). The quest for qualifications: A quick trip without a good map. In Morris, Catherine & Andrew Pirie (Eds.) (1994) *Qualifications for dispute resolution: Perspectives on the debate*. Vancouver: UVIC Institute for Dispute Resolution (pp. 109–129).

Eagly, Alice H. & Blair T. Johnson (1990). Gender and leadership style: A meta-analysis. *Psychological Bulletin* 108:233–256.

Ebright, Malcolm (1994). *Land grants and lawsuits in northern New Mexico*. Albuquerque: University of New Mexico Press.

Edelman, Lauren B., Howard S. Erlanger & John Lande (1993). Internal dispute resolution: The transformation of civil rights in the workplace. *Law & Society Review* 27(3): 497–534.

Eichenbaum, Louise & Susie Orbach (1987). *Between women: Love envy and competition in women's friendships*. New York: Viking Press.

Ellingsworth, Huber W. (1988). A theory of adaptation in intercultural dyads. In Kim, Young Yun & William B. Gudykunst (Eds.) (1988). *Theories in intercultural communication* (Vol XII). Newbury Park: Sage.

Elshtain, Jean Bethke (1992). The power and powerlessness of women. In Bock, Gisela and Susan James (Eds.) (1992), *Beyond equality & difference: Citizenship, feminist politics and female subjectivity*. New York: Routledge.

Emerson, Richard M. (1962). Power dependent relations. *American Sociological Review* October:31–41.

England, Paula (Ed.) (1993). *Theory on gender/Feminism on theory*. New York: Aldine de Gruyter.

Esman, Milton J. (1990). Economic performance and ethnic conflict. In Montville, Joseph V. (Ed.) (1990). *Conflict and peacemaking in multiethnic societies*. Lexington MA: Lexington Books (pp. 477–490).

Etzioni, Amitai (1988) *The moral dimension: Toward a new economics*. New York: The Free Press.

Felstiner, William L.F. (1974). Influences of social organization on dispute processing. *Law & Society Review* Fall:63–94.

——. (1975). Avoidance as dispute processing: An elaboration. *Law & Society Review,* Summer:695–706.

Felstiner, William, Richard Abel & Austin Sarat (1980–81). The emergence and transformation of disputes: Naming, blaming, claiming. *Law & Society Review* 15(3–4): 631–654.

Fisher, K. John, Richard Boyle & Jack Dresser (1995). "Comparison of Australian and U.S. students on cultural theory measures." Presentation at Pacific Sociological Association Meeting, April 6–9, 1995, San Francisco.

Fisher, Karla, Neil Vidmar & Rene Ellis (1993). Procedural justice implications of ADR in specialized contexts: The culture of battering and the role of mediation in domestic violence cases. *SMU Law Review,* 46:2117–2174.

Fisher, Roger & William Ury (1981/1984) *Getting to yes: Negotiating agreement without giving in.* Middlesex, England: Penguin Books.

Fisher, Ronald J. (1990) *The social psychology of intergroup and international conflict resolution.* New York: Springer-Verlag.

Fiske, Alan Page (1991). *Structures of social life, the four elementary forms of human relations.* New York: Free Press.

——. (1992). The four elementary forms of sociality: Framework for a unified theory of social relations. *Psychological Review* 99(4):689–723.

Fiss, Owen (1984). Against settlement. *Yale Law Journal* 93:1073.

Flax, Jane (1993). *Disputed subjects: Essays on psychoanalysis, politics and philosophy.* New York: Routledge.

Folger, Joseph P. & Robert A. Baruch Bush (1994). Ideology, orientations to conflict, and mediation discourse. In Folger, Joseph P. & Tricia S. Jones (Eds.) (1994). *New directions in mediation: Communication research and perspectives.* Thousand Oaks CA: Sage.

Folger, Joseph P. & Tricia S. Jones (Eds.) (1994). *New directions in mediation: Communication research and perspectives.* Thousand Oaks CA: Sage.

Forsyth, Donelson R. (1983/1990). *Group dynamics* (Second Edition). Pacific Grove CA: Brooks/Cole Publishing.

Frank, Ross (2000). *From settler to citizen: New Mexican economic development and the creation of vecino society, 1750–1820.* Berkeley: University of California Press.

Franke, George R., Deborah F. Crown & Deborah F. Spake (1997). Gender differences in ethical perceptions of business practices: A social role theory perspective. *Journal of Applied Psychology* 82(6):920–934.

Frankenberg, Ruth (1993). *White women, race matters: The social construction of whiteness.* Minneapolis: University of Minnesota Press.

Fraser, Colin & Donald Foster (1984). Social groups, nonsense groups and group polarization. In Tajfel, Henri (1984) *The social dimension: European developments in social psychology* (Vol.2). Cambridge: Cambridge University Press.

Frazier, E. Franklin (1947). Sociological theory and race relations. *American Journal of Sociology* 12:265–271. Reprinted in Van den Berghe, P.L. (1972) (Ed.) *Intergroup relations: Sociological perspectives.* New York: Basic Books.

Freeman, Alan (1990). Anti-discrimination: The view from 1989. In Kairys, David (Ed.), *The politics of law: A progressive critique*. New York: Pantheon.

Freidman, Debra (1987). Notes on "Toward a theory of value in social exchange." In Cook, Karen S. (Ed.) (1987) *Social exchange theory*. Newbury Park: Sage.

Frieze, Irene H., Jacquelyn E. Parsons, Paula B. Johnson. Diane N. Ruble & Gail L. Zellerman (1978). *Women and sex roles: A social psychological perspective*. New York: W.W. Norton & Company.

Galanter, Marc (1974). Why the "Haves" come out ahead: Speculations on the limits of social change. *Law & Society Review*, Fall: 95–160.

——. (1983). Reading the landscape of disputes: What we know and don't know (and think we know) about our allegedly contentious society. *UCLA Law Review* 31:4.

Gallois, Cynthia, Arlene Franklyn-Stokes, Howard Giles, Nikolas Coupland (1988). Communication accommodation in intercultural encounters. In Kim, Young Yun & William B. Gudykunst (Eds.) (1988). *Theories in Intercultural communication* (Vol XII). Newbury Park: Sage.

Gans, Eric (1985). *The end of culture: Toward a generative anthropology*. Berkeley: University of California Press.

Gans, Herbert J.(1979). Symbolic ethnicity: The future of ethnic groups and cultures in America. *Ethnic and Racial Studies* 2(1), reprinted in Yetman, Norman R. (Ed.) (1991). *Majority and Minority*. Boston: Allyn and Bacon.

Garcia, Angela (1991). Dispute resolution without disputing: How the interactional organization of mediation hearings minimizes argument. *American Sociological Review* 56:818–835.

Gelfand, Michele J., Marianne Higgins, Lisa H. Nishii, Jana L. Raver, Alexandria Dominguez, Fumio Murakami, Susumu Yamaguchi & Midori Toyama (2002). Culture and egocentric perceptions of fairness in conflict and negotiation. *Journal of Applied Psychology* 87:833–845.

Gelfand, Michele J. & Christakopoulou, S. (1999). Culture and negotiator cognition: Judgment accuracy and negotiation processes in individualistic and collectivistic cultures. *Organizational Behavior & Human Decision Processes* 79:248–269.

Gelfand, Michele J. & Jeanne M. Brett (Eds.) (2004). *The handbook of negotiation and culture*. Stanford CA: Stanford University Press.

Gelfand, Michele J. & Realo, A. (1999). Individualism-collectivism and accountability in intergroup negotiations. *Journal of Applied Psychology* 84:721–736.

Gelfand, Michele J. and Sophia Christakopouloub (1999) Culture and negotiator cognition: Judgment accuracy and negotiation processes in individualistic and collectivistic cultures. *Organizational Behavior and Human Decision Processes* 79(3):248–269.

Gelfand, Michele J., Lisa H. Nishii, Karen M. Holcombe, Naomi Dyer, Ken-Ichi Ohbuchi, Mitsuteru Fukuno (2001). Cultural Influences on Cognitive Representations of Conflict: Interpretations of Conflict Episodes in the United States and Japan. *Journal of Applied Psychology* 86(6):1059–1074.

Giddens, Anthony (1972). Introduction. In Giddens, Anthony (Ed., Trans.) *Emile Durkheim: Selected writings*. Cambridge: Cambridge University Press.

Giles, Howard & Patricia Johnson (1986). Perceived threat, ethnic commitment and interethnic language behavior. In Kim, Young Yun (Ed.) (1986). *Interethnic communication: Current research.* Newbury Park: Sage.

Gilligan, Carol (1982). *In a different voice.* Cambridge: Harvard University Press.

Gire, James T. & D.W. Carment (1993). Dealing with disputes: The influence of individualism-collectivism. *Journal of Social Psychology* 133(1):81–95.

Goffman, Erving (1959). *The presentation of self in everyday life.* Chicago: University of Chicago Press.

Goldberg, Stephen, Sander, Frank and Rogers, Nancy, Eds. (1992) *Dispute resolution: negotiation, mediation and other processes.* Boston: Little, Brown and Company.

Golding, Jacqueline & M. Audrey Burnam (1990). Stress and social support as predictors of depressive symptoms in Mexican Americans and non-hispanic whites. *Journal of Social and Clinical Psychology,* 9(2):268–286.

Gonzales, Phillip B. (1993a). The political construction of Latino nomenclatures in twentieth-century New Mexico. *Journal of the Southwest* 35(2): 158–185.

——(1993b). Historical poverty, restructuring effects, and integrative ties: Mexican American neighborhoods in a peripheral sunbelt economy. In Moore, Joan & Raquel Pinderhughes (Eds.) (1993), *In the barrios: Latinos and the underclass debate.* New York, Russell Sage (pp. 149–171).

Gouldner, Alvin W. (1960). The norm of reciprocity: A preliminary statement. *American Sociological Review,* 25(2):161–178.

Grant, Peter R. (1990). Cognitive theories applied to intergroup conflict. In Fisher, Ronald J. (Ed.) (1990) *The social psychology of intergroup and international conflict resolution.* New York: Springer-Verlag.

Grillo, Trina (1991). The mediation alternative: Process dangers for women, *Yale Law Journal* 100:1545.

Group for the Advancement of Psychiatry (1987). *Us and them.* New York: Brunner—Mazel Publishers (report #123).

Gudykunst, William B. (1985). Normative power and conflict potential in intergroup relationships. In Gudykunst, William B., Lea P. Stewart & Stella Ting-Toomey (Eds.) *Communication, culture & organizational processes.* Beverly Hills: Sage.

——. (1986). Ethnicity, types of relationship, and intraethnic and interethnic uncertainty reduction. In Kim, Young Yun (Ed.) (1986). *Interethnic communication: Current research.* Newbury Park: Sage.

——. (1988). Uncertainty and anxiety. In Kim, Young Yun & William B. Gudykunst (Eds.) (1988). *Theories in intercultural communication* (Vol XII). Newbury Park: Sage.

Hacker, Andrew (1992). *Two nations: Black and white, separate, hostile, unequal.* New York: Ballantine Books.

Hall, Edward T. (1976). *Beyond culture.* New York: Doubleday.

Hall, Raymond (1979). Introduction. In Hall, Raymond (Ed.) (1979). *Ethnic autonomy: Comparative Dynamics in the Americas, Europe and the developing world.* Elmsford, New York: Pergamon Press.

Handler, Joel F. (1978). *Social movements and the legal system: A theory of law reform and social change.* New York: Academic Press.

Hardin, Garret (1968). The tragedy of the commons. *Science* 162(3859):1243–1248.

Hardin, Russell (2004). "The systemic anti-culture of capitalism." Conference presentation at The Ethic and Spirit of Capitalism, Cornell University, October 8–9, 2004.

Harding, Sandra (1991). *Whose science? Whose knowledge? Thinking from women's lives.* Ithaca: Cornell University Press.

——. (1993). Introduction: Eurocentric scientific illiteracy—A challenge for the world community. In Harding, Sandra (Ed.) (1993). *The "racial" economy of science: Toward a democratic future.* Bloomington: Indiana University Press.

Harrington, Christine (1982). Deregulation reform movements: A historical analysis. In Abel, Richard L. (Ed.), *The politics of informal justice,* Vol. 1 (The American experience). New York: Academic Press.

Harrington, Christine and Sally Engle Merry (1988). Ideological production: The making of community mediation. *Law & Society Review,* 22:709.

Harris, M. Kay (1991). Moving into a new millennium: Toward a feminist vision of justice. In Pepinsky, Harold E. & Quinney, Richard (Eds.) *Criminology as peacemaking.* Bloomington: Indiana University Press.

Harris, Marvin (1979). *Cultural materialism: The struggle for a science of culture.* New York: Vintage Books.

Harvey, David L. & Michael H. Reed (1996). The culture of poverty: An ideological analysis. *Sociological Perspectives,* 39(4):465–495.

Hechter, Michael (1987). *Principles of group solidarity.* Berkeley: University of California Press

Hegtvedt, Karen A. (1988). Social determinants of perception: Power, equity, and status effects in an exchange situation. *Social Psychology Quarterly,* 51(2):141–153.

Heinberg, Richard (2003). *The party's over: Oil war and the fate of industrial societies.* Gabriola Island B.C.: New Society Publishers.

Heisler, Martin O. (1990) Ethnicity and ethnic relations in the modern West. In Montville, Joseph V. (Ed.) *Conflict and peacemaking in multiethnic societies.* Lexington MA: Lexington Books. (pp. 21–52).

Henderson, Lynne (1991). Law's patriarchy. *Law & Society Review* 25:411.

Hermann, Michele, Gary LaFree, Christine Rack & Mary Beth West (1992). "*The MetroCourt project final report.*" Washington, DC: National Institute for Dispute Resolution.

Hewstone, Miles & Rupert Brown (1986). Contact is not enough: An intergroup perspective on the "contact hypothesis." In Hewstone, Miles & Rupert Brown (Eds.) (1986) *Contact and conflict in intergroup encounters.* New York: Basil Blackwell.

Hinshaw, Lana M. & Gordon B. Forbes (1993). Attitudes toward women and approaches to conflict resolution in college students in Spain and the United States. *Journal of Social Psychology,* 133(6):865–867.

Hofrichter, Richard (1982). Neighborhood justice and the social control problems of American capitalism: A perspective. In Abel, Richard L. (Ed.). *The politics of informal justice,* Vol 1 (The American experience). New York: Academic Press.

Hofstede, G. (1980). *Culture's consequences.* Beverly Hills, CA: Sage.

Holmbeck, Grayson N. & Patricia Bale (1988). Relations between instrumental and expressive personality characteristics and behaviors: A test of Spence and Helmreich's theory. *Journal of Research in Personality* 22:37–59.

hooks, Bell (1990). *Yearning: Race, gender and cultural politics.* Boston: South End Press.

Horowitz, Donald L. (1990) Ethnic conflict management for policy makers. In Montville, Joseph V. (Ed.) *Conflict and peacemaking in multiethnic societies.* Lexington MA: Lexington Books. pp. 115–132.

Hui, C. Harry (1988). Measurement of individualism-collectivism. *Journal of Research in Personality,* 22:17–36.

Huntington, Samuel P. (1993) The clash of civilizations. *Foreign Affairs* 72(3):22–28.

Hutchins, Edwin (1995). *Cognition in the wild.* Cambridge MA: The MIT Press.

Hyde, Lewis (1979). *The gift: Imagination and the erotic life of property.* New York: Vintage.

Isaacs, Harold R. (1975). *Idols of the tribe, group identity and political change.* New York:Harper & Row.

Janeway, Elizabeth (1980). *The powers of the weak.* New York: Alfred A. Knopf.

Jones, James M. & Kim T. Morris (1993). Individual versus group identification as a factor in intergroup racial conflict. In Worchel, Stephen & Jeffry A. Simpson (Eds.) (1993), *Conflict between people & groups: Causes, processes and resolutions.* Chicago: Nelson-Hall Publishers, pp. 170–189.

Jordan, Judith V., Alexandra G. Kaplan, Jean Baker Miller, Irene Stiver, & Janet L. Surrey (1991). *Women's growth in connection.* New York: Guilford Press.

Just, Peter (1992). History, power, ideology and culture: Current directions in the anthropology of law. *Law and Society Review,* 26(2):373–411.

Kagan, Spencer (1984). Interpreting Chicano cooperativeness: Methodological and theoretical considerations. In Martinez, Joe L. & Richard H. Mendoza (Eds.), *Chicano psychology* (Second Edition). New York: Academic Press.

Kairys, David (Ed.) (1990/1982). *The politics of law: A progressive critique.* New York: Pantheon.

Karst, Kenneth L. (1993). *Law's promise, law's expression: Visions of power on the politics of race, gender, and religion.* New Haven: Yale University Press.

Kashima, Y., Yamaguchi, S., Kim, U., Choi, S., Gelfand, M. J. & Yuki, M. (1995). Culture, gender and self: A perspective from individualism-collectivism research. *Journal of Personality and Social Psychology* 69:926–937.

Kaufman, Sandra & George T. Duncan (1992). A formal framework for mediator mechanisms and motivations. *Journal of Conflict Resolution,* 36(4):688–708.

Kaye, Howard L. (1986). *The social meaning of modern biology: From social Darwinism to sociobiology.* New Haven: Yale University Press.

Keefe, Susan E. and Amando M. Padilla (1987). *Chicano ethnicity.* Albuquerque: University of New Mexico Press.

Keller, Evelyn Fox (1985). *Reflections on gender and science.* New Haven: Yale University Press.

Kidd, Benjamin (1919). *The science of power.* London: Methuen & Co. Ltd (Seventh Edition).

Kidder, Robert L. & Hostetler, John A. (1990). Managing ideologies: Harmony as ideology in Amish and Japanese societies. *Law & Society Review* 24(4): 895–922.

Kim, Young Yun & Brent D. Ruben (1988). Intercultural transformation: A systems theory. In Kim, Young Yun & William B. Gudykunst (Eds.) (1988). *Theories in Intercultural communication* (Vol XII). Newbury Park: Sage.

Kimble, Charles E. & Jeffrey I. Musgrove (1988). Dominance in arguing mixed-sex dyads: Visual dominance patterns, talking time, and speech loudness. *Journal of Research in Personality* 22:1–16.

King, Carol J. (1994). Are justice and harmony mutually exclusive? A response to Professor Nader. *Ohio State Journal on Dispute Resolution* 10(1):65–98.

Knight, George P. & Spencer Kagan (1977). Development of prosocial and competitive behaviors in Anglo-American and Mexican-American children. *Child Development* 48:1385–1394.

Kolb, Deborah M. & Jeffrey Z. Rubin (1989). Research into mediation: What we know, what's left to learn. *Dispute Resolution Forum,* National Institute for Dispute Resolution, October 1989.

Kolb, Deborah M. (1994). Negotiation theory through the looking glass of gender *Institute of Conflict Analysis and Resolution Occasional Paper* (# 9), George Mason University, Fairfax VA.

Korten, David C. (2001[1995]) *When Corporations Rule the World.* Bloomfield CT: Berrett-Koehler Publishers (2nd Edition).

Kramarae, Cheris, Muriel Schultz & William O'Barr (1984). Introduction. In Kramarae, Cheris, Muriel Schultz & William O'Barr (Eds.) (1984), *Language and power.* Beverly Hills: Sage.

Kressel, Ken & Daniel G. Pruitt (Eds.) (1989). *Mediation research: The process and effectiveness of third-party intervention.* San Francisco: Jossey-Bass.

Kritek, Phyllis Beck (1994). *Negotiating at an uneven table: Developing moral courage in resolving our conflicts.* San Francisco: Jossey-Bass.

Kritzer, Herbert M., W.A. Bogart & Neil Vidmar (1991). The aftermath of injury: Cultural factors in compensation seeking in Canada and the United States. *Law & Society Review* 25(3):499–543.

LaFree, Gary & Christine Rack (1996). The effects of participants' ethnicity and gender on monetary outcomes in mediated and adjudicated civil cases. *Law & Society Review* 30(4):767–797.

Lakoff, George & Mark Johnson (1980). *Metaphors we live by.* Chicago: University of Chicago Press.

Lakoff, George (1987). *Women, fire and dangerous things: What categories reveal about the mind.* Chicago: University of Chicago Press.

Larrabee, Mary Jeanne (Ed.) (1993). *An ethic of care: Feminist and interdisciplinary perspectives.* New York: Routledge.

Lawler, Edward J. & Jeongkoo Yoon (1993). Power and the emergence of commitment behavior in negotiated exchange, *American Sociological Review* 58:465–481.

Lazerson, Mark H. (1982). In the halls of justice, the only justice is in the halls. In Abel, Richard L. (Ed.). *The politics of informal justice,* Vol. 1 (The American experience). New York: Academic Press.

Lederach, John Paul & Ron Kraybill (1993). The paradox of popular justice: A practitioner's view. In Merry, Sally Engle & Neil Milner (Eds.) *The possibility of popular justice: A case study of community mediation in the United States.* Ann Arbor: University of Michigan Press.

Leitch, M.L. (1986). The politics of compromise: A feminist perspective on mediation. *Mediation Quarterly,* 14/15:163–175.

Lemann, Nicholas (1992). *The Promised Land: The Great Black Migration and How It Changed America.* New York: Vintage.

Lempert, Richard & Karl Monsma (1994). Cultural differences and discrimination. *American Sociological Review,* 59:890–910.

Lerner, Melvin J. (1980). *The belief in a just world: A fundamental delusion.* New York: Plenum.

——. (1982). The justice motive in human relations and the economic model of man: A radical analysis of facts and fictions. In Derlega & Grzelak (Ed.) *Cooperative helping and behavior.* New York: Academic Press.

Leung, Kwok & Bond, M.H. (1990). Effects of cultural femininity on preference for methods of conflict processing: A cross-cultural study. *Journal of Experimental Social Psychology,* 26:373–388.

Leung, Kwok & Lind, Allan (1986) Procedural justice and culture: Effects of culture, gender, and investigator status on procedural preference. *Journal of Personality and Social Psychology,* 50(6):1134–1140.

Leung, Kwok & Saburo Iwakwaki (1988). Cultural collectivism and distributive behavior. *Journal of Cross-cultural Psychology,* 19(1):35–49.

Leung, Kwok (1987). Some determinants of reactions to procedural models for conflict resolution: A cross-national study. *Journal of Personality and Social Psychology,* 53(5):898–908.

——. (1988). Some determinants of conflict avoidance. *Journal of Cross-cultural Psychology,* 19(1):125–136.

Levenson, Ricki (1984). Intimacy, autonomy and gender: Developmental differences and their reflection in adult relationships. *Journal of the American Academy of Psychoanalysis* 12(4):529–544.

Lewontin, R. C. (1993). IQ: The rank ordering of the world. In Harding, Sandra (Ed.) (1993) *The "racial" economy of science: Toward a democratic future.* Bloomington: Indiana University Press.

Li, Victor Hao & Sally Engle Merry (1987). Cultural aspects of disputing. *Program on Conflict Resolution Occasional Paper Series,* 1987–2, University of Hawaii at Manoa.

Lietaer, Bernard (1997). Global currency speculation and its implications. *IFG News* (July 1997) at http://www.twnside.org.sg/title/nar-cn.htm on August 2, 2005.

Lijphart, Arend (1990). The power-sharing approach. In Montville, Joseph V. (Ed.) *Conflict and peacemaking in multiethnic societies*. Lexington MA: Lexington Books. pp. 491–509.

Lind, E. Allan & Tom R. Tyler (1988). *The social psychology of procedural justice.* New York: Plenum.

Lind, E. Allan, MacCoun, Robert J., Ebener, Patricia A., Felstiner, William L.F., Hensler, Deborah R., Resnik, Judith & Tyler, Tom (1990). In the eye of the beholder: Tort litigants' evaluations of their experiences in the civil justice system. *Law & Society Review,* 24(4):953–988.

Lind, E. Allen, John Thibault & Laurens Walker (1976). A cross cultural comparison of the effect of adversary and inquisitorial processes on bias in legal decisionmaking. *Virginia Law Review* 62:271.

Lind, E. Allen, Tom R. Tyler & Yuen J. Huo (1997). Procedural context and culture: Variation in the antecedents of procedural justice judgments. *Journal of Personality and Social Psychology* 73:767–780.

Lipman-Blumer, Jean (1984). *Gender roles and power.* Englewood, N.J.: Prentice Hall.

Lipton, Jack P., Maureen O'Connor, Craig Terry & Elizabeth Bellamy (1991). Neutral job title and occupational stereotypes: When legal and psychological realities conflict. *Journal of Psychology* 125(2):129–151.

Lorber, Judith & Susan A. Farrell (Eds.) (1991). *The social construction of gender.* Newbury Park: Sage.

Lowry, Ken (1993). Evaluation of community justice programs. In Merry, Sally Engle & Neil Milner (Eds.), *The possibility of popular justice: A case study of community mediation in the United States.* Ann Arbor: University of Michigan Press.

MacCormac, Earl R. (1990[1985]). *A cognitive theory of metaphor.* Cambridge: MIT Press.

MacKinnon, Catherine A. (1984). Feminism, Marxism, method, and the state: Toward feminist jurisprudence. In Harding, Sandra (Ed.) (1984). *Feminism and methodology.* Bloomington: Indiana University Press.

Malpass, Roy S. & John D. Symonds (1974). Value differences associated with social class, sex, and race. *Journal of Cross-Cultural Psychology* 5(3):282–300.

Mantsios, Gregory (2004). Class in America-2003. In Rothenberg, Paula (Ed.) (2004). *Race Class and Gender in the United States.* New York: Worth Publishers (Sixth Edition).

Margolis, Howard (1982). *Selfishness, altruism, and rationality: A theory of social choice.* Cambridge & New York: Cambridge University Press.

Marín, Gerardo, Raymond J. Gamba & Barbara V. Marín (1992). Extreme response style and acquiescence among hispanics: The role of acculturation and education. *Journal of Cross-cultural Psychology,* 23(4):498–509.

Martinez, Valentina Valdez (1994). *Twenty-five years of La Clinica's history.* Tierra Amarilla NM: La Clinica del Pueblo.

Mather, Lynn and Barbara Yngvesson (1980/81) Language, audience and the transformation of disputes. *Law & Society Review,* 15(3–4):775–821.

Matsuda, Mari, Lawrence, Charles R. III, Delgado, Richard and Crenshaw, Kimberle Williams (1993). *Words that wound: Critical race theory, assaultive speech and the first amendment.* Boulder: Westview Press.

Mauss, Marcel (1990/1950). *The gift: The form and reason for exchange in archaic societies.* New York: W.W. Norton (Introduction by Mary Douglas).

Mayer, James C. (1984). Toward an explanation of ethnocentrism vs. ethnorelativism based on reference group orientation. In Verma, Galendra, K. Verma & Christopher Bagley (Eds.) (1984). *Race relations and cultural differences: Educational and interpersonal perspectives.* New York: St. Martin's Press.

Mayhew, Anne (2001). Review of Karl Polanyi The Great Transformation: The political and economic origins of our time. *Economic History Services,* Retrieved May 15, 2005 (http://www.eh.net/bookreviews/library/polanyi.shtml).

McEwen, Craig A. & Richard J. Maiman (1989). Mediation in small claims court: Consensual processes and outcomes. In Kressel, K. & Pruitt, D.G. (Eds.), *Mediation research: The process and effectiveness of third-party intervention* (53–67). San Francisco: Jossey-Bass.

——. (1984) Mediation in small claims court: Achieving compliance through consent, *Law & Society Review* 18:11.

McEwen, Craig A. (1991). Pursuing problem-solving or predictive settlement? *Florida State University Law Review* 19(1):77–88.

McRae, Kenneth D. (1990). Theories of power-sharing and conflict management. In Montville, Joseph V. (Ed.) *Conflict and peacemaking in multiethnic societies.* Lexington MA: Lexington Books, pp. 93–106.

Mead, George Herbert (1934). *Mind, self and society.* Chicago: University of Chicago Press.

Menkel-Meadow, Carrie & Shari Seidman Diamond (1991). The content, method, and epistemology of gender in sociolegal studies. *Law & Society Review* 25(2):221–238.

Menkle-Meadow, Carrie (1991). Pursuing settlement in an adversary culture: A tale of innovation co-opted or "the law of ADR." *Florida State University Law Review* 19(1):1–46.

Menon, Tanya, Michael W. Morris, Chi-yue Chiu & Ying-yi Hong (1999). Culture and the construal of agency: Attribution to individual versus group dispositions. *Journal of Personality and Social Psychology* 76(5):701–717.

Merry, Sally Engle (1982). The social organization of mediation in nonindustrial societies: Implications for informal community justice in America. In Abel, Richard L. (Ed.). *The politics of informal justice,* Vol 2 (Comparative Studies). New York: Academic Press

——. (1989). Mediation in nonindustrial societies. In Kressel, K. & Pruitt, D.G. (Eds.), *Mediation research: The process and effectiveness of third-party intervention* (53–67). San Francisco: Jossey-Bass.

——. (1987). Disputing without culture. *Harvard Law Review* 100:2057–2073.

——. (1990). *Getting justice and getting even.* Chicago: University of Chicago Press.

——. (1992). Popular justice and the ideology of social transformation. *Social and Legal Studies* 1(2):177–198.

Merry, Sally Engle & Neal Milner (Eds.) (1993) *The possibility of popular justice.* Ann Arbor: The University of Michigan Press.

Merton, Robert (1938). Social structure and anomie. Reprinted in Merton, Robert (1968) *Social theory and social structure* (185–214). New York: Free Press.

——. (1968). Manifest and latent functions. In *Social theory and social structure.* New York: Free Press. pp. 73–138.

Miller, Jean Baker (1976). *Toward a New Psychology of Women.* Boston: Beacon Press.

Mirandé, Alfredo (1985). *The Chicano experience: An alternative perspective.* Notre Dame IN: University of Notre Dame Press.

——. (1987). *Gringo justice.* Notre Dame, IN: University of Notre Dame Press

Mizruchi, Mark S. (1994). Social network analysis: Recent Achievements and current controversies. *Acta Sociologica* 37:329–343.

Molm, Linda (1987). Linking power structure and power use. In Cook, Karen S. (Ed.) (1987) *Social exchange theory.* Newbury Park: Sage.

——. (1991). Affect and social exchange: satisfaction in power-dependence relation. *American Sociological Review,* 56:475–493.

——. (1988). The structure and use of power: A comparison of reward and punishment power. *Social Psychology Quarterly* 51(2):108–122.

Molm, Linda, Theron M. Quist & Phillip A. Wisely (1993). Reciprocal justice and strategies of exchange. *Social Forces* 72(1):19–44.

——. (1994). Imbalanced structures, unfair strategies: Power and justice in social exchange, *American Sociological Review,* 59:98–121.

Morris, Michael .W., Kwok Leung, Daniel Ames & Brian Lickel (1999) View from the inside and outside: Integrating emic and etic insights about culture and justice judgment. *Academy of Management Review* 24(4):781–796.

Morris, Michael W., Richard P. Larrick & Steven K. Su (1999). Misperceiving negotiation counterparts: When situationally determined bargaining behaviors are attributed to personality. *Journal of Personality and Social Psychology* 77(1): 52–67.

Morris, Michael W, & Kwok Leung (2000). Justice for all? Progress in research on cultural variation in the psychology of distributive and procedural justice. *Applied Psychology: An International Review* 49(1):100–132.

Morris, Michael W., Kwok Leung & Sheena S. Iyengar (2004) Person perception in the heat of conflict: Negative trait attributions affect procedural preferences and account for situational and cultural differences, *Asian Journal of Social Psychology* 7:127–147.

Morris, Michael W. & Michele J. Gelfand. (2004). Cultural differences and cognitive dynamics: Expanding the cognitive perspective on negotiation. In Gelfand, Michele J. & Jeanne M. Brett (Eds.) (2004). *The handbook of negotiation and culture.* Stanford, CA: Stanford University Press.

Moyerman, David R. & Bruce D. Forman (1992). Acculturation and adjustment: A meta-analytic study. *Hispanic Journal of Behavioral Sciences,* 14(2):163–200.

Nader, Laura (1990). *Harmony ideology: Justice and control in a Zapotec mountain village.* Stanford: Stanford University Press.

——. (1991). Harmony models and the construction of law. In Avruch, Kevin, Peter W. Black & Joseph A. Scimecca (Eds.) (1991). *Conflict resolution: Cross cultural perspectives*. New York: Greenwood Press.

——. (1993). Controlling processes in the practice of law: Hierarchy and pacification in the movement to re-form dispute ideology. *Ohio State Journal on Dispute Resolution* 9(1):1–25.

——. (1994). A reply to Professor King. *Ohio State Journal on Dispute Resolution* 10(1):99–103.

Nagel, Joanne (1986). The political construction of ethnicity. In Olzak, Susan & Joanne Nagel, *Competitive ethnic relations*. Orlando: Academic Press. Reprinted in Yetman, Norman R. (Ed.) (1991). *Majority and minority: The dynamics of race and ethnicity in American life*. Needham Heights, MA: Allyn and Bacon.

Naranjo, Tessie (1992). "Social change in pottery making at Santa Clara pueblo." Ph.D. Albuquerque: University of New Mexico. (unpublished Ph.D. Dissertation)

Nichols, Patricia C. (1984). Networks and hierarchies: language and social stratification. In Kramarae, Cheris, Muriel Schultz & William O'Barr (Eds.) (1984). *Language and power*. Beverly Hills: Sage.

Nicholson, Linda J. (Ed.) (1990). *Feminism/Postmodernism*. New York/London: Routledge.

Nieto-Phillips, John M. (2004). *The language of blood: The making of Spanish American identity in New Mexico, 1850–1940*. Albuquerque: University of New Mexico Press.

Noel, Donald (1968). A theory of the origin of ethnic stratification. *Social Problems*, 6(2):157–172.

Nostrand, Richard L. (1992). *The Hispano homeland*. Norman & London: University of Oklahoma Press.

O'Barr, William M. & John M. Conley (1985). Litigant satisfaction versus adequacy in small claims court narratives. *Law & Society Review* 19(4): 661–701.

O'Barr, William M. (1982). *Linguistic evidence: Language, power, and strategy in the courtroom*. New York: Academic Press.

Oetzel, John G. (1998). The effects of self-construals and ethnicity on self-reported conflict styles. *Communication Reports*. 11(2):133–144.

Ohbachi, Ken-Ichi & Yumi Takahashi (1994). Cultural styles of conflict management in Japanese and Americans: Passivity, covertness, and effectiveness of strategies. *Journal of Applied Psychology*, 24:1345–1366.

Olsen, Cynthia (presenter) (1989). Basic mediation training: A forty hour course. Albuquerque, New Mexico:Albuquerque Mediation Center.

Olsen, Frances (1990). Feminism and critical legal theory: An American perspective. *International Journal of the Sociology of Law* 18:199–215.

Oltman, Philip K., Donald R. Goodenough, Herman A. Witkin, Norbert Friedman & Florence Friedman (1975). Psychological differentiation as a factor in conflict resolution. *Journal of Personality and Social Psychology* 32(4):730–736.

Omi, Michael & Howard Winant (1994). *Racial formation in the United States: From the 1960s to the 1990s* (Second Edition). New York: Routledge.
Orozco, Cynthia (1990[1986]). Sexism in Chicano Studies and the community. In Córdova, Teresa, Norma Cantú, Gilberto Cardenas, Juan Garcia, & Christine M. Sierra (Eds.) (1990), *Chicana Voices: Intersections of class, race, and gender.* Colorado Springs: National Association for Chicano Studies.
Oyserman, D., Coon, H. M., & Kemmelmeier, M. (2002). Rethinking individualism and collectivism: Evaluation of theoretical assumptions and meta-analyses. *Psychological Bulletin* 128:3–72.
Parks, Craig D. & Anh D. Vu (1994). Social dilemma behavior of individuals from highly individualist and highly collectivist cultures. *Journal of Conflict Resolution* 38(4):708–718.
Pearson, Jessica and Nancy Theonnes (1984). Mediating and litigating custody disputes: A longitudinal evaluation. *Family Law Quarterly* 17(4):497.
——(1989). Divorce mediation: Reflections on a decade of research. In Kressel, K. & Pruitt, D.G. (Eds.), *Mediation research: The process and effectiveness of third-party intervention* (pp. 13–42). San Francisco: Jossey-Bass.
Peet, Katherine & John Peet (2002). "Stolen from future generations? The need to move to a political economy of generosity." Presentation at ANZTSR Conference, Unitec, Aukland New Zealand, November 27–29, 2002.
Pettigrew, Thomas F. (1986). The intergroup contact hypothesis revisited. In Hewstone, M. and Rupert Brown (Eds.) (1986). *Contact & conflict in intergroup encounters* New York: Basil Blackwell.
Piliavin, Jane A. & Hong-Wen Charng (1990). Altruism: A review of recent theory and research. *Annual Review of Sociology,* 16:27–65.
Pizzigati, Sam (2004). *Greed and good: Understanding and overcoming the inequality that limits our lives.* New York: Apex Press.
Pruitt, Dean G. & Peter Carnevale (1993). *Negotiation in social conflict.* Pacific Grove CA: Brooks/Cole Publishing Company.
Putnam, L.L. & Folger, J.P. (1988). Communication, conflict, and dispute resolution: The study of interaction and the development of conflict theory. *Communication Research Special Issue: Communication, conflict, and dispute resolution* 15:349–360.
Putnam, Robert D. (2000). *Bowling Alone: The Collapse and Revival of American Community.* NY: Simon & Schuster.
Ra'anan, Uri (1990). The nation-state fallacy. In Montville, Joseph V. (Ed.) (1990) *Conflict and peacemaking in multiethnic societies.* Lexington MA: Lexington Books pp. 5–20.
Rack, Christine (1991). Psyche and image: Figure/ground relationships. *Arts in psychotherapy* 18:97–104.
——. (1994a). Small claims mediation: Findings in a study of ethnicity and gender at MetroCourt. *SGSA Working Paper Series,* 1:10–38, Department of Sociology, University of New Mexico.
——. (1994b). "The reproduction of inequality: The story of minority respondents at the Metro Court." Western Social Science Association, Albuquerque NM, April 21, 1994.

——. (1995). "Cultural disparities in small claims mediation." Contribution to a working seminar in Multicultural Conflict Resolution, National Conference on Peacemaking and Conflict Resolution Minneapolis, MN, May 1995.

——. (1997). *Culture, Structure, and Choice: The Influence of Ethnicity, Gender, Class and Role on Negotiating Behavior in Small Claims Mediation.* Ph.D. Dissertation, University of New Mexico, available from University of Michigan Dissertation Services, 300 North Zeeb Road, Ann Arbor, Michigan 48106.

——. (1999). Negotiated justice: Gender & ethnic bargaining patterns in the MetroCourt study. *Hamline Journal of Public Law & Policy,* 20(2):211–298.

Rack, Christine, Sally Barnes Anderson, & Sally Margolin (1996). "Latino Disadvantage: The linkage of cultural and structural factors in small claims disputes." Presented March 23, 1993 at the Pacific Sociology Association Meeting, Seattle WA.

Ramirez, Manuel III (1983). *Psychology of the Americas: Mestizo perspectives on personality and mental health.* New York: Pergamon Press.

Resnick, Judith (1986). Failing faith: Adjudicatory procedure in decline, *University of Chicago Law Review,* 53:494–560.

——. (1995). Many doors? Closing doors? Alternative Dispute resolution and adjudication. *Ohio State Journal on Dispute Resolution* 10(2):211–265.

Rhee, E., James S. Uleman & Hoon K. Lee (1996). Variations in collectivism and individualism by ingroup and culture: Confirmatory factor analyses. *Journal of Personality and Social Psychology* 71:1037–1053.

Rhee, Eun, James S. Uleman, Hoon K. Lee & Robert J. Roman (1995). Spontaneous self-descriptions and ethnic identities in individualistic and collectivistic cultures. *Journal of Personality and Social Psychology* 69:142–152.

Rheinstein (1969). Weber and law. In Friedman, Lawrence and Stewart Macauley (Eds.) (1969) *Law and the behavioral sciences.* Indianapolis: Bobbs-Merrill Co.

Ridgeway, Cecilia (1997). Interaction and the conservation of gender inequality: Considering employment. *American Sociological Review* 62:218–235.

——. (1993). Gender, status, and the social psychology of expectations. In England, Paula (1993) (Ed.) *Theory on gender / Feminism on theory* (pp. 175–197). New York: Aldine de Gruyter.

Rifkin, Janet (1989). Mediation in the justice system: A paradox for women. *Women & Criminal Justice,* 1(1):41–54.

Rinderle, Susan (2003). "Anglo-Mexican American conflict: A review and critique of current research." *Hawaii International Conference on Social Sciences conference proceedings* (CD-ROM ISSN #1539–7300). Honolulu, HI (June 2003: 16 pp.).

Rodriguez Sylvia (1996). *The Matachines dance.* Albuquerque: University of New Mexico Press.

Rodriguez, Jeanette (1994). *Our Lady of Guadalupe: Faith and empowerment among Mexican-American women.* Austin: University of Texas Press.

Rosaldo, Michelle Z. (1993[1984]). Toward an anthropology of self and feeling. In Shweder, Richard A. & Robert A. LeVine (1993[1984]) *Culture theory: Essays on mind, self, and emotion.* Cambridge: Cambridge University Press.

Rosaldo, Renato (1989). *Culture and truth: The remaking of social analysis.* Boston, Beacon Press.

Rosenholtz, Susan J. & Elizabeth G. Cohen (1985). Activating ethnic status. In Berger, Joseph & Morris Zelditch (Eds.) (1985). *Status, rewards, and influence: How expectations organize behavior.* San Francisco: Jossey-Bass. pp. 430–444.

Ross, Marc Howard (1993). *The culture of conflict.* New Haven: Yale University Press.

Rothenberg, Paula (Ed.) (2002). *White privilege: Essential readings on the other side of racism.* New York: Worth Publishers.

Rotheram-Borus, Mary Jane (1990). Adolescents' reference group choices, self-esteem, and adjustment. *Journal of Personality and Social Psychology* 59(5):1075–1081.

Rothschild, Joseph (1981). *Ethnopolitics: A conceptual framework.* New York: Columbia University Press.

Royce, Anya Peterson (1982). *Ethnic identity: Strategies of diversity.* Bloomington: Indiana University Press.

Ryan, William (1971). *Blaming the victim.* New York: Pantheon/Random House.

Sarat, Austin (1993). Authority, anxiety, and procedural justice: Moving from scientific detachment to critical engagement (a review essay on Tyler, Tom R. (1990), *Why people obey the law,* New Haven: Yale University Press). *Law & Society Review,* 27(3): 647–671.

Scheingold, Stuart A. (1974). *The politics of rights: Lawyers, public policy, and political change.* New Haven: Yale University Press.

Schelling, Thomas C. (1963). *The strategy of conflict.* New York: Oxford University Press.

Schlicht, Ekkehart (2001). "Corporate culture and exploitation." ISNIE Conference presentation, University of Munich Department of Economics, September 8, 2001.

Schofield, Janet Ward (1986). Black-white contact in desegregated schools. In Hewstone, M. and Rupert Brown (Eds.) 1986, *Contact & conflict in intergroup encounters* New York: Basil Blackwell.

Scimecca, Joseph A. (1991). Conflict resolution and a critique of "alternative dispute resolution." In Pepinsky, Harold E. & Quinney, Richard (Eds.) *Criminology as peacemaking.* Bloomington: Indiana University Press.

Segura, Denise A. (1990[1986]). Chicanas and triple oppression in the labor force. In Córdova, Teresa, Norma Cantú, Gilberto Cardenas, Juan Garcia, & Christine M. Sierra (Eds.) (1990), *Chicana Voices: Intersections of class, race, and gender.* Colorado Springs: National Association for Chicano Studies.

Sen, Amartya (1994). The formulation of rational choice. *American Economic Review* 84(2):385–390.

Sewell, William H. Jr. (1992). A theory of structure: Duality, agency, and transformation. *American Journal of Sociology,* 98(1):1–29.

Simmel, Georg (1955). *The web of group-affiliations.* New York: Free Press.

Simmel, Georg (1955/1923). *Conflict.* Glencoe IL: The Free Press.

Singelis, T. M., Triandis, H. C., Bhawuk, D. & Gelfand, M. J. (1995). Horizontal and vertical dimensions of individualism and collectivism: A theoretical and measurement refinement. *Cross-Cultural Research* 29:240–275.

Sinha, D. (1987). Ahimsa as conflict resolution technique and instrument of peace: A psychological appraisal. Paper presented at the seminar on Peace and Conflict Resolution in the World Community, India.

Smedley, Audrey (1993). *Race in North America: Origin and evolution of a worldview.* Boulder: Westview Press.

Smith, Adam & Dugald Stuart (1893). *An inquiry into the nature and causes of the wealth of nations.* London: Routledge.

Smith, Adam (1971[1759]). *The theory of moral sentiments.* New York: Garland.

Smith, Peter B. & Michael Harris Bond (1993). *Social psychology across cultures: Analysis and perspectives.* Hertfordshire/New York: Harvester Wheatsheaf.

Steinberg, Stephen (1989 [1981]). *The ethnic myth: Race, ethnicity and class in America.* Boston: Beacon Press.

Stepan, Nancy Leys (1993). Race and Gender: The role of analogy in science. In Harding, Sandra (Ed.) (1993) *The "racial" economy of science: Toward a democratic future.* Bloomington: Indiana University Press.

Stiver, Irene P. (1991). Beyond the oedipus complex. In Jordan, Judith V., Kaplan, Alexandra G., Miller, Jean Baker, Stiver, Irene, & Surrey, Janet L. (1991). *Women's growth in connection.* New York: Guilford Press.

Stolte, John F. (1987). Legitimacy, justice and productive exchange. In Cook, Karen S. (Ed.) (1987) *Social exchange theory.* Newbury Park: Sage.

Tajfel, Henri (1978a). Interindividual behavior and intergroup behavior. In Tajfel, Henri (Ed.) (1978). *Differentiation between social groups: Studies in the social psychology of intergroup relations.* London: Academic Press pp 27–60.

——. (1978b). Social categorization, social identity and social comparison. In Tajfel, Henri (Ed.) (1978). *Differentiation between social groups: Studies in the social psychology of intergroup relations.* London: Academic Press pp 61–76.

——. (1984). Intergroup relations, social myths and social justice in social psychology. In Tajfel, Henri (1984) *The social dimension: European developments in social psychology* (Vol.2). Cambridge: Cambridge University Press.

Takaki, Ronald (1979). *Iron cages: Race and culture in nineteenth century America.* New York: Alfred A. Knopf.

Tanner, Deborah (1990). *You just don't understand.* New York: Ballantine.

Taub, Nadine & Elizabeth M. Schneider (1990). Women's subordination and the role of law. In Kairys, David (Ed.) (1990/1982). *The politics of law: A progressive critique.* New York: Pantheon.

Taylor, Anita & Judi Beinstein Miller (1994). Introduction: The necessity of seeing gender in conflict. In Taylor, Anita & Judi Beinstein Miller (1994). *Gender and conflict.* Cresskill NJ: Hampton Press.

Tedeschi, James T. (1970). Threats and promises. In Swingle, Paul (Ed.) (1970). *The structure of conflict.* New York: Academic Press.

Thibault, John, Walker, Laurens, and Lind, E. Allen (1972) Adversary presentation and bias in legal decisionmaking. *Harvard Law Review* 86:386.

Thibault, John, Walker, Laurens, Latour Stephen, and Houlden, Pauline (1974) Procedural justice as fairness. *Stanford Law Review* 26:1271.

Thompson, Leigh, Margaret Neale & Marwan Sinaceur (2004). The evolution of cognition and biases in negotiation research: An examination of cognition, social perception, motivation, and Emotion. In Gelfand, Michele J. & Jeanne M. Brett (Eds.) (2004). *The Handbook of Negotiation and Culture.* Stanford CA: Stanford University Press.

Thompson, Michael, Richard Ellis & Aaron Wildavsky (1990). *Culture theory.* Boulder: Westview Press.

Thompson, Richard H. (1989). *Theories of ethnicity: A critical appraisal.* New York: Greenwood Press.

Ting-Toomey, S., Yee-Jung, K., Shapiro, R. B., Garcia, W., Wright, T. J., & Oetzel, J. G. (2000). Ethnic/cultural identity salience and conflict styles in four U.S. ethnic groups. *International Journal of Intercultural Relations* 24:47–81.

Ting-Toomey, Stella (1985). Toward a theory of conflict and culture. In Gudykunst, William B., Lea P. Stewart & Stella Ting-Toomey (Eds.) *Communication, culture & organizational processes.* Beverly Hills: Sage.

Ting-Toomey, Stella (1986). Conflict communication styles in black and white subjective cultures. In Kim, Young Yun (Ed.) (1986). *Interethnic communication: Current research.* Beverly Hills: Sage.

Ting-Toomey, Stella (1988). Intercultural conflict styles: A face-negotiation theory. In Kim, Young Yun & William B. Gudykunst (Eds.) (1988). *Theories in Intercultural communication* (Vol XII). Newbury Park: Sage.

Ting-Toomey, Stella, John G. Oetzel & Kimberlie Yee-jung (2001). Self-construal types and conflict management styles. *Communication Reports* 14(2):87–105.

Tinker, Hugh (1977). *Race, conflict and the international order: From empire to the United Nations.* London: Macmillan Press LTD.

Töennies, Ferdinand. (1963[1957]). *Community and Society (Gemeinschaft und Gesellschaft).* Translated and edited by Charles P. Loomis. New York: Harper & Row. (German publication 1887).

Trattner, Walter I. (1994[1974]). *From poor law to welfare state: A history of social welfare in America* (Fifth Edition). New York: The Free Press.

Triandis, Harry C. (1995). *Individualism & Collectivism.* Boulder: Westview Press.

Triandis, Harry C., Robert Bontempo, Marcelo J. Villareal, Masaaki Asai & Nydia Lucca (1988). *Individualism and collectivism: Cross-cultural perspectives on self-ingroup relationships.* Journal of Personality and Social Psychology 54(2):323–338.

Triandis, Harry C., Hector Bentancourt, Sumiko Iwao, Kwok Leung, Jose Miguel Salazar, Bernadette Setiadi, Jai B.P. Sinha, Hubert Touzard & Zbignew Zaleski (1993). An etic-emic analysis of individualism and collectivism. *Journal of Cross-cultural Psychology* 24(3):366–383.

Triandis, Harry C., Darius K. Chan, Pharm P. S. Bhawuk, Sumiko Iwao & Jai B. P. Sinha (1995). Multimethod probes of allocentrism and idiocentrism. *International Journal of Psychology* 4:461–480.

Triandis, Harry C. & Michele J. Gelfand (1998). Converging measurement of horizontal and vertical individualism and collectivism. *Journal of Personality and Social Psychology* 74:118–128.

Trubisky, Paula, Stella Ting-Toomey & Sung-Ling Lin (1991). The influence of individualism-collectivism and self-monitoring on conflict styles. *International Journal of Intercultural Relations* 15:65–84.

Tucker, Robert C. (1978[1972]). *The Marx-Engels reader* (Second Edition). New York: W. W. Norton.

Tutzauer, F. & Roloff, M.E. (1988). Communication processes leading to integrative agreements. *Communication Research* (Special Issue: Communication, conflict and dispute resolution) 15:360–380.

Tyler, Tom & Steven L. Blader (2004). Justice and negotiation. In Gelfand, Michele J. & Jeanne M. Brett (Eds.) (2004). *The Handbook of Negotiation and Culture.* Stanford CA: Stanford University Press.

Ulin, Robert (1984). *Understanding cultures: Perspectives in anthropology and social theory.* Austin: University of Texas Press.

Valenzuela, Ana, Joydeep Srivastavab, and Seonsu Leec (2005). The role of cultural orientation in bargaining under incomplete information: Differences in causal attributions. *Organizational Behavior and Human Decision Processes* 96(1):72–88.

Van den Berghe, Pierre L. (1981). *The ethnic phenomena.* New York: Elsevier Press.

Van Koppen, Peter J.& Marijke Malsch (1991). Defendants and one-shotters win after all: Compliance with court decisions in civil cases. *Law & Society Review* 25(4):803–820.

Vidmar, Neil & Regina A. Schuller (1987). Individual differences and the pursuit of legal rights. *Law & Human Behavior* 11(4):299.

Vidmar, Neil (1984) The small claims court: A reconceptualization of disputes and an empirical investigation. *Law & Society Review* 18:515–550.

Vila, Pablo (1996). Catholicism and identity on the U.S.-Mexico border. *Occasional Papers in Chicano Studies,* No. 8, Spring 1996, Chicano Studies, University of Texas at El Paso.

Volkan, Vamik D. (1990). Psychoanalytic aspects of ethnic conflicts. In Montville, Joseph V. (Ed.) *Conflict and peacemaking in multiethnic societies.* Lexington MA: Lexington Books. pp. 511–533.

Wagner, J. A. (1995). Studies of individualism-collectivism: Effects of cooperation in groups. *Academy of Management Journal* 38(1):152–172.

Wahrfatig, Paul (1982). An overview of community-oriented citizen dispute resolution programs in the United States. In Abel, Richard L. (Ed.). *The politics of informal justice,* Vol 1 (The American experience). New York: Academic Press.

Wall, James A. & Ann Lynn (1993). Mediation, a current review. *Journal of Conflict Resolution* 37(1):160.

Walsh, Vivian (1994). Rationality as self-interest versus rationality as present aims. *American Economic Review* 84(2):401–405.

Weber, J. Mark & David M. Messick (2004). Conflicting interests in social life: Understanding social dilemma dynamics. In Gelfand, Michele J. & Jeanne M. Brett (Eds.) (2004). *The Handbook of Negotiation and Culture.* Stanford CA: Stanford University Press.

Weber, Max (1958 [1904–5]) *The protestant ethic and the spirit of capitalism.* New York: Charles Scribner's Sons [translated by Talcott Parsons].

Webster, Murray Jr. & Barbara I. Sobiezek (1974). Sources of evaluation and expectation states. In Berger, Joseph, Thomas L. Conner & M. Hamit Fisek (1974) (Eds.) *Expectation states theory: A theoretical research program.* Cambridge MA: Winthrop. pp. 115–158.

Webster, Murray Jr. & James E. Driskell, Jr. (1985). Status generalization. In Berger, Joseph & Morris Zelditch (Eds.) (1985). *Status, rewards, and influence: How expectations organize behavior.* San Francisco: Jossey-Bass.

Weedon, Chris (1987). *Feminist practice and poststructuralist theory.* Oxford, England: Basil Blackwell.

Welch, Sharon D. (1990). *A feminist ethic of risk.* Minneapolis: Fortress Press.

Wellman, David T. (1977). *Portraits of white racism.* London: Cambridge University Press.

West, Candace & Don H. Zimmerman (1991). Doing gender. In Lorber, Judith & Susan A. Farrell (Eds.) (1991). *The social construction of gender.* Newbury Park: Sage.

West, Cornel (1994). *Race matters.* New York: Vintage Books.

Wilden, Anthony (1987). *The rules are no game: The strategy of communication.* London: Routledge & Kegan Paul.

Williams, Colin H. & Elenore Kofman (1989). Culture, community and conflict. In Williams, Colin H. & Elenor Kofman (Eds.) (1989), *Community conflict, partition and nationalism.* London: Routledge.

Williams, Patricia J. (1991). *The alchemy of race and rights.* Cambridge: Harvard University Press.

Wilson, Bryan R. (Ed.) (1970). *Rationality.* New York: Harper & Row.

Wilson, James Q. (1993). *The moral sense.* New York: Macmillan/Free Press.

Wilson, William Julius (1987). *The truly disadvantaged: The inner city, the underclass, and public policy.* Chicago: The University of Chicago Press.

——(1993). Can sociology play a greater role in shaping the national agenda? In Wilson, W. J., *Sociology & the public agenda.* Newbury Park: Sage.

Wise, Tim (1998). Is sisterhood conditional? White women and the rollback of affirmative action. NWSA Journal 10(3). Retrieved June 18 2005 (http://iupjournals.org/nwsa/nws10–3.html).

——. (2005). Race to our credit. *Z Magazine* (January 6, 2005). Retrieved July 21, 2005 (http://www.zmag.org/sustainers/content/2005–01/06wise.cfm)

Wissler, Roselle L. (1995). Mediation and adjudication in the small claims court: The effects of process and case characteristics. *Law & Society Review,* 29(2):323–358.

Witkin H.A. & S. Asch (1948). Studies in space orientation (III and IV). *Journal of Experimental Psychology* 38, 603–614, 762–782.

Witkin, H.A., D.R. Goodenough & P. K. Oltman (1979). Psychological differentiation: Current status. *Journal of Personality and Social Psychology,* 37: 1127–1145.

Witkin, H. A., R. B. Dyk, H. F. Fakerson. D. R. Goodenough & S. A. Karp (1962). *Psychological differentiation.* New York: Wiley.

Wittmer, Jerry M., Carnevale, Peter, Walker, Michael E. (1991). General alignment and overt support in biased mediation. *Journal of Conflict Resolution* 35(4): 594–610.

Worchel, Stephen (1999). *Written in blood: Ethnic identity and the struggle for human harmony.* New York: Worth Publishers.
Wrong, Dennis H. (1988 [1979]). *Power: Its forms, bases, and uses.* Chicago: University of Chicago Press (second edition).
Yetman, Norman R. (Ed.) (1991). *Majority and minority: The dynamics of race and ethnicity in American life.* Needham Heights, MA: Allyn and Bacon.
Yngvesson, Barbara & Patricia Hennessey (1975). Small claims, complex disputes: A review of the small claims literature. *Law & Society Review* 9:219.
Zelditch, Morris Jr. (1985). Three questions about status. In Berger, Joseph & Morris Zelditch (Eds.) (1985). *Status, rewards, and influence: How expectations organize behavior.* San Francisco: Jossey-Bass.

Index

N

For Product Safety Concerns and Information please contact our EU
representative GPSR@taylorandfrancis.com
Taylor & Francis Verlag GmbH, Kaufingerstraße 24, 80331 München, Germany

www.ingramcontent.com/pod-product-compliance
Ingram Content Group UK Ltd.
Pitfield, Milton Keynes, MK11 3LW, UK
UKHW022115190926
475702UK00013B/1460

* 9 7 8 0 4 1 5 6 4 9 6 2 9 *